TESTAMENT OF FRIENDSHIP

VERA BRITTAIN (1893–1970) grew up in provincial comfort in the north of England. In 1914 she won an exhibition to Somerville College, Oxford, but a year later abandoned her studies to enlist as a VAD nurse. She served throughout the war, working in London, Malta and on the Front in France. At the end of the war, with all those closest to her dead, Vera Brittain returned to Oxford. There she met Winifred Holtby and this friendship continued and sustained her until the latter's untimely death.

Vera Brittain wrote twenty-nine books: novels, poetry, biography, autobiography and other non-fiction. Her three "Testaments", *Testament of Youth*—an acclaimed BBC serial —*Testament of Friendship* and *Testament of Experience*, all published by Fontana, are generally considered her greatest works.

In 1925 Vera Brittain married the political philosopher G. E. Catlin and they had two children, one of whom is Shirley Williams.

WINIFRED HOLTBY (1898–1935) was born at Rudstone in Yorkshire. In the First World War she was a member of the Women's Auxiliary Army Corps. She met Vera Brittain at Somerville College, Oxford, and, after graduating, shared a flat with her in London. Winifred Holtby was a prolific journalist, writing for *Time and Tide*, the *Manchester Guardian*, the *News Chronicle*, and many other magazines and newspapers. She published poetry, short stories and works of non-fiction, including a notable critical study, *Virginia Woolf*. Of her seven novels the best known are *Anderby Wold*, *The Crowded Street* and, most particularly, *South Riding* (available in Fontana), published posthumously after her tragic death at the age of thirty-seven.

VERA BRITTAIN

TESTAMENT
OF FRIENDSHIP

The Story of
Winifred Holtby

Afterword by Rosalind Delmar

FONTANA PAPERBACKS
in association with Virago

First published by Macmillan & Co. Ltd, 1940
First published in paperback by Virago Press Ltd,
1980
First published by Fontana Paperbacks in
association with Virago Press Ltd, 1981

Copyright © Vera Brittain 1940
Copyright © Literary executors of Vera Brittain
1970
Afterword copyright © Rosalind Delmar 1980

Made and printed in Great Britain by
William Collins Sons & Co. Ltd, Glasgow

To Winifred in memory
SURSUM CORDA

Unto each man his handiwork, unto each his crown,
    The just Fate gives ;
Whoso takes the world's life on him and his own lays down,
    He, dying so, lives.

Whoso bears the whole heaviness of the wronged world's weight
    And puts it by,
It is well with him suffering, though he face man's fate ;
    How should he die ?

Seeing death has no part in him any more, no power
    Upon his head ;
He has bought his eternity with a little hour,
    And is not dead.

For an hour, if ye look for him, he is no more found,
    For one hour's space ;
Then ye lift up your eyes to him and behold him crowned,
    A deathless face.

On the mountains of memory, by the world's well-springs,
    In all men's eyes,
Where the light of the life of him is on all past things,
    Death only dies,

Not the light that was quenched for us, nor the deeds that were,
    Nor the ancient days,
Nor the sorrows not sorrowful, nor the face most fair
    Of perfect praise.

A. C. SWINBURNE
Super Flumina Babylonis

CONTENTS

AUTHOR'S ACKNOWLEDGMENTS

My deepest gratitude is due to Winifred Holtby's mother[1] and to many friends who helped to make this book possible by lending their letters and sharing their memories.

I am also greatly indebted to Viscountess Rhondda for permission to quote several extracts from her writings, and to Miss Jean M'William for the use of her Introduction to *Letters to a Friend*.

I regret that I was unable to get into touch with Miss Iris Tree and Mr Richard Goodman and trust that they will accept this acknowledgment for *To my Father* and *Poem, 1933*.

Acknowledgments and thanks are due to the editors of *Time and Tide*, *The Observer*, *The Yorkshire Post*, *Country Life* and *The Queen* for kindly permitting the use of copyright poems and articles contributed by Winifred Holtby to their columns.

V. B.

[1] Mrs. Holtby died on July 31st, 1939, the day that the manuscript was completed.

PROLOGUE

In the last year of her life, three leading London publishers invited Winifred Holtby to write her autobiography.

Half interested and half amused, she discussed the project with me during our Easter holiday.

" I don't see how I can write an autobiography," she said. " I never feel I've really had a life of my own. My existence seems to me like a clear stream which has simply reflected other people's stories and problems."

This impression, I told her, was quite untrue. The drama of her life was none the less real because it was not obvious to every acquaintance. Recalling facts, incidents, impressions, I almost persuaded her to undertake the book. Couldn't she do it after she had finished *South Riding*, and been to Liberia, and made her report on native problems in Africa ? We talked and planned as though the time before her were indefinite. I knew, in theory, the danger that threatened her, but I had never quite believed in it. She seemed too vital and radiant a creature for death to touch.

That autumn the task of writing her story fell to me. It is still difficult to achieve reconciliation with the fate that robbed her of the years which were her due, and for this reason I have done what I can, by the use of passages from her books and letters, to let her make her own contribution. The poems that I have quoted are not included for their merit. She wrote them with too little exertion, and they began to count only towards the end of her life, when she really worked on them. Perhaps the series *For the Ghost of Elinor Wylie* — the product of suffering, despair, courage and victory — is alone worthy of permanence. But just because versification came easily her poems sometimes expressed her moods more precisely than her careful writings, and it is for this reason that I have used so many.

Within the framework of this biography I have tried to tell — in the place where it belongs, and there only — the story of a friendship which continued unbroken and unspoilt for sixteen incomparable years. In one sense even death has not ended it, for a writer being dead yet speaketh, and through her work has still new messages to give to those who loved her.

From the days of Homer the friendships of men have enjoyed glory and acclamation, but the friendships of women, in spite of Ruth and Naomi, have usually been not merely unsung, but mocked, belittled and falsely interpreted. I hope that Winifred's story may do something to destroy these tarnished interpretations, and show its readers that loyalty and affection between women is a noble relationship which, far from impoverishing, actually enhances the love of a girl for her lover, of a wife for her husband, of a mother for her children.

The difficulties of this book have not lain in recording the friendship between Winifred and myself, but in the necessary account of her close relations with others. A biographer, in describing personal relationships, confronts a dilemma not experienced by the novelist, who knows — or should know — everything about the characters that he has created, and is on safe ground when he defines the emotions which unite or divide them. The biographer must deal with living persons whom he knows only in part, and of whom at least a few have no desire to confide in him. How far, I asked myself, was I entitled to describe Winifred's relationships with others even when I understood them ? How far, when I knew them only from the outside, should I try to interpret them and to convey their significance ?

In writing of one who was so deeply loved and who received so many confidences, the problem was real. So I turned, as often, for help and advice to Mrs. Gaskell's *Life of Charlotte Brontë*, which Winifred and I had read and admired together. Finding, as I hoped, that Mrs. Gaskell had been confronted by the same perplexity and was equally sensitive to its implications, I offer to Winifred's friends the apology with which she prefaced her portrait of Charlotte Brontë's husband :

" The difficulty that presented itself most strongly to me when I first had the honour of being requested to write this biography, was how I could show what a noble, true and tender woman Charlotte Brontë really was, without mingling up with her life too much of the personal history of her nearest and most intimate friends. After much consideration of this point, I came to the resolution of writing truly if I wrote at all ; of withholding nothing, though some things, from their very nature, could not be spoken of so fully as others."

Mrs. Gaskell suffered bitterly from this endeavour to respect the truth ; she was criticised, censured and driven to the verge of an action for libel. But her book, like its subject, survived these attacks. I can only hope that my humbler experiment in biography, gravely conscious as I am of its defects, may escape the misfortunes of hers, but may add, like hers, to its subject's claim for long remembrance.

I owe a final word to some of Winifred's friends who wanted to see this book published more quickly in order to catch a supposed topical market and to forestall the appearance of half-informed studies. For those who loved her, I fully realise how painful and exasperating it has been to wait for a complete account of her life, based upon adequate knowledge and that growth of understanding which only years of close friendship can bring. My apologies are due to them for the many explanations offered of the simple fact that I did not write this book earlier because I did not want to. And I did not want to because I knew that, if I wrote quickly, I should very soon repent of what I had written.

It would have been easy enough, on the strength of

memory and a superficial glance through the mass of papers which Winifred left me, to construct a readable record of her life within a few months of her death. Anyone accustomed to writing books could produce such a volume ; and she had not been a week in her grave before a number of publishers — though not my own — had invited me to do so. From the standpoint of sales such a course would doubtless have benefited my interests as well as theirs, but I cannot believe that it would have assisted Winifred's reputation.

A hasty portrait may be good journalism, but almost without exception it is bad biography. The chief essential of biography is truth, and truth is seldom served by hurried studies, however topical and efficient. In practice, such work usually proves to be ephemeral to precisely the degree that it is topical. The very public which rushes to buy a book because it is " news " will be the first to drop it when its news value has been captured by something else.

The closer one person has been to another, the greater is the need for time to elapse in order that the bitterness of loss and the arbitrary selections of memory may be modified by perspective and detachment, by the thorough investigation of available material, and most of all by the quiet process of unhurried reflection. Even within the past few months, many facts of Winifred's life and character have become clear to me that I still saw as in a glass darkly a year or two ago.

I can therefore only plead for understanding and forgiveness when I say that I could no more have produced a truthful study of the best friend whom life has given me in the months directly following her death, than I could have written *Testament of Youth* immediately after 1918.

VERA BRITTAIN

October, 1936 — *September,* 1939

CHAPTER I

PILGRIMAGE TO RUDSTON

NO MOURNING, BY REQUEST

Come not to mourn for me with solemn tread
Clad in dull weeds of sad and sable hue,
Nor weep because my tale of life's told through.
Casting light dust on my untroubled head.
Nor linger near me while the sexton fills
My grave with earth — but go gay-garlanded,
And in your halls a shining banquet spread
And gild your chambers o'er with daffodils.

Fill your tall goblets with white wine and red,
And sing brave songs of gallant love and true,
Wearing soft robes of emerald and blue,
And dance, as I your dances oft have led,
And laugh, as I have often laughed with you —
And be most merry — after I am dead.

- WINIFRED HOLTBY, 1923

A HUNDRED YEARS hence, literary tourists will find in
Yorkshire the opportunity for many pious pilgrimages to
places hallowed by association with celebrated writers of
this generation.

Perhaps they will visit first the stocky pugnacious statue
of J. B. Priestley, which may then stand before the Alhambra
Theatre in Bradford where the dramatised version of *The Good
Companions* celebrated its first night, and Phyllis Bentley,
eagerly arriving too soon, waited on the steps for twenty
minutes in the bitter wind. From Bradford, the metropolis of
the West Riding, it is only a short journey to Halifax and the
old-fashioned villa where Phyllis Bentley herself lived with her

mother, screened from intruders by a tree-darkened by-road. Crossing the county diagonally to the North Riding with its wild forbidding cliffs, the pilgrims of the twenty-first century will certainly explore the little sea-coast house where Storm Jameson was born at Whitby. And then, because of Winifred Holtby — younger than these others, yet dead before them — they will turn southward to the wold village of Rudston, in the East Riding.

Centuries of history have passed over this village, folded into a curve of the hills six miles from the North Sea. Earlier than recorded time, some unknown force hurled the giant cone-shaped monolith to the spot where it now stands, a pagan relic incongruously dominating the peaceful church-yard. The Romans knew Rudston, and left their tessellated pavements to be unearthed by twentieth-century archaeologists ; the Angles and Saxons sailed from the Elbe to the Humber and found their way there ; the grey square-towered church at the top of the hill owed its shape to the Normans. But before the Normans came the Northmen and the Danes, who bequeathed to the Wolds a vigorous race with long limbs and golden hair and clear china-blue eyes. Centuries later one of their descendants, still set apart from her fellows by her fair alien colouring and the proud erectness of her northern stature, was to stride the streets of London with the same grand gait that carried the Vikings up the Roman road which runs from York to the sea.

The village itself lies at the bottom of the open cup formed by the rolling uplands of the wolds, a chequer-work of fields and hedges in every conceivable shade of green — emerald, olive and jade. Close to the horizon one long narrow meadow makes a rim of pure gold as the sunshine falls upon it, outlining with light the twisted shapes of isolated elms and sycamores, and throwing into darker shadow the thick clumps of trees on the lower slopes. Tiny feathers of blue smoke curl lazily skyward from the red-brown roofs of farms and cottages which no foreign invasion could make other than " forever England." Around them eddy the small activities of the English countryside — a woman feeding chickens, newly-washed clothes being dried in back yards, an occasional motor passing through the village street, an aeroplane throbbing sleepily overhead. From far away this serene jumble of buildings is crowned and given character by the grey Norman church with its candle-extinguisher summit, and the sloping churchyard where Winifred lies.

I think that the stranger should go there first in late summer, when a golden glow of grain ripe for harvest lies over the wheat-fields beneath the huge open vault of the sky and its slowly marching pageant of cloud. At the end of July the stone church is surrounded by a narrow flower-garden of blue lavender, mauve ageratum, rose-pink ramblers and orange marigolds, and the rough grass of the churchyard gives shelter to small happy creatures that thrive in the sunshine. Brown butterflies quiver above white hemlock and brick-red sorrel ; tall feathery grasses heavy with pollen bend beneath the poised weight of lazy contented bees. As the stranger listens, the quiet air gradually fills with innocent country sounds — the lowing of cows, the throb of a reaping-machine in the valley, the sudden call of a blackbird, the soft chirping of invisible larks. A little leaping breeze carries with it the sweet warm scent of meadow-flowers and newly-mown hay.

From the top of the sloping path that leads from the church porch to the rough hawthorn hedge at the boundary of the churchyard, it is easy to see the long low grave of short grass enclosed within white marble which is the end of the traveller's pilgrimage. If he looks over the hedge as he walks down the slope, he will see, across a stretch of clover-dotted meadow where calves are feeding and hens placidly pecking, the dark hedge of tall trees which hides Winifred's old home.

At the head of the grave the open marble book will tell him that the author of *South Riding* lived out her days in a yet briefer space of time than her countrywoman Charlotte Brontë, whose frail life was extinguished at the age of thirty-nine. In his note-book he will copy the short black-lettered inscription on the smooth white stone :

IN LOVING MEMORY OF

WINIFRED

DAUGHTER OF
DAVID AND ALICE

HOLTBY

DIED IN LONDON
SEPT. 29TH 1935
AGED 37 YEARS

" God give me work
      Till my life shall end
And life
      Till my work is done."

CHAPTER II

THE WOLD FARM

HARVEST AT ANLABY

The heavy wains slow moving go
Across the broad autumnal wold
To great brown-throated men below
Who gather in the glowing gold.
And thus it was they harvested,
They harvested at Anlaby
Before the Danes from Bessingly
Flooded the manor like a sea,
And left Earl Godwin's barley red
    At Anlaby.

The lovers linger down the lane
When moths awake and small owls cry,
Their dresses fade, as pale moons wane,
And glimmer as they wander by.
And thus it was they made their vows,
They made their vows at Anlaby,
When all the wolds were young as they
Among the dusky sheaves they lay,
And kissed beneath the darkened boughs
    At Anlaby.

      WINIFRED HOLTBY, 1920

In MAY SINCLAIR's Introduction to Mrs. Gaskell's *Life of Charlotte Brontë*, two paragraphs occur which have special relevance to the subject of this book :

" By suppressing Haworth churchyard and Charlotte Brontë's relations, it would be possible to write a ' Life ' of her which would be all gaiety and all sunshine. The lives of great men admit of these suppressions. Their relations on the whole do not affect them except as temporary obstacles (more or less offensive) to their career. . . .

" It is otherwise with great women. They cannot thus get rid of their relations. Their lives are inseparable from them, their works in many cases inexplicable without them. . . . A woman cannot get away from her family even in its absence. She may abandon it ; it may abandon her ; but she is bound to it by infrangible, indestructible bonds. It, and all it has done to her or for her, has an enduring life in her memory. However much abandoned or ignored, its persistence there endows it with immortality. Imagine then what its influence must have been on Charlotte Brontë, who never abandoned or ignored it."

Substitute Winifred Holtby for Charlotte Brontē, and you have at least half the truth about her story. The likeness between the two Yorkshire women rests upon something more profound than the coincidence that each died prematurely and each lies buried in her native village within a stone's throw of the house where she was born. Though in Winifred's case the services ungrudgingly given to her family throughout her life were extended to her friends, her acquaintances and humanity at large, we cannot understand her without knowing something of those relatives who created a type of social order from which few writers have sprung.

When Winifred was born at Rudston House on June 23rd, 1898, the young fields of grass, wheat, oats and barley turned the patchwork of the wolds to its vividest green, brilliant against the purple of the dark earth which the grain had not yet pierced. The morning sunshine danced into the front east-facing bedroom of the solid creeper-covered house, and a blackbird sang exuberantly in the thick hedge of ash and sycamore which concealed the garden from the road.

Winifred's parents on both sides came from farming stock ; their families were typical of the old English yeomanry, proud, sturdy and independent, with its roots in the land. Her father, David Holtby, was the son of a farmer

with an ancestral holding at Elmswell, near Driffield, who
planted out his family on smaller farms in the neighbourhood. David managed his holding with skill and economy,
saved a tidy sum while still a young man, and used it to
buy the house and estate at Rudston.

There he lived for two or three years in the company of a
housekeeper, contemplating matrimony but afraid to plunge.
Winifred's mother once told one of her friends among the
village women that her husband came to see her for twelve
years before they actually married, and she never knew
why. She, Alice Winn, was also a farmer's daughter, who
came from Wensleydale and earned her living as a governess
throughout her youth, until David Holtby decided that over
a decade of cautious friendship was sufficient guarantee for
her sterling qualities. His brothers and sisters made similar
late marriages owing to the same wary discretion.

More fortunate than her less-gifted sister Grace, two
and a half years her senior, Winifred had the good luck to
inherit the strong spartan optimism of one parent as well as
the gentle, considerate kindliness of the other. Her positive,
irrepressible vigour was all her mother's ; years later she
explained to a friend that she had never realised the need
for a feminist movement until she went to Oxford, as their
household was a matriarchy. Between herself and her
mother, despite vast intellectual differences intensified by
Winifred's education and the forty years which divided
them, so deep a temperamental sympathy existed that their
relationship was always one of unbroken harmony.

In her early youth Winifred's knowledge of her ancestors
was vague and speculative; they must, she thought, have
had some connection with the village of Holtby, now on
the railway line between York and Market Weighton. But
when she visited Johannesburg in 1926 she learnt more
from a certain Rex Holtby who claimed relationship and
had studied the family history, though his South African
standard of living was considerably beyond the unpretentious
affluence of the East Riding farmers.

At the time of Henry II, he told her, the Holtbys were

respectable Danish settlers living beside the Humber. In the thirteenth and fourteenth centuries they moved north to the Wolds, founded Holtby village and became barons. This tale of growing glory was unfortunately interrupted by the Wars of the Roses, in which they backed the wrong side, lost their title, and split into two groups, one remaining in Yorkshire and the other going to Lincoln. The Yorkshire branch held its head high and registered deeds at York till about 1720, when it married one of its daughters to a Lascelles of Harewood, and, overcome by this triumph of social achievement, faded out of the records and vanished into obscurity.

Winifred's newly-encountered cousin showed her a blue and silver coat of arms which belonged by right, he said, to her family. He also supplied her with a typewritten list of Holtby Wills at York and Lincoln, which went back to a Robert Holteby of York in 1438 and a John Holtbie of Lincoln in 1573.

Whatever the true history of these Holtby forebears, they probably changed as little through the centuries as their own countryside. Up to the War of 1914 the Wold villages were cut off almost as completely as they had been a hundred years earlier from the forces which were creating the modern world. In Winifred's childhood neither radio, cinema, long-distance motor-bus nor even the telephone linked them with those urban areas where the twentieth century had already made itself felt. The process of childbirth was as single-handed a job for the untrained village midwife as it had remained for generations. Sudden illness or imminent death meant a five-mile drive in a pony trap to fetch a doctor from Bridlington, the seaside holiday resort which combined with Hornsea and Withernsea to produce the " Kiplington " of *South Riding*. The tarred, sign-directed highways of to-day were then non-existent, and the doctor rode or drove to his patient over dirt-roads, perilous with potholes, which were all but impassable in winter storms.

The farmers of these isolated regions were, and are, natural Tories ; Winifred once told St. John Ervine that she remembered as a child thinking marigolds vulgar and cornflowers refined, because at the first local election which she could recall, the gentlefolk wore blue cornflowers and the vulgar loutish Radicals wore marigolds.

"There is hardly," she confessed to him, "one political objective which I desire to-day which I was not accustomed as a child to hear derided by my betters."

To Sarah Gertrude Millin, the South African novelist, Winifred wrote in 1932 that if a sympathetic schoolmistress had not persuaded her parents to send her to college, she would never have left that environment of animals, seasons, shooting-parties, the visits of foremen and pig-dealers, the calls of millers and their wives. "Even now," she added, "quite half my life is there, and all my ' roots.' There ' art ' is something as unimportant and incomprehensible as the algebraical implications of the Koran."

In her Yorkshire novels where these granite men and women of the East Riding appear, Winifred describes with humorous understanding their sturdy contempt for fields of knowledge and ways of living outside their own experience. What did impress them was length of acquaintanceship, or familiarity with the same group of people or the same part of the country. Clannish to the final degree, they looked upon those who entered the family from outside as alien intruders. Unfamiliar opinions, however well substantiated, left them quite unmoved. The scene in *South Riding* where Sarah Burton breaks into Alderman Mrs. Beddows's family tea-party to beg the grant of a scholarship to a girl left motherless, and is firmly put in her place, reflects the frequency with which Winifred must have pleaded some cause which seemed vital to her but was totally unimportant to her listeners.

Her relatives regarded most Southerners as poor creatures, particularly when they belonged to those artistic and intellectual types which in Yorkshire eyes were soft and neurotic. The capacity for dramatising persons and situations which is the basis of all artistic achievement was a quality completely foreign to their type. Had they realised its absence, as they never did, they would not have wished to possess it, for it would have seemed to them dishonest, unhealthy and insincere. Their ideal was commonsense ; like the sceptical Midlanders of the Staffordshire Potteries who never appreciated Arnold Bennett until he was dead, they tended to regard literature as high-falutin' clap-trap. When Winifred returned to Rudston as her final home after the triumphant years in London — " comin' back to bide among us all ageean," as an old villager put it — the inhabitants were astonished that the travellers who came to the village to visit her grave were drawn there by the fame of her writings. Her family were equally unimpressed by her literary renown ; to the end of her life she remained " Alice's girl." Proficiency at bridge or folk-dancing would have seemed to them of similar significance.

Nevertheless, for all their scepticism, their loyalty was lifelong to those who won their affection, and Winifred's books are enlivened by their native wit. When visiting uncles or cousins she always carried a notebook, and immediately after the conversation wrote down some phrase or anecdote retailed by her unsuspecting hosts. Their racy farmyard metaphors especially came in useful for novels and stories.

" I can't say I ever liked egg or shell of him," she noted, and added a comment on a hen which had failed to impress the judges at an agricultural show : " Would the Archangel Gabriel himself win a prize if he was in moult ? " In pencil she scribbled down a conversation related by a hard-headed uncle which proved that the contempt meted out to literary mollycoddles was also exhibited with uncompromising justice to unskilled practitioners of important local trades.

" Are you Mr. Holtby ? "

" I am."

" Thank God. We've been looking for you three days. We want to buy some horses."

" Then you've come to the wrong spot."

" Indeed ! And why ? "

" Well, if I tell you I shall only vex you."

" Oh no ; it takes a deal to vex me ! "

" Very well. I met you three years since at a horse show, judging. You gave the first prize to a horse that was never heard of again. A creature that was hardly a horse at all went off with the second, and the one that got the third swept the country after. You're no judge of horses, or else you're a fool. Either way, you'll get no horses from me."

The Rudston estate of nine hundred and forty acres was nearly twice the size of the average wold farm. Before David Holtby bought it, the land belonged to a farmer named Walmisley, who lived in the house next door to his foreman until this became too small for his needs. With the help of £2000 from Lord Londesborough, he then built Rudston House, adding stables to the fold-yards and stack-yards, and laying out flower-gardens, vegetable gardens, a croquet lawn, an orchard, and greenhouses for vines and hothouse flowers. The property came into the market when he died in 1891.

To-day, in the wold villages, the wives of the gentlemen farmers distemper their walls and decorate their light chairs with flowery chintzes, but the solid, oblong house of Winifred's earliest recollection was furnished mainly in red, with brown walls and dark heavy furniture. The architect, unimpeded by limitations of space, had provided in his plan for an extensive family ; dining-room, drawing-room, morning-room and schoolroom were backed on the ground floor by pantries, store-rooms and two large kitchens. One of these was known as the " cooking kitchen " ; it contained both a big range and a large wall oven. The second kitchen also possessed an oven, but was usually given up to meals for the farm workers, who sat round a long table on low wooden benches. In the Holtbys' time, the ten or eleven bedrooms on the upper floor were packed to the limit of their capacity with members of the family, household servants and guests.

As a child Winifred spent many hours reading and

meditating in her bedroom, which looked towards the sunset over the large paddock at the back of the house, where
the hawks hovered watchfully, looking for field-mice, and
the cart-horses were turned loose to graze. Beyond this
pasture the wolds curved upwards like the green slope of a
giant saucer, dotted with isolated elms, chestnuts and sycamores self-sown from seeds blown from the larger clumps
which protected the scattered farmsteads against the pre-
vailing wind.

To the end of her days this view from her window
dominated Winifred's memory, and throughout her youth
it made a permanent background for her stories and dreams.
When she spoke, in one of our first conversations at Somerville College, of her attempts to write the novel which afterwards became *Anderby Wold*, she told me how her whole
life was bound up with " the curves of the hills, the outline
of the wolds." Shortly afterwards she wrote of Mary Robson, the heroine of the story, that " in her lovely childhood,
the fields of Anderby had assumed for her a more definite
personality than any of the people whom she knew."

When the two little sisters were still in the nursery, the
back of the house seemed a long way from the large, imposing bedrooms at the front. In a short vignette called
Harking Back to Long Ago, Winifred describes how she and
Grace, aged four and six and a half, lay awake on Christmas
Eve gazing through the square uncurtained window at the
frosty constellations of the winter stars. The maids clatter-
ing in the pantry below them had at last become silent ;
only the occasional clank of an iron-shod hoof in the horse-
pasture broke the stillness of the night — when suddenly
came the crunch of feet on the gravel of the drive, the soft
flicker of a lantern, and the joyous tumult of a Christmas
carol. In a second the two small girls were out of bed,
scampering barefoot along the nursery passage, up two steps
into a terrifying stretch of unlighted corridor, past the silver
cupboard that harboured ghosts and tigers, on to the front
landing, and through a door into the best spare bedroom.

Peering between the slats of the Venetian blind, they saw

the singers with pale faces and long black coats, standing in moonlight and starlight and lantern-light, and the lamplight streaming from the drawing-room window on to the semicircular sweep of gravel. The chill draught blowing through the cold bedroom was sharp as icy water on the children's small shivering bodies ; they gathered their nightdresses round them and huddled ecstatically together for warmth as the twenty men and boys from the church choir went on singing round the schoolmaster's lantern :

> Mild He lays His glory by,
> Born that man no more may die. . . .

"I can close my eyes and see them," Winifred wrote a quarter of a century later. "I can shut my ears and hear them ; in the warmth of my lighted room I can feel the wind on my bare arms, and the chill boards under my naked feet. I can even smell the queer, cold, frosty smell of the unused bedroom. It is all there.

"But it is mine. Nobody else can ever hear it as I heard and hear it. No other living memory now carries the echo of those particular singers in that particular garden; though a million children have stolen from bed and scampered like mice through a dark house to hear the carollers on Christmas Eve. When I die, nobody will ever again know that particular sweet, fierce exaltation which stirred the rapturous, unblurred imagination of a child."

Perhaps, since both little girls are dead, nobody remembers either the thrill of summer hide-and-seek among the yews and laburnum and weeping ash growing round the semicircle of close-clipped emerald lawn between the garden gate and the gravel drive where the carollers stood. Nobody can recall the excitement of helping the village children to "field" the balls behind the sloping unnetted tennis court, or describe the day when Winifred, aged three, planted the huge weeping elm which can now shelter an entire tea-party from spring rain or summer sun. The cherished rose-bushes which once filled the flower-beds on the front lawn became untidy and have been removed, though Winifred — refusing to visit the house when she spoke to the Rudston Women's Institute in 1934 for fear of reviving the old aching home-sickness — inquired wistfully if the roses were still there. Only the glowing herbaceous border of phlox, antirrhinums, campanula, larkspur and anchusa round the croquet lawn, and the deep hollow dell with its spring carpet of wild flowers and rough tangle of shrubs, remain as they were in the children's time.

To-day, as always, this dell is a refuge for blackbirds, thrushes, yellow-hammers and water-wagtails, but its banks now slope down to a marshy pool, inhabited by small frogs which leap across curious moss-grown stones half concealed by the mud. One stone, of a fantastic gargoyle-like appearance, suggests the use for some long-forgotten purpose of ecclesiastical adornments stolen from the village church in a medieval raid.

An old Yorkshire legend relates that in this part of the East Riding there are underground springs known as " the Wold Waters," which only come to the surface before some national calamity. The dell in the garden is one of the places where the superstitious villagers watch for the emergence of the waters ; they are also said to regulate the flow of Gypsy Race, the narrow stream which runs through the village. Alice Holtby once told the present occupant of Rudston House that throughout the years when they lived there, the bottom of the dell remained dry until the weeks preceding the Great War. According to the Holtbys' successors, it was wet again before the General Strike of 1926 and also at the death of George V, but honesty compelled them to admit that other national calamities had occurred during their tenure which left the Wold Waters apparently unmoved. They must surely, one feels, have flowed when Winifred died, for on that day the Wolds lost their most promising and devoted chronicler. Perhaps the marshy pool in the dell is her Yorkshire's tribute to her memory.

But even apart from the survival of her fame, dependent as it is upon values so far removed from village experience,

Rudston is unlikely to forget either Winifred or her family. Her parents kept a watching brief over the sick and the sad ; her mother looked after the village as assiduously as Mary Robson cared for Anderby and far more judiciously. In the last autumn of her life, Winifred could still recall her mother poulticing a casual labourer's chest in a barn because he was too ill to be carried down the wooden ladder ; she remembered the sunset through the unglazed window and the candles flickering in broken bottles. Years afterwards, when Alice Holtby became the first woman member and later the first woman Alderman on the East Riding County Council, the knowledge of local problems which Winifred was to transmute into universal experience through *South Riding* proved also to be for her mother an abiding source of human wisdom.

At the time it must have seemed ungratefully rewarded, for late in 1918 a farm-workers' strike, from which David Holtby never recovered, caused the family to give up Rudston House and move to Cottingham, a suburb of Hull. The forces which induced agricultural labour to break away from feudalism and take to modern methods of collective bargaining were as baffling as they were bitter to the feudal farmers of a less revolutionary age.

The East Riding remembers Winifred as a slim little girl, tall for her age, with a shining golden head and a long fair pigtail. Quick, alert, spontaneous, very eager and open-eyed with enjoyment of life, she was a vivid contrast to her more sedate brown-haired sister. Friends who were already grown up in her childhood describe her shrieking with merriment as she slid up and down the straw-stacks, or conscientiously endeavouring to subdue her irrepressible vitality when she shared her mother's visits to newly-born babies and bedridden sufferers from asthma or bronchitis.

Her own memories, as related in her books or in conversations with the companions of later years, recalled village sights and sounds and smells with a keenness which we all reserve for our earliest impressions. She wrote of

Yorkshire high teas in the warm kitchen lighted by oil lamps ; of tables loaded with roast chickens and boiled ham, hot buttered tea-cakes, jam tarts, saucer cheese-cakes flavoured with rum, and plates of spiced bread, black and sticky. She spoke of the wild wold flowers in the sun-drenched August hay-fields, ripe for cutting on her return from school, until we who hardly knew Yorkshire could picture the riot of scarlet poppies, golden dandelions, magenta knapweed and mauve scabious, the elder bushes still white in the hedgerows, the pale stars of convolvulus climbing the deep chalk quarry, the hillsides pink and purple with giant willow-herb. In her articles she recorded the persistent farmyard tumult which made a fraud of the town-dweller's cherished illusions about " country silence."

" Let a townsman, accustomed to the hushed hum of urban traffic, sleep near a farm. If he is not awakened by the jugging of the nightingale, the hooting of owls, the howl of a dog at the moon or the love serenades of the stable cats, let him wait for the crowing of the cocks or the early milkers bringing up the cows, or the waggoners calling up their horses, ' Coo-up, coo-up,' in the chill twilight. Then the pigs, then the guinea-fowls, then the geese and the ducks and the clucking hens advertising their new-laid eggs, join the chorus with mooing cows and braying donkeys. Mr. Hore-Belisha may curb the valiant toot of motorists, but just let him try to silence an old rooster in the dawn ! Nature is not silent, and never was a name more derisively inappropriate than when we speak of these non-human creatures who hoot and crow and bray as the *dumb* animals."

Throughout Winifred's childhood the failing health of her father, who had never been robust, kept her mother constantly busy at his bedside or on the farm. She once told me how passionately, with a child's bewildered ignorance of domestic emergencies, she had resented the duties which preoccupied her mother, to whom she was ardently and strenuously devoted. In their earliest years the two little girls were taught by a succession of governesses, of whom " Nuddie," the best beloved, arrived on Winifred's fourth birthday and stayed until she was eight.

Though Grace was docile, Winifred's adventurousness drove her to elude these guardians ; from time to time she escaped them on pony-rides over the rough hills with her father's old shepherd, whose conversation survived in her memory the highbrow utterances of school teachers and Oxford dons.

" So I says, we'll be wanting a cottage, maister. I've found a lass same mind as meself an' we'll away get wed. Tak ceer o' women, maister, and they'll tak ceer o' the men."

Once, with more caution than tact, he inquired : " You bain't afeerd of the ditch, Miss Winifred ? " — to be instantly reproved in the broad Yorkshire which she reserved all through her life for the entertainment of her soft-spoken South Country friends : " If you make that there remark again, Shep, I'll be really mad."

She was tameable only on Sundays, when the family occupied their pew of brown polished wood in the village church, and she memorised with enjoyment a characteristic epitaph on a gravestone in the churchyard, erected by a certain Major John Milner to his wife Dorothy in 1826 :

> *What faults you've seen in me, strive to avoid.*
> *Search your own hearts, and you'll be well employed.*

In the ancient church with its stained-glass windows and abundant memorials, there was plenty to occupy the roving attention of a small imaginative girl. But it did not contain until some years later the remarkable window in the chancel, which shows the surplice-clad figure of the local lord of the manor, Sir Alexander Macdonald of the Isles, seated at the organ surrounded by an unusually pious-looking group of small choir-boys. Sir Alexander, who gave his family name to the larger of the two Rudston inns, the Bosville Arms, held an annual garden party for tenants, local farmers and

other lesser breeds without the County, to which Winifred
went as one of the little village girls and was greeted with
kindly patronage by his wife. In those days there was no
framed Roll of Honour recording the names of one hundred
and fourteen men from Rudston who served in the Great
War. Nor did the War Memorial Cross of white painted
stone stand in the roadside grass at the top of Church Hill
to commemorate the eleven who died, and by its double
inscription to remind alien travellers that Yorkshire pre-
serves an adamant distinction between the natives of a
village and those who merely lived there.

Apart from the village children who " dared " Winifred
to accomplish terrifying climbs to the top of the straw-stacks,
her playmates included her cousins Edmund and Dolly from
Dowthorpe Hall, the home of David Holtby's elder brother
Tom, which in its later and more dilapidated years supplied
the original for " Maythorpe " in *South Riding*. During the
War which competitive imperialisms were already preparing
unsuspected by Yorkshire, Edmund and Winifred were to
spend several war-time " leaves " together when she was
nursing in London and he had become an officer in an
East Yorkshire regiment. Another childhood companion
was Sybil Goulding, the dark, pretty, gifted daughter of a
Bridlington bank manager, who later preceded Winifred to
Somerville and took a brilliant war-time First in French.

But far deeper and more permanent in its consequences
was the children's friendship with two brothers who came
from a neighbouring town to join the games in the stackyard. The younger, whose age matched Winifred's, was
destined to leave home early and become an efficient, self-
confident business man in the Far East. The elder shall be
known for the purposes of this volume as Bill, since years
afterwards, when the long tale of her loyalty and devotion
to his charming incorrigible personality was almost ended,
Winifred recorded it in that story of Jean Stanbury and Bill
Durrant in *Mandoa, Mandoa !*

She had, of course, other and older companions, who
took her to such thrilling entertainments as the agricultural

show at Wetherby, or the performances of the Macdonalds' Theatrical Society at the village theatre, where she found the sounds of hammering behind the curtain " almost unendurably exciting as promise of what was to come." Chief among these friends were the young masters from Bridlington School who at week-ends walked or cycled over to Rudston, where they found the house a second recreation room and the stackyard a supplementary games field. Sometimes they brought the school boarders or the Officers' Training Corps with them for a paper-chase or a route march ; sometimes they helped with the village sports in the Holtbys' paddock, and afterwards sat down with the competitors and the family for a large satisfying tea at the kitchen table.

Familiar as young uncles, their names were a part of Winifred's conversation from the time that I first knew her. I heard of Mr. Warner, the Mathematics master, who wrote her gay, ridiculous letters addressed to " Mrs. Middleton " or " Mrs. Willoughby " ; of Mr. Blagborough, who was killed in action as a war-time Major ; of Mr. Bendall, who became a Colonel in the War but survived it ; of the alarming bachelor headmaster Mr. Thornton, who listened with trepidation in 1934 when Winifred was the first woman ever invited to give the address and present the prizes at the School Speech Day. Most frequently of all she mentioned the School Art master, Mr. Robert Horspool, whose favourite nickname for her was " Bib." One day, not long before her death, when they were walking together up and down the lawn at Cottingham, he found himself unconsciously using the old name, and was startled to see how much it moved her.

" Oh, Robert ! " she exclaimed, impulsively gripping his arm with tears in her eyes, " it's so charming of you to remember that ! So much has happened since I last heard it."

When Winifred was eight years old, she and Grace drove into Bridlington with Scaife, the solemn-faced groom, for lessons in Art from Mr. Horspool. These afternoons gave her the excuse to describe herself as an " Old Boy " of the

School in her Speech Day address. This was, perhaps, the most useful consequence of the lessons, since Winifred's efforts were not of a kind to encourage a teacher hoping for signs of artistic genius. She preferred surreptitious games with the boys, especially one in which the competitors threw lumps of sugar into cups of tea arranged at the end of the long dining-room table. The player who neither spilled the tea nor marked the table-cloth was acclaimed as the winner.

Mr. Horspool's literary co-operation was appreciated far more than his professional instructions, for long before she could read easily Winifred had begun to write, and before she could write she told stories. It was an endowment which proved — as the unexpectedness of human ability has proved so often — that the wind of the spirit bloweth where it listeth, and often chooses the least probable instruments for its finest expression.

At the age of four, Winifred was as implacable a narrator of impossibilities as the Ancient Mariner. Planted on a four-legged wooden stool in the cold stone dairy of the farm, she would " read " interminable narratives to the amiable cook scrubbing the shelves from a book held upside down on her knee. One of these stories, ostensibly related from Nat Gould's *Magpie Jacket* with a favourite picture of a racehorse on the cover, was given by its inventor the title of " Minnie's Berk." What a " Berk " was, she alone knew. She described it later as a portmanteau word, derived from " beck," the shallow, stagnant stream beneath the village bridge, and " murky," which meant something dark and forbidding. Into that sinister Berk, the hapless Minnie was destined to fall. But the story had so many twists, turns and variations that the shelves were scrubbed, the bowls of milk set out, and the pancheon of home-made bread put away, before Minnie reached her hideous destination.

Even when Winifred could read with the effortless rapidity that she never lost, she found her own stories and poems more entertaining than the sentimental pieties of *Christie's Old Organ*, *Jessica's First Prayer* and *A Peep Behind the Scenes.* At the age of seven or eight, she and Grace produced a joint magazine with the vicar's daughters from a neighbouring village who shared their governess. This magazine, written by turns in a half-finished exercise-book, flourished on a basis of mutual admiration until the vicar's younger daughter produced a poem containing the couplet :

> *The herds*
> *Of pretty birds,*

which moved Winifred to an ecstasy of disdain. Similar in its effects to other tactless criticisms, her derisive candour brought the paper to an end.

By this time she herself was writing poetry on the mass instalment principle. When she felt too lazy to put it all down, she recited it to her bored but tolerant sister. Alice Holtby, proud and amused, encouraged her. In domestic and emotional crises Winifred took to exhorting, consoling or admonishing her mother with appropriately pious or didactic verses written in pencil on scraps of paper and solemnly laid upon her desk. One very juvenile but still decipherable experiment apparently refers to the recent death of an uncle :

> *On the sad Ascention day,*
> *Mouring Mother weep no more*
> *O'er my uncle's death so sore,*
> *Others need your care much more*
> > *Than he.*

> *He in heaven is at rest*
> *Leaning on Lord Jesu's brest,*
> *He is now forever blest*
> > *Up there.*

> *Far 'way ore the cristle sea*
> *There a place is kept for thee,*
> *Father, Kitty, Grace and me*
> > *With him.*

As Winifred grew older her scansion, though not her spelling, improved, but the quality of her youthful verses remained unaltered.

" I regret to confess it," she wrote in one of her liveliest articles, *Mother Knows Best*, " that quality is execrable — priggish, derivative, nauseatingly insincere. I was, between the ages of seven and twenty-one, a creature of completely uncritical piety and sentimental convention. One of the earliest efforts runs thus :

> *Only a rose-bud*
> *Tender and soft,*
> *Dropped from a rose tree,*
> *Waving aloft.*
>
> *Only a kind thought*
> *Spoken by Love,*
> *Dropped like the rose-bud*
> *From Heaven above.*
>
> *But the wee rose-bud*
> *Once pleasure gave ;*
> *The kind thought's remembered*
> *Unto the grave."*

Shortly afterwards it evidently began to strike her that even noble sentiments could have too luscious a quality, for an effusion of similar date ends with the heart-rending query :

> *Oh, why should I suffer ?   Oh, why should I struggle,*
> *When fame is a-calling to me ?*
> *Oh, why should I toil in the murk of the city*
> *When I hear the grand roar of the sea ?*

At this time Winifred had seen only two cities, Hull and London, and she adored them both. But the idea of urban toil as an alternative to fame and freedom produced almost

as satisfactory a sensation of triumphant gloom as the immense blank-verse poem which she began to compose at the
age of eleven, scribbling with terrified urgency amid the
shadows of a box-room half-lighted by a lantern smuggled
from the stable :

> *Why should we mortals, rulers of this world,*
> *Bow down ourselves to One who went before*
> *And is long dead — One Who has passed before,*
> *Whom we have never seen, nor neer can see*
> *Till the last trump shall sound, proclaiming all*
> *At end ?   Both land and sea, and beasts and men,*
> *All mortals to be ended, and the world,*
> *And all the universe, one bare blank space,*
> *Devoid of light, of life, of everything*
> *Save His own presence, making all things day ;*
> *And life and love perpetually there,*
> *The end of all things, save of Him Himself.*

Much to Winifred's embarrassment, this turgid soliloquy
was included in the published edition of her juvenile verses
and given the title *In Milton's Footsteps*. For, surprising as
it may seem to other literary aspirants who have used up
reams of perfectly good paper without the satisfaction of
seeing themselves in print, published these verses were. In
Mother Knows Best she describes how the astonishing event
occurred.

One afternoon in 1911, when she had been at boarding-
school for two years, she accompanied the school matron
into a stationer's shop to buy some Christmas presents.
And there, beside the counter on a special stand, she saw a
quantity of elegant little pink and pale-green gift books,
bound in paper and tied with purple ribbon, entitled : *My
Garden and Other Poems*, by Winifred Holtby.

 " I felt — well, what would you have felt ? I paid my
sixpence — borrowed from the matron, who also, properly
astonished, bought a copy. I returned to school — on
air ? No, in the air, a creature transformed (and doubt-

less most unpleasant). I might be plain, I might be bad at hockey, I might be delicate, tiresome, naughty and unpopular ; but I had done something now that no girl in the school, no girl of my acquaintance (except a horrid little prig, whose photograph I had once seen and hated in the *Girl's Realm*) had ever done before. I had published a book.

" And what a book ! The publication had been arranged (for a sum down, I imagine, though I have never asked) with a local firm. My mother's intention was, I think, to present me with a copy for Christmas ; but the ways of publishers are not those of mothers. Commerce frustrated her. But what cared I for her intention ? I have known since then countless moments of pleasure, several of rapture and a few of pride, but as I walked back to school with my first published work I knew so dazzling an ecstasy of achievement that nothing experienced since has ever approached it."

Recently, in the mottled blue exercise-book, still cherished by Winifred's family and known as " The Album," in which the manuscript originals of *My Garden* appear, I found a receipted bill that gave me the information for which she never inquired. Dated December 13th, 1911, it was rendered by a well-known Yorkshire bookseller to Mrs. David Holtby, Rudston House, Bridlington, for " Producing 500 copies containing 48 pp. of Poems in Art Cover tied with col⁴˙ ribbon as per our Estimate of 30/9/XI. £10.15.0."

It seems a modest charge for publishing and distributing so unique a collection of masterpieces.

CHAPTER III

"FILIA REGIS"

Q.M.S. SCARBOROUGH

There's a long grey school on a wind-swept hillside,
  Where over the garden the wild sea-birds cry ;
There's a red-roofed town that the waves wash ever,
  And a castle stands guarding it regally high.
And far away from the eastward coastline,
  Where the wind from the moorland heights blows chill,
We suddenly pause in our work to remember
  That red-roofed town at the foot of the hill.

When the valley lies still in the soft morning sunlight,
  And the looped river gleams like a silver snake,
And the misty clouds that enwrap the shoulders
  Of the mountain giants grow tattered and break,
Then we think of the waves in the golden morning,
  When the great sun rises beyond the sea,
Throwing living flame on the grey, cold water,
  And the fresh salt sting of the wind blowing free.

WINIFRED HOLTBY (aged 16½)
Q.M.S. Magazine, Pitlochry, 1915

THE PUBLICATION of Winifred's poems was valuable
chiefly for the assurance that it gave her. In bringing them
out her mother anticipated the methods of modern parents,
who are taught at the lectures on infant psychology
which they humbly attend that if a child has confidence
and a sense of security, everything else shall be added unto
him.

Alice Holtby was no theorist, but her intuition was sound.
It taught her that, whatever temporary outburst of ebullient
pride might result, nothing but good could come in the long

run from such a criticism of *My Garden* as the review published in the *Bridlington Gazette*. This notice concluded with the encouraging words :

> " From a mind so gifted and a fancy so delicate the world will be justified in expecting much in the future when time and thought and study have done their work upon the fruitful ground, and we shall be much mistaken if the world of poetry shall not be the richer for the existence of Miss Winifred Holtby of Rudstone."

When Winifred went to Queen Margaret's School, Scarborough, in September 1909, she possessed several disadvantages which might have given a sense of inferiority to a less affirmative child.

She was very thin, and tall for her age ; her lanky limbs and large pale features gave as yet no hint of the Dantesque profile and fair vivid colouring which were to make her so handsome and brilliant in her twenties and so beautiful and impressive in her thirties. She could not spell, or do arithmetic, or sew with patience ; neither was she capable of those athletic achievements which inspire adolescent heroine-worship in schoolgirls. Hockey bored her and she played it execrably. At lacrosse her long arms and legs made her a useful player in spite of her natural prejudices, but her occasional membership of the team was a reluctantly accepted obligation. She preferred the Girl Guides, where she rose to be a Patrol Leader, and acquired practical knowledge which was to be useful in Queen Mary's Army Auxiliary Corps during the War. Later in life her opinion of the " ball games " which have made the English what they are (and account even more, perhaps, for a great deal that they are not) was forcibly expressed in *Mandoa, Mandoa !* and innumerable articles.

In addition to her athletic deficiencies, Winifred was never strong. During the bleak northern winters she endured agonies from the cold. The Scarborough winds blew too keenly for her delicate constitution, and thirty years ago school sanitation was not all that it has since become. Outgrowing her strength, she developed poisoned glands, the removal of which left a lifelong scar. In moods of self-derision she sometimes entertained the friends of her adulthood with graphic descriptions of the pallid, gawky schoolgirl whose claims to the homage due to beauty were not enhanced by the cotton wool and bandages which swathed her long neck for weeks on end.

Probably the glands and the operation lowered her resistance, for throughout her schooldays at Scarborough she caught one infectious disease after another, and was even known to develop two or three in such rapid succession that their symptoms were almost simultaneous. The London specialists who attended her in her last illness believed that its origin might have lain as far back as an acute attack of scarlet fever, with complications, at the age of fifteen. During the four years of strenuously resisted invalidism which preceded her death, her doctors talked mysteriously of "renal sclerosis" and "adjustment to abnormal conditions"; they did not mention the simple if unscientific name of Bright's Disease, which we should sadly have understood, knowing how often it proves fatal to its younger victims. Medical science has now established the fact that a severe attack of scarlet fever can sow the seeds of Bright's Disease if its after-effects are left unchecked — and nobody thought of investigating the after-effects of schoolgirl ailments in pre-war Yorkshire.

Notwithstanding her plainness, her illnesses and her antipathy to games, Winifred was happy.

" I am not surprised to read," her second headmistress wrote in the school magazine just after her death, " that in spite of her sensitiveness to the sorrow of the world, what struck her friends in later life was her happiness, though it is not perhaps what one would guess from her books. And the self-forgetfulness which is universally noted, and which no doubt was the root of her fundamental happiness, that too, one could trace in her childhood."

Perhaps, at eleven, self-assurance is a more direct well-spring of joy than self-abnegation. Because she felt sure of herself, Winifred's bubbling delight in life was quite irrepressible. Her sureness made her intensely interested in certain lessons and occupations. Half instinctively she knew what she wanted to do, and was unashamedly indifferent to everything else. When she arrived at school with Grace she was put straight into Form IIIA, where thirteen was the average age. Here neither bad marks, derisive contemporaries, nor the critical comments of her elders could subdue her.

When placed before a wooden board at a drawing-lesson, she informed the Art master that she had already learnt everything that he was trying to teach her from Mr. Horspool at Bridlington. A contemporary clearly remembers her in her blue overall and red school tie a year or two later, standing up in VA form room to argue some point determinedly with the mistress taking the class. She had a habit, comments her schoolfellow, of introducing brilliant but irrelevant variations into a lesson. To the end of her life she cherished and quoted her house-mistress's comment in one of her earliest school reports : " Winifred would do better if she would learn not to express her opinions so freely in front of her elders ; and her writing, spelling and general tidiness leave *much* to be desired."

In 1909 Queen Margaret's was still under its first headmistress, Miss Agnes Body. Four years later, when Winifred, though only fifteen, was already in the Upper Fifth, her place was taken by Miss Rosalind Fowler, who remained a lifelong friend.

Queen Margaret's had been founded, as one of the Woodard schools, in 1901. It stood just below Oliver's Mount on a hill above Scarborough, looking north over the unplanned jumble of the town with its grey-roofed buff or red Victorian houses, to the wide sweep of the bay round the Castle. The grey, gabled building had first been a hotel and then a boys' school. It was not so much sheltered as cut off from the southern sun by the wood-covered heights of Oliver's Mount, which created a funnel down which the bitter winds swept over the cold hillside. To-day the warm red brick of the new buildings — with modern windows, central heating and clean light walls — adds a glow of colour to the school's bleakness, and a bright flower-garden climbs the adjacent slope which in Winifred's day was rented to various holders and turned into an untidy conglomeration of allotments. Just below the long grass path which now skirts the garden and ends in a narrow white road, stands a flourishing small beech-tree planted by Princess Mary in a shell-hole made during the Scarborough bombardment.

Like all girls' public schools of the period, Queen Margaret's beauty was not, during Winifred's childhood, its outstanding quality.

Years afterwards, when Winifred was a member of our household at Glebe Place, Chelsea, my husband told her that she furnished her sitting-room according to the standards of a hospital matron. Unlike her usually charming clothes, her furniture was chosen for utility rather than effect. We never persuaded her to get rid of a cheap and hideous cardboard filing cabinet, which gradually faded from crimson to rusty brown, and at last could be induced to stand erect only by a judicious adjustment of its overflowing contents.

If this simplification of Winifred's crowded life by indifference to the claims of interior decoration dated back to her schooldays, the result was not surprising. Before the War the founders of church schools regarded neither beauty nor comfort as necessary aids to the morality and religion which they desired for the young women whom they set out to educate. Hence the old school-house, with its huge draughty windows and tiny antiquated grates, was a cheerless study in green, white and brown. White butter-muslin curtains divided the bedrooms into small unlovely cubicles. Although there was a second house, the school already contained one hundred and fifty girls, and these rooms must have been uncomfortably crowded. Furnished with white-painted chests of drawers and heavy white counterpanes, they gave, like all cubicled bedrooms, the impression of a comfortless, unpatterned disorder. Throughout the school the floors were covered with brown oilcloth, the walls painted a dark olive green. Its chill, stuffy, lysol-pervaded ugliness was more than sufficient to account for the late development of aesthetic standards in its pupils.

The true spirit of the school was to be found, not in its external appearance, but in its aims, the quality of its teaching, and its motto, *Filia Regis*. Its education was designed for middle-class girls of moderate means with their living to earn ; even in Winifred's time it was assumed that the majority would follow some professional career and strive to make themselves independent. Winifred never ceased to be thankful for this early inculcation of modern ideas, and in gratitude bequeathed her library to the school in her Will.

Most of her contemporaries who chose one of the more scholarly professions went on to Lady Margaret Hall at Oxford. Winifred was one of the few to go to Somerville, an undenominational college which her mother felt would provide a stimulating change from the Anglican atmosphere at Scarborough. Queen Margaret's had a special psalm for ceremonial occasions which was used when Canon H. R. L. Sheppard, who was to follow Winifred to the grave two years afterwards, conducted her Memorial Service at St. Martin-in-the-Fields on October 1st, 1935. It was, perhaps, more appropriate to Winifred than to any of the other outstanding girls who passed through the school :

My heart is inditing of a good matter : I speak of the things which I have made unto the King.

My tongue is the pen : of a ready writer.

Thou art fairer than the children of men : full of grace are thy lips, because God has blessed thee for ever. . . .

Winifred's communications to her family from school appear to have been a mixed collection of eager letters and semi-fictitious anecdotes. Her correspondence was interspersed with poems, still reminiscent of late Victorian piety, which boasted such titles as *The Sin of Omission, A Vision at Night* and *The Quest.*

" Mother dear," runs one early attempt at epistolary consolation for natural shortcomings, " dont worry about not been able to sing. God maybe thought that you could do plenty of things without. You see, he made you just sweet and dear instead, and you did not want a voice too."

Besides adding variety to the weekly letters her perpetual spate of verses rapidly burst its way into the school magazine, though this fresh guarantee of publication did not conspicuously improve their quality. But she was already experimenting with another form of expression — the form that throughout her life most fascinated her, gave her the greatest pleasure and brought her no single vestige of success. She was writing plays, to be performed in the holidays by herself, her sister, Sybil Goulding, and the boy companions who took the place of brothers at the farm.

Chief among these was, as usual, Bill, now at a famous public school. Soon he was to begin working for the Cambridge scholarship which — like so many brilliant boys whose careers were to be smashed at the outset by death or disillusion — he was to win in the very summer that the first Great Insanity brought decade upon decade of chaos and ruin to the Europe of our generation. Another adopted brother was a Russian boy, George de Coundouroff, who was also to be a victim of history's irrelevant but devastating intrigues. The son of wealthy parents, already dead, who had owned copper mines in Georgia, he had come to England at the age of fourteen to study agriculture and estate-management. His elder brother, a tutor in Manchester and a friend of Major Blagborough, sent him to Bridlington School as a boarder for a few years of preliminary education, and the Holtbys, finding that he had nowhere to go for the holidays, characteristically invited him to spend them at Rudston.

The plays initiated by Winifred, and produced by herself and her companions, were seldom written down in full. Experienced charade-players, the children discussed and rehearsed them, composing the dialogue between them in the process. The boys liked noise and martial vigour. Grace, pretty and gentle, preferred dressing-up and love scenes. Sybil Goulding, a witty child, added most of the jokes. Winifred enjoyed drama, and saw to it that the script contained as many opportunities for its manifestation as literary ingenuity could devise.

They acted the plays in the front kitchen, an admirable place for amateur theatricals. Built in the days when the farm hands " lived in," it was a long, bare room with three doors opening off one end, and a fourth near the fireplace. Of the three end doors, two opened into cupboards, the third on to stairs leading up to the maids' bedroom and the box-room which had been Winifred's study and now became a green-room. Sides of bacon, hams in muslin bags, and Christmas puddings hung on hooks from the whitewashed kitchen ceiling. On those hooks the performers fixed their curtains ; in the cupboards they kept their " properties " and changes of scenery ; up the stairs they fled to transform themselves into the numerous characters which each had to represent.

The first two plays, *The Highwayman's Curse* and *Grizelda's Vow*, contained nothing more alarming to parental solicitude than a few murders and duels, and one superb suicide when Grizelda (having accomplished her vow to murder her father's enemy) leapt from the kitchen window and flung a croquet ball on the stones below to represent the cracking of her skull. So during the third Christmas holidays after Winifred went to school, her mother thought that the annual performance might have a more exciting audience than the couple of maids and an aunt or two who had applauded the earlier dramas. Possibly she had watched them with divided attention, for she was a busy woman, and did not suspect the macabre possibilities lurking in juvenile minds. Optimistically she invited the children from two or three neighbouring families and a few local adults to watch the play and have supper afterwards.

Spurred by the prospect, Winifred rose to the occasion.

She wrote a drama word for word, and they all laboriously learned it.

The drama was called *A Living Lie*. It ran for four long acts, and contained, among its milder entertainments, one elopement, a strong scene of adultery, a case of leprosy and two murders. The "Lie" was lived by a lady who contracted leprosy under most shady circumstances, and murdered both the doctor — who was also her lover — and her husband in order to avoid deportation to Robben Island; before she stabbed herself across her lover's body.

When the second act was over, one horrified mother removed her family from the "theatre." Throughout the third, the audience appeared distinctly apprehensive. At the end of the fourth, the lurid "curtain" brought scant applause. The following year, Winifred's mother insisted that they should perform a nice little comedy from French's acting edition called *Two Sharps and a Flat*. But who wanted comedy? Winifred was only consoled by a promise to play the heroine in one of her mother's best evening dresses, and to have an adult male friend — an experienced amateur to whom she was much attached — to make her up.

She compensated herself during her last year at school, in 1915, by writing a play called *Espionage* which grossly but superbly plagiarised *Diplomacy*. The brown exercise-book (marked "Strictly Private. *Strictly*") in which it was composed still exists with its eccentrically spelt title *Espinage — A Drama of 1914*, and its imposing list of seventeen "Dramatis Personnae" with "Colonel Sir Robert Burley (retired)" at their head. A mournful ditty, which was set to music and sung as a prologue, opened the performance :

> *The harvest fields of fair Lorraine*
> *Were crowned with yellow corn,*
> *And midst the gold were crimson heads*
> *By poppy stems up borne.*

> *In dewy morn the peasants reap,*
> *In quivering heat of noon,*
> *Till o'er the purple hill-top glides*
> *The primrose harvest moon.*
> *The harvest fields of fair Lorraine*
> *Are not so gold as then,*
> *And midst the gold are crimson stains,*
> *The blood of slaughtered men ;*
> *And by the light of one lone star*
> *And the chill wind's sobbing breath,*
> *A reaper gathers his harvest there —*
> *And the reaper's name is Death.*

Winifred produced the play with the entire Girl Guide Company in aid of the Red Cross. Out of a passion for originality and revolt against mob-emotion, she made her spy a beautiful but venal American and her German suspect guiltless.

Before she wrote *Espionage*, Winifred had already blossomed into print with two typical journalistic efforts, inspired by an event which was for ever to remain a high spot of Queen Margaret's history.

It has been suggested that Winifred was " amazed " by the bombardment of Scarborough on December 16th, 1914. Actually the attack had been so accurately predicted that more than half the school, establishing a precedent for A.R.P. " evacuations " twenty-five years later, had already departed in anticipation. Winifred remained because, living so close to Bridlington, her home was as much within the range of German shells as Scarborough itself.

About three weeks before the end of the Christmas term, there was unmistakable alarm and tension along the East Coast. In November 1938, one of Winifred's school contemporaries, Mrs. D. M. Lucas, knowing that I should want my story to be completely accurate, sent me a letter received at the time from Winifred describing the bombardment, and herself gave me an account of the preparations made by their headmistress to meet the danger. It is from this account that I quote :

"Miss Fowler had been warned (whether by Scarborough authorities or the War Office I do not know) of the possibility of East Coast raids. She had sent a letter to every parent warning them of this, and also telling of the precautions the school was taking. They were asked to decide whether they would like their children home or prefer them to stay at school.

"From the beginning of term she had made preparations, and in those last few days little bags of money and rations were stored ready for any emergency. Out of 170 girls, I think quite 130 of us left in 36 hours — amid *anger* and *scorn* and *contempt* for the cowardice of our parents ! I felt I could never forgive them, but 14 days later they were more than justified."

The abundance of their justification was proved by another letter from Winifred, written the day after the bombardment to the head girl of the school, who had been among those recalled. This youthfully eager and detailed description, subsequently extracted from the head girl by Winifred's mother, became a "hot topical" of its day. The *Bridlington Chronicle* not only published it, but arranged for its syndication in Australia. Prints of it were taken and sold by Winifred and her mother at threepence each for the Red Cross, which made a useful little sum.

As this letter is now unobtainable, and gives a vivid first-hand impression, by a girl of sixteen, of an event which Yorkshire history is unlikely to forget, it seems worth while to reproduce it here :

"When I got up on Wednesday morning, if somebody had told me it was going to be the most exciting day I ever had, I should have laughed and said ' Rats.' I went down to breakfast in high spirits. There was an end-of-termy feeling in the air, and breakfast was at 8 A.M. I was sitting next to Miss Crichton, and I distinctly remember she had just passed me the milk, and I was raising my first spoonful of porridge to my mouth.

" I never tasted that porridge ! Crash ! Thu-u-d ! I sat up, my spoon in the air, all the nerves in my system suddenly strung taut, for the noise was like nothing I had heard before — deafening, clear-cut, not rumbly — as though a heavy piece of furniture had crashed in the room overhead. I looked at Miss Crichton, saying with a laugh, ' Hello ! who's fallen ? ' when the look on her face arrested me. She was deathly white, and with fixed eyes was looking towards Miss Bubb. Suddenly I felt a tightness across my chest and an icy hand laid on my spine. I could see the hand that held my spoon trembling, and yet I had not realised what was happening, only something caught at my heart and for an instant it stopped beating.

" I was about to speak, when Cr-r-ash — a sound more terrific than the first — and then all the windows danced in their frames ; each report was doubled — first a roar, and then an ear-splitting crash as the shell exploded. Then someone whispered ' guns.' The word, like magic, passed from mouth to mouth as we sat white-faced but undismayed, with the uneaten food before us. Another crash, and two mistresses rose and spoke together a moment and went out. Still not a girl moved or spoke ; all sat as under a spell. Another crash, and another ; then one by one the girls rose to their feet ; that was the moment — the only moment — when panic could have occurred.

" We did not know, we could only guess what was happening, but a steady voice brought us to our senses.

" ' Lead out to the cloak-room and wait there.'

" We led out ; yes, but not as sedately as usual ; quite slowly and quietly, and then we stood awaiting orders. If anybody felt fear, and I know that some did, no one showed it save by a white face or an excited laugh. We talked quietly in awed tones. Each time a shot was fired some started and flinched, others stood calm and motionless. Then Miss Bubb appeared on the stairs, with her dear, familiar smile and her steadying voice, and we seemed to have caught in a bad dream on to something that was safe, and real, and solid. She was our saviour. And yet the words she said were so absurdly familiar and common-place : ' Put on your long coats, tammies and thick boots ; we are going for a walk into the country till it is over.'

" We dressed and started, Nellie calm and placid as ever, waiting till we were all in line. Just as we got through the gate another shell burst quite near, and ' Run ! ' came the order — and we ran. Ran, under the early morning sky, on the muddy, uneven road, with that deafening noise in our ears, the echo ringing even when the actual firing stopped for a moment — it never stopped for more ; ran, though our hastily clad feet slipped on the muddy road.

" Over the town hung a mantle of heavy smoke, yellow, unreal, which made the place look like a dream city, far, far away. Only the road was real, and the tight pain that caught us across our breast — it was not fear, but something inexplicable that hurt, and yet in some strange way was not wholly unpleasant. Round the corner leading down to the Mere we ran — now all puffing. Someone was down ; with a bang they fell full length on the road and lay winded ; then somebody picked her up and they ran together.

" In an instant's pause I looked round. I heard the roar of a gun, and the next instant there was a crash, and a thick cloud of black smoke enveloped one of the houses in Seamer Road ; a tiny spurt of red flame shot out. Then I was swept on down the hill to where the Mere lay grey and placid in the cold morning light. Where the road joins at the foot of the hill we hesitated a second ; we were moving to the level crossing, when a shell struck the ground some 50 yards away, throwing up earth and mud in all directions. ' Back, back ! ' came the cry, and we turned and ran with dragging feet along the Mere path. It was all so like a bad dream, I wondered if I should wake and find myself in my dormy ! Well, we just had to jog on, and we tried to keep our spirits up by singing ' Tipperary,' but it took too much breath.

" We left the Mere path where it turns, and went along ' No Man's Land,' strewn with old tins and broken crockery ; we tripped on the pottery and slipped on decaying refuse and staggered along through the mud. Miss Trethowan still ran behind, helping stragglers, encouraging, laughing, and being just the brick she is. It was an awful responsibility but she bore it capitally.

" We crossed the line into the Seamer Valley. Along the road was a stream of refugees ; there was every kind of vehicle, filled to overflowing with women and children ; yes, and men too. I saw one great brute, young and strong, mounted on a cart horse, striking it with a heavy whip, tearing at full gallop down the road, caring nothing for the women and children who scrambled piteously out of his path, with the fear of death on his craven face. I could have killed him with pleasure.

" Oh ! those poor things on the road. There was a young mother with a tiny baby clutched in her arms ; an old woman, only partly dressed, with her pitiful little bundle of worldly goods on a rickety perambulator ; there were mothers with tiny children clinging to their skirts, crying for fear of this unknown horror. There was one particularly touching old couple, tottering along side by side, perhaps the last time they would ever walk together. I think I shall never forget them — those people of the Dream that was Real. With white faces they passed on. Whither ? Where to go ? Only an instinct urged on their weary feet, and fear lent wings to the old and tired.

" We paused at the foot of the hill that leads to Seamer to rest for a moment, for shells had been bursting not far from the top, and we knew that when we were half-way up we must run for our lives ; all our strength was needed for that, so we stood for a moment and watched the living stream sweep past. I saw a rulley laden with children pulled at an unsteady amble by an old, old horse, driven by a young girl ; then a motor built for two with at least five in it ; then a country cart with old women and children driven at full gallop ; then with a warning honk ! honk ! a splendid car swept by at a terrific speed with one occupant — a woman wrapped in costly furs, alone in that great car, yet she would not stop to take up one of the poor old women who staggered on weary to death, yet fleeing for their lives.

" Here, also, some of the girls found four tiny mites, half-dressed and almost mad with fear, yet not understanding in the least why. They had lost their mother, so we took them with us ; some put coats round them and carried them. At the top of the hill we found their mother. The poor thing was almost wild with joy when she saw her ' bairns ' safe and sound.

" Just outside Seamer we sat down, tired out. As we sat, new comers came with dreadful tales. ' The School was shattered ' — (two mistresses had stayed in !) — ' The Grand Hotel was in flames ' — ' The South Cliff lay in ruins ' — ' The Germans had landed.' All this we took with salt, and waited for the mistresses to come — they had carried on their hands a mistress who was ill. Some of the servants came up and told us Miss Fowler was on the road with our breakfast. Our breakfast ! At this awful moment they had stopped to get chocolate, dates, and biscuits, parcels of which they had ready in case of emergency. How good those biscuits were, eaten as we sat by the side of the road and shared them with other refugees.

" While we sat there a nice looking officer, who seemed to be directing the traffic, came up and said he was the Vicar's son, and we were to go to the Vicarage. Miss Fowler demurred ; how could she land fifty dirty, tired schoolgirls and maids on the Vicar's wife ? But he waved away her hesitation with a kindly gesture, saying, ' Tell them I sent you.' Bless him ! we went, and the kindness of the Vicar of Seamer and Mrs. Stapleton will never be forgotten by any of us. They set us to make tea and cut bread and butter, knowing that occupation was the best thing for our overstrained nerves.

" Then Miss Fowler appeared, armed with a time table, and read out the names of the London girls who had to be put on the train just due. The Leeds girls had to wait some time, so the Vicar had a fire put in the parish room and turned us in there to give vent to our high spirits in songs and games ; and some of us he took to see the quaint old church.

" How strange it all seemed ! Only an hour or two ago we were sitting calmly at breakfast. Another few minutes — seven, to be correct — we were running for our lives in the chill morning twilight, and here we were in the peaceful village street, which seemed miles and miles away from guns. Finally we returned to School by train to find a meal ready for us. I just can't describe the cool way everything was arranged. Poor Miss Miller had been brought back by car and put to bed again. We set to work to pack, and then walked round the town to see the havoc."

In the letter to Mrs. Lucas, that havoc was further described :

" The South Cliff looks pretty bad. The poor old Prince of Wales (Hotel) has a good many shells through it, and the darling Hall has had its hat knocked off by a German shell. . . . Don't you wish," she added — doubtless to the exasperation of her correspondent — " you'd stayed at school ? " She had already concluded her letter to the head girl with a characteristic aspiration : " I can only finish with an earnest hope that never again will England suffer as she did on that awful December 16th, 1914 — but if she does, may I be there to see."

This experience, and the publication of her impressions, roused Winifred's always keen sense of responsibility to further action. Fired with high-minded ambition, she wrote a long letter to the Press, earnestly and rhetorically protesting against a policy of reprisals.

" It is the boast of England," she urged, " that hitherto she has preserved her honour untarnished. Shall she because of the brutal disregard of all honour and humanity on the part of her enemies be cowed into destroying her soul ? Supposing for an instant that by means of her cruel devices Germany did temporarily, at least, become victorious in this War ; supposing that England was for a time defeated through having refrained from the employment of like methods, would that defeat be half so shameful as if she stooped to actions which she has condemned so bitterly ? The day that sees the loss of England's greatness is not the day that sees the fall of London but the day that sees the Allies marching victorious into Berlin through the use of criminal and barbarous methods of warfare.

"The penalty of any wrong decision made by the Government to-day will be paid by the rising generation ; it is the boys and girls of to-day who are too young to make their voices heard who will suffer the loss of prestige which must inevitably follow such a course of action."

Winifred lived just long enough to realise, through the gathering of the storm which was to overwhelm her contemporaries for the second period within their lifetime, how truthfully she had prophesied the consequences of a vengeful policy, whether pursued during or after a war. In pathetic hope of adult human wisdom, she signed her letter " One of the rising generation."

After the Scarborough bombardment the school was moved away from the range of enemy shells to Pitlochry in Perthshire, where it took possession of the Atholl Palace Hotel. Here the health of all the girls rapidly improved, and Winifred, now a senior, found herself at last free from infectious diseases. Still more to her delight, the lack of playing fields and equipment released her from games. Instead she was allowed to go for long walks with her friends over the Highland hills and wild moors rough with gorse and heather.

Two of these friends were unusually exotic types for a Yorkshire public school. One, Edith Mannaberg, a naturalised Austrian, belonged to a family richly endowed with the musical ability of her lively, tragic nation. She herself was a gifted 'cellist, and most appropriately married Jan Smeterlin, the pianist, in 1925. During her school days her father, Maximilian Mannaberg, was manager of the Frodingham Iron Works, near Leeds, where he owned a large and sumptuous house. Winifred often related how, when she stayed there during one holiday feeling an awkward, half-fledged country girl, she managed through sheer nervousness to shatter the pane of a large plate-glass door.

Her other friend, Osyth Harvey, was the daughter of the British Consul in Ostend. To save Osyth from constant Channel crossings, the Holtbys invited her to spend some of her holidays at Rudston. In Winifred's second novel, *The Crowded Street*, Osyth is portrayed as the decorative, exuberant singer, Clare Duquesne. An early chapter in which the chief characters are still children gives an entertaining picture — not far removed from the facts — of her sudden arrival at school in the middle of a term. More than ten years afterwards, Winifred still keenly remembered the impression made upon her by Osyth's dimpled cheeks, bubbling laughter, and clipped, precise voice speaking English as though it were a foreign language. She described the surprising bow on Osyth's sleek brown hair, the shining buckles on her trim patent shoes, and recalled how cheerfully her short dress of pleated tartan with its muslin frill repudiated public school sartorial conventions.

But Osyth married an airman who took her off to South America on an aeroplane-selling expedition, and a pleasant, amusing companionship vanished with her. It was Edith through whom the friendships of " Q.M.S." lived on ; Edith who invited Winifred after the War to listen to music in a luxurious Knightsbridge flat, and later, when she was Madame Smeterlin, to stay in her apartment at Monte Carlo. And, at the last, it was Edith who visited Winifred when she was dying, addressed her gruffly by an old pet name, put an exquisite bunch of lilies of the valley into her hands, and went away quickly to remember her always.

Winifred's final year at school was memorable for many events apart from the War which had sent them all into exile. In her last Christmas term she played the beautiful rôle of the Young King in Miss Buckton's *Eager Heart* — another small bond between us when we first met, since during my own last term at Kingswood I had taken the silent and less exacting part of the Madonna in the same symbolic nativity play. And at Easter she sat for the Somerville entrance examination — to learn later that her papers had reached a much higher standard than the entrance level.

She would have gained a scholarship or an exhibition, she was told, had she chosen to sit for one.

Winifred had never contemplated a scholarship for the simple reason that, unlike most of her contemporaries, she took Oxford in her stride. It did not occur to her that even then, when the competitive intellectual dog-fight of feminine Oxford approached nowhere near to its present degree of intensity, the winning of a place, and still more of a scholarship, at the most impregnable of the women's colleges, represented an achievement. Only when she arrived at Somerville did she begin to realise the struggle with adverse financial circumstances or disapproving families that many girls had to encounter before they reached the University.

She used to say that she was one of the very few women who went to Oxford because their mothers wished it, rather than from any strong personal impetus or family tradition. The wisdom of Alice and David Holtby as parents was never perhaps more clearly shown than in their readiness — out of a circumscribed society almost as far removed from the peaks of art and scholarship as from the mountains of the moon — to accept the fact that their younger daughter was a " sport " of the most unexpected variety, and to act without criticism on the advice of teachers who predicted a distinguished future career.

Winifred left Queen Margaret's in July, 1916, head of the school in work, but only a prefect in order of merit. She was still too effervescent, too fond of vehemently expressing her views, too deeply preoccupied with matters that she thought essential and too unrepentantly indifferent to everything else, to make the typical competent, executive head-girl.

At the end of that summer term, Queen Margaret's was still far from any prospect of return to Scarborough. Books, paper and funds being scarce in war-time, the girls elected to receive Honour Cards instead of prizes. Winifred, who was awarded the coveted Sixth Form prize, thus missed the star pupil's usual chance to form the nucleus of a personal library. The cards were symbolically inscribed with the Gaelic motto : *Am fear aig am bi an Roimh, bidh an Roimh aige ri chumail suas* — " He that hath Rome must maintain Rome." In the school magazine for the following term, Winifred produced an ode on this motto. Despite her protest on the subject of reprisals, it was replete with current imperialistic sentiments about death and glory.

On July 5th, 1916, Miss Fowler gave a remarkable Speech Day address. Whether Winifred consciously recalled them or not, the headmistress's words must have strongly influenced her in the work to which she turned when she left college.

" What will matter most in the reconstruction that must follow the War," Miss Fowler concluded, " is not specialised skill, but the setting up again of those ideals on which Christian civilisation has been built. With that aim all educationalists are concerned, for it is the young generation that will have to attain to it, and parents and teachers must work together to see that they go into life with principles of justice, service, and mutual responsibility engrained by long practice at home and school, in work and play. . . . If we have taught the children in our schools that in national and international life the ultimate test of every act is ' Is it fair ? ' we have laid deep and true the foundations of a nobler civilisation. Without this, all our Hague tribunals, our courts of arbitration, our international guarantees, are valueless ' scraps of paper.' Unless the treaty that closes this war is founded, not on revenge, or the balancing of interests, but on justice, there is no hope for European civilisation. And it is our work as teachers to mould the outlook of the men and women of the future. . . . In the long run every nation has the politicians and diplomats it deserves. A rightly educated nation, desiring justice even more than peace, may lead the nations towards true peace, for peace will only flourish out of the earth when righteousness looks down from heaven."

Unhappily, it was neither the school-children of 1916 nor their teachers, but the self-same elderly men for whose tradition-ridden minds the catastrophic last resort had always been war, who were to mould the " new world " in which, for over twenty years, that young generation was to struggle and strive against the self-interested forces of power politics. As T. E. Lawrence — Winifred's senior by only ten years and always the object of her fascinated admiration — was to write in *The Seven Pillars of Wisdom*, which she reviewed shortly before she died :

" When we achieved and the new world dawned, the old men came out again and took from us our victory, and re-made it in the likeness of the former world they knew. Youth could win, but had not learned to keep, and was pitiably weak against age. We stammered that we had worked for a new heaven and a new earth, and they thanked us kindly and made their peace."

CHAPTER IV

YOUTH AND WAR

THE SARABANDE

A Coward's Apology

So you are angry, will not take my hand,
Nor laugh to me again with loving eyes ;
But lift your charming head with hurt surprise,
Half scornful. Dear, you do not understand.
Down music-haunted halls we bow and sway,
Moving in measured figures, gravely planned ;
Not knowing what wild air the minstrels play.
You hid your anger with disdainful face
Thinking 'twas I who gave the sidelong glance,
Tortured your soul upon a turn of chance.
Because I trod my measure out of place
You thought I wittingly forwent your grace.
It was not I, dear heart. It was the Dance.

WINIFRED HOLTBY, 1920

THE WAR came to Rudston in the shape of agricultural
pressure, half-trained land-girls taking the place of male
farm workers, nervous young sentries on picket duty in the
village, and bored Territorial officers perpetually craving
for light entertainment.

In 1914 Winifred had two more years of school in front
of her. But she came home for the holidays nearly a week
before August 4th, and never forgot the oddly unfamiliar
appearance of the village on the summer evening that England's ultimatum to Germany expired.

There was no wireless then to announce that the over-
hanging disaster of the past few weeks was now unavoidable
or to carry war's declaration to the public in a statesman's
living voice, but somehow the news travelled to the remotest

corners of England. In Rudston little knots of people stood
in the half-light round the open doorways of shops that would
normally have closed hours before. Unexpected shadows and
whisperings moved and rustled in the tense, quiet air. Noises
from the road — a motor horn, the shouts of children playing, their bedtime forgotten — broke with shattering effect
upon the stillness. In a far-away farm-house, a dog barked
persistently. Above the counter of the small crowded newspaper shop, large moths flopped clumsily round the swinging
paraffin lamp. An old drunken woman wearing a man's
cap planted herself in a chair beneath it.

"War's bloody hell," she remarked in mild conversational
tones. "Ah'm tellin' you God's truth. Two o' my lads went
i' South Africa. Bloody hell. That's wha' 'tis."

At Rudston House, hospitality and common sense drove
away the hell to a safe distance. The Holtby family
responded to "England's call" with a variety of miscellaneous services. Their smooth well-rolled croquet lawn
was dug up and turned into a potato patch. The young
sentries apprehensively watching for Zeppelins in the moonlight were cheered with hard-boiled eggs and mugs of tea.
Territorial soldiers, enrolled for more serious duties than
the Bridlington schoolboys on O.T.C. route marches,
crowded round the solid table in the long bare kitchen.

At the front of the house their officers amused themselves with choruses shouted from Gilbert and Sullivan or
the Globe Song Book to Grace's adaptable vamped accom-
paniments. On mild autumn evenings the young men
fought duels with oranges across the wide stretch of semicircular lawn. Winifred, who had run and laughed with the
rest, described in her second novel the great harvest moon
hanging low above the elm trees, the gay figures leaping
out of the black shadows before the dark, carefully curtained
house, the oranges glittering like golden metal in the silver
moonlight. There was a madness in the air of those war-
time summers, which was to intoxicate her with bewildering
emotion when a young officer with his arm in a sling stood
beside her to watch the wild games that he could not share.

In a lecture on " The Psychology of Peace and War " delivered a few months before her death, Winifred included " the erotic impulse " as third among the war-making instincts.

" I am qualified to speak here . . ." her rough notes stated. " Sixteen when the War started. The first thing it made me do was to fall in love. Brevity of life makes passion more insistent. The youngest and fittest in uniform. The erotic attraction of death."

In common with others upon whose adolescence the year 1914 burst like a thunderstorm, Winifred belonged to a generation of women which — however sincere its subsequent urge towards peace — identifies its memory of first love with the sight of a uniform and the sound of " Tipperary." It was of herself, as much as of certain wives and mothers amongst her friends, that she was thinking when she wrote for *Good Housekeeping* in 1935 a review of Pamela Hinkson's novel, *The Deeply Rooted* :

" There are to-day in England — and in France and Germany and Austria and Italy, one imagines — women peacefully married to men whom they respect, for whom they feel deep affection and whose children they have borne, who will yet turn heartsick and lose colour at the sight of a khaki-clad figure, a lean ghost from a lost age, a word, a memory. These are they whose youth was violently severed by war and death ; a word on the telephone, a scribbled line on paper, and their future ceased. They have built up their lives again, but their safety is not absolute, their fortress not impregnable."

For all the distinguished men that Winifred met later who would gladly have made her wife or mistress, she never outlived the compulsion of this memory — associated, for her, with one individual. At the outbreak of War, Bill had joined a West Yorkshire Regiment, and relinquished for ever the undergraduate life at Cambridge to which his scholarship would have admitted him the following October. Already he possessed a gay, virile attractiveness which his later

years of rootless wandering were never to destroy. In his
khaki uniform he looked tall and very slim. Long brown
lashes, a little deeper in colour than his bronzed cheeks,
curled lazily over his amused blue eyes, and his vivid,
humorous smile creased his thin face into characteristic lines
of cynical benevolence.

In the Easter holidays of 1916, Bill was sent back from
France to Yorkshire with a wound in his shoulder. Through
him, as she wrote long afterwards, Winifred had vicariously
endured " all the enormities he had seen at the front — the
mouthless mangled faces, the human ribs whence rats would
steal, the frenzied tortured horses, with leg or quarter rent
away, still living ; the rotted farms, the dazed and hopeless
peasants ; his innumerable suffering comrades ; the desert
of no-man's-land ; and all the thunder and moaning of war ;
and the reek and freezing of war ; and the driving — the
callous, perpetual driving by some great Force — which
shovelled warm human hearts and bodies, warm human
hopes and loves, by the million into the furnace."

When he came, convalescent, to stay at Rudston House,
Winifred found in dressing his wounded shoulder an ecstasy
of relief from the half-adult anxiety and suspense which had
lain, a dull intermittent ache, beneath the excitement of the
Scarborough raid and the move to Pitlochry. The slow
process of recovery that kept him back from the front gave
him, in turn, time to think and to dream. Before many
months had passed he was writing her a sequence of love
sonnets, for it was he who was first moved — as so many
boys barely out of their 'teens were moved beneath the
shadow of that doom — to feelings and expressions of
romantic adoration.

In those days Bill's writings betrayed the noble impulses of religious-minded boyhood ; the youthful aspiration for a life of service, the mood of sublime self-dedication
which was so readily exploited by the war-mongers of 1914.
The very intensity of that consecration and the cold disillusion of the post-war years were to change him, as they
changed so many others, from an ardent idealist into a soul

still benevolent but without purpose or integration, capricious, perverse, incalculable, a war casualty of the spirit.
If he had clothed his vulnerability with the defensive armour
of callous indifference, if the pure flame of his sacrificial
ecstasy had leapt less brightly to heaven, he might have kept
his foothold more securely upon the lampless everyday earth
where the War flung its exhausted survivors.

His love-poems, though neither powerful nor original,
were musical and infinitely touching, sincere and tender
with the gentle illumined tenderness of a serious-minded
boy's first emotional awakening. They spoke of loveliness
and longing, of grief at the beauty of autumn in war-time ;
they challenged the imminent death which might leave
unconsummated the holiest desire of earthly passion, but
could not prevent the final union of two young lovers in
the arms of God.

Shyly he offered his verses to an eighteen-year-old
Winifred who, captivated though she knew herself to be,
had not yet grown sufficiently mature to understand their
moving significance. She was the product of a rational
education, the offspring of a family which took a stalwart
pride in its hard-headed sanity, and the difference in their
ages was just sufficient to render still incomprehensible to
her the religious, erotic mysticism of twenty-one. Partly
to cover the embarrassment of her own awakening passion,
she received his tribute with a breezy schoolgirl scepticism
and told him a little scornfully not to be sentimental.

He was deeply, irretrievably wounded. In later years
Winifred believed that the casual indifference with which
he often treated her was due to some half-conscious memory
which could not forgive her the pain of that uncomprehend-
ing rebuff. She, at any rate, never forgave herself. For the
rest of her life her conscience, as well as her emotions, was
aroused on his behalf. Because she had once disdained
his poems, she humbly accepted as her due the many occasions on which he scorned or ignored her devotion.

One late evening in the dim firelight of our rooms
at Oxford after the War, she turned from reading aloud

to me Swinburne's *Super Flumina Babylonis* — a favourite poem associated in her mind with war-time loss and all premature death — and opened the notebook which contained her copies of Bill's verses. I can still see her blue dressing-gown, the glow of the fire on her golden hair and the sparkle of tears in her eyes as she recited his sonnets ; still hear the self-reproachful sadness of her voice, as though she uttered a requiem for someone dear and departed. It was the mood which produced, at the same period, her reminiscent lines *The Sarabande*. A more mature and bitter comment on Bill and his poems went ten years later into her novel *Poor Caroline*, in the form of *Epigram on the End of Love* :

> *You said that death was not the end ; most true.*
> *Death was not stronger than my love for you.*
> *But since sweet love so lightly goes, my friend,*
> *We are not dead, and yet — this is the end.*

It would be, I think, impossible for any late-comer in Winifred's life to realise the extent to which these youthful experiences captured her imagination and moulded her standards of conduct. Although I knew her comparatively early and remained close to her till the last, I can judge of their influence only from the account of them that she gave me and their immediate after-effects which I saw. When her career grew more definite and her work and responsibilities increased, this influence, though perpetual, became less obvious. Those who knew her only in London may well tend to overlook or underestimate these controlling memories of the past.

At the end of July 1916, a number of mothers from Bridlington belonging to a local club known as " The Babies' Welcome " were entertained with their families at Rudston House. They came over in charabancs for one of their periodic outings, and Winifred, just back from Queen Margaret's with Edith Mannaberg as her guest, was called in as usual to take her share of social obligation. At Rudston House the practice of feudal benevolence marched steadily on irrespective of tastes, temperaments and tragedies. The fact that Edith Mannaberg adored her 'cello and detested babies did not absolve her from taking charge of shrill and fractious infants while their mothers enjoyed a holiday. Nor could the function be postponed because only that day one member of the party had seen her husband off to the front, and felt that her heart was dead.

This preoccupied victim of enforced separation was Edith de Coundouroff, for George, the Russian boy, was now grown up, and in khaki, and married to a young English wife. In 1912 he had left Bridlington School and gone to Cirencester Agricultural College, where he fell in love with the Principal's pretty curly-haired secretary. Three years later he took his degree and joined the Royal Fusiliers — in which, being Russian, he could only enlist as a private. After he and Edith were married in December 1915 they took a temporary house in Oxford, and Winifred stayed with them when she went up for the Somerville entrance examination the following Easter.

Now, because George was going to France, Edith had been invited to Rudston. She came to the Holtbys for a few months ; she stayed with them for over twenty years. Bound to the family by those profound emotional experiences which are more compelling than ties of blood, she was closer to Winifred in every way than the well-meaning but too gentle Grace. Efficient, reliable, intelligent, but comfortably unafflicted by the restless urge of ambition, Edith neither pretended nor desired to be a " highbrow." But her tolerant acquaintance with many tempestuous intellectuals was to give her an affectionate sympathy — enhanced rather than diminished by freedom from competition — with their problems and preoccupations. To a recorder of Winifred's life the value of her accurate memories and honest impressions is beyond all gratitude.

The two Ediths, temperamentally as different as a couple of young women could be, but united by the shared intensity of boredom and grief, helped each other to endure the long nightmare of the hot and exhausting July afternoon. Edith

de Coundouroff, not caring whether the customary habits
of babies might ruin her pretty summer frock, sat miserably
on the lawn with one Bridlington infant after another on
her lap. Edith Mannaberg, brusque, laconic, infinitely
kind, assisted her with endearing inexperience. Winifred,
only too well aware how much the interminable ordeal
was costing them both, hurried anxiously between them in
the intervals of cutting sandwiches and pouring out tea.
But, long before she expected it, she too was to be removed
from the brisk atmosphere of war-time philanthropy to
cruder and more urgent occupations.

A day or two after the " Babies' Welcome," Alice Holtby
received a letter from a fashionable London nursing-home.
The secretary and partner in this enterprise was a daughter
of the school matron who had taken charge of Grace and
Winifred at Queen Margaret's. She now wrote to explain
that because of the demand for trained and V.A.D. nurses
in military hospitals after the battle of the Somme, the home
found it difficult to get enough probationers. Could Mrs.
Holtby perhaps spare Grace for a short time to make herself
useful to the staff and patients ?

But Grace, as it happened, was no longer available.
Having completed a normal and irreproachable school
career a year or two before Winifred, and being further
equipped with a brief training course in domestic economy,
she had now left home to work in a military hospital at
Darlington. It was Winifred, seated at the breakfast table
with shining eyes and eager, parted lips, to whom the unexpected invitation came as a clarion call.

" Oh, Mummie ! " she pleaded urgently, " do let me
go instead ! "

Winifred was then only a few weeks past her eighteenth
birthday, and her knowledge of life may be deduced from her
published *juvenilia* and her tactless treatment of Bill. But a
private nursing-home, her mother calculated, was not, after
all, a military hospital, and Winifred would only be required
for elementary probationers' work under the eye of a family
friend. Alice Holtby did not reckon on the enforced ex-

pedients to which private nursing-homes were driven during the War by overwork and the shortage of qualified women. She did not foresee — and probably was not told until long afterwards — that Winifred would be required to help with the dressings of acute cancer cases, or would find herself alone in the room when a distinguished patient died suddenly in her arms. So she gave her consent, and Winifred rushed excitedly to the village dressmaker to order some cotton frocks in a becoming shade of lavender blue which showed her pale skin and fair hair to their best advantage. A fortnight after leaving school, she went to London for a rapid initiation into what are known as the facts of life.

In *The Land of Green Ginger* — the only one of her novels in which she ventured upon a self-portrait — Winifred describes the first weeks of her new rôle and her own attitude towards it.

"Joanna thus left school for ever, bought three grey overalls and a fountain pen, pinned up her thick fair hair and set herself to learn the mysteries of petty cash, night specials, and reduced terms. Because she was, beyond all her other loves, in love with life, she found it very interesting.

"She was, moreover, an unexpected success, for though she sometimes forgot messages, or sorted linen into the wrong bundles, the nurses liked her. And even when she charged 4d. twice for soda-water, the patients liked her too. Her capacity for endowing the commonplace with transcendental qualities enabled her to see South Park Nursing Home as the Best in England, her work there as Part of the Great Effort Made by Gallant Women to Win the War, and Sister Warren as a splendid Leader and Chief — an attitude of mind commonly appreciated by employers."

Very soon, the shortage of nurses brought Winifred other duties than this placid secretarial assistance. For the best part of a year, in which she went home only at intervals,

she polished sterilisers, made beds, helped to give patients
blanket-baths, handed swabs in the operating theatre, and
in other ways familiar to all nurses endeavoured to earn the
£18 a year (£2 less than the pay of the V.A.D.s in the
military hospitals) which was known as " uniform money."
She also picked up a great deal of miscellaneous information,
including the fact that a celebrated gynaecologist had served,
somewhat inappropriately, as the specialist communicating
his doom to the middle-aged gentleman in the famous
pre-war problem picture "Sentence of Death." When
this gynaecologist actually came to the nursing-home,
Winifred scalded her fingers nearly to the bone from sheer
reverent excitement while pouring out the water for him
to wash his hands.

Long before her nineteenth birthday, her nursing experience went far beyond the making of beds and the care
of sterilisers. *The Land of Green Ginger*, with its accurate and
sometimes gruesome descriptions of tuberculosis and other
diseases, indicates a close acquaintance with the less agreeable manifestations of mortal sickness. It suggests, too, that
the latent pity for human suffering which was to struggle
throughout Winifred's life with the ruthless consecrated
egotism so necessary to artistic achievement, began to pro-
claim its inconvenient presence when the dying victims of
incurable illness sought consolation from the warm vitality
of her youth.

"Don't let him touch me. I can't bear it," she makes
the girl Joanna cry. But the shadows in the fictitious nursing-
home jeer at Winifred's imaginary counterpart. "You've
got to bear it. You can't hurt the poor old thing. You
can't escape from pity. Pity will pursue you always. If
you run away from here, it is out in the streets, it is on the
battlefields. It is in your private room, everywhere. It
has marked you down. You can't escape, ever."

Whatever knowledge she acquired or conflicts she suffered
during this period, Winifred's external appearance of fresh,
naïve eagerness never left her. The speed of her domestic
performances, it was true, did not always equal the measure

of her enthusiasm. A long-cherished family story originated when an aunt of Lady Diana Manners, who had been in the home as a patient, left half a crown for "the tall slow maid who cleans the washstand." But though Winifred might fall into day-dreams over her less exhilarating duties, her appearance must have been a delight to eyes failing from age or pain if it resembled her own description of Joanna Burton at the Kingsport Nursing Home.

"She was tall and grandly proportioned, like an immature young goddess. Soft golden hairs curled graciously against her firm, milky neck. Her full lips, parted eagerly, belied the severity of her nose and brow ; her blue eyes, deep-set below heavy lids, laughed at a pleasant world. She appeared to be a singularly happy and healthy creature."

When Sir Herbert Beerbohm Tree, as a patient at the nursing-home, died suddenly in Winifred's arms, this golden vividness must have been his last earthly impression. He had gone there to recover from an accidental fracture of the leg, and no one suspected the clot of blood making its way towards his heart. One afternoon Winifred was peeling a peach for his tea when he asked her to open the window. As she turned back towards the room, he collapsed against his pillow. For years she was haunted by the nightmare memory of her efforts to support the heavy body and simultaneously reach the bell to summon the Sister-in-Charge. In the same notebook which contains her manuscript copies of Bill's poems, I found transcribed the following sonnet by Sir Herbert's daughter, Iris :

IN MEMORIAM

HERBERT TREE

July 2nd, 1922

I cannot think that you have gone away.
You loved the earth — and light lit up your eyes,
And flickered in your smile that would surmise
Death as a song, a poem or a play.

You were reborn afresh with every day,
And baffled fortune in some new disguise.
Ah ! can it perish when the body dies,
Such youth, such love, such passion to be gay ?

We shall not see you come to us and leave
A conqueror — nor catch on fairy wing
Some slender fancy — nor new wonders weave
Upon the loom of your imagining.
The world is wearier, grown dark to grieve
Her child that was a pilgrim and a king.

As later years were to prove, Winifred's deceptive appearance of strength concealed a vulnerable constitution. In the middle of her twelve months of nursing, she was obliged to return home with a bad attack of shingles and septic poisoning. Perhaps the severe cases that she had attended were responsible ; perhaps the shock of Tree's death overcame her resistance. Government rationing and private economies had also reduced the quality of the food supplied to civilian nurses, and the half-days spent with her cousin Edmund or her mother and Edith de Coundouroff were not frequent enough to compensate for its deficiencies. Bill, too, had gone back to the front. He was in Flanders now, and in constant peril, with the violent ordeal of Messines Ridge before him in the summer.

Winifred was not the only invalid at Rudston, for George de Coundouroff, who had been wounded in November 1916, was there convalescing in his turn. His injury had not been permanent, and he now sat day after day beside Winifred's bed, talking to her about Russian literature and reading aloud from *Crime and Punishment*. He had barely returned to camp at Dover when the Russian Revolution burst from the chaos of Eastern Europe, transforming him into an alien who was obliged to leave the British Army. He became naturalised, applied for a commission, and had just begun his officer's training when Winifred finished her year's nursing in July 1917. She had now "done her bit," her family decided, and it was time to continue her postponed education.

So Winifred went up to Somerville in the autumn of 1917.

"I spend my time," she reported to a school friend, "tearing about Oxford streets on a very rusty cycle, flying from lectures, tea-parties, concerts, lacrosse matches, and all the thousand and one other things that insist on taking place at the very farthest possible point from my headquarters. This is a terribly strenuous life — and in the new rations we are chronicled under the heading of 'Sedentary Occupations'! If they only knew!"

Somerville College, its buildings commandeered by the War Office for use as a military hospital, was then going through its period of exile in the St. Mary Hall Quadrangle of Oriel. The half-empty men's colleges now housed only the unfit, the incurably wounded, and a number of juvenile cadets. Winifred remained at Somerville for a university year, made friends with Hilda Stuart Reid who was afterwards to write historical novels, fell in love with her work for the Honours School of Modern History, acquired a lifelong interest in the career of the Emperor Frederick II (" *Stupor Mundi* "), and obtained on the strength of it a Distinction in the History Previous examination.

But she felt, with her young eager vitality, unbearably marooned in this half-dead war-time city of elderly dons, women students, and wounded men on crutches. The same 1935 lecture-notes which emphasised " the erotic impulse " as a war-making force put " the masochistic impulse " into the same category. Under this second heading she described two separate mental attitudes :

" (a) The desire to suffer and to die —especially when suffering is associated with glory.

(b) Fear of immunity from danger when our friends are suffering, *e.g.* Oxford in 1917–18. March offensive of '18. Oxford seemed intolerable."

It was evidently at Somerville that Winifred first began to
experience that horror of " immunity " which, as her books
and articles show, was to haunt her throughout her life.
Being among the youngest of those who could claim to be
called " the war generation," she constantly witnessed
physical suffering and mental torment which she was still
too juvenile to share on equal terms. The claim of this
human agony upon her overwhelming compassion led her
to underestimate her own periods of shock and suspense,
though all her novels bear witness to the permanent impression that they made upon her. So great always were
her feelings of compunction and remorse when her friends
suffered and she did not, that in one sense she welcomed
her last illness for the kinship that it gave her with other
victims of pain. It was well for her peace of mind that she
foresaw only at intervals the advancing epoch of international
nightmare of which her premature death was to spare her
the misery.

Long after her first year at Oxford, she wrote to me about
those unhappy months of " anguished indecision." She
longed for Army service, but her duty as presented to her by
the persons whom she most respected — the Oxford authorities, the Minister of Education, her headmistress at Queen
Margaret's — appeared to lie in remaining at college.

" It always seemed to me then," she confessed afterwards,
" that I yielded to desire to join the W.A.A.C., a desire
which my poorer contemporaries, who had to hurry through
with their preparations to earn livings, could not afford to
indulge in. . . . I had been so infinitely happier both
nursing and in the W.A.A.C. than I had been in that ghastly
year at Oxford in 1917, that it never occurred to me that
Army life was anything but a fortunate privilege."

By the summer term of 1918, academic conceptions of
" duty " had become insupportable. Her childhood companions serving at the front, her dead friend among the
Bridlington masters, Bill who had been wounded a second
time by a bullet which barely avoided permanent damage
to one of his eyes, all seemed to summon her to abandon

the worthy but glamourless security of a college student. Flinging reverence for middle-aged exhortations to the winds, she obtained leave to go up to London for the supposed purpose of visiting a relative, and joined Queen Mary's Army Auxiliary Corps.

CHAPTER V

"FOR KING AND COUNTRY"

TRAINS IN FRANCE

All through the night among the unseen hills
The trains,
The fire-eyed trains,
Call to each other their wild seeking cry,
And I,
Who thought I had forgotten all the War,
Remember now a night in Camiers,
When, through the darkness, as I wakeful lay,
I heard the trains,
The savage, shrieking trains,
Call to each other their fierce hunting-cry,
Ruthless, inevitable, as the beasts
After their prey.
Made for this end by their creators, they,
Whose business was to capture and devour
Flesh of our flesh, bone of our very bone.
Hour after hour,
Angry and impotent I lay alone
Hearing them hunt you down, my dear, and you,
Hearing them carry you away to die,
Trying to warn you of the beasts, the beasts!
Then, no, thought I;
So foul a dream as this cannot be true,
And calmed myself, hearing their cry no more.
Till, from the silence, broke a trembling roar,
And I heard, far away,
The growling thunder of their joyless feasts —
The beasts had got you then, the beasts, the beasts —
And knew
The nightmare true.

WINIFRED HOLTBY
Time and Tide, 1931

IN THESE DAYS, when patriotic exhortations on the
importance of "civilian morale" are used to persuade

young women to enlist in many varieties of semi-military activity, it is strange to recall that in 1918 the experiment of employing women other than nurses in the Army was considered extremely daring. Before the recruiting began which was ultimately to mobilise fifty thousand " Waacs," the project had been discussed interminably in official circles, and its opponents persisted in their glum criticisms right up to the end of the War. The French, characteristically sceptical with regard to the actual functions of a Women's Army, inquired with amiable interest : " *Mais que feront-elles avec les bébés ?* "

Despite Gallic incredulity, Winifred's initial military occupations appear to have been innocent to the point of tedium, which was redeemed only by the idealistic fervour of her day and generation. Her earliest description of the work to which she was first posted at the New Zealand Officers' Club in Hill Street, Mayfair, reflects in its guileless sentimentality countless thousands of letters written to their relatives by young nurses, canteen workers and ambulance drivers throughout those four years.

" Perhaps washing dishes and counting linen is very uninspiring, boring sort of work, but when you are in the Women's Army there is always a chance that you may suddenly be taken away from your sink, or your linen cupboard or your dustpan into something big and noble and beautiful, that takes the little bothering things right away, and gives one strength from its vastness and its beauty. It's rather jolly starting one's proper work on the fourth of August like I'm doing, because it sends you off with a swing."

A few days earlier, a newly-enlisted recruit, she had been sent to Connaught Club in the Edgware Road for medical inspection, vaccination and equipment as a hostel forewoman. She had now reached her full height of five foot ten, and black Army boots, size seven, turned her long narrow feet into miniature canoes.

" We had considerable trouble fitting me up," she reported, " as the longest size coat frock was too short, and when I was told to lengthen it, we found that then the biggest coat in the store would not cover it, so I go about with a fair exhibition of khaki ankle."

The house in Hill Street, where she and the girls over whom she was "Sergeant" waited upon the New Zealand officers, had once belonged to a wealthy family of German Jews. Its equipment, like that of so many buildings commandeered by the War Office, appears to have been singularly unsuited to its purpose, for she described it as "a place of dim gold and green and pale grey, with carpets that reflect the latest comer's footmark, and many mirrors and lifts and large sofas in £1 : 10 per yard chintz, and stairs that twist for ever, and chandeliers, and magazines luxuriously strewn about large sofas and officers luxuriously ditto."

These elegant quarters were allocated neither to her nor to her colleagues, most of whom had previously been "in service" in private houses or wage-earning in factories. Her name defeated them, and they addressed her alternately as "Dear," "Miss" and "Love." Like the rest of them she entered the house through the basement, and lived on the other side of that green baize door which in many households divides the Family from the Maids. Now, she related triumphantly, she knew exactly what happened to the strawberry-fool when it retired in its silver dish beyond the kitchen passage. Fortunately her normal diet was more substantial ; she breakfasted on porridge, tea, bacon, bread and margarine, and assured her family that she had never seen so much food since the War began. Even the habitual excess of official supervision could not quench her naïve delight in exchanging Oxford's dejected privations for the lively discomforts of war service ; it was just one more subject for gay comment in her letters to Rudston.

"Mrs. R., the housekeeper, superintends me, and I superintend the girls, and Captain T. superintends Mrs. R., and Miss S. puts in an occasional appearance and superintends everyone, so we ought to be well looked after ! "

Mrs. R., it appeared, was a civilian, a Nice Woman, who

knew how to put Servants in their Place. Regarding Winifred as a poor Yorkshire girl who must be lonely in London, she even took the trouble to find her a New Zealand orderly to walk out with on her days off duty. Winifred and the orderly did walk out once together, and finished up with tea at Lyons', where they discussed Mrs. R. in a physiological and psychological detail which would have left the respectable lady gasping with embarrassment. Sometimes, in her post-war dreams at Oxford, Winifred would still hear a shrill voice summoning her back as she was hurrying out for her half-day.

" Holtby ! Holtby ! Did you forget to dust the drawing-room mirrors ? Come here at *once* ! I can nearly write my name on them. Go and get a duster so that I can *see* you do them ! "

And Winifred would be late for her rendezvous at Peter Robinson's or Swan & Edgar's in order to polish once more the gilt-framed atrocities which reached from the floor almost to the top of the lofty ceiling.

But there were other occasions, graver and more dignified, which made the twenty-year-old girl soldier re-dedicate her newly released spirit to that " something big and noble " which seemed to her to lie just beyond the outward seeming of everyday life. One Sunday she heard Maude Royden preach at the City Temple on the text : " How shall we sing the Lord's song in a strange land ? " The famous preacher's reputation was now so high that Winifred went apprehensively, fearing disappointment. But the gracious tolerance of the sermon struck a responsive chord in the developing mind which had repudiated the idea of reprisals for the Scarborough bombardment, and she came away filled with an inspiration not yet wholly understood. Another afternoon, she took her squadron of girls to a memorial service at St. Martin-in-the-Fields for all the women from the London Area, Q.M.A.A.C., who had died while serving in the War.

" I cannot describe it," she wrote, " excepting that it was one of the most wonderful things I ever saw or heard in my life. There were fifteen thousand of us there, all in khaki. The band was splendid, and I wish you could have heard those 1500 girls all singing ' Fight the Good Fight,' with the rolling drums of the military band. The preacher " (surely Dick Sheppard ?) " was very good and very simple. Many of the girls were sobbing when he had finished."

She soon had need of the disciplined assurance given her by these experiences, for the coming of harvest-time to Rudston brought news from home which astonished and dismayed her. Although she had studied the feudal system at school and college, she had not realised that under the strain of the War and the growing strength of labour, the old Yorkshire feudalism was creaking and cracking. Agitators had been in the village that summer, and their machinations finally produced a local strike of agricultural labourers similar to the strike described in Winifred's first novel, *Anderby Wold*.

Like John Robson in her story, David Holtby was ready to give way to the strikers and pay the higher wages demanded, but the smaller farmers could not afford them. Confronted by an unfamiliar type of economic strategy disconcerting to employers who had been masters for generations and understood no other relationship, David, panic-stricken, decided that he had grown too old to adapt himself to the new conditions. On the spur of the moment he resolved to retire from farming, and sold the only home that Winifred had ever known.

When her parents actually left Rudston House on February 26th, 1919, she had gone to France, so she did not fully realise for several months how sharply her deepest loves and loyalties had been torn up by their roots. It was George de Coundouroff, home for a short leave before joining as interpreter one of the Allied " missions " of intervention in South Russia, who helped the family to move to Cottingham.

The new house was satisfactorily distant from the many interrogative and critical relatives who lived on the other side of the East Riding ; it was also convenient for Alice

Holtby, who had been serving since 1916 on the East Riding
War Pensions Committee, which met at Beverley a few
miles away. But she could not immediately adapt herself to
the loss of the village which for a quarter of a century she had
mothered and befriended. Some sense of failure, some
measure of self-reproach, must have crept into her correspondence with her absent daughter, for an answering letter
testifies to that warmth of sympathy between them which
Winifred's maturity and success were to leave unspoiled.

"You mustn't talk as you did in the beginning of your
letter about the way you treat me," wrote Winifred with
anxious affection. "What is there to reproach yourself
for in the wonderful trust and love and understanding that
you have always given me ? Don't you know that I understand and am always close, close to you, even though we
are miles apart and though we may not write much and
often to one another ? Don't you know that I realise that
such love as ours does not need constant communication,
because it holds us together for all time ? Don't you know
that your love and your example are to me an everlasting
inspiration and support ? Oh, my more than dear, I
know you know, because I feel you present in my heart
always. You cannot help but understand."

The early autumn of 1918 found Winifred at Folkestone,
where she arrived just in time for one of the biggest air
raids of the War. That year's expensive campaigns had
caused an acute shortage of nurses everywhere, and as she
rubbed sore throats, bandaged cuts and scalds, took suspected temperatures and administered Number Nines, she
thanked the probationer's experience which enabled her to
combine the work of a V.A.D. nurse with the duties of a
hostel forewoman.

By this time she enjoyed giving orders and making her
girls march smartly in line ; a glow of exaltation ran
through her whenever she drew herself up to her impressive
height and cried : " Squad, 'shun ! Right turn ! Quick
march ! By the left, left wheel ! Eyes right ! " And unlike

the unhappy V.A.D. nurses who were expected to behave as officers when they were with the Tommies but were not allowed the companionship of officers themselves, she was free to associate with men of her own rank both in England and in France.

After a short period of waiting at Folkestone, she and her squadron crossed the Channel. In Boulogne it rained, as it always did when anybody arrived there for the first time, and they spent the day in a hostel waiting for their orders. At nightfall they were marched into a goods van, which was then shunted and left in a siding while train after train went by. Lying half asleep in the stuffy, uncomfortable darkness, Winifred listened to the trains in a nightmare of sick apprehension for Bill and other boys at the front. Years afterwards, on a journey home from the Riviera, the memory of this waking dream came back to her and inspired the poem *Trains in France*.

When the girls arrived, half suffocated, at Camiers just before morning, Winifred imagined that they had travelled many miles from Boulogne instead of covering hardly more than walking distance. In the grey semi-light of dawn, they dragged their kit uphill from the village, and fell into bed in a huge warehouse-like hut with the gratified sense of having already contributed their full share towards winning the War.

Some hours later they rose reluctantly to hear a lecture by a plump W.A.A.C. administrator, tightly buttoned into a tunic with her chest puffed out like a pigeon and her cap pulled over one eye. She talked to the girls about their duty to King and Country, exhorted them to remember the honour of their uniform, and forbade them to speak to officers or walk in the woods with Australians. Then, being a gourmand by nature, she sent Winifred to a nearby farm to fetch new-laid eggs, fresh vegetables and a chicken for her dinner. To Winifred's critical Yorkshire eyes the French farmstead with its mud-plastered walls resembled a pigsty rather than a farm, but once inside she had to admit that it was clean enough.

Winifred did not stay long in Camiers. After a few days she was sent up the line to a Signals Unit at Huchenneville, eight kilometres from Abbeville. Throughout that spring and summer Abbeville had been severely bombed, and the Signals Unit once stationed there was now hidden in the orchard of the Château of Huchenneville so that communications might not be destroyed.

The women in the unit included twenty-five telegraphists, eight telephonists, four cooks, four waitresses, two stenographers and three clerks. They were housed in tents under the apple trees, and a gardener's cottage provided messroom, kitchen and a tiny bedroom for the W.A.A.C. administrator. Officially the administrator belonged to the staff of the Colonel at the Château headquarters, where he and four officers controlled the trains run by the British on the southern section of the French railway line. On the other side of the orchard from the women's tents was a men's camp of telegraphists, electricians, chauffeurs and orderlies. Among the native feminine inhabitants of Huchenneville village, the proximity of the male and female camps caused French opinion of British morality to become even lower and still more articulate.

The isolation of the unit made it difficult to administer, and eight weeks was the usual limit of a W.A.A.C. officer's residence. When Winifred went to Huchenneville the administrator in charge was Jean Findlay McWilliam, a former Somervillian of Celtic temperament and striking appearance. Winifred never ceased to be fascinated by the wild splendour of her abundant chestnut hair, her redbrown eyes, alternately passionate and melancholy, her superb figure, even taller than Winifred's own. With the rich hair and brave stature went the cultured, academic mind of an Oxford-educated student of English literature. It was to Jean McWilliam in South Africa, first as lecturer at Rhodes University College, Grahamston, and then as headmistress of Pretoria High School, that Winifred after the War wrote the series of letters now collected in the volume *Letters to a Friend.*

In her Preface to this collection, Jean McWilliam describes how Winifred was sent to Huchenneville.

"At W.A.A.C. headquarters in France there was a Somervillian called Haythorne who was second in command in France and an old friend of mine. She was anxious that I should stay longer than eight weeks at Huchenneville and rang me up one evening and asked if I was lonely. I told her I was rather and she said there was a girl in the ranks who had been a year at Somerville but was too young to have a commission. She would have her brought out to be my hostel forewoman.

"A few days later I had orders to go to Camp Three in Abbeville to fetch my new hostel forewoman. The colonel lent me his car, for he was always kind about giving the W.A.A.C. lifts. When I arrived at Camp Three I found a tall, pale, tired-looking girl waiting for me.

"'Are you Holtby?'

"She saluted smartly and answered, 'Yes, ma'am.'

"'Then you are to come to my unit.'

"'Yes, ma'am.'

"'I hear you have been a year at Somerville, and I was there years ago.'

"'Oh! were you?' with relief.

"'Yes, and now you are coming to a very uncomfortable unit. If you step off the duck-boards your shoe will be sucked off by the mud. The women are in tents. I have a small room in the gardener's cottage. There is a loft above it without doors or windows. You can have that as a habitation if you like. All the water we have is carted, and when one of the horses is ill it is limited. Baths are difficult. But I suppose Rosalind and Celia had difficulty in getting baths in the Forest of Arden.''

This conversation explains why throughout the *Letters*, Winifred addresses Jean as Rosalind and signs herself as Celia. It also gave her the idea for a series of sketches on W.A.A.C. life in France, which she wrote by candle-light at the kitchen table and called *The Forest Unit*. These sketches followed the theme of *As You Like It* in the same way as Barrie's *Dear Brutus* borrowed its inspiration from *A Midsummer Night's Dream*. Their light phantasies describe the orchard unit as, in Winifred's words, " it was throughout the ' dream night's day ' that was its year of life."

In her naïve pages the forest passes from the sunlit somnolence of late summer through gusty autumn winds and falling fiery leaves to the dark mornings of icy winter. The later sketches, with unusual justification, become frankly lyrical over the first post-war spring at Huchenneville, with its lavish treasure of cherry blossom and budding trees beneath the cloudless azure skies of Northern France. The arcadian beauty which encompassed the young members of the orchard unit drew a luminous veil of unreality over the stark tragedies of the War, and fortified Winifred against the glum disillusionment which turned Bill and many others into the lost victims of a too complacent peace.

This first attempt to write a full-length book sparkled with the uninhibited vivacity which no work of Winifred's could lack, but the style of the sketches betrayed the same young, derivative sentimentality which had been more crudely evident in the saccharine verses of *My Garden and Other Poems*. Obviously written under the influence of *Peter Pan* and *Dear Brutus*, *The Forest Unit* abounds in Barrie-like whimsicalities, but the author of *Mary Rose* cannot be held responsible for the arch *clichés* and popular magazine sentiments which fill its pages like the excess ingredients of an over-sweetened cake. There can hardly have been another forest in France so lavishly endowed with mossy swards, stately trees, bright little squirrels, wise old donkeys, rosy little Waacs, and Australian soldiers with " white teeth gleaming and eyes a-dance."

" I will sing," runs a typical passage, " under the greenwood trees alone, of the charming world of Arden and the men and maids who dwelt there, and, like Rosalind in her epilogue, I will pray all women to listen to me for the love they bear to men, and all men to harken for the love they bear to women, and if any of those who have cast the shadow of their disfavour over the small and isolated units of the Corps should still uphold their hands in righteous indignation at the irregularities of the Forest Unit, let them look for a moment at its claim to immortality ; for *As you Like It* ended in the Masque of Hymen, and our forest comedy shall live on in the hearts of healthy, happy children whose mothers were taught lessons of womanhood under the trees of a fairy orchard."

Should some adolescent would-be writer, struggling to overcome a redundant style and a commonplace outlook, wish to encourage himself by learning how much a dozen years of practising his craft can accomplish at the period of maximum development, I suggest that he compare this product of conventionally moralistic youth with the zestfully Rabelaisian " Rules for Mandoans " on page 216 of Winifred's brilliant satire, *Mandoa, Mandoa !*, published in January 1933. Though it lacked the quality of universal application which made the greatness of *South Riding*, *Mandoa, Mandoa !* remains the wittiest and most scintillating of Winifred's novels. It is not surprising, perhaps, that as early as 1926 she told Jean McWilliam, with whom she was then staying in South Africa, that *The Forest Unit* was too sentimental and bad to publish.

Its immature young author was nevertheless the spiritual parent of the woman who wrote the ruthless and vivid satire on British imperialism, and when she can forget her stock-in-trade of orchard fairies, eldritch laughter, wide-eyed daisies and magic pens made from the veins of skeleton leaves dipped in dew, Winifred's sketches give an almost realistic picture of the humours, discomforts and temperamental problems of the Huchenneville camp.

By 1919 her appreciation of ludicrous situations and her capacity for selecting the elements which made them funny were already fully developed. *The Forest Unit* gives evidence of this gift in her description of the masculine jealousies and romantic feminine perturbations which followed the coming of an Australian contingent to rest at Huchenneville after ten months in the line.

Huchenneville village was only three minutes' walk from the orchard unit, and Jean McWilliam has confessed that she awaited the arrival of the Australians with apprehension. She was not mistaken in supposing that the plain, under-sized British group of orderlies and engineers, who had come to take for granted their monopoly of the Waacs as companions, would suffer by contrast with the tall bronzed figures in slouch hats who rode through the forest blowing kisses to the girls from the high saddles of their magnificent horses. But she admits that from the beginning the Australians proved to be generous friends who increased the enchantments of life at Huchenneville without appreciably adding to her problems.

"When they arrived," she writes, "we had only one hut which we used for recreation. We usually danced because the Colonel's batman played splendid dance music on the accordion. The sound of revelry drew the Australians to our unit, and I found an Australian officer standing by me.

"'You ought to have more than one candle,' he said.

"'Yes, but our ration of candles was short this week,' I answered.

"He said nothing, but the next day he sent me a bag of candles."

In the late autumn of 1918 the Australian division, by arrangement between their captain and Jean McWilliam, gave a dance in the new recreation hut of the orchard unit. Many of the Australians had not seen a woman for months, and keen masculine competition for the favours of the small W.A.A.C. group suggested the injudicious exclusion of their British rivals. In *The Forest Unit*, Winifred describes with obvious enjoyment how the jointly owned piano so necessary to the success of the dance was twice kidnapped by the determined antagonists.

"Next morning Celia saw the wagon that was one of the most cherished possessions of the Orchard office at the door of the new recreation hut.

"'What's happening?' she asked the rabbit-mouthed corporal.

"He looked uneasy but defiant.

"'Oh, we are just coming to remove the piano to our hut for a little sing-song that we are having to-morrow night.'

"'Oh, but you can't do that! We're having a dance here.'

"'I know nothing about no dance. Those are my orders and I shall proceed to fulfil them.' The corporal expanded his already somewhat spreading chest.

"'But you can't.' Celia wrung her hands with feverish anxiety. 'We must have it for the dance.'

"'Excuse me, but orders is orders, and the dance is no concern of ours. The piano is ours by rights, which you 'ave 'ad the privilege of making use of owing to kind permission of the colonel. If you want to dance to-morrow night, you must find your own music. Some of you girls is fond of singing, I've noticed. Let your friends bring their hown piano. We 'ave a 'ymn practice at our 'ut to-morrow night and the work of the Lord cannot be put off for vain and frivolous amusements. Carry on, boys.'

"And Celia, wringing her hands on the steps in furious impotence, watched the piano disappearing across the orchard."

The Australian-bewitched Waacs were not defeated. Without the official knowledge of their administrator or her hostel forewoman, eight of them took an old farm-cart to the men's Mess Hut that night and, at the cost of barked shins and broken finger-nails, jubilantly brought back the piano to their recreation-room. But in the end Cockney cunning triumphed over Colonial virility, for half-way through the dance the electric light went out with malicious suddenness. As Winifred, in the excitement of preparing refreshments, had forgotten to indent for candles, the exuberant dancers were plunged into chaotic darkness — " while Sapper Bright, diligently searching for the fault with conspicuous piety, failed to find it."

Winifred and Jean soon made their own friends amongst the Australians. One of them — still known to me only as " Ken," the name by which she always spoke of him — lent Winifred a horse for her afternoons off duty. Her country upbringing had made her a fine horsewoman, and they rode together over the placid Somme country in the golden autumn, and cantered through the anemone-carpeted woods in the early spring, exhilarated by the sudden lifting of death and terror from a suffering world. Later in the year Ken spent a few days at Cottingham with Winifred and her family, but whatever hints he may have dropped to her about the distant attractions of a pioneer Dominion, they made no progress against the anticipated return of a demobilised Bill who appeared to have brought both life and health safely out of the War.

Winifred's growing friendship with Jean McWilliam was destined to occupy a more permanent place in her memory than her rides with Ken. The Somervillian administrator at W.A.A.C. headquarters had been wise in her precautions against official loneliness, for in spite of differences of both age and background, the similarity of their education caused them to co-operate with affectionate understanding in the various small enterprises of a women's camp. Winifred's pages gaily describe the homely attractions and fantastic discomforts of their primitive cottage, the canteen which they ran at a profit for the unit after borrowing the Colonel's big Vauxhall car and spending four hundred dollars in Abbeville, the sing-song washing-up parties which they supervised at the military Mess, where the girls wiped the plates to " Give me the moonlight ! " and scraped the pans to " K-K-K-Katie ! "

The ending of the War, and the enjoyment of this congenial comradeship, which was to continue all her life and to give her the reputation of a letter-writer after her death, made a fairy-tale of Winifred's final months in France. From the time that the Waacs and Tommies toasted the first post-war Christmas in claret-cup under the trees of their orchard to the August day when Winifred returned to England, there seemed to be nothing more to fear from the future.

In one sketch she describes the 19th of July, when the Forest Unit — mercifully spared foreknowledge of the Europe which was to leer at the Treaty-makers two decades later from the ruins of their Carthaginian peace — went mad with the rest of France on its day of rejoicing at the official conclusion of the War to end War. Calling, during the day, on the plump French Madame who had done her laundry, Winifred found the gay, voluble little woman sobbing beneath a cherry tree in her cottage garden for the son who would never return to gather the ripe fruit from the laden boughs. Did this sudden recall to reality bring back to her mind the old drunken woman who had told her at Rudston on August 3rd, 1914, that war was " bloody hell " ? At any rate, she returned to Yorkshire to find that for some — amongst whom she did not yet include herself — the War's tragedies, far from being over, had hardly begun.

It was a strange and damping experience to go back to Cottingham instead of her beloved Rudston, and to accept as home a solidly built suburban house which she had not yet seen. In her post-war room at Oxford she hung above her desk a little engraving, which I have inherited from her, of the Norman church at Rudston and the Roman road running like a white ribbon across the wolds, but she did not see the village again for four years, and could never bring herself to revisit the wold farm. Her mind, she told me, was a confused muddle of emotions and memories that afternoon when she went back in 1923, but she did wish that

I could have seen the wind on the silver barley and the hills that she loved. We planned to go there together some day, but I actually went for the first time on the morning of her burial.

For Hull, and the flat enormous landscape of patterned fields and clustering trees round the estuary of the Humber, Winifred came later to feel an affection which revealed itself in the description of Sarah Burton's 'bus-ride through "Kingsport" in Book I of *South Riding*.

"Hull has ⌐ character and you will find it," she wrote in 1930 to Phyllis Bentley, who was about to lecture there. "What you can't discover from a few days' visit is the deadening effect of low altitude and snobbish idleness on its suburban population — but that applies to most cities and has little to do with Hull itself."

The blow which was to strike the Cottingham household barely awaited Winifred's return from France. She had only been home for a few days when news came that George de Coundouroff was missing in Russia. Since Edith was helplessly tied to the baby daughter born a month after he left, Winifred went up to London and wrestled with every Government department which undertook to answer inquiries about officers serving in Russia.

It was one of those heart-breaking tasks which she so often shouldered because nobody else could endure them. News came slowly from the wild Georgian country where the White Armies had sent their "mission," and for months the household in which the Russian boy had lived as an adopted son did not know whether he was dead or wounded, imprisoned or insane. Two years later — as a letter dated October 23rd, 1921, to Jean McWilliam testifies — Winifred's inquiries from the War Office, the Foreign Office and occasional Secret Service agents were still going on.

"At least," she wrote, "it takes away that horribly impotent feeling that comes of sitting still and doing nothing, and it would be so much better to learn that he had been shot in the first instance, than for Edith to sit waiting, apprehensive of every shadow that crosses the doorway, of every voice that echoes from the road. . . . She has suffered enough. I want her to learn he is dead, have one good weep, and then be at peace."

Winifred was never to have the sorrowful satisfaction of that conclusive knowledge, and Edith and her daughter — now a beautiful girl just beginning her career as an actress — are waiting for it still. But time and the gradual discovery of George's possessions in the primitive shops of remote Russian villages did bring some information. He had been sent, it appeared, with a group of thirteen British soldiers to find the haunts of the Green Guards, a band of brigands which infested the country where the mission was stationed. On July 25th, 1919, this expedition was ambushed by the Green Guards themselves. Eleven of its members escaped, but George and a private had their horses shot under them and were captured.

Imagination could — and did — supply the rest of the story. Often, looking at Edith and the fatherless baby during the sad weeks before her return to Oxford, Winifred reproached herself for the feeling of happiness that could not be resisted now that Bill had come back. She was still to learn how much of him also the War had taken away from her.

CHAPTER VI

SECOND APPRENTICESHIP

THE DEAD MAN

I see men walk wild ways with love,
Along the wind their laughter blown
Strikes up against the singing stars —
But I lie all alone.

When love has stricken laughter dead
And tears their silly hearts in twain,
They long for easeful death, but I
Am hungry for their pain.

WINIFRED HOLTBY
Oxford Poetry, 1920

THE OXFORD to which Winifred returned in October 1919 had nothing in common with the dispirited remnant of a University which she had left fifteen months earlier to join the W.A.A.C. Vital, controversial and experimental, its renewed life became for the next two years a mental and spiritual tug-of-war between three incompatible groups.

To the first belonged those members of Senior Common Rooms who had lived from 1914 to 1918 in an ever-deepening academic twilight, barely illumined by occasional visits from younger or more enterprising colleagues who had joined the Army or taken posts in Government offices. It included most of the College Principals and older tutors, a few specialists whose rarity value had given them exemption from military service, and practically the whole body of women dons. Almost unanimously these senior members of the University had contemplated the War with extreme discomfort, not as a rule from any innate pacifist sentiment, but because it flung the shadow of chaos over their peaceful scholarly pastures, and threatened their decorous intellectual routine with the wild disruptions of tragedy and emotion. But even the War itself had not roused their nervous apprehensions so acutely as the anticipated invasion of tough, experienced, prematurely hardened youth.

There was adequate cause for these middle-aged trepidations. The group of ex-soldiers and other war-workers now returning to finish their long-interrupted studies had known four years of peril, independence and extreme responsibility. Having proved their mettle on the battlefield and elsewhere, their attitude towards the cautious elderly regulations which restricted the liberties of undergraduate Oxford was one of cynical, amused impatience. Since their older members included rapidly promoted ex-colonels and majors who had already entered their late twenties, the problem of enforcing college discipline kept many worthy recluses awake at night.

The third university group disliked and resented the second almost as keenly as the apprehensive dons. To this youthful contingent of schoolboys and schoolgirls who had spent the War in classrooms and on playing-fields, the transformation of normal Oxford by their disillusioned seniors became a cause of conflict and animosity. The Armistice, and the illusory prospects of a European Renaissance which the Old Men at Versailles were even then in process of destroying, had fired these eighteen-year-olds with more than the common aspirations of extreme youth to build the New Jerusalem. They were not prepared to relinquish the choice of its architecture to their sophisticated predecessors without a battle which raged for several terms in Junior Common Rooms, lecture halls, college debating societies and the editorial offices of university magazines.

Feared by sheltered age and resented by inexperienced youth, the surviving members of the Oxford war generations tended more and more to become a class apart within the University until they went down in 1920 and 1921. These maturer undergraduates were almost exclusively masculine, for in the later years of the War the women students provided the chief *raison d'être* for the remaining holders of academic posts, and patriotic volunteering had therefore — as Winifred found — been sedulously discouraged at the women's colleges. The few female rebels were a tiny minority, and only one or two, having once defied tutorial exhortations, had ventured to return to Oxford at all.

At the beginning of the Michaelmas term 1919 Winifred and I were totally unaware of each other's existence, but even before we met we were invisibly linked by the unique bond of our war service and the attitude towards it of mingled pity and disapproval which we sensed rather than observed on the part of the Somerville dons. We were, perhaps, especially conscious of it in the Principal of the College and our young History tutor.

In 1919 the Principal of Somerville College was Miss (now Dame) Emily Penrose, whose austere personality and dominant mind were probably, through their grim concentration of purpose, more responsible than anything else for the fact that Oxford took advantage of post-war legislation to give Degrees to women while Cambridge refused them. Early in the War Miss Penrose's sympathies had been stirred by those students whom anxious grief or restless propaganda-ridden consciences drove into active service, but her attitude towards them changed when the limited franchise granted to women in 1918 brought the Mecca of her life within reach. From that time onwards, equality for women at Oxford became for her a more important objective than the victory of the Allies.

How far this Olympian determination had influenced our History tutor, Maude Clarke, I shall now never know, but to Winifred and myself, with our still raw memories, her elegant dark-eyed youth lent an inhuman emphasis to the serene detachment with which she seemed to view the tragedy that had dislocated our lives. She had become a member of the Somerville Senior Common Room after brilliant First-Class Honours taken in Dublin and later at Oxford during the very years which had destroyed our own powers of concentration. When we returned to Oxford, she was still only twenty-seven. With her smooth dark hair, attractive wedge-shaped face and soft Irish voice, she did not appear inhuman, but though her keen incisive mind could be moved to sympathy by intellectual struggles, the emotional conflicts of those whose work she directed seemed to leave her singularly unmoved.

To many of her former students, the memory of Maude Clarke — who died prematurely, as Vice-Principal of Somerville, only a few weeks later than Winifred — remains an enigma which time is unlikely to solve. When she was teaching or correcting essays, it appeared criminally wasteful that so rare and scholarly an intellect should spend itself upon coaching cocksure adolescents, but as soon as she attempted to put her knowledge into a book, the dry bones refused to live. Hardly more successful on platforms, she evidently lacked the supreme gift of interpretation, without which the best equipped mind is apt to resemble a phial so tightly corked that none of its valuable contents are able to emerge.

I cannot now recall whether it was Winifred or myself who contributed, in January 1924, a letter to *Time and Tide* signed " Post-War Woman Graduate," which complained that the eager, immature, bewildered students at the women's colleges did not receive sympathetic guidance from female dons who appeared to place themselves on pedestals and to regard the perplexities of adolescence as beneath their dignity. But our critical reactions at this period towards our Somerville education may be deduced from an unpublished letter written on September 14th, 1923, by Winifred to Jean McWilliam, who had criticised adversely the Oxford scenes in my first novel, *The Dark Tide* :

" Oxford is adopting most seriously a policy of *laissez-faire* between student and don. Students come up fresh from school, inexperienced, keen, idealistic often enough, but accustomed to direction. At school and at home other people hitched their aspirations on to their everyday life for them. They come up to college and are told by the dons from the moment they come to the moment they go down, that the only thing that matters is intellectual success. . . . There aren't any ' Patricias ' at college — as I know it, anyway. There are people with commanding personalities like Miss Penrose, and people with charm and splendid intelligence and exquisite taste like Miss Clarke. When I was at college there was not a soul to whom one could go to ask for advice about knotty points, or even who held up any sort of suggestion about behaviour — only about brains. I know that the idea is that interference is unjustifiable. The more I remember what I was like at college in the light of my own small experience as a teacher, the more convinced I am that I needed a thorough good scolding, and then a thorough good talking to. . . . I am quite sure that it was not always like this. I believe it is just a phase ; but it is a dangerous phase, and the sooner people realise what is happening, the better."

Many of these criticisms I still feel to be justified of the University that Winifred knew. It was perhaps truer of Somerville — where the influence of Miss Penrose had created an almost impassable gulf between Senior and Junior Common Rooms — than of the other women's colleges. Whether the same lack of human compassion for youth's fatiguing perplexities is still to be found there I cannot say. It will never, perhaps, be wholly remedied until teaching posts in schools and universities are opened to married women who have known the humours, exasperations and minor tragedies of normal family life.

In the difficult University of 1919 to 1921, there was certainly need for a greater measure of personal wisdom than most of us encountered. But in after years Winifred and I both recognised that the conflicts of post-war Oxford sprang out of the false values and abnormal activities with which war interrupts the customary processes of life and thought. The atmosphere of tension was not entirely due, as we had critically believed, to the inability of stay-at-home dons to sympathise with our griefs or share our memories ; it arose from the natural incompatibility of outlook, over-emphasised by catastrophe, which must always exist between the nobly impetuous, untutored young, and their elders whom time has endowed with the capacity to discern the facts behind the plausible exterior of accepted standards.

Gradually we perceived the jagged rent made by four years of chaos in the fabric of civilisation so painfully woven by the workings of human reason. We realised, too, how often the instruments of this constructive achievement were the sheltered, contemplative academics whom we after our dramatic period of hectic action had so lightly despised. With time we also understood that to the older Oxford the War had presented, not the crude black-and-white choice between self-interest and self-sacrifice in terms of which we ourselves had seen it, but a series of acute philosophical problems, to be wrestled with in mental anguish because the future of mankind depended upon their right solution.

In the end, Winifred was to remember her years at Somerville with gratitude. By way of paying her debt, she made the College a benefactor under her Will from any posthumous works of her own which her literary executor might publish. Thanks to the cruel irony of the fate which deprived her of full recognition when fame was so near, these posthumous publications included *South Riding* ; and the sum which she thought of as a small contribution towards a scholarship already amounts to nearly £5000 and will soon have founded not one scholarship but two.

Winifred's sense of obligation to Somerville was largely based upon its value as an apprenticeship to her life as a writer, but in 1919 very few people at Oxford suspected that she would ever write at all. Her tutors, indeed, frequently regretted that she could neither write nor spell, and owing to her energy and the magnanimous generosity which even then was infinitely susceptible to remorseless exploitation, her contemporaries regarded her as a useful, efficient and much-enduring committee woman. At various times she was President of two debating and two dramatic societies, and a member of at least a dozen college committees. She also qualified for the female counterpart of Rose Macaulay's pleasant but too impartial hero in *The Making of a Bigot* by belonging to all three political parties.

" But how can I know," she asked ingenuously when a partisan fanatic protested, " which I like best till I've tried them all ? "

At Oxford, unlike Queen Margaret's, Winifred was not compelled to take part in games, though she was once induced to play lacrosse for Somerville—with consequences so deplorable that her performance became a college tradition. Thanks to a bicycle accident caused in her schooldays by a hen which, like most hens, inconsiderately lost its head at the critical moment, she even detested cycling. During the post-war Eights Weeks she enjoyed the gay parties on the men's barges in the May sunshine, and shared with undisguised zest the vicarious excitement of running and shouting along the Isis towing-path when " Toggers " (the Easter term boat races more sedately known as Torpids) were rowed in the cold March wind. But her real recreations were walking — a taste which I fortunately shared — and the old enchanting occupations of writing and producing plays and acting in amateur theatricals.

In the first term of her reincarnation as a student, she played with vigorous and appropriate sentimentality the part of the hero in *The Professor's Love Story*, and during her second and third summer terms wrote columns of resourceful doggerel for the Going Down Play. She seemed, her tutors complained, to spend more time composing these vivacious masterpieces than in reading for her Finals. Incredible as their surprise now appears, most of her contemporaries were astonished when she only just missed an entirely un-foreseen First in the Honours School of Modern History by her ribald replies to the well-intentioned questions of the examiners conducting her *Viva Voce*.

In retrospect Winifred's college career appears as a prelude to the struggle — which was to be the chief spiritual conflict of her life — between the social reformer whose

benevolent common sense cautiously treads the earth, and
the artist whose imagination recklessly scales the heavens.
Many of her critics, judging her solely by her external
activities, still believe that she preferred a well-filled engage-
ment-book to creative literary effort. Others who knew her
better, and recognised that her greatest happiness sprang
from the quiet intervals of thought and writing in which
she produced her books, wondered why she was apparently
content that these periods should be so limited. Only the
few who saw her upbringing for themselves and realised the
strength of the influences which inspired her passion for
justice, understood that the greatest obstacle to her achievements as an artist was the sensitive and implacably trained
conscience which she could never decide whether to treat
as an enemy or a friend.

Brought up in a philanthropic household which regarded
the demands of the intellect as negligible compared with
the claims of human need, Winifred had a stern moral battle
to fight every time she resisted the summons of a good cause
or ignored an unfortunate fellow creature. Some who are
familiar with the finely truthful character study of Alderman
Mrs. Beddows in *South Riding* imagine that the vigorous
practical qualities bequeathed to Winifred by her mother
were the chief source of this conflict. I believe this judgment
to be an underestimate of the truth. Winifred inherited
with her East Riding blood that feudal sense of responsibility
which is part of the English agricultural tradition. Her
creative imagination was at war with not one but twenty
generations of farmers and landowners who regarded the
welfare of tenants and labourers as part of their personal
obligations.

At college Winifred's anxious solicitude was aroused by
every student who suffered from problems, poverty, disappointment or ill-health. Into the last of these categories
came her first-year friend, Hilda Reid, who had also been
absent for twelve months owing to a serious operation.
Buried in the *Paston Letters* or the *Memoirs of Philippe de
Comines*, the meditative future author of *Ashley Hamel* fre-

quently forgot to eat her meals or to go to bed, and would probably have perished of starvation or insomnia but for Winifred's watchful and persistent care.

The other students to whom she extended her generosity were not always so graciously unobtrusive as Hilda Reid. Winifred had hardly settled into her bed-sitting-room in the West Building, with its pleasant view over the college garden, when she was invaded by cavalcades of her first-year contemporaries who demanded anything from biscuits to good advice. In one letter to Jean McWilliam she confesses that " there were, when I wrote the last page, about five other people in my little room, so I finally had to abandon the attempt." At Somerville, as throughout her life, the instinctive magnanimity which so deceptively concealed her keen sardonic intelligence made her an immediate target for everyone with a want, a grievance or a dilemma.

" I'm suffocated," runs a heartfelt comment scribbled in a notebook of this date. " People have been pouring their emotional crises all over me till I can't breathe."

When an unoccupied graduate who had come to Oxford in the hope of finding a job took to bringing her sewing and settling down in Winifred's room for the day, Winifred escaped to the cold college library — where the fire was hardly ever lighted, and never burned properly on the few occasions when the weather defeated Somerville economy — and worked on one of the long tables for the rest of the term. Her friends, left in possession, borrowed her kettle, her saucepan, her tea, her sugar and her coal. They held parties in her room and often were still there when she returned from the library at midnight.

Most of these winter evenings were spent in a painful struggle to improve her college essays. Her work on the sketches which composed *The Forest Unit* had proved to her, beyond all possibility of doubt, that she wanted to be a writer, but the criticisms passed by her tutors on her compositions did not suggest any immediate prospect of realising this ambition. The severest, and therefore perhaps the most ultimately valuable, came from Mr. C. R. M. F. Cruttwell, then Dean and now Principal of Hertford College. He coached Winifred in " Period 8," the epoch from 1789 to 1878 so surprisingly regarded by Oxford as the most modern period of European history in which its students of inter-national politics could expect to be instructed, and though he praised her weekly essay for its industry, he also alleged, with challenging reiteration, that her style was laborious, her sentences confused, her writing clumsy and her spelling abominable.

Winifred accepted these strictures with resolute humility. To the end of her life she never learned to spell and her handwriting remained half-formed, but she started at once with diligence and distress to remedy the shortcomings of her style.

" I was told," she relates in *Mother Knows Best*, " that an essay should have a beginning, a middle and an end ; that its argument should be capable of division into points, one, two, three, four and five ; that these points should be stated briefly, lucidly and without undue decoration. Term by term I set myself to produce from my fuddled, nebulous and fragmentary impressions of the past, some-thing more neatly and concisely designed to satisfy my tutors. I thought I was learning how to Get a First and please my mother and my tutors. I did neither. What I was learning was how to earn my living as a journalist and please myself."

Not until years afterwards, in reply to a letter in which I told her how much I always envied her popularity at Oxford, did she acknowledge the many tears that this process of learning her craft had cost her.

" I used to boast to you and everyone about my parties," she admitted, " and then go and howl in my room because I was not the talented young woman I had hoped to be ! "

The confession had its piquancy, for I too began to study " Period 8 " with Mr. Cruttwell in the Michaelmas term of 1919, and it was at the beginning of our joint classes, known to Oxford as " coachings," that Winifred and I first met.

We did not, to begin with, like each other at all.

The opening of that Michaelmas term had found me in the uttermost depths of post-war depression. The most iniquitous patriot amongst the renegade women students, I was back at Somerville — the only woman in the University with so uncomfortable a record — after four years of war service. I had returned because, like Winifred, I regarded Oxford as a valuable prelude to a writer's career, and the successive deaths of my fiancé, my brother, and his two greatest friends on European battlefields had deprived me of the alternative lives that I might have lived. Exhausted by the griefs and experiences of these years, and immersed in a fathomless pessimism typical of the youth which I had forgotten that I still possessed, I completely underestimated my own powers of recuperation. In that bitter mood, Winifred's high-spirited presence overwhelmed me like a powerful gust of crude north country wind.

No one who remembers only the stricken fragility of her later years and the pale ethereal glow of the face which confronted death without fear or self-pity, can picture Winifred as she was in October 1919. The vigorous outdoor activities and the rough but plentiful Army rations of her year in the W.A.A.C. had finally banished the lanky, white-faced girl who won school prizes with bandages round her neck ; her splendid height and majestic proportions were now those of a radiant young goddess. A delicate bronze, the legacy of her open-air life, disguised the natural pallor of her skin, and her clear blue eyes danced and shone with the vivacity of good health and unquenchable spirits. Not even her retrospective sorrow for George de Coundouroff and the unpromising behaviour of a war-obsessed Bill could subdue the joy of beginning at last to realise her ambitions in a world released from the terror which had darkened her schooldays.

As she came into the room, her golden hair seemed to

illuminate the decorous dimness of Mr. Cruttwell's study
like a brilliant lamp irrepressibly shining in a dark corner.
Her choice of clothes was then colourful rather than judicious;
the admirable taste which she developed after several years
of life in London had not yet lost its provincial exuberance.
She wore, I remember, a coat and skirt of striped brown
cloth, and a felt hat in a bright shade of emerald green.
This vivid costume seemed to exaggerate both her impressive
size and her glowing animation, which reduced Mr. Cruttwell,
like myself, to the temporary dumbness of subdued astonishment. I did not realise, and he never knew, that the weeks
which she might have given to preparing for Oxford had been
spent upon consoling Edith and trying to trace George,
and her air of breezy indifference to the prescribed books
which she had not read was perhaps the origin of his critical
attitude towards her essays.

For several weeks of coachings, the contrast between
Winifred's gay, stimulating popularity and my own isolated
depression provoked me to barely concealed hostility, not
mitigated by a college debate in which, with the humourless
bitterness of that miserable year, I believed myself to have
been mocked for my war service by a number of heartless
juniors at Winifred's instigation. But the link which the
War had forged between us was too strong to be broken by
these trivial hurts and temporary resentments. It drew us
into the Cathedral together on the first anniversary of
Armistice Day, and by the following term it was sending
us out on long walks to Wood Eaton or Marston Ferry, or
on bicycle rides to the wet primrose-starred hollows of
Tubney Wood. Another unpublished letter to Jean
McWilliam describes our discovery, on a still later expedition
to Boar's Hill, of the then notorious " poets' colony."

" We go long walks together and get lost wonderfully,"
wrote Winifred. " To-day we went beyond Cumnor and
got lost among the minor poets on Boar's Hill. . . . The
poets live on goat's milk and cheese and bread from the
co-operative stores. They never use buses except by accident,
and their slippers are of red leather. One of them keeps a

shop in a wooden hovel, made like a shepherd's hut. It is a wet shop, for the roof leaks on these wet autumn afternoons. The oranges in the window are always a little shrivelled and the tins of sardines have rust on them. But it is so much more elegantly aesthetic to buy one's sardines in a Boar's Hill shop, kept by a minor poet who draws ' Faire Ladies ' all over the accounts, than to cycle down to Sainsbury's or the Market. There are goats everywhere, do you know, and some babies, but not so many, chiefly goats. The poet who kept the shop looked at us with plaintive eyes, as he picked up the shop door. It had fallen out on to the road. These things will happen in a poets' colony. They all worship Masefield. . . . I wonder if they give him cheese and goat's milk when he goes to tea."

A large number of embryo poets were at Oxford that year, though they did not all live on Boar's Hill. The surviving literary " lions " of the seven Oxford " Years " which were now all collected together taking shortened courses in the turbulent University, their names included those of Edmund Blunden, Roy Campbell, Charles Morgan, Robert Graves, L. P. Hartley, Alan Porter, L. A. G. Strong and Louis Golding. Of the last Winifred wrote prophetically to Jean : " Louis Golding is an Oxford poet of sorts — you saw his things in *Oxford Poetry*. He's rather an interesting person, though. I think we shall hear more of him."

The promising quality of these young men's productions, which we both read and criticised, induced Winifred to tell me on our walks and rides of her own aspirations. But it was not until the next academic year, when we had finished with the stimulating but captious Mr. Cruttwell and were coaching together with the Master of Balliol, Dr. A. L. Smith, that the sudden illumination came which gave her the idea for her first novel.

One day, at a coaching on economic history, the Master had described the ruthlessness of economic processes ; the new phases driving out the old, the good of yesterday becoming the evil of to-day, the past making way for the future. He was then over seventy, dwindled and a little shrunken, though brilliantly alive. Watching his lined, mobile face with its twinkling judicious eyes, Winifred, in a flash of revelation, all but exclaimed aloud : " Yes, that's it ! That's true ! That's what happened ! "

In spite of Oxford's engrossing occupations, she often grieved over her father's departure from the farm that she loved and his withdrawal to a provincial suburb where he would not have to cope with post-war agricultural problems. She realised now that he was delicate and growing old ; that he could never have learned how to deal with the new phenomena of government inspection, statutory laws, wage boards and trade unions. But she still felt that when he retired, part of her heart had been broken.

And suddenly, as she listened to A. L. Smith, she realised how the breach could be mended through that supreme form of consolation which life offers to those who are fortunate enough to be born articulate.

" I went back to my room," she records in *Mother Knows Best*, " and began at once to make notes for the novel I determined to write about it, to instruct myself in the reason for that change which had previously seemed to me an unmitigated tragedy. I forced myself to read histories of agriculture, of trade unionism, of Socialism. I tried to see the drama of rural Yorkshire as I knew it, as it had filled my whole horizon until the War destroyed a small and settled world, against the background of historical change and progress, and gradually, reading and thinking, I comforted myself, and invented a story of a young woman (twenty-nine I made her, and, God forgive me, thought her middle-aged !) married to a much older farmer, and confronted by circumstances similar to those which had proved too much for my frail and gentle father."

From that time onwards, the life that mattered most to Winifred centred, not in debates nor Going Down Plays nor her work for the History School, but in the growing sheaf of notes inside her desk. In *The Leviathan* of Thomas Hobbes, one of the seventeenth-century philosophers whom we had studied in our classes on Political Science, she found for her quotation page a passage which exactly fitted the theme :

" Felicity is a continual progresse of the desire from one object to another, the attaining of the former being still but the way to the later . . . so that, in the first place, I put for a generall inclination of all mankind, a perpetuall and restlesse desire of power after power which ceaseth only after death . . . and there shall be no contentment but proceeding."

Before that illumined moment of rich inspiration, Winifred had been experimenting with other kinds of writing, and studying such treasure-troves of style as the travel books of Sir Walter Raleigh and the prose works of Milton.

After the publication of *Letters to a Friend* in 1937, one critical reviewer too cleverly deduced from the numerous books and poems mentioned there that Winifred admired only second-rate literature. Another stated that the correspondence continued " for fifteen years," and inferred from the note of consistent appreciation produced by the over-conscientious editorial omission of every comment which might hurt or offend persons referred to in the letters, that Winifred was just a charming girl with an undiscriminating, " late-flowering mind." Actually, except for a few hurried notes belonging to later years, these young high-spirited letters ended when Winifred went to South Africa at the age of twenty-seven. What they do illustrate is not her critical powers, but the versatility of her interests and the Elizabethan adventurousness which drove her to test every experience that life offered.

Even when this correspondence began in 1920, Winifred understood very clearly the difference between first-rate and second-rate literature. The fact that she could not yet write well herself only gave her the greater reverence for those

who did. During our Oxford years the works to which
she turned most frequently were Shakespeare's *Richard II*,
Raleigh's *Discovery of Guiana*, Milton's *Areopagitica*, the writings of John Wyclif, Blake's *Minor Prophecies*, and the plays
of Bernard Shaw. Her quotation books of the period are
filled with extracts from Browning, Bridges, Swinburne,
Matthew Arnold, Masefield, Kipling, Walter de la Mare,
Alice Meynell and W. B. Yeats. But it was hardly to be
expected that Winifred would subject a lecturer in English,
who was presumably familiar with the titans of literature,
to long dissertations on the classics. The matters discussed
between them, as in most regular correspondences, were the
trivia of everyday life, the small pleasant episodes lying on
the surface. It was not therefore of the treasured books on
her own shelves that Winifred wrote, but of novels sampled
from the local library, or verses casually discovered in
magazines which sometimes gave her ideas for her own.

By the middle of 1920 she was sending poems to University journals and sketching occasional short stories,
though that hectic, emotional summer term was too full
of perturbing interruptions for concentration to be easy.
The national background added to the general feeling of
disturbance. Letters to Jean appreciatively describing performances by the Oxford University Dramatic Society of
Antony and Cleopatra at Easter and *As You Like It* the following
term in Wadham College garden, refer also to railway strikes,
coal strikes and industrial unrest. If the " horrid mess "
in which Winifred perceived England to be struggling inspired her often-expressed desire to travel " and see strange
things and people," the unsolved problems of herself and
her friends filled her with a longing for Jean's decorative
presence and the comforting wisdom of her mature advice.

" I would give much," she wrote, " to see you, tall and
fine and trusty, with your boy's hair and your face brown
from African sun."

Two of Winifred's visitors that summer had their own
private dilemmas, in which, both explicitly and tacitly,
they sought her assistance. The first to arrive was Dorothy

McCalman, who had shared Edith de Coundouroff's school-days in a Belgian convent. Good-tempered, courageous and penniless, the daughter of an Indian Army colonel who turned her adrift when she adopted Roman Catholicism, Dot McCalman had earned her living for many years as an unqualified teacher in elementary schools. But her life-long ambition was an Oxford education, and though she had already reached her thirties, she still hoped to obtain it.

That summer she came to Oxford to discover whether she could take the Somerville entrance examination while still teaching at a school in Forest Gate. With her pleasant face redeemed from plainness by its eager honesty, and her boundless enthusiasm for agreeable trifles apt to be overlooked by favourites of fortune, Winifred found her an attractive guest. Her problems, too, since they were created merely by financial stringency, seemed refreshingly simple after the obscure spiritual torments then so common amongst ex-patriots facing the difficult process of readjust-ment. Moreover, she had a limitless capacity for intrepid persistence, first revealed by a unique little school adventure which Winifred related years afterwards in *Time and Tide*.

At Dorothy McCalman's Belgian convent an elderly nun had suffered badly from rheumatism. Solicitous, sym-pathetic and practical, the young Dot inquired into its cause, and discovered that the nuns wore only cotton under-clothing. Distressed by the thought of her old teacher shivering through the Belgian winter, Dot offered to buy her some woollies. The nun gently refused; combinations had not been invented when her Order was founded, and it was against the rules to wear them. Dot then went to the Mother Superior, who told her that she had no power to revise the regulations. Who had? No one, it seemed, but the Bishop himself. Where was the Bishop? In Brussels.

Quite undaunted, Dorothy McCalman went alone to Brussels on her next free day, found the Bishop and demanded an interview. Expecting to be consulted on some abstruse religious dilemma, he consented to see her, and she indignantly pressed her claim to be allowed to present her nun with warm underclothing. Taken by storm, the astonished Father in God gave his permission. After that, nothing ever intimidated Dot McCalman again. Entering Somerville without time to work for the examination or money to pay for it was nothing to getting the consent of a Catholic Bishop for a Belgian nun to wear woollen combinations.

The financial help which Winifred gave Dorothy McCalman, and her triumphant attainment of a place at Somerville in 1922 at the age of thirty-three, are now matters of college history. Like Winifred, she was destined to be the victim of life's pitiless irony, for she too died prematurely when her goal of university teaching had just been attained. By Winifred's wish the first of the scholarships founded from her bequest to Somerville stands in Dorothy McCalman's name. It is reserved for students who have been obliged, as Dot was, to earn a living for several years before going to college.

Winifred's other visitor was her sister Grace — a less straightforward proposition. Since the end of the War Grace had been living at Cottingham, unsettled, half-anchored, vaguely discontented, a source of perplexity to her mother. In the hope that Oxford would provide a change of atmosphere, Alice Holtby sent her south to spend a few weeks with Winifred.

The tense post-war University might hardly have appeared a consoling environment for a dissatisfied spirit. But Alice Holtby's intuition, as so often, was justified, for Grace proved an unexpected success. Soothingly indifferent to the competitive intellectual fervour which surrounded her, she was usefully content to do Winifred's shopping, take punting parties on the river, and design costumes for the Going Down Play. Even the romance-ridden atmosphere did not oppress her, for though her real objective in life was marriage and a family, from her twenty-four-year-old standpoint these student dramas were mere temporary ebullitions of immature restlessness. Half-pitying and half-amused, she regarded the wrought-up actors with placid toleration, and was therefore in great demand as a " chaperone." University regulations still required these supernumerary gooseberry-players at mixed expeditions, and Grace, with her languid youth, her serene manner and elegant willowy prettiness, was far more congenial to rebellious privacy-seeking students than the reluctant overworked tutors or cautious neutral-tinted dons' wives who usually filled the thankless office.

The pseudo-eroticism of that uncomfortable term ran through Somerville like a high-powered epidemic. From one friend or another, Winifred must have received as many confidences about passionate interludes and their attendant quarrels as even she could endure, and their emotional effect was not mitigated by the melancholy neglectfulness of Bill, who was drifting between Yorkshire and London half-heartedly exploring the discouraging possibilities of free-lance journalism. Perhaps feeling that even the excruciating love-affairs of her contemporaries were better than one which refused to declare itself a " love-affair " at all, Winifred sent a bitter little poem called *The Dead Man* to the 1920 volume of *Oxford Poetry*. Though it surprised the readers of her usual facile lyrics, it was entirely typical of the disillusioned, sardonic element in her character which always lay beneath the benevolent surface but only began to reach its full intellectual expression in her final years.

When the term ended we escaped with relief from our emotional aberrations and spent a peaceful fortnight together in Cornwall, walking through honeysuckled lanes or along the rocky coast, and preparing our Special Subjects for the following term. Winifred had chosen to study the reign of Richard II. She was already deeply engrossed in the story of John Wyclif, whose teaching was to haunt her imagination for five years and to inspire her only unpublished novel, *The Runners*. In the sitting-room of the cottage lent to us at West Pentyre, she sat half concealed by huge dingy volumes of monastic chronicles written in the rambling dog-Latin

of the fourteenth century, while I meditated upon the cyni-
cisms of Machiavelli as a prelude to International Relations.

It was the beginning of a shared working existence which
was to keep us continuously together for the next five years,
and was to last, with only one or two long intervals, to the
end of Winifred's life.

CHAPTER VII

OXFORD OUTGROWN

EPILOGUE TO ROMANCE

I would not honour Love the less,
Who know myself to be
Unworthy of the tenderness
Of your sweet constancy ;
But walk more proudly on my way alone,
Because you once loved me.

I shall go gaily all my days
Where skies are wild and blue,
Finding the flowers about my ways
Are clad in richer hue—
And in the darkest night one star will burn
Because I once loved you.

Why should I weep for one short day
That you have passed my door ?
No changing time can snatch away
The joy that went before.
I shall be thankful all my life for love
Although we love no more.

WINIFRED HOLTBY, 1921

In August 1920 I went for the first time to Winifred's home, and met her tall, kindly, self-effacing father and her imposing white-haired mother, whose powerful personality always recalled to me the strength and stature of Martha Washington.

Edith de Coundouroff was there too, her sweet sorrowful face with its aureole of pale-brown hair still wearing the withdrawn expression of one who communes with a secret grief. Morning after morning beneath my bedroom window she walked silently up and down the garden pushing the sleeping fair-haired baby Margaret, then at the crawling, clambering stage when open doors and slippery stairs are a source of perpetual apprehension to mothers.

It was after that visit that I began, like Jean McWilliam, to keep Winifred's letters, but I remember less what we said and did together than the teas, tennis parties and crowded conversational suppers which followed one another in animated succession. The social life at " Marshington " with which Winifred provided Muriel Hammond in her second novel, *The Crowded Street*, bore a distinct family resemblance to her own hectic vacations. For the first time I realised what it must mean to contend with exacting mental work in a hospitable household where the bedrooms were always full and every hour of privacy meant a discreet battle with circumstance.

The house at Cottingham, appropriately enough, had been christened " Bainesse," an Indian word meaning " welcome." To its generous, convivial owners Winifred was not an eagerly watched prospective " First " working in rigorous competition with men students who spent their vacations on reading parties and dedicated their entire energies to preparations for Schools ; she was merely the youngest member of the family, who could be made to sleep on a sofa when beds ran short. I can still picture her with an armful of books, wandering round the house in search of a quiet corner for uninterrupted work. Her parents had shown exceptional imagination in sending her to Oxford ; the inexorable claims of high scholarly standards lay beyond their experience. Consequently these too sociable Yorkshire interludes foreshadowed the expensive lifelong struggle between Winifred's well-fostered gregarious instincts and her intellectual need for solitude, which impaired her literary output and confused her less-informed critics.

" I pretend I enjoy them tremendously," she wrote to me of the Bainesse tennis parties during one period at home, " but more than often I am a little resentful about them — because I have so much to do, from which they keep me ;

because there is a table here covered with books waiting to be read and *Anderby Wold* waiting to be written. I'm busy with my old game of snatching minutes, and hours, and half mornings, to do the things I want to do, while the parties that sound so gay and are often rather boring — though I pretend even to myself they are glorious — crowd upon me like the surge of a tide from which there is no escape."

The following term we were moved out of college to rooms in Bevington Road, where Winifred occupied a lofty attic with windows overlooking the scarlet and gold of Oxford back gardens in autumn. Our work that term was stimulated by the final attainment of Degrees for Women, the victorious result of a battle half a century old against academic masculine prejudice. Winifred and I were amongst the first women students to take part in the matriculation ceremony, which had hitherto been required only for men.

After the first Degree-giving in the Sheldonian Theatre, when honorary M.A. Degrees were granted to the five Principals of the women's foundations, Oxford became suddenly filled with unfamiliar feminine figures cycling up and down the High Street in scholars' and commoners' gowns. Numerous apocryphal legends sprang up round the historic function and its aftermath. One story related that on Degree-giving Day a lady standing outside the Sheldonian Theatre turned to an undergraduate and, taking him by surprise, exclaimed ecstatically : " I have waited forty years for this ! " " Madam," he replied, with a gallantry not always typical of Junior Common Rooms, " seeing you, I can hardly believe it ! "

During the Christmas vacation, Winifred reported a new invasion of relatives.

" Grace and I are on show to-night. It will be ' Dear Grace, dear Winifred ' — and when we've gone, ' My dear, that younger girl of Alice's grows more gawky and weird every day.' "

But before the new term started, she had to confront an experience still more bitter than the perpetual undermining of her examination prospects by family claims.

A few weeks earlier, Bill had found suddenly intolerable his undirected post-war existence. On the spur of the moment he accepted the post of tutor to the two nephews of a Mexican bishop, and sailed for South America. The boys' parents intended to send them to Europe with Bill to finish their education, but their father was captured in the rebellion against Villa, and after his ransom had been paid there was no money left for the trip. So Bill went from Mexico to Demerara, found a temporary job on a sugar plantation, worked his way intrepidly to a Canadian lumber camp, and for a time disappeared so completely that Winifred did not know whether he was alive or dead. For months he never communicated with her, but for this his absence was not solely responsible.

On the boat going out to South America, Bill had met a young woman pianist, pretty, fragile, penniless, dependent. Her helplessness appealed to those protective instincts which Winifred's independence seldom invoked, and on arrival at his destination he reported himself engaged to be married. In January 1921, Winifred wrote from Cottingham to tell me the news. In her letter she enclosed the poem *Epilogue to Romance*, which seemed a sad sequel to *The Sarabande* of the previous year. She then did her best to deny the implications of her verses.

"I knew, you see, in my heart of hearts, that what he loved was a dream woman whom he called by my name because he knew no one else. And I would not accept his identification of me with his dreams until we had both proved ourselves, for if he was uncertain of his love for me, I was still more uncertain of mine for him. . . . I set myself at work to leave him perfectly free from the first moment I knew he loved me. I am not hurt. The only thing I am disillusioned about is my power of holding others."

She felt glad, she concluded, that he had struck out for himself, and had not just chosen someone whom his family thought suitable. Above all she was thankful that she had not spoilt his life, for she realised now that she had loved him merely as a friend.

It was a rationalisation which not only the distant future but the very next term was to prove an example of wishful thinking. Through the depressing weeks of that cheerless spring, all Winifred's literary inventions centred round the idea of love departed. One sonnet entitled *The Robber*, published in the *Oxford Outlook* of March 1921, especially expressed the sense of grief which her letters repudiated.

> *If dreams were true, then you would come to-day*
> *And find Love's habitation desolate ;*
> *I think his wayward fancy would not wait*
> *For your return, when you were far away.*
> *But I sit lonely with my heart all bare ;*
> *When others come and knock upon the door*
> *Only their shadows cross the empty floor,*
> *And fade again, because you are not there.*
> *For when you went away, Love said good-bye,*
> *Fled from my heart, and left the door ajar,*
> *Seeking your fleeting form from star to star*
> *Until he find you, or, not finding, die.*
> *And I have neither happiness nor pain*
> *Until you come and bring me love again.*

But the ultimate distresses of that term could not be assuaged by the melancholy satisfaction of writing love-poems. With astonished pain Winifred suddenly found herself a victim of the close psychological relationship between sex and religion, for the loss of Bill united with the theological implications of Wyclif's teaching to undermine those orthodox Anglican principles which she had hitherto accepted without question. Three years afterwards, when much mature experience seemed to have passed over our heads, she recalled to me in a letter " those nights that you thought madness, that were mad, when I would lie face downwards on the floor in searing agony, hearing in mythical church bells the call to a devotion that my intellect would no longer allow me wholly to offer."

One afternoon some exasperating failure of comprehension on my part produced a vehement outburst of temper

which passed swiftly into a passion of tears. All that evening
I sat in front of her fire while she knelt beside me with her
face in my lap, and poured out the pent-up torment of her
religious conflict. I could only listen with the compassion
born of similar knowledge and assure her that in time her
mental anguish would pass, for I knew that there were no
consoling replies to these bitter intellectual questionings.
Just after leaving school, I had been plunged into the same
tumult of agonised inquiry by reading Mrs. Humphry
Ward's *Robert Elsmere*. Then the War, with its desperate
personal preoccupations, had eclipsed those bewildering
mental problems. By the time that the hurricane was over,
my theological self-torturings had either answered themselves
or ceased to matter. In 1921 they seemed to have occurred
half a lifetime before, and Winifred's attack of spiritual
awakening appeared curiously belated. She was then only
twenty-two, but her commanding stature and mature
appearance — which hardly changed during the sixteen
years that I knew her — made me forget how young she was.

We seldom spoke of Bill during our remaining weeks at
Oxford, but soon after we went down I learnt that his engagement to the girl musician had been as ephemeral as his
tutorial post. By that time Winifred had recovered her
optimism. Both then and later her work absorbed her far
too deeply to be wrecked or even overshadowed by an
unsatisfactory emotional relationship, but Bill's invisible
influence constantly reasserted itself the moment that she
returned to Yorkshire. She must have written to me about
him directly after our Final Schools, for though she kept
little of my earlier correspondence, a letter still exists dated
June 27th, 1921, in which I ventured upon a prophecy that
was to be strangely and sorrowfully fulfilled.

" I always wonder whom you are most hard on — Bill
or yourself ! You haven't really much mercy on either. I
always feel certain that you and he will come together in the
end. You may not marry, but you'll come together eventually. . . . But not yet. At present you both suffer too
much ; you wouldn't help each other."

Our last term at Oxford vanished in frantic, belated revision, of which the progress had hardly been assisted by shattered romances and religious doubts. The magnitude of the ground to be covered so absorbed our energies that the attempts of the Senior Common Room to shepherd us into academic careers seriously taxed our powers of resistance. Soon after going down, Winifred was offered the History tutorship at St. Hugh's College. But though periodic attacks of conscience suggested that just because she enjoyed writing she ought to try instead for a South African school inspectorship and help Jean McWilliam to civilise the youth of Pretoria, she refused the Oxford post. I too had declined to consider a London University lectureship at Westfield College, Hampstead. We compromised with the tutorial opinion which deplored our inexplicable preference for popular forms of literature by promising to collaborate in a work of historical research, which we thankfully abandoned as soon as we discovered how unfavourable were its chances of making any impression.

Winifred, like myself, had no real doubt where her dearest ambitions lay. We both pictured a vague but wholly alluring existence of novel-writing and journalism, financially sustained by the barest minimum of part-time teaching, and varied with occasional excursions into lecturing and political speaking. The synthetic task of scholarship offered insufficient scope for Winifred's overflowing creative force ; as she explained to Jean McWilliam, " too much Oxford would make me think the world was made for the benefit of historical research."

Long before we actually started to look for a modest flat suited to our limited incomes, Winifred had agreed to share with me the adventurous, experimental London life on which we proposed to launch ourselves the following January. Her attitude towards it was expressed by the first verse of a rhyme which she wrote to the tune of Yum-Yum's Sun Song in the *Mikado* for that summer's Going Down Play. It was intended — as she afterwards told Lady Rhondda — " to trample down all nasty little giggling feminine inferiority-complexes."

We mean to run this show.
We are not shy.
We'll make the whole world go —
My friends and I !

It was probably fortunate for Winifred that she did just miss getting a First, for had she achieved one the pressure upon her to take up academic work would have been vigorously renewed, and her over-sensitive conscience might well have responded. But when the telegram announcing our disappointing results arrived in the middle of an August tennis-party at Cottingham, where I was again staying, the advantages of an undistinguished class were not immediately apparent.

" Not very nice — both Seconds," Winifred whispered lugubriously to me as she crushed the orange envelope into the pocket of her sports-coat. For the rest of the afternoon we had to practise the technique — which lecture platforms were later to make so familiar — of concealing our private feelings in front of an audience. Some days afterwards Winifred learnt that before her too spirited *Viva Voce*, the ten examiners of that year's outsize History School had carried her untidy, exuberant, well-informed papers about with them for days, unable to decide on their merits. A Hull friend, Commander Regan — known to the family as " Uncle Mickey " — finally wrote for further details to one of the examiners who had worked with him at the Admiralty during the War. He received a sympathetic reply which indicated how near to a First Winifred had been.

" It is a pity," the letter concluded, " that she is quite illiterate, but I do not think that this affected the verdict of the examiners."

When she began immediately afterwards to correspond with me about writing, lecturing, teaching and the possibilities of speaking for the League of Nations Union, Winifred's irrepressible spirits had again recovered from their temporary set-back. On the tenuous basis of a published volume of poems and my friendship with the writers,

Robert and Marie Connor Leighton, I poured out letters of advice about marketing stories, visiting agents, and obtaining introductions to the whole barrage of middle-men who seem in youth so necessary a stepping-stone to success, though every established author eliminates as many as he can.

Like the rest of Winifred's friends, I discovered that she was a gay, grateful, infinitely responsive letter-writer, whose correspondence suggested a long, vivid, unbroken conversation.

" Why is it I always have to sit down and answer your letters at once ? " I asked her that summer. " Is it because of that irresistible conversational quality, or because I have so much to say to you that five minutes after I have written I could always sit down and write another letter, just as long ? "

Already, during a week with me in London, Winifred had met Clare Leighton's literary parents, who had been friends of Sir Herbert Tree, and were moved by the thought that he had died in her presence. They regarded her as a superb young Viking, full of strength and vitality, and were surprised to learn that her delicacy as a child had lingered on in baffling periods of ill-health which had even impaired her work during Schools.

" I liked her especially for the laughter in her," Marie Leighton said to me afterwards. " What's more, she knows when to laugh ; she'll never laugh at the wrong things. She's got a tremendous reverence for almost everything."

But it was her intellectual attainments, rather than her appearance or her moral qualities, which impressed the Yorkshire estate agent at the block of flats where my parents lived in Kensington. The agent had known David Holtby in Yorkshire, and forcibly expressed to my father his views on Winifred's emergence as a " sport " in her family.

" Fancy Mr. 'Oltby 'aving a daughter like that ! "

" Why shouldn't he ? " inquired my father, characteristically adding, " They're very nice people."

" Ay, I know. But they're the old yeoman stock, not the brainy sort at all. I wouldn't 'ave expected 'im to 'ave a daughter fit to go to college."

Perhaps David and Alice Holtby still secretly shared the same opinion, for a letter from Winifred in the late autumn described her mother's pleasure in a ceremony at Queen Margaret's, where the Archbishop of York had presided and Winifred's Oxford Honours were announced to the School.

"An old lady now living in Scarborough was present who had known Mother's mother and father. . . . After Miss Fowler had said about me and the school had clapped, old Mrs. Dale turned and said, ' That's your Winifred, isn't it ? ' And Mother said humbly, ' Yes ; just think of my daughter — of John and Anne Winn's granddaughter — being clapped by an Archbishop ! ' And the old lady said, ' Of course, I always say that brains are hereditary.' And Mother came home with, not a feather, but a whole aviary of plumes in her cap ! "

Winifred herself had not been present at this function, for at the end of August we went away together on that six weeks' holiday in Italy which has been so fully described in *Testament of Youth* and *Letters to a Friend*. From the standpoint of the guide-books, all the portents were most inauspicious. The season was wrong, for we ventured into Italy during the hottest August of Europe's recollection. The mosquitoes were wrong, our finances were inadequate, and we did not know Italian. We travelled by classes which varied from crowded Seconds to garlic-smelling Fourths ; we could only afford cheap hotels, and our tour was so planned that half our trains seemed to leave at five o'clock in the morning. Even so, they always arrived hours behind schedule, for this was happy-go-lucky pre-Fascist Italy, which had not to save a dictator's face by pretending to be efficient.

The result was the most perfect holiday of all my experience and, I believe, of Winifred's ; a holiday which we both remembered long after more politically adventurous journeys to Geneva, and Occupied Germany, and the Succession States, had been almost forgotten. I can still recall St. Mark's Square beneath a star-studded sky of indigo velvet; still feel the exquisite coolness of the evening hour when we leaned out of our pension window in Florence and saw the shining banks of the Arno grow mellow beneath the beneficent glow of the autumn sunset. We spent our last week in Rome, and knew — as I had known during the War when travelling home from Malta — that no experience quite equalled the consciousness of having been there. For Rome then was still the centre of the world; not of this new, ugly world so long politically dominated by a war-like Axis, but of an older world in which all Rome-ward roads led to intellectual beauty and the treasures of the spirit.

We parted in London until the New Year, and Winifred returned to Yorkshire. That night she wrote me a letter which still glows like a gentle lantern through the shadowed corridors of memory.

" Now I am undressed, and have unpacked, and the family is safely tucked in bed, so I can sit down and talk to you without fear of interruption or delay. It has been a wonderful time. . . . But you know, the best thing of all was finding out from day to day how dear you are. The journey would have been pleasant in most circumstances, and interesting in any, but because you were there, it was wholly delightful. Whatever things may happen in the future of good or evil, at least we have had one perfect time which nothing can take away.

> *Our actions all have immortality ;*
> *Such gladness gives no hostage unto death.*

Thank you, thank you, thank you, for being so completely satisfactory, you most sweet woman.

" And we will go again. There are heaps of lovely places to see and things to do. Never doubt that I want to see and do them, and that I ask no better travelling companion than you."

CHAPTER VIII

THE NINETEEN-TWENTIES
(1)

THE DEBT

I owe so large a debt to life,
I think if I should die to-day
My death would never quite repay
For music, friends and careless laughter,
The swift, light-hearted interplay
Of wit on ready wit, and after,
The silence that most blessed falls
Across the room and firelit walls
And quells our flame of jesting strife.
I owe so large a debt to life
No gift can wipe it quite away,
Nor any tears that I can borrow
From watching all the world's wild sorrow,
As Autumn never can allay
The promise of a sunlit morrow
We had as legacy from May.

WINIFRED HOLTBY, 1923

BETWEEN 1922 and 1923, Winifred and I first occupied a ground-floor studio and then a top-floor flat in Doughty Street, the long straight road not far from the British Museum which links Theobalds Road with Mecklenburg Square.

In the autumn of 1923 we moved into a spacious mansion flat in Maida Vale, without in the least realising that we were exchanging the choice habitation of intellectual Bloomsbury for a district with quite another reputation. Winifred was always gaily indifferent to the peculiar snobbery which attaches importance to " good " note-paper and a " good " address, and the lugubrious comment of a New

College friend — " Why are you leaving the neighbourhood of Tawney and Eileen Power for a place called Maida Vale ? " — left us both undisturbed. Our sole object in moving to the unfashionable end of the Edgware Road was to acquire space for a housekeeper who would shoulder all domestic obligations, and leave us more time for our ever-increasing work.

In retrospect those years seem further away than the pre-ceding period in which the national mood was similar to that before the present war, for in spite of their dislocation and re-membered grief they were years of stimulating hope. Our outlook, like that of many of our contemporaries, was re-presented by an optimistic comment in one of Winifred's letters to Jean McWilliam : " The day of imperialism is passed. I heard its curfew sound when the guns startled the pigeons in Huchenneville orchard on Armistice Day."

Nothing is now left of those nineteen-twenties, with their exhilarating certainty that mankind could learn from experience in one or two decades. We felt so old after the four lifelong years which had ended only yesterday ; we were in fact still so young in our fond belief that humanity would never again resort to its evil historic paraphernalia of secret treaties, economic injustices and balances of power, or again deceive itself with the recurrent conviction that one more war would destroy militarism for ever.

In Doughty Street we had few comforts and no luxuries except a tortoise called Adolphus, which died prematurely because we anxiously roused and fed it when it should have been hibernating. Rents in Bloomsbury were then so high that the bed-sitting-room standards of college were beyond our means ; even the garrets in the house to which our chilly habitation was attached fetched 32s. 6d. a week without food. Winifred's letters to Jean refer enthusiastic-ally to this partitioned " studio " with its cold skylights and miniature penny-in-the-slot gas fires ; they describe the pleasant trivialities of our daily routine with its strenuous arguments over mop and duster, its egg and cheese suppers cooked on a gas-ring, its adornment by coloured bowls of bluebells or wallflowers picked up cheap from a pavement flower-seller.

The real luxury of our strenuous and economical life lay in its comparative freedom from disturbing responsibility, an asset which we had both lost by the latter end of that post-war decade. Although her small successes were trivial compared with her subsequent achievements, Winifred was invariably happy because she was doing work that she chose for herself; it was not yet laid upon her by the many who found her useful, efficient and obliging, and naturally preferred her to further their interests rather than her own. Never again, too, were family claims to lie so lightly upon her. She was still far from those later years which were not only to be shadowed by her own approaching end, but darkened by the illness and death which destroyed the convivial family circle where in spite of its interruptions she had known so much happiness.

In the early nineteen-twenties the news from Yorkshire fitted the brightening post-war scene, for it was nearly always pleasant and encouraging.

" Mother's been elected to the East Riding County Council ! " Winifred announced to me excitedly one breakfast-time in March 1923. " She's the first woman they've ever had on it ! "

Two months later she ran up Doughty Street to meet me, joyously waving a telegram which contained one of Alice Holtby's cryptic messages :

" Engaged last night. Both very happy ; we also."

From this we gathered that Grace was to marry the Scottish doctor from Hull who had recently become a frequent visitor to Cottingham. He was a widower and many years her senior, but we knew that the man who brought her the only vocation she desired would have no disadvantages in her eyes, and we rejoiced that her mother's problem was solved at last.

Neither Grace nor her future husband wanted a long engagement, and their wedding was planned for September. International politics meant even less to her than the sporting events of her own county, and she chose a date which not only disconcerted many of the Yorkshire guests by coinciding with the Doncaster races, but came right in the middle of the League of Nations Assembly at Geneva which Winifred and I had arranged to attend. In those days, when the Assembly had real drama and significance, the opening week was usually the most exciting, but that autumn Mussolini's bombardment of Corfu gave a startled world the first indication of methods which were to become familiar in the next dictator-ridden decade. We travelled, hurriedly and reluctantly, straight from Geneva to Cottingham while Signor Salandra of Italy was still engaged in acrimonious verbal warfare with M. Politis of Greece.

On the morning of the wedding I found myself able, for the first time, to be really useful to Winifred's family.

"We don't know what to do with Grace," Edith confided to me. "She hasn't finished her packing, and she won't get dressed or have any lunch. If we try to help we only seem to get on her nerves, and we're supposed to start for the church in an hour. Do see if you can do anything with her! She might listen to you."

Without much confidence I said that I would try, for Grace, I knew, had no special affection for Winifred's ambition-driven friends from Oxford. I went upstairs to find her trailing aimlessly from room to room, wrapped in a long coat because her dressing-gown was packed. As always, she reminded me of an elegant drooping lily on an overlong stalk. She was quite incapable of outward excitement, but it was obvious that concealed agitation had simultaneously deprived her of the ability to finish anything, and inspired her with resentful antagonism against the efficient family which wanted to take everything out of her hands.

Because I was not one of them, she actually hailed me with undisguised relief. Quite how I helped her to pack and persuaded her to eat I cannot recall, but I remember sitting in her bedroom amid the chaos of her luggage, racking my brains for soothing small-talk over a plate of cold chicken and a bottle of champagne. Eventually she allowed her bridesmaids — Winifred and a cousin — to help her into her wedding dress, and we all set off for the church at a reasonable approximation to the time arranged.

Never, I think, have I seen anyone whom the conventional white robe and veil of a bride suited so well. With her languid dark-eyed beauty and the huge sheaf of crimson roses that she carried (" No maidenly lilies for me — I'm twenty-eight ! " she had said, no longer reluctant to acknowledge the passing of time), she looked like a graceful princess in a medieval pageant. Being even taller than Winifred, she topped by several inches her short sandy-haired bridegroom, but even this major incongruity was diminished by her stately dignity, by the filmy hydrangea-shaded draperies of the bridesmaids as they stood in the aisle with four-year-old Margaret between them, and most of all by the grand Gothic proportions of Cottingham parish church, the architectural sister to Beverley Minster.

We returned to a marquee-covered lawn, cheerfully crowded by a large contingent of Holtby relatives. At the wedding theatre-party in Hull that evening, a male guest who had already taken full advantage of the reception effectually completed the process, and was escorted home to his lodgings, more firmly than gently, by Edith and Winifred.

After such incursions into family life, we were more than ever glad of our strenuous, independent, enthralling London existence. Neither of us had ever known any pleasure quite equal to the joy of coming home at the end of the day after a series of separate varied experiences, and each recounting these incidents to the other over late biscuits and tea. Our conversations were irradiated by Winifred's delight in small, absurd trifles. She used to sit on the floor in front of the tiny gas-fire, the light on her hair and her blue eyes sparkling with enjoyment, eagerly imploring : " Tell me some more ! "

Those years with Winifred taught me that the type of friendship which reaches its apotheosis in the story of David and Jonathan is not a monopoly of the masculine sex.

Hitherto, perhaps owing to a lack of women recorders, this fact has been found difficult to accept by men, and even by other women. Some feminine individualists believe that they flatter men by fostering the fiction of women's jealous inability to love and respect one another. Other sceptics are roused by any record of affection between women to suspicions habitual among the over-sophisticated.

" Too, *too* Chelsea ! " Winifred would comment amiably in after years when some zealous friend related the newest legend current about us in the neighbourhood.

After a year or two of constant companionship, our response to each other's needs and emotions had become so instinctive that in our correspondence one of us often replied to some statement or request made by the other before the letter which contained it had arrived. When I wrote Winifred from America at the beginning of May 1927 that I thought I was going to have a child, she replied that during the previous week she remembered having an unusually vivid dream about a baby of mine. She called it " the beloved and lovely child " — a sentiment which she always felt for my son John Edward from the time that he was born at the end of that year.

The only personal experience of telepathy that I have ever known occurred in connection with Winifred. One day in 1923, when I was out of London on a periodic teaching expedition, a class was cancelled and I arrived back at our Doughty Street flat before tea-time instead of the usual supper-time. Not knowing that Winifred was out, I ran up the stairs and called gaily, " Hullo, my dear ! " as I opened the door.

Shortly before supper Winifred returned from an afternoon's shopping in the West End. As soon as she saw me she inquired rather oddly : " Look here — did you come back to-day at the usual time ? "

I explained that I had been early, and she then asked : " Well, did you go straight to the flat ? "

" Yes," I replied. " I came on the 'bus from London Bridge as usual. Why do you ask ? "

"Because," she said, "I had the queerest experience this afternoon. I was in Berkeley Street, going to Piccadilly, and suddenly I heard your voice just behind me calling, "Hallo, my dear!" I turned round quite startled — and found you weren't there."

"When exactly did that happen?" I asked.

"It was just about four o'clock," she said.

I then told her that precisely at that hour I had run up the stairs and called my greeting to the empty flat.

Passionately as I desired Winifred's friendship, deeply as I needed it with the starving need of an individual whose earlier loves had been prematurely and violently shattered, the building of it was her achievement rather than mine. In the years which followed the War I was not easy to live with, and I often wondered even then why Winifred showed no sign of wanting to leave me. The heredity inconsiderately bequeathed me by nervous irritable ancestors, combined with the loss of every person for whose life I feared during the War, had implanted a habit of apprehension which I now accept as a lifelong burden, since twenty years have not sufficed to remove it. To-day I can conceal and sometimes forget it, but in the nineteen-twenties it was perpetual and acute. Every hour of suspense, however slight its cause, meant unmitigated agony. Every minor set-back, criticism or disappointment upset me at least twice as much as any sane person. Our stimulating life in London, with its constant surprises and excitements, was probably the worst that I could then have lived, for whenever we spent a country holiday together at Whipsnade or Cornwall or Burgh Heath, the sense of strain began to disappear. But that London life was inevitable if a beginning was ever to be made with the writer's career that I had already postponed for seven interminable years, and Winifred, realising this, resolved that since the surroundings could not be changed the companion chosen must act as compensation.

Her own capacity for swift exasperation was not negligible; I once saw her take an inefficient secretary, who had bungled an important telephone message, firmly by

the shoulders and shake her like a child. But it was chiefly
fools whom she would not suffer ; provided that intelligence
and goodwill existed, she was ready to forgive every accom-
panying disadvantage. With me her generosity and for-
bearance were unfailing ; patiently she consoled my lunatic
anxiety over adverse reviews, rejected manuscripts, family
ailments, and other minor everyday annoyances which
to her must have seemed absurdly trivial. Sometimes,
ruefully seeing myself as others saw me, I asked her half
sadly and half amusedly why she put up with it. She would
then answer quite seriously that she was a debtor to life, and
therefore felt under an obligation to repay with love and
service a friend whose personal history had given less reason
for gaiety and confidence than her own.

" I didn't have to fight to go to college like you," she
would explain. " Mother just sent me, and everything
came of its own accord. And then I didn't lose anyone in
the War who was really necessary to my happiness."

When I asked her if she did not regard Bill and her
comfortless relationship with him as a species of war-time
tragedy, she would reply that at any rate he wasn't dead,
or even any longer missing in South America. Soon, now,
he would be back in London, and if she found that after
all she had lost him, she had only herself to thank.

The quality that she called her " immunity " persistently
oppressed her. So many of her associates seemed to be
unhappy or frustrated, racked with domestic anxiety,
forced by poverty into uncongenial jobs, stricken by the War
and still secretly mourning for friends lost in battle. Remorsefully she dwelt upon her own good fortune, her
exemption from fate's cruellest blows, the freedom to do her
chosen work which her small private income gave her, her
health and vital energy, the opportunities brought her by
her inexplicable popularity.

" I would rather shriek like a rat in a trap," she wrote
to me in the spring of 1924, " than impose a new form of
torture upon those whose pain has reacted so long upon
me with a sort of dull urgency of distress until my own

becomes preferable in any form. Remember I speak as one who has nearly all experience upon the debit side of fortune. I still owe to life much more than I have paid, and if there were any way to rid myself of my debt without calling upon others who have already paid too dearly to share it with me I would do so. . . . I am torn between the exacting demands of love, and my invincible belief that no person should lay too heavy claims upon another. To let each one of one's beloveds feel completely free, even the most beloved of them all, to interpose no barrier of pity or tenderness between them and their destiny — that needs a little careful schooling."

Like the man with the tender heart in her fable, *The Queen's Justice*,[1] Winifred did not realise that some aspects of her life would have seemed bitter to an egotist with a grievance, nor understand that it was her own charity and humour which caused her to regard her personal disappointments as less catastrophic than other people's. She felt that she had bought her happiness at the expense of all who suffered and were sorrowful, and her conscience-stricken sense of this indebtedness runs through all her books and stories like a *motif* in a minor key.

In her novel *Poor Caroline*, she causes Eleanor de la Roux, the young heroine who is an obvious near relative of herself, to perform ridiculous financial sacrifices in order to " shake off this intolerable burden " of exemption from poverty and ignorance. At the end of another fable, *The Comforter*,[1] she makes Judas Iscariot say in hell : " Heaven is only tolerable for those who have learned how to forgive themselves. So I came here, where, if we are in torment, we may at least share the pain we have inflicted. We are not called upon to suffer the horror of immunity."

Some day, she felt, she must pay for this exoneration from life's worst catastrophes in order that justice, in which she passionately believed, might exist. And behind all her gaiety, her sense of well-being and delight in life, lay the subconscious intuition that this payment would take the

[1] Now collected in the volume of short stories, *Pavements at Anderby*.

form of early death. It recurs at intervals in her letters to Jean McWilliam ; it appears in various poems such as *No Mourning by Request* and *Invocation to Time*.

At some very early stage this intuition must have communicated itself to me, for in a letter written to her in August 1923, on the premature death of Elizabeth Murray, Professor Gilbert Murray's beautiful daughter and our Somerville predecessor, I find the sadly prophetic comment : "You know, you're just such another as she was in your own way ; you don't or won't realise your physical limitations either. You forget that mental fire and imaginative effort are just as tiring as knocking about in trains and buses. I hope you are on the moors now, being blown about. . . . Come back with brighter eyes and more colour, and take away the compunction your tired-lookingness always worries me with the moment you are gone."

Searching through my letters, I find expressed again and again this fear of losing her, and I still remember the agony of my growing panic one afternoon in Maida Vale when she returned from some expedition two hours later than the time she had given me. At the moment I attributed this anxiety to my established bad habit of apprehension, but now I believe that some deep-rooted instinct beyond all reason senses the coming of danger to those whom we love, and is even aware of constitutional defects unknown to their possessor. I realise now that I do not feel this intuitive anxiety for all who are dear to me, and that whenever I have felt it, it has invariably been justified.

When Winifred's Will with its apparently large total capital was published, many people wondered why she had seemed so impecunious at the outset of her career, and even during her last illness continued strenuously to earn her living.

Actually, the size of her " estate " was entirely deceptive. Owing to the curious calculations of legal procedure, it was made to include amounts which she would ultimately have inherited from various sources, but which were still in other people's possession at the time of her death. When she first came to London a small income of under £200 a year, made over to her by her father from his own estate, represented her only private means. The same measure of wisdom which had caused David and Alice Holtby to send Winifred to Oxford now enabled them to accept her judgment that London alone would give her the work that she wanted to do in the world. They realised that in the cut-throat competition of capital cities the worker who need not earn his actual bread starts with a favourable handicap ; they also knew that an income which has to be supplemented adds a salutary incentive to the urge of ambition.

In order to have the maximum freedom for writing, Winifred decided to do the supplementing by a variety of small teaching and lecturing posts until literary work could be made to pay, rather than tie herself for half each week to one employer. Her first engagement, offered on the strength of my eager if daring recommendation, was a course of lectures on Italian personalities at my old school, St. Monica's, Kingswood. The six personalities chosen — Frederick II, St. Francis of Assisi, Joanna of Naples, St. Catherine of Siena, Savonarola and Leonardo da Vinci — were united by the parts that they had played in the medieval struggle between the secular and religious ideals of the *Summum Bonum*. We had spent many hours of our Italian holiday searching for pictures and stories to illustrate their careers.

Our exertions were justified, for the first address proved Winifred to be both a born lecturer and an adornment to any public platform. Many of the letters which I received after her death came from strangers who had heard her speak only once, but had never forgotten her. At her request I went to one of the St. Monica's lectures to act as critic, and watched her as she stood on the platform of the school gymnasium in a long picture dress of heavy blue silk, her golden hair an aureole beneath the light over her head. She lectured quietly, her pale face serene, benevolent and dignified. Beside her on the desk stood a vase of daffodils,

the same pale gold as her hair. The whole setting might
have been a study by a Renaissance artist, and the mistresses
sitting at the back of the hall silently drew one another's
attention to the gracious picture that she made. It was
inevitable that she should be asked, when the lectures were
over, to take a series of weekly classes at the school. People
who once engaged Winifred always continued to do so ;
her difficulty after the first few months was to avoid an
embarras de richesses of jobs.

A recommendation from one school soon led to engagements at others. For some time she coached several girls
in the top form at Notting Hill High School for their entrance
examinations to Oxford, and had the satisfaction of seeing
one of them — Sonia Hambourg, the eldest daughter of
Mark Hambourg the pianist, and now editor of the
Albatross publications — win the History Scholarship at
Somerville. After Winifred's death it was Sonia who
arranged with me for the inclusion of *South Riding* among
the Albatross novels, and who presented Winifred's mother
and myself with a beautiful hand-printed edition of the
book specially bound for us in primrose-coloured leather.

At one private school which Winifred visited in the
country, she learned the disadvantages as well as the merits
of modern history teaching. She was asked to use " outlines "
of enormous scope as text-books, and found that the girls
suffered in consequence from an extraordinary poverty of
historical imagination. Having lost what she called " the
good proteins of fact and vitamins of picturesque legend,"
they confused Napoleon with Alexander of Greece, and
Alfred the Great with Alfred the Good, in a manner impos-
ible to the benighted generations reared on apocryphal
stories.

" I'm not sure that Alfred and the Cakes wasn't a
better method after all," she observed ruefully, though she
recalled with justice that she herself, by skipping two forms
at school, had done the Civil Wars three times, but had
never heard of the Industrial Revolution. So she endeavoured to combine both methods in coaching a lovely and

brilliant American society girl, whose wayward ambition led her to aspire to the entrance examination at Newnham College, Cambridge.

Winifred went two or three times weekly to the wealthy household in Mount Street and was paid at the rate of fifteen shillings an hour, a fee which we both considered enormous. The money was thoroughly earned, for the girl, though gifted and charming, was sometimes wayward and petulant. She once gave Winifred a violent cold through her disposal of her own used handkerchiefs by the simple expedient of throwing them on the floor.

Since Winifred was only a few years her pupil's senior, she determined after the first fit of temper to establish her authority at an early stage. The next time the young American peevishly refused a difficult test paper, Winifred picked her up and quietly shook her as she was later to shake our astonished secretary, until common sense returned. This drastic treatment produced the desired result and the girl eventually passed her examination, but by that time her enthusiasm had moved from scholarship to woodcuts and Left-wing politics. A few months later she married a foreign diplomat and invited Winifred to the wedding. Winifred was then going through an impecunious period and could not afford a wedding garment, so she borrowed a squirrel fur coat given me some years earlier by my father. It was full length for me, but appeared on Winifred as an elegant three-quarters. The wedding guests, she reported afterwards, were the strangest conglomeration that she had ever encountered of Mayfair society with Comrades wearing the red ties and long hair of highbrow Communism.

Winifred's lectures, after the carefully prepared series at St. Monica's, were sometimes adventurous rather than discreet. When Dorothy McCalman asked her to suggest a lantern lecturer on Gothic architecture for her school at Forest Gate, Winifred enthusiastically recommended herself, but forgot that in the darkness required by the slides she would not be able to see her notes with the names of the pictures. For five minutes during the lecture she talked

about Lincoln Cathedral in the belief that it was Ely — a
feat only rivalled on a speaking tour some years afterwards,
when she lunched in one Lancashire town under the impression that it was another.   Probably no one but myself —
again present at the lecture as a source of critical reassurance
— noticed the relief in her voice when a slide appeared
which she could recognise without hesitation, and she
exclaimed delightedly : " Allow me to introduce you to St.
Paul's Cathedral ! "

She soon conquered these shortcomings of inexperience,
and in the autumn of 1923 was appointed by the Oxford
University Extension Delegacy to give three courses of north
country lectures at Kendal, Seascale and Windermere.   Although she was then only just twenty-five, her eager youth
and humility delighted the Secretary to the Delegacy, and the
lectures were so successful that he invited her, during the
next few years, to give more courses than she had time to
accept.   It was at Seascale, sitting in a tea-shop waiting
for the hour of her lecture, that she met the crazy little
woman, half lunatic, half child, who told her the tale of
fear and desolation which she afterwards related in the
short story *A Windy Day*.[1]

Confidences of this type were a common experience for
Winifred ; her personality carried with it an aura of
sympathy which led complete strangers to tell her their
intimate histories in railway carriages or at dances, and
brought her into perpetual contact with those minor but
time-demanding accidents and tragedies which most of us
manage to elude.   One typical incident happened on the
afternoon that my son was born, four days before Christmas
during a period of sudden thaw between two weeks of
paralysing cold.   After leaving me at a Kensington nursing
home she was walking back to Earl's Court, feeling anxious
and miserable owing to a doctor's diagnosis which had been
carefully withheld from me, when a small elderly woman
slipped and fell on the icy pavement in front of her.   The
stranger turned out to be helpless, hysterical, considerably

[1] In *Pavements at Anderby*.

damaged by the fall, miles away from her home in the East End and unable to afford a taxi. In any case taxis were infrequent in that quiet section of Kensington, and the best part of an hour elapsed while Winifred found a policeman, discovered a taxi, took the querulous victim to a chemist for First Aid, and finally sent her home in a second taxi after paying the fare in advance.

On another occasion Winifred was buying stamps at a West End Post Office when an agitated girl rushed in, looked frantically for a number in the telephone book, gave up the attempt in despair and burst into tears. Inevitably the person beside her, Winifred asked what was the matter. Could she do anything to help?

The girl sobbed out : " My only brother's just been killed. My father's dead, my mother's away staying with friends, and I've got to tell her."

It was, of course, Winifred who found the number, put through the call, and gave the catastrophic message. I have never known anyone upon whom the burden of vicarious responsibility fell so repeatedly, yet it never seemed to reduce her readiness to shoulder obligations for friends and relatives whose claims, if seldom excellent, were at least better justi-fied than those intermittently made by a long sequence of haphazard strangers.

CHAPTER IX

THE NINETEEN-TWENTIES
(2)

ART AND SCIENCE

("Science has *absolutely nothing* to give to Art."—
An American Critic)

Must we complain of beauty who have seen
The wakening woods unfold their gowns of green,
Or the day's loveliness serenely die
Below the pale pavilion of the sky?

These having seen, are we so blindly bold
To say that beauty's little tale is told?
Rather we walk with eyes that cannot see
Her revelation in the days to be.

We shall make pictures, when we have the skill,
Of the clear crystals that the rocks distil,
And draw fair pictures to enrich our night
With the inexorable curves of light.

We shall weave traceries as fine as lace
Of the minute events of time in space,
And hear through silence, with enchanted ears,
The silver music of the turning spheres.

Then shall we glory, with enfranchised sight,
In smallest wonder or superb delight,
And marvel with compassionate amaze
At these lost, blind, inert, unhearing days.

WINIFRED HOLTBY
The Observer, August 3rd, 1930

WINIFRED HERSELF was not, as some of the critics have
imagined, slow to perceive the danger to her work of the

natural humanitarian so instinctively recognised by persons with sorrows, grievances and problems. In her summary of the ideas underlying her unpublished novel *The Runners*, she writes with heartfelt knowledge of " pity, the deadliest enemy of art." Like the bedside meditations of the girl Joanna, her rough notes for *The Land of Green Ginger* reflect the permanent clash between her desire to help the inhabitants of the real world, and her longing to escape to the society of an imaginary one.

" I want my name to live ! " cried the voice of her youthful aspiration. But immediately her conscience confronted her with the practical question : " Yes — but as what ? You want to be a writer, an artist. Must art then be ruthless and pitiless, its bright preoccupations undimmed by the chilling miasma of human sorrow ? Because some would-be artists contemptuously describe the civilised achievements of compassion as ' questions ' and ' causes,' the fact that children are starving from malnutrition is not altered. Nor does war cease to threaten the community — which includes artists, though they do not always appear to be aware of it."

Was she to aim at being a Charlotte Brontë or a Josephine Butler ; the truthful contemplative chronicler of her countryside or the eloquent humanitarian, impressive with precisely the glowing inspired radiance which produces the most effective results in public life ?

" The difficulty is," she confessed to Jean McWilliam, " to what can one dedicate one's self. I am blown about by a wandering wind of great pity and sorrow and desire."

During her last years the problem was still troubling her. " I shall never quite make up my mind whether to be a reformer-sort-of-person or a writer-sort-of-person," she wrote to Lady Rhondda towards the end of her life. " Only I trust my judgment as writer " (so far had she progressed in one decade) " much more than as a worker for movements, and I actually enjoy writing more."

Whenever she stopped to think of herself and the direction of her own endeavours, this question preoccupied her beyond all others. It seemed to her, rightly enough, to

be the special concern of the writers and thinkers of her
generation, whose minds had been so largely moulded by
world events and great political movements. The perpetual
argument with herself in which it involved her is fully
expressed in the notes for a lecture on " Art and Journalism "
which she gave about a year before her death. Here she
faces both the artist's contempt for the " mere journalist "
(" So-and-so has gone Fleet Street ") and the journalist's
dismissal of the " pure artist " as a secluded visionary out
of touch with current tendencies of life and thought. She
refers to Virginia Woolf's condemnation of nineteenth-
century women writers, because they wrote with " a mind
which was pulled from the straight and made to alter its
vision in deference to external authority." And she quotes
R. A. Scott-James in *The Making of Literature* :

> " The business of the artist is to provide us with an
> experience and . . . any end he may have beyond making
> that experience vivid and complete is an alien end,
> destroying his singleness of purpose, wholly disruptive of
> his art and destructive of his energy."

She goes on to inquire : " But what sort of experience ?
How shall the artist select one experience from another ? "
and at the end of her lecture she attempts (as in her own
mind she was always attempting) to reconcile the artist's
self-dedication to the eternal values with the journalist's
knowledge of contemporary opinion and the propagandist's
sense of social responsibility.

" Behind this choice lies . . . the circumstances of the
day — something to do with morality — with a judgment
of ethical values.

" We may cling to the doctrine of pure aesthetics as
closely as we choose, but the thing is round us. The watch-
dogs of the Lord bark at our heels ; the yoke of His burden
is laid upon our shoulders.

" While our souls rest in our bodies, absolute and contingent are bound up together. We cannot live on bread
alone nor without bread. We cannot see truth when

frightened by starvation. We cannot extend our vision of reality when we have no freedom. Saint Augustine's cry still holds us : ' Thou madest us for ourselves and we have no rest until we rest in Thee ' ; but we are bound in mortality, prisoners in a world of compromise, where politics and aesthetics meet. . . .

" Do not be afraid of the daily event, the passing emotion. If the spirit is clear, the love profound, the artisan's hand steady and well-trained, the artist's ecstasy of creation may occur, the ephemeral may be seen in the light of eternity, the moment seized, recreated, made immortal. Do not despise the humble foundations from which great literatures rise."

Because she herself refused to scorn those humble foundations, she could not resist any cause that appealed to the sense of justice which, apart from her creative impulse, was her strongest instinct and the main source of her spiritual warfare. She was not, of course, alone in this conflict. All creative writers would undoubtedly be more productive if they had no sense of justice. Most of them, unfortunately for themselves, possess it to a high degree, but I have never known anyone whom it dominated more than Winifred.

Of the three causes which she served most consistently, two claimed her devotion through direct personal experience. To the third she was compelled to offer allegiance as the logical conclusion of her intellectual philosophy.

Her lifelong and untiring work for peace sprang spontaneously out of her own war-time history — her anxiety for Bill, the death of George de Coundouroff, her years in the nursing-home and the W.A.A.C., the war-tarnished Oxford of 1919 and her vicarious participation in the stories of war and grief which I related to her. The realisation that the power of the modern war machine had outstripped man's moral control, the recognition that civilisation depended for its survival upon the maintenance of perpetual peace, caused her to sacrifice time, health and even her own novels in the attempt to bring home their responsibility to the apathetic and the unconvinced.

"As the Christian ethic was to our fathers," she said,
"so is the idea of world unity to us to-day : a standard to
appreciate, a necessity to acknowledge and a policy to
neglect. . . . Those who prepare for war get it." She
would add with a rational downrightness characteristic of her
mother : "There's never been a lack of men willing to die
bravely. The trouble is to find a few able to live sensibly."

The urgent impulse to broadcast this conviction drove
her to take part in political meetings which varied from
loquacious open-air gatherings on Hampstead Heath to
decorous assemblies in north country Congregational
chapels. It persuaded her, immediately she went down
from Somerville, to join and speak for the League of Nations
Union, in the belief that she was working with a group of
genuine pacifists who were prepared to sacrifice national
pride and imperial privileges in the cause of world peace.
It led her, through a meeting in Bethnal Green, to work and
speak during two General Elections for Sir Percy Harris,
who has been the Liberal Member of Parliament for South-
west Bethnal Green since 1922, and was a strong supporter
of the League of Nations in its early experimental years.
It sent her to Geneva to attend the annual meetings of the
League Assembly throughout those nineteen-twenties in
which we believed that the hope of the future shone through
the Covenant.

Behind all her advocacy of a new internationalism lay
the idea put into words by Johan Bojer, whom she often
quoted : "I went and sowed corn in my enemy's field that
God might exist." Her consciousness that here lay the
practical application of religious experience and the secret
of magnanimity in human relationships, contributed very
largely to the courageous peace policy of *Time and Tide*
during the decade in which she was a Director of the paper.
The ardent and intelligent resolution of her campaign to
eliminate war was equalled only by the passionate determination with which, after her visit to South Africa, she
espoused the cause of the native races exploited by imperialism.

Compared with the burning sense of pity which summoned Winifred to seek justice for the victims of war and racial oppression, her belief in the equality of the sexes was a cool intellectual conviction. To the end she maintained that the realisation of sex inequality first dawned upon her at Oxford, and that I was its source. Her little volume *Women and a Changing Civilisation*, in John Lane's Twentieth Century Library, is dedicated to two veteran advocates of women's rights, but in my personal copy she wrote on the flyleaf : " For Vera, who taught me to be a feminist."

During my schooldays, which coincided with the dramatic climax of the suffrage movement, I had read Olive Schreiner and followed the militant campaigns with the excitement of a sympathetic spectator, but my growing consciousness that women suffered from remediable injustices was due less to the movement for the vote than to my early environment with its complacent acceptance of female subordination. Winifred never went through any such reaction against her surroundings. Apart from her occasional exasperation with family claims upon her time and energy, she not only accepted but gloried in her background. In her early experiences lay her strength, and her mother's domination over those early experiences formed part of the picture against which she grew to adulthood.

Throughout her life Winifred was never made to feel a personal sense of feminine inferiority. At home, a woman ruled. At school, both she and her contemporaries were trained to take their places beside men in the professional world. In the Army, women had been so much in demand that they were surrounded by a constant and flattering competition for their favour. When we first knew each other at Oxford, Winifred learnt with astonishment of the low estimate of women's intelligence by Staffordshire business men who regarded the entire female sex as constitutionally incapable of managing money.

Hardly had she begun to be incredulously convinced by my convictions, when her theoretical acceptance was rein-forced by the final stage of the struggle for Women's Degrees and the battle in various professions to get the Sex Disqualification (Removal) Act interpreted as its sponsors had intended. She became politically conscious that, while women over thirty were now voting, she, though a B.A. of Oxford, was still voteless. The outset of her life in London found her joining the campaign for equal political rights, and becoming a member of the small but vigorous Six Point Group which Lady Rhondda had founded.

But her own feminist opinions knew no bitterness, since they had not originated in any sense of grievance. Never having found it a disadvantage to be a woman, she brought to the service of women ideas which were positive and constructive, inspired by her own wide interests and her natural versatility. Ardently welcoming all adventure, she could not bear to think that women less fortunate than herself suffered from a restriction of experience through the mere accident of their sex.

"I am a feminist," she once wrote in the *Yorkshire Post*, "because I dislike everything that feminism implies. I desire an end of the whole business, the demands for equality, the suggestions of sex warfare, the very name of feminist. I want to be about the work in which my real interests lie, the study of inter-race relationships, the writing of novels and so forth. But while the inequality exists, while injustice is done and opportunity denied to the great majority of women, I shall have to be a feminist with the motto Equality First. And I shan't be happy till I get . . . a society in which sex-differentiation concerns those things alone which by the physical laws of nature it must govern, a society in which men and women work together for the good of all mankind, a society in which there is no respect of persons, either male or female, but a supreme regard for the importance of the human being. And when that dream is a reality they will say farewell to feminism, as to a disbanded but victorious army, with honour for its heroes, gratitude for its sacrifice and profound relief that the hour for its necessity has passed."

In spite of these diverse occupations, Winifred finished her first novel in the late spring of 1922. After Cassell's had refused it, it was accepted with enthusiasm in August by John Lane and published the following March. Neither the pacifist, the feminist nor the anti-imperialist wrote *Anderby Wold* ; its author was the Yorkshire-born artist who endeavoured from the beginning to see her creatures in the round, as God sees them, and with the true artist's detachment to do even more justice to the characters with whose outlook she disagreed than to those who shared her opinions.

By a strange coincidence which gives (as she herself recognised when dying) an unusual unity to her brief career, the dominant theme of this first novel — the victory of young, strident, progressive social forces over the beloved and tradition-hallowed old — is the same as that of her last, *South Riding*. In the beautiful and tender story of the tragedy which time and change brought to the Robsons of Anderby, Winifred's own outlook is approximately reflected in that of the eloquent red-haired young Socialist, David Rossitur ; he plays a similar part to the one fulfilled in *South Riding* by the crude, eager, courageous schoolmistress, Sarah Burton. But her reactionaries, John and Mary Robson, are portrayed with the same loving sympathy, the same understanding of the reverence due to the ideals of a vanishing society, which made Robert Carne of Maythorpe the most attractive character in *South Riding*.

Recognising the gratitude which she owed to her parents for both the theme of *Anderby Wold* and the heredity which enabled her to write it at all, Winifred dedicated " To David and Alice Holtby " the book which she described, by a prevarication customary amongst fiction writers, as " this imaginary story of imaginary events on an imaginary farm." Perhaps the least fictitious of all these " imaginary " properties was the character of John Robson, who is a portrait of her father so faithful that even such illuminating details are recorded as David Holtby's habit of washing himself for days without soap unless someone put out the new cake which he required, though the soap was kept in a drawer of his own dressing-room. Mary Robson, though she fills at Anderby the same philanthropic, feudal rôle as Alice Holtby fulfilled at Rudston, bears no real resemblance to Winifred's mother ; she is a younger, less positive type, owning many of the uncertainties and half-blind good intentions of which Winifred was conscious in herself.

Tentatively she sent the book to her proud but not unnaturally agitated parents with a characteristic letter :

My Dearest Mother and Father,

(I put you this way round because you were the other way round in the book !) Here is your first grandchild. For all that it is worth I send it to you with my love, knowing how much of it is already yours. Some people have asked me about the dedication, saying ' Why did you not write it " To my Father and Mother " ? ' But I pointed out that I had a strong objection to the type of young person who thinks their parents only worth noting because they are their parents, and that you were two very dear people with two very nice names and that I loved you very much, and should like to think that I should love you as my friends if you were not my parents — which seems to be a sufficiently rare thing in these days — and therefore it is to David and Alice Holtby, who are so very much more than just my father and mother, that I have dedicated my story.

My love to you —

Winifred.

Winifred had begun *Anderby Wold* in 1920, when she was twenty-two, and she finished it before she was twenty-four. Her publishers let slip a first-rate opportunity to advertise the youth of their new discovery ; they described her in their publicity notices as " a well-known Yorkshire lady," thereby suggesting a formidable combination of headmistress, county-councillor and hospital matron. Her immaturity appears chiefly in her dialogue, which is too often self-consciously epigrammatical. Especially she makes David Rossitur (not without some justification, since he was supposed to have been sent down from Oxford for his revolutionary activities) talk like the editor of the *Isis*.

David, young and doomed, was the first of the many characters destined for premature death who appear in Winifred's novels. Like Connie Hammond in *The Crowded Street* and Teddy Leigh in *The Land of Green Ginger*, Rossitur owns close kinship to the group of *prédestinés* in *South Riding* — Robert Carne, Joe Astell, Lily Sawdon, Mrs. Holly. It seemed as though, long before she knew her own fate, Winifred deliberately courted the mingled pain and delight of describing the heightened consciousness, the peculiar zest for experience, which so often distinguishes those whose days are numbered. Though she makes Rossitur's age the same as her own, her youth treats his with commendable detachment ; she remarks that " he was still young enough to believe habit to be amenable to reason."

To David's background, then unfamiliar to her, of Manchester journalism, she refers only occasionally and indirectly ; she was never guilty of the error, committed by many much older first novelists, of going beyond her own experience. Mary Robson's kinsfolk and friends are Winifred's Yorkshire relatives ; her agricultural labourers are the beloved villagers whose dialect she often rendered for the delight of her companions. The scene throughout is that of the familiar East Riding to which she turned again and again, and at last enshrined, surely for permanence, in her one triumphant classic. " Market Burton " is recognisable as first cousin to Driffield ; " Hardrascliffe " as a combination of Scarborough and Bridlington ; " Anderby " as Rudston by " the sweeping curves of the wolds ", " the sturdy outline of the Norman church on the hill," the " salt sting in the wind from the sea six miles away."

Anderby Wold received some remarkable notices, even though Winifred did confess gloomily to Jean immediately after its appearance : " What with the reviews of critics, the sarcasms of one's friends, the reproaches of one's own taste, there's precious little peace after publishing a book, and the first result of progress is to make one hate one's work."

This first novel definitely put Winifred on the map as a young writer to be watched with expectation. It was finally " remaindered " in 1930, but the publishers re-issued it after the success of *South Riding*, and it had a good sale in its second incarnation. Robert Leighton, Winifred's first adviser, thought well of it, and liked especially the way in which she took her metaphors from the country life that she knew. In *Time and Tide* Mary Agnes Hamilton wrote that she showed " a degree of mastery over her material and a knowledge of how to present it that are rare even in the hands of much more practised writers." But Winifred was not deluded nor even greatly encouraged by praise, for she was already wrestling painfully with the opening chapters of *The Crowded Street* (then known as *The Wallflower*). Her attitude towards her literary achievements remained much the same as it had been when she wrote to Jean McWilliam a few weeks after *Anderby Wold* had been accepted :

" I've got your letter of the 5th and you make me ashamed. You say that I've got to write and write and one day I shall find myself expressing a great idea and then I shall write a great book. But oh Rosalind, I doubt my own capacity most truly. I want to write epics and I write like parish magazines. I want to write an epic about modern civilisation and the duty of happiness, no not exactly the duty of happiness so much as the duty of creating happiness in the world. How sweeping and naïve this sounds ! But in my idea it is, as the *Athenæum* says of me, ' a little less crude, though the artifice is still apparent ' ! "

Strangely enough, Winifred's first efforts in journalism were less successful than her venture into novel-writing. She had a determined and well-justified reverence for the journalist's art, but I have always felt that it was the efficient, social-reformer half of her personality, rather than her imaginative power, which produced her lively topical articles. Only a few of her contributions to periodicals — her short stories, and the poems and miscellanies having no particular topical relevance — are recognisable as products of the artist, who cannot write to a time-table or be guided by topical demands rather than by what he wants to say and how he wants to say it. A letter to Sarah Gertrude Millin in December 1934 suggests that Winifred herself took this view of her journalism.

"I write all these articles and things to make money, not to 'keep a standing,'" she admitted with typical self-disparagement. "People who only write very rare things — like Virginia Woolf — have a far higher standing than prolific journalists like myself. I have no illusions about my work. I am primarily a useful, versatile, sensible and fairly careful artisan. I have trained myself to write quickly, punctually and readably to order over a wide range of subjects. That has nothing to do with art. It has quite a lot to do with politics. I am, primarily, a publicist. At odd moments I write works of the imagination — stories, satires, poems and plays. They are very uneven in quality. They have moments of virtue. But I feel that a pedestrian gift like mine must apply itself to quantity, because quality is a gift of the gods which is only rarely given."

Even the methods which Winifred brought to the two divisions of her literary life were utterly different. When she was writing a novel, no expenditure of time was too long, no trouble too great. She liked to sit in a low armchair with her notes beside her on a table, and a block of cheap paper on her knee. After an hour or two of preliminary torment, she would cover the pages at terrific speed with the large sprawling calligraphy which always suggested that she was too hurried to form her letters. Often she wrote the same paragraph half a dozen times over, discarding sheet after sheet until the floor was covered with crumpled balls of illegible hieroglyphics.

"Every good piece of writing I have done that has given me in retrospect the slightest satisfaction," she once told Lady Rhondda, "has been done after hours and hours of labour. I must retire into myself and fight and fight to get form and thought hammered hard together."

To her journalism Winifred never brought one-tenth of this pain and perseverance. Towards the end of her life, when she was called "the most brilliant journalist in London," she seldom made more than one draft of the topic on hand. As she hated typing and only occasionally had a secretary, she even arranged with many of her journals to accept these manuscript drafts as they stood. In her books she was always painfully pursuing an elusive perfection ; in her articles she was satisfied with a vivid efficient statement of the case at issue turned out capably to time.

Winifred's early and voluminous experiments brought so many rejection slips that I sought desperately for an explanation, though my attempts at constructive criticism were somewhat hampered by the fact that her novel was already published before mine had even succeeded in finding a home.

"I don't know what it is about your articles," I told her. "Or rather I do know, but cannot put it into words. I can only call your attention to little errors of prepositions or punctuation which aren't really the mischief. Somehow you have a heavy hand with them — they don't read quite finished or polished. They are much more like extracts from a long book than articles. I *wish* I could explain — though I have no right to try when you are the authoress of *Anderby Wold* and I am nobody."

By 1923, though I was attempting with a less exuberant vitality of creativeness to tread the same discouraging path, I had become quite anxious lest the most promising editors should be prematurely exhausted by her importunity. In a letter written on April 9th, I earnestly urged her to "leave *Time and Tide* alone for a bit ; you mayn't be quite their style and there are heaps of other papers."

This judgment reads strangely now, for it was *Time and Tide*, the weekly review of which she later became the youngest and most active director, which gave Winifred her first permanent footing in London journalism.

At the end of her autobiography, *This Was My World*, Lady Rhondda has described the origins of *Time and Tide*. She relates how, one evening in 1918 at the Ministry of National Service, when the end of the War was near, she and Mrs. Chalmers Watson, the founder and first commandant of the W.A.A.C., stopped late in the office to discuss what they hoped to do afterwards. As the only child of Viscount Rhondda, the wealthy coal-owner and war-time Food Controller, Lady Rhondda had the means to fulfil any reasonable ambition.

" I want," she said, " to found a paper. That's what I have always wanted."

And immediately she sat down and sketched the journal of her dreams. " I could see," she writes, " that the old ideas had failed us, but what exactly were the new ones that were to save us ? How could they be ventilated ? . . . I wanted to find, to test and to spread the customs and the ideas that would be health-giving and life-saving."

In 1920 *Time and Tide* was founded by a like-minded group of women, of whom Lady Rhondda was leader. They included Mrs. Chalmers Watson, the paper's first editor Mrs. Helen Archdale, Miss Jean Lyon of *Punch*, and three outstanding novelists, Rebecca West, E. M. Delafield and Cicely Hamilton. The odds, as Lady Rhondda knew, were heavily against success, since the people for whom the paper was provided — the people who talked the same language as herself — were only a small group at best. Even among these, as time was to show, quite a surprising number possessed temperaments and ideas which did not fit in with her own approach to life, and were therefore to prove uncongenial. In 1924, when Winifred first began to know her, Lady Rhondda was still in the process of learning her job. It took her, as she has admitted, about eight years to learn it properly, and much of the experience was expensive and painful. But it never ceased to seem worth while, for no woman had attempted such a task before. None had been accepted on equal terms by the masculine world which ran weekly reviews and had hitherto supplied the bulk of their readers.

One of the first groups of possible subscribers to receive specimen copies of *Time and Tide* were the students at the women's colleges, so Winifred and I already knew of the paper's existence before we went down from Somerville. As a journalistic innovation made exclusively by women the experiment intrigued us, and we often bought copies to read in Doughty Street. It was through *Time and Tide* that we first heard of Lady Rhondda's other foundation, the Six Point Group, and at a mass meeting of the Group in Queen's Hall that we both saw her for the first time.

She appeared, that evening, a personality very different from the relentless organiser of the war years or the formidable editor whose authority was to increase as the years went by. On the Queen's Hall platform, as on most platforms, her intimidating qualities were not in evidence. We heard only a gentle, rather hesitant voice; saw a round young-looking face, a pair of unexpectedly benevolent blue-grey eyes, and an abundance of plainly-dressed light brown hair. The sympathetic impression that her speech created encouraged Winifred to make yet another attempt to penetrate *Time and Tide*'s defences.

During 1922 and 1923, when Winifred was working in Bethnal Green with Sir Percy Harris, she had become a " school manager " for one or two London County Council schools in the East End, and belonged to a group of after-care committees for school children. She had already planned a series of articles on the " human side " of the L.C.C. educational machine, and now sent the first one, entitled *The Human Factor*, to *Time and Tide*'s office. This time the manuscript was not returned. Instead, Lady Rhondda invited Winifred to lunch at her flat in Chelsea.

" Directly I read that article," she stated in the memorial essay which appeared in *Time and Tide* after Winifred's death, " I knew that here was someone who counted and whom I must at once get hold of. . . ."

In more than one of Winifred's articles and stories, that luncheon, in different guises, has been faithfully recorded. For the powerful, diffident and lonely woman who had recognised her quality, Winifred had the instantaneous magnetic attraction which the warm-hearted, highly-intelligent extrovert always possesses for those who are naturally reticent and shy. In the last few years of Winifred's life she displayed critical, satirical and ruthless characteristics quite other than those of an extrovert, and developed the maturity which comes from the secret endurance of pain and the certainty of frustration by death. But in 1924 she was overflowing with vitality and superb undaunted confidence ; she never doubted that people would like her because they always did.

In spite of these advantages she felt " morbidly shy " at the *tête-à-tête* luncheon and could not stop talking. Moreover, there was lobster for lunch, and though she had flourished on Army rations and even, as a youthful pantry-pilferer, had eaten with relish an accidental mixture of treacle and potted turkey, lobster was still more than her Yorkshire-disciplined stomach could manage.

" Still," she relates in the final paragraphs of *Mother Knows Best*, " there it was. There was the first editor who had ever shown a sign of taking my work seriously, and there was the lobster, rich, pink, formidable, on lettuce leaves. I had a feeling that if I rejected her lobster, she had a right to reject my articles. I ate what was set before me. When offered more, I took more. I endured throughout the interview. I departed no sooner than was seemly. And then I fled to Sloane Square Station, where I was very, very sick. But *Time and Tide* took the articles ; Lady Rhondda soon appointed me a regular note and leader writer, first on educational, then on general political subjects. . . . Four years later, I became a director of the paper."

Before many months had passed, this new work and the

influential acquaintance who was so soon to become a friend appeared to Winifred as one of life's rare uncovenanted mercies. With less than the usual degree of warning, an occurrence totally if naïvely unexpected by both of us seemed to threaten — though only, as it happened, quite temporarily — the joint existence which we had built up together. By the middle of that summer, to my own astonishment, I was again in love, and this time the consequences were permanent. On July 5th, 1924, three weeks after he had landed in England and taken me to a performance of Bernard Shaw's *St. Joan*, I promised to marry the young university professor with whom, as the result of a "fan-mail" letter about my novel *The Dark Tide*, I had been corresponding for a year during his absence in America.

With the characteristic selfishness of lovers I completely forgot that this arrangement would mean a period of loneliness and heartache for Winifred, confronting her again with the fundamental question which renders all of us ineffective until we have answered it satisfactorily : "How shall I live ? " Before I recovered a little from the self-absorbing shock of surprise, I even overlooked the fact that Winifred must inevitably compare G.'s persistent devotion with the perfunctory indecisiveness of Bill — for whom, she confessed to me with sorrowful candour a month later, "I must sublimate an emotion that I may not otherwise expend." It was, typically enough, her mother who sent her a brief word of affectionate sympathy, and who generously lent me the now tattered fragments of Winifred's reply.

" My Dearest Dear, Thank you so much for your under-standing card. Your letters always give me a curious sense of satisfied companionship that must surely be very rare for daughters in this workaday world. I grow a little less restive. . . . She may drop me, but I don't think that she will dupe me. . . .

" As for suffering, dear heart, don't you see that long ago I saw that this was inevitable ? It is a thing that one cannot escape from unless one hides from life. Do you think for a moment that when I see what I do see of human sorrow . . . that I should want to take the easy road? I ask nothing better than to be allowed the very high privilege of ' writing with my heart's blood,' if that may be. I only ask that I may suffer for those things which are high and brave and lovely, and that I may not be weak when suffering comes. For the end, success, failure, ruin or achievement, I think that it matters so little. The stuff of life that matters is experience. I ask that I may be permitted to love much, to serve to the utmost limit of my capacity, and to keep faith with that high vision which men call God. I shan't do it wholly. Nobody does that. I only want never to stop caring. The other things don't matter."

Years afterwards, when it was too late to ask for her forgiveness, I recognised the emotions that Winifred had concealed from me with so loving and self-forgetful a magnanimity. Going through her library the week following her death, I found these words written on the flyleaf of her copy of *St. Joan* :

" *Ave atque Vale.* July 5th, 1924. W. H."

CHAPTER X

A PARTNERSHIP INTERRUPTED

EPIGRAM TO V. B.

(Written on the flyleaf of a presentation copy of *The Crowded Street*)

Sweet pilgrim, since awhile I walked with thee,
My fortune's thine, while thine brings wealth to me.
Now so enriched am I that I remain
Not poorer, sweet, but richer for thy gain.

WINIFRED HOLTBY, 1924

BUT WINIFRED and I did not, after all, lose each other's society as quickly as she had expected.

Since G. and I had so recently " become acquainted " (a much slower process than falling in love), and since we had in any case no money to marry on, we decided to postpone our wedding until his return from America the following summer. So in September he sailed for the United States again, and Winifred carried out with me the plan that we had made before he came to England of spending three months in Central Europe. Although the demand for our literary work was still slow and discouraging, we were cordially invited to make so many voluntary political speeches that we wanted to check for ourselves the statements, derived mainly from books and pamphlets, to which we had committed ourselves on League of Nations Union and Party platforms. Then, as always, we both preferred first-hand information.

We spent the night in Paris under the auspices of the American Women's Club, where the organisers had obviously never heard of us and, since their house was full, found somewhat embarrassing the introductions which we had forwarded in advance. As Winifred, who could never survive the calmest Channel crossing, was still quite ill after a very bad journey from Newhaven to Dieppe which we had taken for the sake of economy, I implored the harassed Americans to put us in somewhere. Eventually they found us a room in a strange little back-street hotel with primitive bedrooms and sheets like rough sacking.

Winifred had hardly recovered by the time that we reached Geneva, which in those days seemed the inevitable preliminary to autumn travel. There we saw Edouard Herriot and Ramsay Macdonald, the leader of the British delegation, optimistically talking Arbitration, Security and Disarmament. Another Labour delegate was Mrs. H. M. Swanwick, disarmament expert and the editor of *Foreign Affairs*. She became afterwards a good friend to us both, and gave us articles and reviews to write for her paper.

From Geneva, by way of Basle, we went on a sorrowful and all too instructive tour of investigation through the Saar Valley, British-occupied Cologne and the French-occupied Rhineland and Ruhr. In the Ruhr we found Essen a haunted, half-alive city, with Krupp's huge works almost silent and a red wrath of autumn sunset reflecting the smouldering rage of the repressed population. The previous November, Winifred had written to Jean with epigrammatic lightness of the international situation : " Italy and Spain are drawing together. France and England are drawing apart. Germany seems to be drawing to a close." Now, chastened by even the briefest experience, she wrote more sadly : " Not a generation nor a dozen generations will heal the breaches made by centuries of folly here. . . . There is a special hunger of the heart that comes from reading too much history and being surrounded by politics."

A few weeks had taught us both that in our earnest second-hand statements about the effects of blockade, the secret calculating vengefulness of the conquered, the vain belief of the triumphant victors that they could keep a proud and efficient people subdued for ever, we had underestimated rather than exaggerated the truth. Already it was obvious that the Treaty of Versailles had brought Europe not peace but a sword ; the lusty Satanism of Georges Clemenceau had been coldly carried to its logical conclusions by the pitiless lawyer-Beelzebub, Raymond Poincaré. Germany in 1924 was a tragic land, whose post-war miseries and humiliations we have now forgotten — though Herr Hitler, to our scandalised astonishment, has gone on remembering them and taking his ungentlemanly revenges. That autumn the callousness and brutality of German Fascism was already implicit in the vicious resentful cartoons appearing in the " comic " papers *Simplicissimus* and *Lustige Blätter*.

In Cologne, in Saarbrück, in Essen, in Berlin, even we, political novices as we were, could perceive that those who were sowing oppression and hatred would end by reaping hatred and oppression. Inevitably the small boys and girls whom we saw in Cologne wistfully watching cheerful English Tommies eating beef-steaks inside the windows of Army canteens marked " No Germans allowed," are now members of Nazi youth organisations conditioned by the savage propaganda for which past British crassness injudiciously supplied unlimited material. We met all types of individuals — rich and poor, official and unofficial, influential and insignificant — who told us independently and so frequently about the children suffering from rickets and tuberculosis in German hospitals, that every British canteen soon filled Winifred with the same compassionate rage as she was later to feel at the sight of an exploited African negro.

Wherever we went the local pastors — worthy, under-nourished men with a strong sense of responsibility — discovered our existence by some infallible instinct, and travelled miles to tell us the grievances of their little parishes. Resolutely and strenuously they escorted us round slums, hospitals, clubs, embankments, reputable and disreputable areas, until we nearly fainted from exhaustion and the endeavour to follow a language in which we were only semi-proficient. Their main topics of conversation were food shortage, reparations, the chaos produced by inflation, and the " persecutions," varying from pin-pricks to real atrocities, of the French authorities in the Rhineland and Ruhr. The one place where the shadows did not lie darkly was Düsseldorf, a cheerful friendly town ; the one occasion on which we felt light-hearted an evening spent discussing the League in our halting Anglo-German with a group of razor-makers at Solingen, the Sheffield of Germany, near Cologne.

By half-past eight that night the library of the Solingen pastor, who had arranged the meeting, was almost filled with members of the local Communist Party, though some of the audience were Socialists, and even one or two Nationalists came out of curiosity. We sat on chairs, the floor, a table, and the pastor's camouflaged sofa-bed. After he had given, in German, a short account of us, I started off with a solemn explanation of the aims of British peace-makers who wanted to meet and mix with their former enemies. Winifred followed. Her German was even worse than mine ; it turned the solemnity into a friendly comedy, and we were all still arguing about " war-guilt," the Dawes report, and hours of labour, until ten minutes before the last tram to the station left at 11.30 P.M.

Discovering then that we were quarter of an hour's walk from the tram terminus, we ran like a couple of young hares for half a mile, with a pursuing trail of men, girls and our clerical host still bombarding us with questions, explanations and good wishes. We caught that tram and arrived at Cologne in the early hours of the morning, only to lose our luggage next day in the Ruhr on the way to Berlin. So drab, angry and miserable was the once vainglorious capital that Winifred was startled one evening by the shining yellow glory of the lime-trees in the Tiergarten ; a gift of nature, less ruthless than man, to a stricken people starved of light and colour.

It was balm for troubled, remorseful spirits to go on to

Prague ; to exchange confidence for depression, an appreciative welcoming friendliness for the harsh, despairing reiteration of grievances. Already, at Geneva, we had seen Edvard Beneš, small, young, boyish, alert, his face grey with fatigue and determination, acting as *rapporteur* for the Disarmament Protocol, and explaining to England's gentle representative, Lord Parmoor, the father of Sir Stafford Cripps, those problems and prejudices which were tearing Europe to pieces behind the decorous façade of the League. Now, from a park on the top of a hill, we looked down over his old, ramshackle, beautiful capital, its crooked hilly streets mellow with age and history in contrast to the geometrical oppressiveness of Berlin. The day was one of mingled mist and sunshine, with strange dark shadows as though there were an eclipse of the sun ; we saw towers, roofs and palaces as in a mirage, darkly silhouetted against a dim background of changing light.

We stayed at the Hotel de Saxe in the Hybernska Ulice. At first we thought it was dirty, but later decided that its dark appearance was due merely to shabbiness and age. It resembled, we told each other romantically, a ruined palace in a back street. This impressive antiquity was, indeed, responsible for a minor catastrophe that occurred on the very night of our arrival.

To make the money we had saved go as far as possible, Winifred and I had arranged to share bedrooms in the various hotels, and we settled down to sleep comfortably enough in a couple of imposing if rickety beds massively decorated at top and bottom. With characteristic provincial foresight we had endeavoured to pull them away from the wall as a precaution against bugs, but the attempt proved fruitless and we soon abandoned it. In the middle of the night I was awakened by a colossal crash, followed by a roar resembling a titanic earthquake. Thinking that the whole hotel was crashing to the ground I sat up in terror — to see Winifred struggling helplessly with the rocking ruins of a bed of which the end and the lower legs had already deposited themselves on the floor. Next day she swore that, murmuring complacently, "Better come over and share my bed if you're not comfortable there," I merely lay down again and, exhausted by the previous day's long journey from Berlin, drifted back into peaceful slumber.

Evidently she took my advice, for the next morning the chambermaid found us occupying the same bed while the remnants of the other — intended to hold a small Czech occupant, and not a Yorkshirewoman of Viking proportions — lay beside us with its mattress cocked over the wreckage of its heavy carved decorations. Pointing to the ruin, we observed unnecessarily in the language which we had been told would be the most appreciated, " *Voilà que le lit est cassé pendant la nuit.*"

With her hands on her hips, the little plump woman observed the wreck.

" *Das ist gut !* " she exclaimed in the forbidden tongue, a broad grin spreading over her face, and she offered to fetch the carpenter to mend the bed at once. We murmured apologetically that " *Vielleicht später* " would be more convenient. When we finally dressed and emerged from the room, we found a small army of smiling chambermaids and gay little page boys lined up in the passage waiting to see the large Englishwoman who had broken the big bed. They were short, cheerful and happy-go-lucky, with fair hair, high cheek-bones and humorous uptilted noses.

Again, as in Germany, we were strenuously seized, escorted up and down the city and indigestibly provided with miscellaneous facts, but the guides were quite different guides, and the information was very different information. Our charming, affirmative, highly intelligent escorts were members, like ourselves, of the International Federation of University Women — amongst whom, one day, we met Madame Franciska Plaminkova, afterwards Czechoslovakia's distinguished feminist Senator and one of the first to be arrested by the Gestapo when Hitler marched into Prague. A large, fair, kindly woman, she talked of her country's affairs with the benevolent vitality which the whole people seemed to possess. Like her colleagues she agreed that the

Czech Fascist movement was negligible; small as it was, it had already split into three parts, and every member wanted to be President.

Proudly our friends accompanied us through streets in which every foreign word or name was slightly altered to give it a Czech complexion. We passed studios anxious to take our "foto," and observed numerous copies of the works of "Elinor Glynova"—who appeared, in company with "Tarzan," to be the chief representative of English literature in Czechoslovakia. From the Ministry of Education near the Baroque church of St. Nicholas, with its restless grotesque figures of saints and popes, we were taken to the Ministry of Foreign Affairs in the hill castle of Hradcány, once the home of the Kings of Bohemia, whence President Masaryk now looked over the city and the circling Vltava river. There we saw his library, with its thirty thousand books in the ten languages that he could read and speak, and on his desk the photograph of his American wife as the beautiful young student whom he had met at the University of Leipzig.

We were shown the offices of the Red Cross, of which Masaryk's eldest daughter was President; we interviewed the secretaries of the Czech and German League of Nations societies; we watched a performance of Smetana's *The Brandenburgs in Bohemia* from the private box of the Foreign Minister; we were deluged with beautiful illustrated pamphlets written in strange but vivacious English. From each and all of our eager hosts we heard details of Czechoslovakia's relations with France, with Germany, with Hungary; her minorities, her religious problems, her Slovak Question, her half-built Parliament house, her new culture, her plans for the future. Above all, her plans for the future.

"How optimistic they are!" I said to Winifred on our last day in Prague. "It's quite obvious that this little state is going to play a great part in the New Europe."

"Yes," she said, "they *are* excited about their country, aren't they?—and I like their human desire to display it."

She added in her diary of our tour: "Everyone in

politics works. . . . They seem to work because they like it, and are proud and interested. They do not worry like the Germans, philosophise like the Russians, nor commit suicide like the Viennese. Life is for them a hopeful affair."

Unhappy Czechs ! — whose subsequent fate she was never to know.

At five o'clock on a cold October morning, we drove to the station in an open two-horsed carriage under a chill little moon. The dawn air smote our faces with an icy sharpness, and we huddled together for warmth in the unheated train as we passed through enormous pine forests, broken by deep blue tarns like sapphires, on our way from Prague to Vienna.

In the charming dilapidated city — cold, leaf-blown, beautiful, indolent and sad — we found at last that nobody wanted to educate us or give us political information. The difficulty was to get any response at all to our questions in surroundings where the really controversial problems were not political but musical, and all conversations, wherever they started, invariably ended with music or books. In the gay colourful restaurants, at the animated tea-parties where everybody ate with unashamed enjoyment the cream-filled cakes and incomparable open sandwiches, the only topics which roused the gathering from its lazy good humour were the dispute between Strauss and Alwin at the Opera, and the latest animosities of the music critic Korngold in the *Neue Freie Presse*.

The gaiety of the guests and the luxury of the refreshments gave no clue to the real conditions under which Vienna's upper and middle classes were living. We soon discovered that her aristocracy had no money and her bourgeoisie no future ; that they and the workers all suffered alike from high prices, low wages, overwhelming taxation and a terrible housing shortage which obliged families to occupy rooms rather than houses. To us the strange vacillations of the inflated kroner — which caused a meal to cost 100,000 kronen and a tip of 1000 kronen to be inadequate — were merely part of the complicated account-keeping which obliged us to add more " noughts " the further east we went. But we learnt that for the victims of financial gymnastics, inflation had meant a long period of cheating and trickery.

Even of this they did not complain. Where Berlin had been haughty and resentful, Vienna displayed only dignity and regret. Her citizens sighed with reminiscent sadness for the spacious days before the War, but they showed no self-pity ; the bitterness of Germany had here given way to a gentle resignation. In so far as they were capable of disliking anyone the Viennese disliked the Czechs, but without animosity ; they all admitted that the Czechs had been their best workers, whose departure contributed to the ruin of the country. In those days when Austrian finance was benevolently controlled by the League of Nations, nobody guessed that the cheerful optimism of Prague and the charming melancholy of Vienna would alike be quenched in the next decade by the dark night of an avenging Attila's tyranny.

Winifred and I lived for the month of November in a cheap pension kept by two half Scottish, half Austrian sisters in a central quarter of the city. Besides being economical it was clean to the point of chilly bleakness, the bare rooms swept and garnished like the spotless uncarpeted bedrooms of a Dutch country hotel. Our pleasant, obliging hostesses told us that a current quarrel between landlords and tenants over which should pay for central heating had led to its complete abolition as the line of least resistance. For a week we worked in our room enveloped in eiderdowns until a stove was provided which smoked at intervals to the point of suffocation, but at least protected us from the biting autumn cold. For this, as for practically every other amenity, the pension-keepers were taxed. They also paid luxury taxes for occupying a central position, for electric light, telephone and lift, and for central heating even when, as at our own pension, it did not heat. Visitors in addition had to pay tribute to the municipality for baths, fires, meals in bed, and a window balcony which " occupied space."

For the first two or three days we spent our afternoons walking in the Prater or beneath the pale ochre trees of the Stadtpark, where the closed cafés, the falling leaves and the fading bronze and purple of chrysanthemums and asters wore the same mournful charm as the population itself. From the Gloriette at Schönbrunn, Maria Theresa's small fantastic refuge on the top of the wood-crowned hill behind the castle, we looked down one evening at the soft extended beauty of Vienna, dominated by the tall grey spire of the Stefanskirche like an old engraving against a calm, even sky.

Another short journey, on the day following All Saints, took us out to the Zentralfriedhof — of which, thirteen years afterwards, when Winifred was dead, an All Saints' Day spent in the Métairie Cemetery at New Orleans was so strangely to remind me. At the gates of the Viennese burial-ground stood booths crowded with buyers, purchasing candles, cakes, paper flowers, roast chestnuts and succulent-looking sausages which we longed to sample. Inside, the huge cemetery stretched away from a jolly-looking chapel which, Winifred said, resembled a dance-hall.

" Look ! " she observed, " all the little electric lights have diamanté fringes. They seem to be saying ' O death, where is thy sting ? ' to a rag-time tune ! "

We had not been more than a day or two in the city when a sprightly voice rang us up at our pension.

" Jan Smeterlin speaking ! Edith told me you were coming to Wien, and I want to take you both out to lunch."

In Germany Winifred had received a letter from Edith Mannaberg, now an accomplished amateur 'cellist, announcing her engagement to the Polish pianist. It would make, we felt, an unusually appropriate marriage, and as soon as we saw Jan we knew that we were right. Lovable and vivacious, he possessed the happy affirmative temperament and brilliant childlike naïveté of the born musical artist. I saw grief only once on his pleasant mobile face, when years afterwards we met for a moment in the nursing-home where

Winifred lay dying. During those weeks in Vienna, his newly acquired fiancée was never out of his mind.

" She's got black hair and gr-reen eyes ! " he would cry delightedly, and with each exuberant roll of the " r " Edith's handsome sophisticated face and figure seemed to grow more beautiful.

After our first luncheon together we met him several times at the Reisbar in the Dorotheergasse, where we drank Turkish coffee and chocolate cocktails. One evening he gave us tickets for his Chopin concert in the gilded Musik-vereinsaal, which aroused so much enthusiasm that he was obliged to play five or six encores before the shabby, excited audience would allow him to go home. Later, when he was visiting the Mannabergs, we heard him give another concert in London, where, as Winifred remarked in a letter to Jean, " even an audience at the Aeolian Hall looked as though its first sleep was broken."

Amongst other Viennese friends to whom Jan introduced us, we visited several times some cousins of Edith's who lived in a magnificent flat with red silk wallpaper. The father was a distinguished banker, and the whole family, like all the survivors of Vienna's plutocracy, was gay, cultured and intelligent. At their house one afternoon we discussed Bernard Shaw's plays, for *St. Joan*, which had also been running in Berlin, was then playing to crowded houses in Vienna. The banker's sons and daughter were baffled by Shaw ; wit, they thought, should be kept in one mental watertight compartment and serious reflections in another. When Winifred explained that it was our habit, as a nation, to conceal our feelings by laughing at many things that we cared for deeply, the daughter Grĕtl inquired, with a troubled expression :

" But surely you would not laugh at sorrow ! Would you laugh at death ? Would you laugh at Christ ? "

And she appeared deeply shocked at Winifred's reply that the trouble with most Christians was the lack of humour that they brought to the study of Christianity.

This charming family, like their city, were doomed. A

few months after we left Vienna, we heard that the son who had accompanied us to the circus had first embezzled money for his mistress, and then killed himself in exile abroad. The father, who had sent him there, died broken-hearted ; the daughter, slender and lovely, relapsed into melancholia for vain love of the handsome, much-married man whose sinister fascination obsessed her. A malign fate seemed to shadow the lives of many Viennese households during those inauspicious post-war years ; they inhabited a world of nightmares which the solid British family rein-forced with middle-class respectability neither knew nor imagined.

Late in November, the ten days that we had promised ourselves in Budapest were reduced to five by an Austrian strike of railway employees against the limited wages allowed by the Railway Companies under League of Nations super-vision. Dr. Seipel's government fell ; trains stopped at the frontiers ; boats were overcrowded and car fares became prohibitive. The few aeroplanes, which we could not in any case have afforded, were booked up several times over, so we had no choice but to stay where we were. Going out to observe some political excitement at last, we saw two crowds close to the Rathaus.

" Let's join them, " Winifred said to me. " They're probably watching the fallen Ministers leave the various departments."

She had forgotten that this was Vienna. One crowd, we discovered, was waiting to see a bride leave a fashionable church ; the other was watching a piece of machinery for the Rathaus clock being hauled by a pulley to the top of the tower.

Two of our five days in Budapest vanished upon the eight-hour journey from Vienna across the Hungarian plain, cold and vast in the early morning, brilliantly white until midday with hoar-frost like the icing sugar on a titanic birthday cake. Beneath the trees the autumn earth glowed red-brown from the fallen leaves ; the frosted grass at the edge of the woods appeared by contrast a brilliant greenish-blue. Scarcely a house broke the flat monotony of the rich agricultural country ; only occasionally a rough path ran through the dark, gently sloping fields to the foot of distant shadowy hills. An hour's journey from Budapest, the landscape changed abruptly ; rounded hillocks, like crouching beasts, jerked suddenly out of the plain. As we reached the city, we saw, for the first time, the Danube, grey, wide and slow-flowing, beside the railway embankment.

Its pace, we discovered, was the pace of everything in Budapest but the vehement Hungarian temperament. Life, like all mechanical forms of transport, instinctively adopted the speed of Europe a hundred years ago, and no one expected a function, festival or entertainment to begin within half an hour of the time specified. But the inhabitants of the city were lively with riotous resentment, as far removed as Czech optimism from German bitterness and Viennese melancholy. Politically-minded monarchical aristocrats with their roots in the past, these Hungarians resembled the restored Bourbons in having learnt nothing and forgotten nothing. Like all strangers, we provided a heaven-sent target for their grievances, which they described with a zestful, angry enjoyment. They also told us how to start a revolution, though we questioned whether the information would ever come in handy for either of us. Their formula contained only three injunctions : seize the telephone headquarters ; get control of the police ; make everyone go home. A handful of conspirators — as the world has since learnt from others who practised what the Hungarians preached — could then carry through a revolution in a few hours without opposition.

In Hungary we found that manual labour now commanded better pay than intellectual work, for the few cities were flooded with unemployed professionals from the ceded territories. In every bank, office and restaurant, maps of these lost areas crowded the walls, and the conversations which eddied round them were long and very violent. With aching heads we escaped at intervals to the hills and terraces of the cold, beautiful city, where the derelict grass-

grown streets were grey with slush from the light snow which
had fallen just after our arrival.

"They're worse paved than the lanes round Rudston,"
observed Winifred, as we passed a number of thin scraggy
hens scratching forlornly in the mud outside the imposing
doorway of the Ministry of Finance. But just beyond our
pleasant small hotel in Old Buda stretched the grand
rampart of the Fisher's Bastion, with its view of the Gothic
towers and Byzantine palaces climbing the ancient hills,
and beneath them the flat commercial miles of Pesth
stretching along the grey Danube to the violet horizon.
When the sun suddenly shone upon the snow-covered roofs
the look of breathless rapture which beauty always inspired
in her illumined Winifred's face, and lines came into my
head from Rossetti's *Blessed Damozel* :

> *It was the terrace of God's house*
> *That she was standing on.*

The evening before we left Buda, a young woman doctor
invited us to a tea-party which began at her home with tea
and rum at 5.30 P.M. and ended after midnight in a restaurant
where we drank Tokay with a group of riotous youths from
the National Students' Federation. These boys were fiercely
nationalistic, furiously anti-Bolshevik and closely in league
with Italian Fascismo, but the political diatribes which
rent the smoke-laden atmosphere seemed as remote from
reality as the breaking of angry waves on a distant coast.
We listened instead to the *tziganes* playing Liszt's Hungarian
Rhapsodies with a wild, bizarre lilt which made them
strangely unfamiliar, until the tense music and suffocating
air drove us out of the restaurant into the moonlit street.
There Winifred saw her last view of Budapest, blue-white
under the snow ; a city frozen to silence save for the faint
echo of music behind the closed door. She remembered,
too, that to-morrow we were starting back to England, and
might never again set out together on journeys abroad.

"Never mind !" she said, with a stubborn courage of
which we both felt in need. "It'll be worth while if you get

to know America." She added, taking my arm as we began to walk back to our hotel up the dark snow-covered hill : " Perhaps I'll go to South Africa myself and see Jean again ! "

In Vienna we had missed two events of which the second, though trivial for everyone else, had more importance for us than the first. The one was the "Zinovieff Letter" General Election ; the other the publication of Winifred's second novel, *The Crowded Street.*

The central theme of this book turned upon the part played by the marriage market in the lives of provincial young ladies ; it described " woman's inhumanity to woman " in the matrimonial game. Based upon Winifred's own experience of middle-class standards in a Yorkshire suburb, the story perhaps reflected, in the contrast of its treatment with the swifter movement of *Anderby Wold*, the difference between her instinctive affection for Rudston and her more critical attitude towards Cottingham.

In her fifth chapter she writes of a railway journey taken by her heroine, " After the ringing splendour of the wind-swept wolds, the stale flatness of the plain seemed doubly depressing." Something of this depression evidently communicated itself to John Lane's reader, whose trenchant style suggests that then, as later, he was J. B. Priestley.

" It has no passion, not even for freedom," he wrote of the theme. " As a love-story it is cold as the north pole. The unattractive heroine will appeal neither to the sexually unattractive, who will be repelled by this ruthless but calm analysis of their failures, nor to the sexually attractive, who will ignore her, as they do in life."

In spite of this unfavourable comment, John Lane published the book for its " quiet power and scenes of unusual merit." It also contained one or two noticeable portrait studies. In addition to the exhilarating picture of her school friend, Osyth Harvey, as Clare Duquesne, Winifred produced in Delia Vaughan a partial and less successful imaginary reconstruction of my war-time self.

Except for the minor character of Rachel Harris in *The Land of Green Ginger*, she never again attempted to interpret me in a novel.

Although she dedicated her story to Jean McWilliam, Winifred herself was never satisfied with it.

" It's like a jelly that won't jell — cold, flabby, formless," she complained to Jean soon after she began the book in 1923. " Oh, I write like a cook, a jellyfish or a porpoise would write. I deserve to make omelettes and dresses all my natural life."

Even after the novel had been accepted, she confessed that she could summon up no interest in its appearance.

" Somehow I feel that all this work is only a prelude," she admitted, and decided that she would not describe suburban life again ; it repelled her so much that she could not do it justice. Only the anaemic author whose powers are waning cares more for the book that is past than for the one which is to come, and Winifred, like all writers of vitality, lost interest in the fate of the story she had written in the surge of new ideas for the next on the list. She now proposed to move right away from Marshington-Cottingham to the far-off romantic roads of the fourteenth century and the brilliant tortured clarity of John Wyclif's Yorkshire mind. With her head full of scenes from the Peasants' Revolt, the meetings of the Lollards and the Earthquake Council, she wrote to Jean eagerly : " I am mad and violent with the theme. . . . I feel that if I don't write it, it will write me, or I shall explode."

Her estimate of her second novel was substantially true. In spite of many beautiful passages, and a power to evoke suspense which gives the Thraile chapters an atmosphere akin to the brooding darkness of *Wuthering Heights*, there is a slow, laboured quality in *The Crowded Street*. Its joints creak and it moves on pedestrian feet with its negative, colourless heroine, lacking the tender spontaneity of *Anderby Wold*. An explanation of its failure is not difficult to find, for the book was written twice.

When Winifred finished the first version we were spending

a holiday together at Whipsnade. Its total effect did not please her ; she thought it, not unjustly, too long and verbose for its everyday theme, and constantly applied to it Mr. Cruttwell's criticisms of her Oxford essays. Finally, unable even by revision to produce the result that she wanted, she flew into one of her rare fits of temper, and nearly broke her chair by lifting it up and banging it violently on the floor. Then, the rage of her anguished exasperation still unspent, she tore the book in half and crushed it into the waste-paper basket so that no remnant of the original should tempt her to imitation in the task of rewriting.

The gesture was a grand one ; it provided the best possible evidence of a capacity for self-criticism and the true craftsman's courage, which spares itself no uttermost pain and will drastically destroy in order to re-create. Nevertheless, judging from my own experience that one says most nearly what one wants to say when the inspiration is fresh, I believe that the first version would have been swifter and more illumined. The spiritual theme of the story as distinct from its ostensible topic — the search of the burdened, frustrated soul for some magic experience lying just beyond the confines of daily life — is one which cannot be developed laboriously. It was a theme that constantly haunted Winifred's earlier novels and short stories ; she was to repeat it two years later in *The Land of Green Ginger*.

Winifred made less than £20 from *The Crowded Street* — a sum easily exceeded by the recent cheap edition — but the poverty of this financial result was compensated during the early months of 1925 by her growing success in journalism. Not only, now, was she writing regularly for *Time and Tide* ; her articles had penetrated behind the editorial barrage of several other journals. Already, the previous August, I had congratulated her upon placing in the *Saturday Review* an essay with the engagingly misspelt title of " Eutopias and Paradises," but her conquests included also the *Manchester Guardian*, *Cassell's Weekly* and *The New*

Leader. To the last paper, then under the editorship of H. N. Brailsford, she contributed some of her best short stories, illustrated with striking, virile woodcuts by Clare Leighton.

Not only was Winifred making progress herself; it seemed to her far more important that Bill, now back from South America, had also come to London and was making it too. Throughout the previous year his unanchored existence had stirred her conscience and roused the dominant pity which did battle with her love ; she knew that he resented it, yet could never resist the solicitude to which he moved her. Had he mattered more she would have been brought face to face with the unprofitableness of their relationship and would probably have let him go ; had he mattered less, the memory of his poetic affection for her as a boy officer would not have kept her faithful to the spoiled simulacrum of that romantic image. As it was, the intensity of her compunction allowed her to miss no chance of serving him, and an opportunity had recently presented itself through a casual encounter.

Lunching together at an Express Dairy soon after we went to live in Doughty Street, Winifred and I had plunged into an argument about the probable conduct in a crisis of the exhibitionist clerical hero in my second novel, *Not Without Honour*. So absorbed were we that we did not notice a small dark-haired man with shrewd blue eyes, who had seated himself at our table and was listening with interest to the conversation. Finally, during a pause, he leaned across to us and asked in an incisive American voice : " Is it a story ? Couldn't I help ? I write a little too." For an hour the three of us dissected the curate's flamboyant psychology, and before we left the restaurant the American had taken our names and address.

Two years afterwards, when we had long forgotten his existence, a letter came to say that he had founded a school of journalism and would gladly be of use to us. Whether he wanted us as pupils or as assistants was not entirely clear, but though we had now as great a variety

of work as we could manage, we took him at his face value
and invited him several times to our flat. Of his actual
value I still have my doubts, and if Winifred's portrait of
Clifton Roderick Johnson, the proprietor of the school of
journalism in *Poor Caroline*, may be taken as evidence, she
apparently began to share them at an early stage. But for
Bill's problems as Winifred saw them, the dynamic little
American seemed to provide a heaven-sent solution.
Eventually she persuaded him to employ Bill as his assistant
at an apprentice's salary, and Bill, temporarily tired of
wandering over the earth's unresponsive surface, came to
London to start his new job.

There were limits, however, to his willingness to be organised by two over-zealous young women. When I tried, through
a relative interested in the movement, to find him a room in
a Toc H hostel for the sake of companionship and economy,
he quietly but tenaciously resisted and eventually turned up
equipped with lodgings at Peckham. During the year in
which he worked for the American, he frequently " dropped
in " at our flat for meals. Sometimes he joined our informal
Saturday evening coffee parties, where he sat on the floor
smoking his pipe and listening, usually in silence, to the
conversation. When the other guests had gone, he helped
us to tidy the room and wash up the coffee cups. Occasionally he stayed so late that he had to walk from Maida Vale
to Peckham, arriving there in the early hours of the morning.

One engagement that Bill failed to keep that year was
my own wedding. After I had assured him that ceremonial
garments, which he did not possess, were quite unnecessary,
he promised to come. I persuaded a family friend of his own
age to wear a lounge suit to keep him company, but when I
looked for him at the reception I found — to my disappointment, for I had hoped that he would cheer Winifred after
my departure — that he was not present. We learnt later
that he had actually arrived at the door of the church —
St. James's, Spanish Place — but seeing various young men
in morning coats acting as ushers, he literally took to his
heels and vanished.

" It was all too posh for me," he explained afterwards to Winifred. " I decided I couldn't live up to it, so I went back to Peckham."

The day before I was married, Winifred gave me as her wedding gift a long fine platinum chain studded with small seed-pearls. With my wedding dress and for years afterwards I wore it as a necklace, but later, twisted two or three times round my wrist, it looked more effective as a bracelet. Two days before Winifred died I took the chain to the nursing-home, twined as usual round my arm. Her illness had already made her blind, but I closed her fingers over it. Recognising her gift, she smiled. " It was too little," she said characteristically. " It ought to have been bigger. . . ."

On the June day of my marriage ten days after G.'s return from his American university, Winifred drove before me to the church beneath a quiet clouded sky, with sudden gleams of sunshine casting a gentle momentary radiance over its grey canopy. Since G.'s mother was dead and Winifred was my only bridesmaid, she went in the same car as my elderly clerical father-in-law. Soft mauve draperies shaded her blue dress ; her large feathered hat, in the fashion of that year, almost covered her eyes, and she carried an enormous bouquet of blue and mauve delphiniums. For a young woman only four days past her twenty-seventh birthday, it was, perhaps, an unexpectedly imposing array. As she alighted from the car, she heard a whispered discussion among the onlookers crowded round the church porch.

" Who's that ? "

" Why, the bride's mother, of course, you silly ! "

As she waited for me at the door, the lovely organ began to roll triumphantly from the vaulted roof, passing imperceptibly from a Bach Prelude into the jubilant rhythm of the bridal march from *Lohengrin*. When I stood with G. before the altar, I felt rather than saw her standing behind me in her blue dress, golden, Madonna-like, reassuring, her personality alight with a luminous tenderness which seemed to glow like the rose-pink peonies on the chancel rails as a long shaft of sunlight pierced the tall, high windows.

That night, when all the festivities were over and she returned home to the realisation that I was actually married and gone, she told me later that she became violently conscious of the ticking of the clocks in the empty flat. We had quite a number, usually wrong, and I had been accustomed to wind them all. Too tired to go to bed immediately, she sat down at the large sitting-room table which we had shared for our work, and wrote a short poem called *The Foolish Clocks*. She afterwards ascribed its invention to Joanna in *The Land of Green Ginger* :

> *Now she is gone, but all her clocks are ticking*
> *With gentle voices, punctual and polite,*
> *Their thrifty hands the scattered moments picking*
> *Tossed from the careless bounty of the night.*
>
> *Oh, foolish clocks, who had no wit for hoarding*
> *The precious moments when my love was here,*
> *Be silent now, and cease this vain recording*
> *Of worthless hours, since she is not near.*

CHAPTER XI

PRELUDE TO NEW ADVENTURE

THE FROZEN EARTH

("*Edward's Funeral March*")

As I come through the garden,
Suddenly all the birds seem to cease their singing :
The tight-curled buds like birds on the branches swinging
Silently shrink and harden
On the naked trees that were once green fountains springing.
And you are not there, not there, not there,
Your laughing face and your wind-blown hair
Leave not even a ghost in the garden.

So how can I remember
What you were like in the spring when the birds were crying,
And the call of your voice, and the sound of your footsteps flying ?
The garden in December
Is frozen too hard for the lads in the dark earth lying
To wander again, again, again,
As blithe as bird-song and light as rain
That I may see and remember.

Not a ghost in the garden,
Not a touch that brushes my arm like the wing of a swallow.
Not an echo of laughter as clear as a flute and as hollow.
The earth would never pardon
A fugitive ghost who broke from the grave to find me and follow
You have grown too cold, too cold, too cold
To lift your limbs from the frozen mould
And come to me here in the garden.

WINIFRED HOLTBY
December 1925

FOR SOME DAYS the aftermath of my wedding was so
strenuous that Winifred had no time to fall again into the

167

mood of sentimental reminiscence in which she wrote *The Foolish Clocks*.

The convention which sends young men and women away on honeymoons at the very time that their lives are passing through a period of maximum reorganisation (and which has its wisdom for this very reason) leaves much to be done by those who are left behind, and it is always the unselfish who suffer. Amused, resigned, and exasperated, Winifred wrote me that she was no longer a person but A List. As usual, everyone exploited her — not least of all ourselves by our inevitable absence. One of many small obligations was the recovery of the gloves which G. had left in church. Thanks to his incorrigible absent-mindedness, Winifred's genuine affection for him had begun to acquire an almost maternal quality. Those gloves were the first of a long series of miscellaneous objects which she was to spend quite a large proportion of her life in helping him to retrieve.

When she arrived the following week for her work on *Time and Tide*, "somewhat hot and dishevelled and in exceedingly dirty gloves," Lady Rhondda, correctly deducing from these unusual symptoms a condition of strain, fatigue and loneliness, whirled her off to lunch in a Soho restaurant with Cicely Hamilton and Olga Lindo, then playing in Somerset Maugham's drama *Rain*. Other friends rallied round her too. Hilda Reid, also a guest at the wedding, invited her to meet Edith Sitwell. At a private school where she still gave some classes, she was invited to stay for the week-end. In the garden, she wrote to me, the soft bunches of pink roses were as deep as cushions, and the syringa blossoms made a Milky Way of stars against a dark sky of green silk leaves.

The headmistresses, who were shortly retiring, implored her with tears in their eyes to take over the school. This type of request was not unusual. Persons who employed Winifred soon acquired the habit of regarding her as their heaven-sent successor ; it seemed natural to them that she should prefer doing their work to getting on with her own.

"How could I explain," she inquired ruefully, "that it is one of my intentions to remove such schools, however admirable, from England altogether? I could only say 'Impossible' and be very sorry."

In two or three weeks, when she had found time to think, she wrote me her views on the possibility of her own marriage, and sent me her conclusions about the dissolution — more temporary than either of us then supposed — of our working partnership.

"I think . . . that I might one day marry, simply because detatchment [sic] is negative, and contacts, experiences and so forth, the stuff of life. I believe that life is intended to be corporate as well as individual — only I think with you that marriage is probably no more enchanting than any other great emotion — religion, the early days of the War. It is an enriching rather than an impoverishing thing at least. I do not mean that it is all the things that the sentimental or even the sincerely entranced say of it — but it is experience, completion, what Mrs. H. calls 'coming inside.'. . .

"I am happy. In a way I suppose I miss you but that does not make me less happy. . . . I find you in all small and lovely things ; in the little fishes like flames in the green water, in the furred and stupid softness of bumble-bees fat as laughter, in all the chiming radiance of warmth and light and scent in the summer garden. . . . When a person that one loves is in the world and alive and well, and pleased to be in the world, then to miss them is only a new flavour, a salt sharpness in experience. It is when the beloved is unhappy or maimed or troubled that one misses with pain. But even pain is perhaps not wholly undesirable. I feel of pain as Plato felt of death : 'For to fear death, sirs, is simply to think we are wise when we are not so ; it is to think we know what we know not. No man knows whether death is not the greatest of all goods that can come to man ; and yet men fear it as though they knew it was the greatest of all ills.'

"This alone is to be feared—the closed mind, the sleeping imagination, the death of the spirit. The death of the body is to that, I think, a little thing. I do not know whether the spirit survives the death of the body, but I do know that the spirit can be killed while the body lives, and most men walk the world as skeletons. . . . I believe in the communion of saints and in the life of the spirit. Amen."

She had said that she was happy, but when we returned from our honeymoon abroad to spend two or three days with her in the flat before she went for a so-called holiday to a Yorkshire household smitten with an untimely epidemic, we found her pale, tired and restless. She told me, with an air of laconic indifference, that Bill had failed to telephone at a time appointed, and the school of journalism reported his sudden unforeseen departure. But Bill's disappearances were now proverbial, his hankerings after the disciplined irresponsible life of the Army or Air Force perpetual, and I did not at first attach much importance to this information. Instead, I was seized with a belated panic of self-reproach ; G. and I, my conscience insisted, must have seemed complacent, exasperating and altogether abominable in our preoccupation with each other and our new relationship.

"What was it really?" I asked her in a remorseful letter to Yorkshire. "Was it the thought of going home into the mumps, when you had hoped for complete peace and quiet? or your hair not pleasing you and costing so much more than you had intended? or that our invasion of the flat gave you more work to do than you ever said and made you tired? or that Bill went off without telling you and without realising, after all your efforts on his behalf, that whatever it was, you would have understood?"

She wrote from Cottingham in reply : "All your reasons but one were wrong. Bill, I think—and the few hours of what was a very real suspense until I heard that he was safely in existence—perhaps tired me more than I knew. You see, with people like him I always dread the ultimate despair . . . but to-day even that is past with a really

charming letter from him—all apologies and thanks and full
of happiness. . . . Curious how, though I do not love nor
respect as lovers love, I yet feel my personality so strangely
linked to him. I do not particularly want to see him, and
in his company I am a little bored, but the thought of disaster
to him oppresses me beyond words, and for the three days
since the Friday when he should have telephoned me, till
the time when I went seeking him in a sort of comic nightmare from Leicester Square to Peckham and back to the
Air Ministry, I was more terrified than my sane senses let me
realise."

I did not inquire why she—always so full of work, so
much in demand and already beginning, though still in a
small way, to have a distinguished reputation—should so
uncomplainingly endure this capricious treatment, for I
thought that I knew. Had I asked her, I believe she would
have replied that, after all, she owed to Bill her knowledge
of love. She used to say that the education of the spirit
lay, not in being loved, but in loving, and because through
him had come the supreme emotional experience that
many people never knew, she could only repay him with
understanding, with patience, and with unrebuffed affection.

For the rest, she said, she was " heavy with notions "
for *The Runners*, and though it might be absurd to make so
much fuss over her mediocre productions, she had never
learnt that miscarriages were much less uncomfortable than
the production of sound infants.

" You are quite, quite wrong," she concluded, " if you
think that either you or G. were complacent, or that I find
your happiness painful. What matters is that happiness —
the golden day — should exist in the world, not much to
whom it comes. For all of us it is so transitory a thing, how
could one not draw joy from its arrival ? "

A fortnight before G. and I sailed for America, Winifred
gave me the opportunity — for which I had hardly dared
to hope — of meeting Stella Benson at our flat.

For years she had been moved by the exquisite perception of beauty in Stella Benson's novels, by their tenderness for lovely things no less than by their sorrowful scorn for their foolish, pitiful characters. After reading *Living Alone* in 1923, Winifred wrote Stella a letter of appreciation. When no answer arrived she concluded that Stella Benson, like so many authors, put her " fan mail " in the wastepaper basket, but months afterwards a reply came from South China. Across more than half a world, they began to correspond and to like each other. Winifred longed to know her. " The thing I cannot understand," she wrote humbly to Jean, " is that she seems to want to know me."

During the summer of 1925 Stella Benson came to England with her husband, a Chinese customs official, for a few months' leave, and the long-imagined meeting was now at hand.

We waited for her nervously, for her books suggested that she was critical and alarming.

" She's ill most of the time, though she seems to take it as a matter of course," Winifred warned me. " I often forget," she added, " what a strange distance there is between ill people and well ones."

Stella Benson arrived so quietly, ushered in by Winifred's old nurse who was then acting as our housekeeper, that we both sprang to our feet in speechless embarrassment. She was dressed in a charming, expensive wool suit which belonged entirely to the gay world of extravagant reality, but she herself did not " belong," though it was a world that she loved. Delicate, witch-like, remote, with her penetrating blue eyes and the chill whisper of a voice that her deafness gave her, she seemed a spirit from some distant planet temporarily inhabiting a crude, material universe.

I can recall nothing of that afternoon's conversation, for I was too much intimidated to take it in or even to join it. But I remember watching Winifred and Stella talking to each other, two young women of rare quality both doomed to early death. With Stella, her fate was obvious even then ; with Winifred not yet. Perhaps, like Maeterlinck's

Prédestinés, they were drawn to each other by some intuitive knowledge of that steadily approaching end.

Stella Benson only came to our house once again, during the summer of 1932 when Phyllis Bentley was staying with us. By that time she was even deafer and still more terrifying, a withdrawn half-ghost whom it was disconcerting for a stranger to meet. But in 1925, by way of contrast to the isolation of China, she loved " binges " and still felt well enough to arrange them. Winifred was invited to several of these parties ; she also spent a morning at Stella's house going through her new book, and was delighted to find that Stella had scrapped its first version as ruthlessly as she herself had destroyed *The Crowded Street*.

When she came home she described to me excitedly the commonplace Kensington room made so strangely exotic by the possessions of its temporary owner — a collection of little china horses, an elephant with a scarlet trunk, a Chinese vase full of brilliant dahlias standing beside Stella's manuscript on the polished table. These treasures gleaned from a distant civilisation fired her anew with an eagerness to go to South Africa, to travel to China, to live until she had seen for herself the unknown glories of far-off lands, the colours and sights and shapes of beauty as yet unwitnessed by her mortal eyes. In her letter of thanks to Stella, she enclosed one of the most anxiously prescient of the poems inspired by her love of life and adventure — the brief and pathetic *Invocation to Time*.

Since Winifred, with an autumn's earnings to gather in, could not afford a journey to South Africa till January, she decided that on the day I sailed for America she would go as usual to Geneva, in order to avoid being " left " again. G. and I spent the night before our departure at my parents' flat in Kensington, and Winifred came over from Maida Vale to say goodbye. We were all resolutely cheerful, discussing plans which then seemed improbable, though ultimately we carried them out. He only intended, G. said, to remain in his American post for a year or two longer ;

then we would return to some part of London where Winifred could share our home.

With an early train to catch in the morning, Winifred departed soon after supper, smiling a little sadly and incredulously at our determined optimism. She waved her hand as she ran downstairs to the street, wishing me well in the adventure that was to begin before her own. When she had gone, I found a bottle of rose-scented perfume and a tiny gold powder-box left for me on my dressing-table. At the boat next day a large bouquet of Ophelia roses with pink petals and golden hearts awaited us in our cabin. It was yet another of her last-moment gifts.

At the same hour that G. and I left Euston for Liverpool, Winifred caught the morning train from Victoria to Paris. In France she shared her second-class carriage with a Russian woman, a Greek boy, and three bearded, slow-smiling Arabs who talked to her about Lord Balfour's recent visit to Palestine. She found Geneva unspectacular and business-like beneath the spell of Sir Austen Chamberlain's frosty personality. Lord Cecil, she wrote to me, was there as usual, " looking more than ever like an amiable tortoise," and Mrs. Woodrow Wilson appeared at the Assembly " in a little black hat and a cloud of glory."

She heard Dr. Harry Emerson Fosdick, the famous American preacher, give the Sunday sermon at the Protestant Cathedral, and Count Apponyi of Hungary denounce the one-sidedness of a disarmament policy in which the Central Powers did all the disarming and the rest of the world did nothing. She collected the well-authenticated story of a lady from the Dominions who remarked, after being shown round the lower rooms of the Secretariat, " It's all very nice and comfortable, I'm sure. No wonder you always have the bedrooms full ! " She listened to Dr. Nansen reminding Britain of her facile promises to the Armenians and other refugees, " and the Duchess of Atholl intervening as ever on the side of caution, economy and common sense " — not a characteristic which the Duchess was to retain indefinitely. Finally, in an article on the Assembly for *Time and Tide*, she permitted herself an all too accurate prophecy which rings sadly to-day : " The coming fate of southern Central Europe depends very largely upon how far the moderation of Beneš and Masaryk, backed by the League, may impose itself upon the ebullient nationalism, the protracted memories and misplaced enthusiasms of Slavs, Rumanians, Greeks and Croats."

Significantly enough, she omitted — as we all did in those days — to mention the still more ebullient nationalism of the Sudeten Germans.

On a mild Sunday afternoon, she wrote to me, she climbed alone to the top of Mt. Salève, and lay meditating in the sunshine on the smooth green turf, " with all the kingdoms of the earth spread below, and the Swiss, like the souls of the blessed, wandering about picking heather and wild thyme. From the pastures below the benevolent little cows made a happy sort of Sunday noise with their bells, calling one to a perpetual worship. Then, as evening falls, there is ambrosial food to be eaten and nectar-like chocolate to be drunk outside a cafe, *Les Treize Arbres*, from tables covered with scarlet check cloths, and then an easy walk down, with clouds and sunset making rainbows across the Alps, and as a grand finale an apocalyptic sky spreading right across from the Jura."

Wherever she went in Geneva, she added, she was haunted by my ghost. I wrote in reply from the little American town where too few human presences peopled the forest-clad hills and the gorges whose only voices were waterfalls : " Am I a ghost who ever calls your name aloud behind you, as once the ghost of me did in Berkeley Street ? I surely should be, for your name is often enough on my lips . . . but perhaps the Atlantic is too big to be a sounding-board."

Winifred came back to London to find that " Nursie " had fallen ill in her absence and had returned for a time to Yorkshire. She was obliged to look after the flat herself, sweeping and dusting it each morning just as I — five hours earlier because of the difference in time between the two hemispheres — had swept and dusted our country apartment on the other side of the ocean. She found herself entertaining gas - men, electricians and Franciscan Sisters, who called one morning to sell exquisite East End embroideries. They had breakfasted lightly because it was Friday, and she gave them tea and bread-and-butter while they discussed Marie Corelli, the Holy Church, modern underclothing and Monsignor Benson.

England, that autumn, basked in the pleasant warmth of a mild and lovely October. The Thames shone mellow and golden beneath the blue haze of St. Luke's summer ; orange and scarlet dahlias glowed from the flowerbeds of Paddington Recreation Ground near the Maida Vale flat, and the fallen leaves rustled gently about the pavements. Did she miss me, Winifred asked herself, as she ate her lonely teas and went for her solitary walks.

" I do — and don't," she wrote. " I cannot describe it. I am, as I said, very very happy, but it's a sort of autumn empty happiness. I miss the feel of your fingers round my left arm when I walk through the evening streets, and the lamps are golden flowers among the sycamore trees."

In the last few days of the month, Winifred was invited to spend the first of many week-ends at Stonepitts, Lady Rhondda's country " cottage " among the woodland hills of Kent. Actually, she found, it was a fifteenth-century house with oak beams, peat fires and three oast-houses beyond the garden. When she arrived at Sevenoaks, the nearest station, a youngish couple standing beside a car called out : " Are you for Lady Rhondda ? "

" Yes, I am," responded Winifred, and thankfully climbed in.

" Our name is Ervine," said the young woman.

Winifred remarked that hers was Holtby, and said no more as the car whirled them through the yellow Kentish woods in the mild sunshine. Then, from her companions' labelled suitcase, she suddenly realised that she was in the presence of St. John Ervine, the *Observer's* famous dramatic critic and the author of *Jane Clegg*.

It was the first stage of a friendship which brought Winifred the warm regard of a distinguished man whose pugnacious honesty gave no quarter to those who failed to win his esteem. St. John Ervine was to criticise Winifred and scold her, to pour scorn on some of her writings while insisting that she herself failed to perceive the outstanding merit of others, but his appreciative recognition of the radiant generosity which she brought to the service of her friends was to last to the end of her life and beyond.

The week-end was so warm and fine that they all went about without coats or hats. On the Sunday they walked together in the garden after a tea-party at which — to Winifred's excitement which ran to three pages of vivacious description — one of the guests was the actor Henry Ainley. Her hostess, she discovered, possessed one quality held by psychologists to be essential in gathering a large circle of friends. She was a perfect listener.

" I like her more and more," Winifred told me. " She gets to look about eighteen at the end of a Sunday. She told us how Miss Faithfull, of Cheltenham, when she went to help entertain the American women's hockey team, mistook her for one of the team, to her great joy. . . . I never knew a woman draw people to talk so much. She always makes me garrulous — I can't help myself. St. John absolutely effervesces under her. He began a monologue at tea which has continued at intervals ever since. . . . He is very kind, gentle, obviously loves goodness and nice, honest ' that sort ' of people, adores Hardy. To-night we heard the 3rd Act of ' Tess ' over the wireless, and he cried — and wasn't at all ashamed of it. We talked about quite ordinary things like houses, and then about Pacifism and the Military Tattoo — on which he said my views were sound — which meant that they agreed with his."

At the beginning of November Winifred finished her novel *The Runners*, and sent it to John Lane. She had spent her Yorkshire holiday in July reading about Wyclif, and wrote despairingly to Jean McWilliam of her " gallumphing,

clod-hopping bucolic style." Half sorrowful and half
amused, she described the " semi-philosophico-politico be-
wilderments " which overcame her when she tried to imagine
herself amid the medieval squabbles of a hot, petulant
fourteenth-century Oxford, and to depict the agony of a
fierce intellect driven by love and hatred and sorrow.

" Can I, who am nothing save water blown by the wind,
write of such tempests ? " she asked, yet went on to confess :
" I am fierce for work. Without work I am nothing. It's
glorious watching the scenes and meeting the people. But
to write—that is grief and labour ; and to read what one
has written — how unlike the story as one saw it ; how
dull, how spiritless — that is enough to send one weeping to
bed."

By August she reported that *The Runners* was writing
itself, and that she enjoyed doing it as she had never enjoyed
a book in her life. " I am frightened of hurrying it," she
wrote in October when she reached the last chapter, " but
now that the end is coming near I sweat at nights for fear
lest it may be all rot."

In mid-November John Lane rejected the book as it
stood, and she told them sadly to return it and let her re-write
it when she came back from South Africa. The disappointment was bitter, for all her eager love of history and humanity
had gone into the story, but she blamed only herself.

" The thing is too big for contempt. I probably rushed
too hard at it. It deserved better treatment. . . . I must
rewrite it. It is not quixotism but vanity. . . . I could not
bear it as it is."

During her absence in South Africa her agent tried other
publishers, but the result was always the same. In February
Jonathan Cape reported that though the book would be well
reviewed and highly recommended by a few specialists, it
would not get through to any considerable public. She
wanted to curse him, she wrote me from Grahamstown,
but instead bought a copy of St. Augustine's *Confessions*,
had her hair shingled, went to a dance and felt better. By
the following summer, when Heinemann also rejected the

story, her mind was aflame with new themes after her South African tour, and the desire to rewrite it had gone.

" Two years' writing wasted," she commented, " — or possibly not wasted. I believe that there are some good things in it, and I may have gained experience even if it never sees daylight."

The book never did see daylight, yet in one sense it illuminates Winifred's mind more clearly than any of her writings except *South Riding*, for in the contrasting personalities of those whom she called " runners " and " leaders " it embodies her own conflict between the claims of art and the demands of social service. Not long ago I found, in one of her notebooks, the original summary of the idea underlying the story, which perhaps explains her view of this conflict more directly than anything that appears in her published work.

" The poets and artists and men of vision are the runners who leap ahead untrammelled towards perfect beauty. In their running sometimes they hold up a mirror that the world may catch a glimpse of beauty. The teachers and politicians are those who have been touched by ' pity, the deadliest enemy of art.' They cannot leap ahead untrammelled, but must turn back to help along the weaker travellers, and bring them forward on their journey towards beauty. Progress does not lie with the artist. At all times some men have grown close to beauty. So we find the highest thought of all the ages akin, and Greek beauty as rare as that of to-day. But progress lies in the slow levelling up of the race, so that there may be fewer that lag behind. In the ancient empires none thought that slaves could yet be runners. Empires have risen and fallen. Civilisation goes forward as an incoming tide, with waves that rise and slide again towards the sea. But slowly the mass of humanity moves forward, led by the Leaders, towards the good shown in the mirror of the Runners. This is progress. Often the leaders pay for their pity by loss of vision. They cannot run so close to the goal, being bound by cares and sorrows of the unseeing."

The last sentence embodied her own half-conscious purpose—a final reconciliation of the two ideals.

" But the rarest spirits, those who knowing pity yet go forward, those who loving the sightless yet do not lose their vision, who both Run and Lead and See and beckon those who follow, these are Gods, and of such was Christ the greatest, and Buddha and St. Francis and the saints."

When Winifred had finally dispatched *The Runners*, my family invited her to stay with them until she sailed for South Africa. Eventually she accepted, not, as she carefully explained to me, from loneliness (though she had discovered that solitary evenings could be lonely and found herself going out on unnecessary expeditions in order to escape from the solitude) but because cleaning and the constant preparation of meals interrupted her work. So she let the flat to a Russian family—who left it anything but clean when they relinquished it six months later—and moved her books and papers to Kensington.

One morning she was visiting a bookshop in the High Street when suddenly in the doorway she encountered John Lane's reader and her fellow Yorkshireman, J. B. Priestley, whom she had met at a party earlier in the autumn. He looked ill and distressed after a cruel bereavement and she was about to pass him with a word of greeting when, to her surprise and embarrassment, he stopped her and asked : " Are you doing anything special ? "

" No," she said. " I'm only going to the bank."

" Then can you spare quarter of an hour ? I've just read your book for John Lane, and I want to talk to you about it."

They went into a restaurant which Winifred described as " a curious underground café, where apparently lady shoppers drink morning coffee in an obnoxious atmosphere and listen to a most deplorable orchestra." There they argued for an hour on a strange variety of topics—Yorkshire, sex, the post-war generation, Rose Macaulay and the Sitwells.

" He did not want to talk about my book," she related.

" He just wanted to talk. We laughed a great deal. He was furiously witty, pungent and ruthless. Then, quite suddenly, he began to tell me the story of his life. It was one of the bitterest that I ever heard."

When the tale of hard work and unconquerable tragedy was over, Priestley informed her that he was just leaving for a journalist's tour to the Canaries and Madeira, to make money and see a new part of the world. Then, he said, he meant to come back and write novels and plays. He had no certainty, no foundation of faith ; only a determination never to run away from life. He talked to her about politics and art, and the need for an artist to abandon all " axes " lest he should begin to grind them on his work despite himself.

" I read *The Runners* last week," he continued, and told her that he had advised John Lane to refuse it. Parts of it he had thought very good indeed, but judged as a whole it was bad, since it did not " hang together " ; the first half was a romance and the second half a chronicle-biography. He advised her to rewrite the theme and make two books of it if she could. Finally, she reported, " he scolded me roundly for my ' Six Point Group feminism,' my ' propagandist attitude ' and ' this running about after politics,' all of which I accepted without protest because he so obviously wanted to scold somebody. . . ."

After one o'clock a waitress turned them out of the café, and they walked together along the High Street and parted abruptly.

" And probably," wrote Winifred in conclusion, " I shall never see him again for years and years. And that is that. And excepting for the fact that Lane's have refused my book it is really none of my business. But I liked him better and felt more sorry, inexperienced and inadequate than I could have imagined. I wished then as I have wished so often, that I had some of that power for comfort which only experience would give. I could do nothing but sit and let him scold me, and I felt all the time that if ever a man needed real friendship he needed it then."

One December day while Winifred was staying with my parents in Kensington, my mother began to play the piano in the drawing-room next to the bedroom where she was working. She chose Beethoven's No. 7 Sonata ; it had been a favourite of my dead brother, and the slow movement was always known to my family as " Edward's Funeral March."

I had often played this movement over to Winifred on the piano at our flat, and when she heard my mother — an infinitely better pianist than myself — Winifred laid down her pen and started to listen. The idea of Edward, whom she had never known, often possessed her imagination ; instinctively she was attracted by the clear, purposeful austerity of his musician's mind, and sometimes dreamed that if he had survived the War she might have loved and married him. There was nothing incompatible in this semi-fantasy with the still poignant affection that she felt for Bill, who, though living, was also identified in her thoughts with loss. Sometimes their dead romance seemed to fuse in her mind with the picture of the dead musician, and become one single tragedy, one combined grief, in the sorrowful story of War's frustration.

When my mother had finished playing, Winifred came out of the bedroom and silently handed her a sheet of paper. It contained a poem entitled *The Frozen Earth*, of which the theme was a winter threnody for " the lads in the dark earth lying." I have always read into it her lament, not for Edward alone, but for Bill, as though she had lost him through death instead of the mutability of war-tarnished human nature.

My mother sent the poem out to me in America, and I cried for a whole afternoon when I had read it, though whether I cried because I missed Edward or missed Winifred I hardly knew. The images used in her poem must have haunted her throughout that winter, for at the beginning of January she wrote to me from Cottingham :

" Do you know those very still winter evenings, when the sky wears serene Quaker grey, and there is one star, a

faint primrose growing above the elm tree? Then suddenly
in the bare, black garden the birds start singing — clear,
cold winter music, austere and cloudless as the trees and
the sky and the calm twilight. I love this winter singing
far more than the clamorous summer jangle of larks and
wrens and cuckoos and warblers. To-night we had a missel-
thrush and one queer bird whose name I do not know,
but who sings three high questioning notes, then pauses,
then repeats his question."

The activities of that Christmas-time were regulated, for
Winifred, by the visit to South Africa which was to begin
in January. The plans for this journey had been forming
in her mind since the autumn of 1923, when Ethelreda
Lewis, the author of *Trader Horn*, came to London with an
introduction to Winifred from Jean McWilliam in order to
find a publisher for her first novel, *The Harp*. Winifred and
I had tea with her at her Earl's Court boarding-house and
talked publishers for hours. Her intense, serious mind (which
nevertheless conveyed so successfully the salty, ribald humour
of Aloysius Horn) was then, as always, deeply preoccupied
with the welfare of the African natives, and her tales of
their exploitation stirred Winifred's dominant passion for
justice into a longing to go to their aid.

Only two months afterwards Jean McWilliam herself
had arrived in England, tall and Diana-like with her un-
controllable copper-tinted hair. A sudden alarm at her
appointment as headmistress of Pretoria High School had
sent her to England to make contact with friends and acquire
reassurance. She stayed at the same boarding-house as
Mrs. Lewis and several times visited our flat, sitting on the
fender seat beside the hearth with her long thin hands
clasped behind her head as she talked. The four of us
discussed South Africa, inspiring Winifred with a determination to see the country as soon as she could. For months
the thought of South Africa haunted her; she constantly
met people who had just been there or who were about to
go. In those days I meant to share the trip with her;
though I was already corresponding with G., I never

imagined that he would so radically alter my plans. Our engagement the following summer renewed Winifred's resolution, and she made up her mind to go to South Africa when I had sailed for the United States.

Throughout December her preparations continued. Owing to seamen's strikes in Australia, which held up a number of ships, she had some difficulty in booking a passage. There were clothes, too, to be bought for the League of Nations Union lectures in South Africa which she had arranged to give in order to meet part of her travelling expenses. So preoccupied was she with these sartorial problems, that when a friend who wanted to know the name of her boat inquired : " What are you going out in ? " she replied cheerfully, " Oh, a mole and blue silk knitted thing." In the midst of her shopping she found time to see Cicely Hamilton's drama *The Old Adam*, and came away with a sentence spoken by the War Minister in the play ringing through her head : " If you want to end war, you must end the righteous cause." With the long letter that described the play she sent me her Christmas gifts — a new shoulder-knot for my best evening dress, a green fountain pen with a green and gold pencil to match it, and a copy of Stella Benson's new travel book, *The Little World*.

Our presents must have crossed in mid-Atlantic and I cannot recall the details of mine : I remember only that in a Czechoslovakian shop in our small university city I found a blue and yellow painted bird with an unutterably idiotic expression, and sent it to her for a mascot on the journey. Winifred christened it " Vsvdyl," and carried it with her on her travels for the rest of her life. Strange babies encountered on railway journeys could always be amused by it, and its blue and yellow paint soon disappeared.

Before leaving for South Africa, Winifred spent three days with Grace and her husband at Bridlington. More than two years had passed since their marriage, and, knowing that Grace wanted children, Winifred had begun to fear that her ambition to become an aunt was not to be fulfilled. She learnt now that a baby was expected in April, and

found her sister very happy. Throughout her life Grace
had longed to be loved by men, and now she had two at her
feet — a husband who had always approved and now openly
beamed upon her, and their delicate, capable chauffeur,
an ex-slum child from Hull, whom the doctor had cured of
tuberculosis. This quiet, domestic complacency was hardly,
Winifred supposed, the kind of marriage that would satisfy
G. and myself, but at least, she reflected with thankfulness
for Grace, there were some who wanted nothing more.

"*Laus tibi Domine*," she wrote to me, "who sendeth unto
each man his portion in due season. Some of us, of course,
don't make use of it — but that is not the fault of *le bon Dieu*.
I heard of Dot's old confessor, Father Bernard, who used to
tell her : '*Mon enfant, la vie qui n'a pas son Calvaire est un
châtiment de Dieu !* '"

CHAPTER XII

SAILING SOUTH

INVOCATION TO TIME

O Time, deal gently with me.
I cannot see the colours of the wind
Where green lands blossom from unshadowed seas.
Their music beckons, but I cannot find
The dark cathedral of the forest trees,
Nor from the night's deep chalice for my healing
Drink wine of strange communion, blindly kneeling
To pray from your omnipotence one hour
That will not perish, one immortal flower.
O Time, deal gently with me.

WINIFRED HOLTBY, 1925
Country Life, 1928

WINIFRED sailed for South Africa from Tilbury on January 14th, 1926, an ungraciously cold and dreary afternoon. The tender which carried her across the river made its way between black tugs and small motor boats amid a whirl of grey sea-birds and wind-blown snowflakes. For a moment the snow made ships and land appear startlingly clear in the wan, greyish light ; then it suddenly came down like a curtain, blotting out the landscape and postponing their voyage for several hours. Winifred did not care, for she was reading Conrad's *Suspense* — a noble and spacious book which made the early nineteenth century come alive for her in a clear yet faint glow like candlelight.

The next morning the orchestra played, causing her to feel as excited as a small child at a party. As the *Grantully Castle*, white beneath three inches of snow with icicles dripping from the rails, began slowly to slide down the river, she walked round the deck looking for yesterday's acquaintances. Finding only a few, she realised that though the tender, like the grave, had known no distinctions, class divisions vehemently reasserted themselves the moment that the liner's passengers embarked. A conversation between two young ship's officers, discussing icebergs seen on a voyage round the Cape, arrested her with the momentary illusion that they had stepped straight out of the book she was reading.

" The icebergs were breaking up just then," one officer said to the other. " They were nasty, but very beautiful to look at. At night they seemed to glow with a lambent light — a sort of dangerous beauty."

So sailors really do talk like that, she thought. It isn't just Conrad.

Gradually the boat gathered speed, until the low white coast with its miles of frozen roofs seemed to rush past her. The water too hurried by with a silent dark intensity. Above the grey-brown sea a canopy of purplish-grey sky was faintly illumined by a small orange sun, flat like a gold disc on a grey silk tablecloth. The ship ran westwards for several hours ; then she turned south and headed for the Bay of Biscay. This unprepossessing stretch of water behaved in a manner so traditional that Winifred, always a bad sailor, soon abandoned the unequal struggle. For three days she lay prostrate, rousing herself only to bury in a wine-dark sea the last of the carnations that I had ordered for her. Her helpless inability to eat or read gave her plenty of time to meditate on the object of her journey and the experiences which she hoped to gain.

For Winifred this voyage to South Africa was to fulfil a function not dissimilar from the part played by the Great War in the lives of young men and women two or three years her senior, who were just old enough when it broke out to adventure forth on their own initiative. Hitherto she had always been in tutelage to authority or constantly associated with some intimate companion ; now she was launched, an independent, questing personality, without supervision upon an unfamiliar world. Though her months in South Africa did not involve a complete break with the past, they acted as a watershed, dividing the earlier half of her career from the later. She went out an eager, uncritical girl, full of enthusiasms, a little sentimental; she returned a young woman, balanced, experienced, confident, mature.

Perhaps the most unexpected contributor to this development was the League of Nations Union and the meetings that she addressed under its auspices. She had, it was true, arranged these lectures with determined perseverance, driving Jean McWilliam to unaccustomed fury by her obstinate refusal to contemplate a " sunshine holiday." Sensibly she insisted that the best way to break down the ring-fence of hospitable politeness was to be a lecturer who ceased to rank as a visitor, and became a target the moment that she appeared on a platform.

" A lecture," she explained, " is a good thing to give, because it gives an entrée, a starting-point. I go to a town or a village to lecture. I stand on a platform and give my piece of information. That is only the beginning. I come down and we talk. I go into one or other of their houses. We sit up till midnight. We talk about shoes and ships, and Austria, and cabbages and kings, and whether widows should have State pensions, and whether hating Germany does any good. And before we have finished, I have generally learnt twice as much as I ever said."

She had not, however, regarded these lectures as important in themselves. Their function was to help her pay her way, acquire knowledge and make contact with strangers. She expected nothing more intimidating or impressive than the small provincial meetings and unreported Nonconformist gatherings to which the Union was accustomed to relegate its younger speakers. The Overseas Department of its Grosvenor Crescent headquarters attached, it was clear, no earth-shaking importance to her visit; even when she returned from her triumphant tour and presented a detailed and efficient report on League of Nations Union branches in South Africa, the London officials recalled with surprise the fact that she had been there. At the outset of her journey she had no idea that the South African branches, after a long period of comfortable sleep, had suddenly awakened from their stagnation and decided to use her visit as an excuse for a great push on a Dominion-wide scale. There was nothing to indicate that she would be met by deputations, lionised by organisers, be invited to address some of the largest and most distinguished gatherings in the Union, and have engagements piled upon her until even her exceptional powers of endurance began to wilt under the strain.

Like every period of fame and responsibility, these experiences helped her to grow up. However circumscribed the society in which an individual moves, more can be learnt in a week from its high places than from months of grovelling on the ground floor. All ground floors are much alike ; it is only from the peaks that the true configuration of the landscape appears. South Africa gave Winifred poise and self-confidence ; it inspired the theme of *Mandoa, Mandoa !* and *The Land of Green Ginger*, and furnished her with new topics for innumerable articles.

Nevertheless, her months there struck a more formidable blow against the artist in her than any other adventure, for they provided the social reformer with an overwhelming programme of wrongs to contest. South Africa represented for her " The Land of Green Ginger," the magic always lying just beyond the surface of life, yet by the strangest of ironies it became identified with obligations which drew her away from that magic. She went to preach the gospel of peace to white South Africa ; she returned to plead, with passion and pertinacity, the cause of black South Africa to an indifferent England.

Six days after sailing, Winifred could no longer believe that the month was still January, for she was wearing a summer dress without a coat through days in which cobalt seas lay calm beneath sapphire skies. From being unable to swallow a mouthful, she found that she was very hungry and had completely lost all capacity for intellectual work. So she sewed, read, slept, and spent many hours on the third-class deck. She preferred this to the first-class, where normally sane and admirable women in their thirties and forties pursued pleasantly embarrassed schoolboys with a wholesale abandonment which astounded her. The inhabitants of the more democratic quarters—farmers, school-masters, actresses, demobilised officers, doctors from Rhodesia, women veterinary surgeons, French, German, Polish and Russian emigrants—seemed to her far more entertaining. She was soon " adopted " by an ex-captain, his young wife and their three small children, and became —neither for the first nor by any means the last time in her life—an accommodating " auntie " drawing dragons and building " bungalows."

" I don't know how it happened," she wrote to me, " except that my plebeian taste naturally makes me gravitate to a third class anywhere. . . . I understand that my reputation here (we all have a stock label) is ' quiet, domesticated, fond of children, *not* a " modern girl " ! ' I rather like this character for a change. It is so restful. I have advised ladies how to wash crêpe schappe with a touch of red ink in the water, how not to rust needles, and of cures for babies with inflamed eyes (all genuine memories of your mother and Edith)."

She did, nevertheless, make a number of agreeable friends among the first-class passengers, and was apparently the only member of them who had the unchallenged freedom of both decks. Her letters describe some of her companions —a woman tutor from Wellington University, good-looking, breezy, intelligent ; a handsome, urbane aristocrat of seventy-nine ; the classics professor from Pretoria University with whom she discussed the Socratic *daimon* and the conflict of reason and emotion in human life.

" He tells me," she reported, " that too much thinking has made me inhuman and is robbing me of charm and common sense. Is this true ? Never, never ! "

One of Jean McWilliam's friends who was travelling on

the boat remembered years afterwards Winifred's infectious gaiety; the delight of the other passengers in her society; the demands as usual made upon her to organise charades, write pantomimes which would give the right young man the chance to embrace the right young woman, and present prizes at the children's sports. She recalled that Winifred, dressed as " The Sheik " in three sheets, two scarves, a peaked basket and some bronze paint, had won the first prize at the fancy dress dance. The basket increased her commanding height and the ship's competitive flirts assumed her to be a man. They treated her to coy glances, and were furious with both her and themselves when they discovered her identity. Jean's friend lent her George Moore's *Héloïse and Abélard*—" one of the loveliest; all that my Wyclif book should have been and was not," Winifred confessed, lamenting that she was required to present prizes just when she wanted to finish it. In spite of the novel's length and these interruptions, its owner reported that Winifred returned it, read from cover to cover, within a couple of days.

On January 21st, across a sea of pale steel whipped into silver by a small soft wind, Winifred saw the white walls and flat roofs of Santa Cruz, sliding down the green precipices of Teneriffe into a deep blue bay. The mountains—green and jagged, striped with terraces and tufted with cactus— seemed to play a game of " ring-a-ring-o'-roses " round the ship. Between the large tugs in the harbour, tiny cockle-shells of rowing-boats carried bare-legged Spaniards wearing red handkerchiefs and little boys in blue shirts, sitting amid piles of lemons and bananas.

Winifred and five of her friends landed, hired a car and drove from Santa Cruz to Laguna, through white sun-drenched squares filled with palms and babies, tumbling intrepidly outside villas half hidden by purple convolvulus, wax-white magnolia and milk-blue plumbago. Scarlet poinsettias flamed in the gardens; muleteers jangled cheerfully through the streets. The car threaded its way dextrously between ox-wagons, Ford motors, waddling trams, elephants, photographers, monks, women with market-baskets, Jews selling ebony, and soft-footed camels with tasselled shawls and little ringing bells on their mournful heads. Once free of the town, the motorists flew up hairpin bends, careened over watercourses and collided with donkeys. Gasping for breath, they compared the respective merits of green houses with blue and yellow doors, blue houses with green and pink doors, and magenta houses flanked by cobalt and emerald barns. Winifred felt that she was really seeing life. A noticeable contrast exists between the excited admirations of her voyage out, and the humorous, balanced descriptions of the journey home.

" There is nothing reticent about Teneriffe," she told me. " Its colours do not glow softly through a mist ; they shout, they riot, they positively hurl themselves at you. Ooo-er. If it is all as lovely as this. . . . It can't be. I don't believe that flowers can be so amazing anywhere."

That evening, as she watched the island glimmer and disappear like a pricked green and opal bubble, Winifred was scolded by a lady from Cape Town who had noted and disapproved of her unrestrained enjoyment.

" You're going to South Africa for a six months' visit and I know what will happen to you there," the stranger remarked severely. " You'll sit in the corner of a first-class railway carriage ; you'll look at the Rhodes Memorial and the Union Buildings and de Beer's mines at Kimberley ; you'll perhaps take a train trip up to Rhodesia to see the Victoria Falls ; you'll go for picnics, and surf-bathe at Durban, and eat mangoes, and then you'll begin to think you know everything. You'll tell farmers in the Karoo to water their crops after a nine months' drought. You'll tell the Native Affairs Department how to run Bantu education. And then you'll sit down and write articles about us all for the English Press."

Winifred did not attempt to argue. She fully intended to travel second and let Colour Bars take care of themselves, but her enthusiasm was a little damped. It returned next day when the ship passed Cape Verde, its reddish cliffs crowned by a lighthouse, its white native houses glistening on the shore. Looking at the palm-trees, the dolphins, the boat-loads of Senegalese, the small rocks in front of the Cape like a row of children paddling, she told herself exultantly : " Now I have seen Africa ! "

One night when the liner was near the Equator, drifting lazily through motionless blue seas encircled by sweeping albatrosses, Winifred lay on deck watching the brilliant enormous stars sway slowly backwards and forwards behind the long mast of the ship. Suddenly from the darkness a tenor voice rose into the quiet air, melancholy, pure, exquisite. It sang a song of reiterated melody, each verse ending in a chorus which was taken up by a deep-throated choir singing in harmony. The voice rose to a high note of wild protest, then died away in a sigh which melted across the water into the dark, velvety night.

" Jove, what was that ? " exclaimed a first-class passenger. But Winifred dropped her book, hurried through a familiar labyrinth of passages, ran down one flight of steps, climbed another, and emerged as usual on the third-class deck. There, in the shadows, she saw the passengers gathered round an open circle of lamplight where a small ungainly man played a guitar. Beside him a slim boy in shirt sleeves stood with flushed cheeks and parted lips. He sang song after song while the dark-skinned Poles and Latvians and Lithuanians, who slept in the hold beneath the third-class dining-saloon which smelt of Condy's Fluid and looked like a public lavatory, laughed, clapped and stamped. Two black-haired youths stepped into the ring of lamplight and danced, with arms locked, in clumsy, rhythmical abandon. Two girls thrust their arms through those of the men, and suddenly closed the line in a magic circle. Wildly and more wildly they danced ; louder and louder rose the Jewish chorus. So David might have danced before the Ark of the Covenant ; so the followers of Moses might have danced their way into the Promised Land. Poor, despised, and fugitive, the exiles' kinship of suffering, their exultation of defeat, their secret communion of race, made the outer ring of Gentiles seem desultory, boastful, heterogeneous.

" By God ! " breathed Winifred to herself, " I'll tell the world ! "

And she did, for a few months later she made the music, the songs, the dances live again in her description of the Finnish foresters' camp on the Yorkshire wolds in *The Land of Green Ginger*. But that night she sought out one of her friends among the demobilised officers in the third-class quarters.

" Look here," she said, " the first-class passengers are bored stiff with their own amateur performances. Why don't you put on a show and ask them to come and see it ? You've got talent enough down here to fill the Queen's Hall."

The gallant captain, gratified by the suggestion, set to work immediately. A few days later, the invitations to the concert arrived. Stirred to expectation by Winifred's description of the wild folk-music, the first-class passengers, jewelled, scented, surrounded by the whiff of excellent cigars, streamed through the gates which separated the well-to-do sheep from the penurious goats. One by one the performers took their place in the middle of the deck above the hatches, with two vivid arc lights turned on to their faces. A Russian tenor sang a melancholy oriental song in a beautiful well-trained voice. A German Jew played a competent piano solo. A Scotch girl, the professional dancer of highland flings, came in full tartan with a real piper ; she cut her capers on deck and her shadow danced with her. Two Englishmen gave deep-sea chanties ; the inevitable genteel lady sang " Because " and " Until."

That was all. The Jewish emigrants had not even been invited. The captain, a little hurt, found it difficult to believe that their ragged, uncouth presence could possibly have been desired. He called them " the Sqwugs."

On January 26th, the *Grantully Castle* passed the Equator. A soft, hot Trade Wind was blowing ; dolphins leapt in and out of the sea ; flying fish like small tropical birds skimmed the surface of the water. The next evening, wrote Winifred in ecstasy, " a most lovely, lovely thing happened. We were dancing on deck. It was a marvellous moonlight night, the moon almost full, the sea one dancing, glimmering sheet of iridescent silver. Some people were talking about the *Garth Castle*, our sister ship, known to be passing us about twenty miles away.

" Suddenly on the horizon, turning in the turn of the waltz, we saw a light that was no star. We went to the rail, and slowly along the dark rim of the sea, into the scattering silver of moonlight, rode the *Garth*. She was lit brilliantly from end to end, and the light through her portholes against the light sky beyond gave her a marvellous transparency. Her movement was so silent, so inevitable, as she came straight towards us, that she looked like some ghost ship, some glimmering lovely fate, riding upon us out of the moon. She came so close that we could hear the band upon her deck and see the little black people against the cream radiance of her lighted sides. Her music answered ours, and when we called, faintly across the water came her answer."

Winifred described the passengers' sudden realisation that both ships had stopped and were gently rocking side by side under the stars. Just as the more sophisticated among them were conjecturing the reason, a boat from the *Garth Castle* danced towards them, a black fleck on a ribbon of moonlight, and an officer with a bundle of papers in his mouth climbed up a rope-ladder to their deck, left his documents and returned. Gradually the two ships began to move away from each other as the passengers cheered and roared, the sirens whistled " Goodbye " and the orchestra played exuberantly : " Tea for two, two for tea ! "

The unusual encounter was never explained to the travellers, but this meeting of sister ships in the moonlight left with Winifred an image of loveliness which haunted her for the rest of her life. She often spoke of it afterwards. It had, she said, " a significance, a secret-something quite beautiful, with a strange, unearthly beauty that I cannot explain. We do not know why it happened nor what it was. At least it was something that only happens once in a lifetime of travel, and it happened to us."

Two days afterwards they landed at Ascension Island, the volcanic outpost with its Eastern Telegraph station which made it resemble a ship, and its strange stories of men who spent a night among the extinct volcanoes and never returned. The island was eclipsed in her mind by the memory of St. Helena and Napoleon's magic prison at Longwood, where she picked a spray of blue plumbago, and sent it to me across the world on a five weeks' journey. We were now more widely separated than we had ever been, or were ever to be again until death divided us.

" Never be sorry for Napoleon," she wrote. " St. Helena is exquisite—a symphony of blues. Longwood is glowing and dancing in blue. Blue sea on three sides nearly 2000 feet below, blue heliotrope, plumbago, potato plant, and blue flax in his garden, blue butterflies fluttering in his porch, and on the hills cobalt shadows. His tomb lies in a gully, with a circle of cypress and firs standing hand in hand very gravely round. There is no inscription on the flat white stone. But never be sorry for Napoleon."

A week later, the boat began to pitch and toss on the crest of the " Cape swell." On February 9th the enchanted voyage ended, and Winifred looked down from the deck of the *Grantully Castle* to the white fringe of Cape Town, like foam tossed on to the green shore of Table Mountain from the deep blue water.

CHAPTER XIII

AN IMPERIAL PEOPLE DISPLAYS ITSELF

THE TRAVELLERS

See, I have cast my nets
  Over the ball of the world.
Wherever my friends sail out on the wide seas,
  Wherever their sails are furled
In hill-girt harbour, or swinging river-mouth,
  My nets are hurled.

The ships bring news for me,
  And the wind their words,
For my friends have enslaved the trees as their messengers,
  The slow-moving herds
Of cattle, the wind-blown seeds, and the running streams,
  And the homing birds.

Now all the world is mine,
  China and Labrador,
Hungary, Africa, Washington, Rome,
  And a hundred more
Tall cities, and many a sudden-flowering isle
  And a rocky shore.

For I have part in the land
  Wherever my friends go.
Wherever the hills of their pilgrimage break and their cities
      tower
  And their red roads glow,
I have cast my nets and drawn them home to my mind,
  Though they never know.

Now am I rich indeed
  Who hold half earth in fee.

> There is not a flowering field in all the world,
>   Not an almond tree,
> But its beauty has gladdened the heart of a friend of mine,
>   And enriches me.
>
>   WINIFRED HOLTBY, 1926

NOT IN ENGLAND, not in Central Europe, not even in Italy, had Winifred ever seen a city which filled her with the same ecstasy as Cape Town. She could hardly land for the excitement of trying to take in, all at once, the dazzling white sand and the purple-blue background of mountains ; the green forests of fir and pine crowned with peaked and jagged rocks ; the long white town straggling with its suburbs for fifteen miles along the indented coast. The moment that she left the boat she felt drunk and dazed with the shouting chorus of colour—the vivid turquoise water, the deep cobalt shadows, the purple, grey and rose-pink of the rocky hills.

Two eager friends came to meet her at the quay—an old family acquaintance, and the half-German secretary of the Cape Town League of Nations Union, deaf, charming, a graduate of Newnham. But though she listened to them with the interested attention that all strangers received from her, her mind, like her eyes, was given to the riotous extravagance of the summer flowers—the plumbago, morning glory, bougainvillea and pink oleanders which frothed exuberantly over shining white walls, the lobelia and geraniums growing in wild luxuriance, the tall watsonia with their flame-coloured spears. As they drove to the seaside suburb where the secretary lived, every street seemed to have purple mountains behind it and the turquoise ocean in front. Winifred noticed too—just as I had observed in America a few months before—that even the handsomest streets had an unfinished appearance ; the line of imposing shops and sophisticated cafés would suddenly be interrupted by a broken hovel with a corrugated iron roof. Evidently, she thought, this tendency of luxury to end unexpectedly in squalor is characteristic of all new countries.

She had imagined that she would arrive in South Africa

unheralded, a private tourist of no importance to anyone but a few affectionate friends and the secretaries of tiny League of Nations Union branches. Cape Town soon undeceived her. Before she had time to change her travelling dress after a hurried early breakfast and the usual struggle with the customs, "Lady Peggy" of the *Cape Argus* society column carried her off for an interview lasting nearly an hour. After three days she was receiving so many invitations that she spent half her time in writing polite notes of refusal. She had hardly begun to unpack when her friends rushed her across the city to the Archbishop's garden-party at Bishopscourt, where the lawns were kept fresh in the midsummer heat by tiny streams dripping from terrace to terrace below the long white house.

Attired in her blue bridesmaid's dress with the large feathered hat, she carried the gold bead bag which G. had given her as his wedding gift, and wondered, as she walked between hydrangeas as tall as herself and scarlet cannas flaming against terraces covered with morning glory, why everyone stared at her and inquired her identity from his neighbour. Everything seemed strange, transformed, exaggerated, in that vigorous, astounding, exuberant air.

"It was like an English garden gone to heaven," she wrote me in rapture.

If her privacy had indeed existed outside her imagination, that garden-party put an end to it. Her modest little programme of League of Nations Union talks suddenly multiplied by five, by ten. With the League as the flimsiest excuse for a lecture, she found herself addressing Rotary clubs, students' unions, Jewish guilds, University women, boys' and girls' high schools, training colleges, synods of clergy and Sons of England. At the end of her tour, when she counted up the speeches that she had made during her two short visits to Cape Town, she found that they amounted to forty in that city alone. Her Press interviews increased with her public meetings, and leading South African newspapers invited her to contribute articles to their columns.

"I live," she reported, with half-amused bewilderment,

" on peaches, flattery and amazing views."

It had been, she confessed, a relief to get away from it all for a few hours and go for a long walk with the young son of Sir George Paish, who had once spoken at Bethnal Green for Sir Percy Harris and came back afterwards for tea and buns at our Doughty Street flat. His son was now editing a financial newspaper in Cape Town. He took Winifred to climb the lower slopes of the Devil's Peak above the Rhodes Memorial and showed her the enormous tree-covered plain beyond the city, where the distant mountains looked like faint opalescent bubbles against the horizon.

When she exclaimed with delight at seeing a springbok leaping through Rhodes Park on the side of Table Mountain, he told her how Cecil Rhodes had loved and collected the beautiful animals for whose benefit this vast garden had been planned. Once, he said, when Rhodes had a number of zebras, bucks and gazelles, he sent his hunters up country to find a giraffe. The hunters captured one and began their journey home, wiring reports on the giraffe's progress to Rhodes from every station. It arrived safely in Cape Province, but at the last station broke its lovely slender neck against a railway bridge. Rhodes was so much upset that he galloped straight off into the country. He spoke to no one all day, and never again attempted to collect a giraffe.

Travelling north in mid-February to Kimberley, Winifred tried to occupy the long hot journey through the barren wilderness of the Great Karoo by writing an article on " Women and World Peace," but concentration was difficult in the midsummer heat and her thoughts wandered. Through the windows she gazed upon the low scrubby land, its stunted bushes casting their sharp-edged black shadows for hundreds of miles unrelieved by green fields. Occasionally a mud hut broke the monotonous landscape, its contingent of black babies seeming to spring like the scrub from the sandy soil. Upon the horizon the crouching hills, their violet shadows substantial as drapery, rolled back against the clear blue sky. One, she decided, was a lion, another a sphinx, a third the huge uplifted torso of a headless giant.

As the train covered mile upon forbidding mile, Winifred meditated upon the valour of those pioneers who had first trekked their way northward into this harsh, hostile country. No wonder, she thought, that their descendants were sensitive to the good opinion of chance visitors like herself, who came from an old civilisation to judge, with little background of knowledge, the achievements of the new. Already the Yorkshire resolution tacitly taken when she was scolded by her fellow-traveller after leaving Teneriffe — " See all, hear all, say nowt " — had been violated by the question which confronted her at the end of every lecture and the beginning of every party.

" And what do you think of South Africa ? "

At first it had disconcerted her, for how was she to keep her vow of silence, how avoid expressing those uninformed opinions which her fellow passenger had scornfully assured her that she would broadcast, if like the enchanted princess in the fairy tale she was to be trapped at any moment into speech ? But after a day or two she had realised that the question was almost mechanical, a part of the ritual of South African greeting, and she had chosen a harmless formula in reply.

" I think the climate is perfectly delightful ! "

Ah ! she reflected after a few weeks in the country, if that were all ! If the entrancing loveliness of those early mornings, those golden afternoons, those dark star-pricked nights freshened by cool winds when the lights of Cape Town twinkled as though in the sky's inverted cup, if that were all, South Africa would be unmatched, save by California, in beauty and peace. If there were no more to tell, newcomers to the country would not be beleaguered by such eager questioners.

" Anxiety to learn the opinion of others is a mark of uncertainty," she wrote in an article for a South African paper. She continued in words which, by the strange coincidence that so often caused our thoughts to flow together though we were hundreds of miles apart, were almost identical with the words of an article on America which I was simultaneously submitting to *Harper's Magazine*:

" In Paris, in Vienna, in London, visitors are rarely catechised about their impressions of France and Austria and England. Who cares a toss for their opinions, anyway ? These old countries have the superb insolence of tradition. But in the new Czechoslovakia I found that anxiety for reassurance. I am told that it exists in New York and Melbourne. It is a mark of the new countries, and the disarming modesty of the new countries. South Africa is no more sure of herself than New South Wales is sure. So she questions her visitors in search of more self-confidence."

True to the instinct which Winifred described as her " plebeian taste," she had decided to travel by second-class " sleepers " whether she shared them with her coloured sisters or not. These second-class sleeping cars held six passengers — three to a side, sleeping on shelves one above another — and at one end had a wash-basin which became a table by day. The charge for the sleeping berth, including bed-clothes, was only three shillings beyond the ordinary second-class fare. Winifred never changed her mind about this method of travel. English trains might be cleaner, French trains faster, German trains more punctual, Italian trains more convivial, Hungarian trains more unexpected, but South African trains gave you the best for your money.

The memory of that journey through the Karoo never faded ; it appears again and again in her articles, and inspired one of the finest short descriptive passages in *Mandoa, Mandoa!* When the day came up hotter and hotter, she found that she had to fold a rug between herself and the scorching leather cushions. Like the breath of a dragon, the fiery wind rushed through the open window and blazed along the corridors. Then, quite suddenly, she learnt that in tropical countries there is a moment when the sun, having done its worst, begins to give way ; when the prickly pears grow a tiny fringe of shadow on their eastern side, and the long day turns and looks towards the cool of the evening. For the first time she understood the truth of Stephen Hawes's words :

> *After the day cometh the dark night,*
> *For though the day be never so long*
> *At last the bell ringeth to Evensong.*

Now, if ever, she thought, watching the pale twilight come from behind the hills as she was to watch, nine years later, the quiet advance of inevitable death, now, if ever, I shall know rest after weariness, refreshment after drought, peace after turmoil. Such a royal sunset flamed, as she gazed, above the black heads of the kopjes, that they seemed to bow abashed, trailing their heavy shadows. Suddenly the sweet chill of the night wind blew down the corridor against her hot temples, and beneath the first faint points of stars, darkness stretched over the Karoo.

At Kimberley Winifred was met by an ex-Waac who had gone to South Africa to train as a maternity nurse. Here, she learnt, she would escape the fiercest fervours of lionisation, for they had been directed elsewhere ; she had arrived at the same moment as Alan Cobham and Anna Pavlova. She watched Cobham fly round the town ; the descent of his aeroplane out of the sunset gave her another picture which she carred in her mind until she finally crystallised it in *Mandoa, Mandoa !* Six miles out of Kimberley at a dance in a country hotel, she thankfully yielded to Cobham the position of guest of honour. The city's youth and beauty assiduously displayed itself for his benefit ; but Cobham was chaperoned by the local mayor and introduced to the daughters of the town councillors while youth and beauty languished.

In de Beer's diamond works Winifred heard the shrieking of crushed stone and watched the yellow uncut diamonds falling over the rollers on to a sloping table spread with vaseline. The white foreman who took her over the mine displayed with pride the native foreman's compound of bare asphalt surrounded by tin huts. The coloured " boys," she gathered, were engaged for four months ; during that period they were let down into the mines from the compound, prisoners who never saw the outside world.

" But they like it," the foreman assured her. " At the end of the time they always sign on again."

" *Do* they ! " Winifred exclaimed incredulously.

Afterwards a friend provided the explanation.

" My dear, they're kept five days under guard when their contract ends to make sure they don't steal the diamonds. They're only allowed soft clothes, because they used to hide the diamonds in their boot-heels — or even make holes in their legs. One native once got a diamond away by swallowing it. He escaped before its loss was noticed, but since then the natives are not only searched, but given stomach-pumps and enemas before they leave. No wonder they sign on again ! The apparatus terrifies them so much, they prefer years of captivity."

Winifred listened. It was her first experience of white South Africa's behaviour to natives. Later she told me that Kimberley struck her as the dustiest place in the world. It was a brittle town with no roots of vitality, as though its heart had been hollowed away in the search for diamonds.

She had no lectures in Kimberley and without waiting there went on to Durban, travelling through the kindly green land of the Orange Free State and the spacious Drakensberg mountains to the veld country of Natal. At the station she was greeted by a deputation which had risen at 5.30 A.M. to meet her, and then had to wait for three hours because the train was late. She saw a great bay enclosed by emerald hills, the tree-covered Bluff with the sea on either side, the Berea where clean white houses blossomed like the flowers which half smothered their long verandas. Among them she noticed scarlet hibiscus, pink and feathery Pride of India, and frangipanni with heavy exotic scent and stiff waxen petals. A charming seaside place, she told her family, where she ate yams and mangoes and grapes picked sun-warm off the heavy vines ; and found the girls in gay cotton frocks, with their bare brown arms and laughing boyish faces, so pretty that they looked like flowers themselves.

But she had little time for eating mangoes or admiring girls, for between February 22nd and February 25th Durban presented her with a programme of fourteen lectures and a broadcast, and kept her alive by cups of tea which appeared on seven occasions each day. At one meeting, she reported to Grace, her chairman was the father of Roy Campbell, the poet. So far, she told her, she had found very little anti-German feeling in South Africa because of the Dutch element, but there was a good deal of anti-French suspicion, and a fear of the League interfering with the " Indian question." In spite of these engagements and a record collection of mosquito bites, she managed to attend the Congress of Indians who packed the Town Hall to protest against the Asiatic Bill — " seven thousand heathen praying that a Christian government may see light."

" My most conspicuous importance," she related, " I enjoyed not from any merit of my own, oh dear no ! but by the very simple action of walking through Durban with an Indian. It is true that he was a highly cultured and respected Indian. It is true that he had been appointed to conduct me, as an interested but neutral spectator, to the Town Hall Indian Congress. It is true that I was a lecturer for the League of Nations Union, and therefore debarred from any barrier of race or colour. Yet as I went, I think that everyone in the street turned round and stared, stopping their conversations. I suppose that such a sight as that of . . . an obviously *quite* white Englishwoman walking and talking with an Indian in the street had hardly been seen before. You have no idea of the race feeling here. The only people who attempt to bridge it are the missionaries and the League of Nations Union. I believe that I am the first lecturer asked to address the Indians on the League of Nations."

Winifred went on from Durban to Maritzburg, travelling

through a tropical thunderstorm so violent that the vivid blue lightning stopped the train. Later she visited Lady-smith, driving into the heart of a golden sunset towards Spion Kop among the battlefields of a war contemporary with her babyhood.

Early in March she arrived at last in Pretoria, and made her peace with Jean McWilliam in spite of having, for the moment, only a week-end to spare. From the suburb of Arcadia she wrote to her father about " the most beautiful school in South Africa," with its three large buildings and seven hundred pupils. Jean, she reported, was " just as sweet and friendly and dear as ever," and just as unlike a headmistress, with her adventurous car-driving and her fiery hair. The staff of Pretoria High School, she observed, had much more freedom and dignity than most English teachers ; they too drove their own cars, lunched at the country clubs of Pretoria and Johannesburg, and suffered no cloistered exclusion from social life.

She found that the forgiving Jean, whose disapproval of her lectures was so emphatic, had nevertheless procured her a number of engagements; indeed, she assured her family, she was " living quite like a grand lady. One lady invited me to lunch on a day when I could not go, and when I asked her to change the date, she was terribly upset because she had hired a special cook to come in and cook the lunch. This is colonial hospitality ! I can't get used to it at all. It is all too grand for me."

Winifred did not describe her programme very fully to her father. She never committed the common error of supposing her correspondents to be more interested in her affairs than in their own ; instead, she made a point of going over one or two farms in order to tell David Holtby about them. How would he like, she inquired, to manage three thousand acres of baked sandy soil, growing cactus and prickly pear and tufts of thin cactus-like grass where sheep could graze only at the rate of one to eight acres ?

"There are no turnips," she wrote, "and not much artificial feeding of any kind on most of the farms. The great ox wagons that they use for transport are delightfully varied by strings of twenty donkeys. Donkeys can be bought in some places for sixpence each after a drought. I am thinking of buying some."

Three weeks later she returned to Pretoria to give away the prizes at the High School Speech Day. (" Darling Rosalind," she had characteristically inquired when first invited, " oughtn't you to get a big nob to do this ? ") The journey from Johannesburg gave her the new experience of night motoring in South Africa. Still intoxicated by the sinister beauty of the land after nightfall, she described for me the long avenue of blue gum trees barring the straight ribbon of road with velvet stripes, and beyond the trees the soft dark hills crouching beneath a sky grown black as iron, but still glowing in the west like a red-hot oven door. The air vibrated with the shrill music of owls and cicadas ; the rough tracks were broken by tiny streams looking black as the bottomless pit but actually only a few inches deep. Along the road she passed wagon-loads pulled by ten to eighteen donkeys ambling along on small quiet feet, or a great string of oxen swaying before a hooded wagon such as Lyndall used for her last journey in *The Story of an African Farm*. Innumerable obstacles constantly stopped the car ; bemused owls descended in front of them and blinked at the headlights ; rabbits no larger than rats scuttled ahead in zigzag flight ; sleeping dogs lay beside the fires which guarded the Kaffir kraals ; tame cows came close enough to be patted on their hairy haunches; flocks of sheep crowded together in panic, their myriad astonished eyes giving a strange effect of glistening water in the lamplight.

Although Pretoria, like every centre of education and government, contained numerous officials, university professors, lawyers and teachers, Winifred's critical audience at the High School prize-giving described her speech as " one of the finest ever delivered in Pretoria." Many young women in South Africa must remember the tall fair-haired writer from England, junior then to themselves to-day, who enjoined them, not to win prizes or pass examinations, but to " hold beauty fast," and went on to assure them : " She is the most certain solace for so many human sorrows. She is the first secret teacher of the child's inquiring mind, as her creation is the supreme achievement of the human spirit."

Winifred herself was astonished and a little embarrassed by the minor sensation which this address created and by the exuberant reports of it that appeared in the Press.

" Mother darling, don't take notice of South African papers," she urged Alice Holtby, and added both to her and to me : " Little donkeys become big lions here . . . they like to feel that the big guns fire here, so when only little rifles come, they say, ' Hark to the thunder of the great big gun ! ' "

When Speech Day was over, Winifred and Jean McWilliam escaped from the limelight to a motoring holiday in the Transvaal. With them went Margaret Huxley, Winifred's Somerville contemporary and the sister of Julian and Aldous Huxley, who was now on the staff at Pretoria High School.

The rolling grassy tableland of the High Veld reminded Winifred of the Yorkshire region which lies between the moors and the wolds, but its motoring roads were very different. Occasionally rain-storms washed them away in yards as the car drove over them, and their pot-holes meant a long sequence of adventurous bumps. Whenever the motorists encountered a ford or a difficult sandheap they merely deviated, taking their choice of three or four rutted tracks.

They fried their beans and bacon over methylated stoves at the roadside, and at night stayed in primitive hostelries with resplendent names like " The Imperial Hotel." These glorified inns, according to Winifred, were " all bars and spittoons ", but their women guests appeared in the bare dining-rooms attired in pink velvet and cream lace as though they had stepped from a Cynthia Stockley novel. In the morning Indian boys brought early tea, returning half an hour later to retrieve the cups while the visitors were washing themselves.

Although Jean drove her within four miles of the Game Reserve in Transvaal East, Winifred saw no lions, but at night she heard baboons barking among the prickly pears in the moonlit valleys, and by day observed brilliant butter-flies large as saucers and rainbow-hued dragonflies bigger than humming-birds. At Sabie she put her hand in the purple shadow of a stone, and it flew up into her face as three enormous cobalt-winged butterflies striped with iridescent black and speckled with crimson.

The trip came to a premature end owing to the sudden death of the school secretary, who had been at Pretoria for over twenty years. The three of them returned for the funeral, and Winifred spent the remaining ten days of the Easter holiday in Pretoria. Here she was offered a number of academic teaching posts, including History lectureships at Wellington and Rhodes Universities, but her conscience had ceased to be susceptible to tempting proposals from the world of education.

" I am growing a little tired of colonial lionisation," she wrote to me in the middle of April, " and it will be nice to return home and become a plain London donkey again."

CHAPTER XIV

AN IMPERIAL PEOPLE IS AFRAID

HILLS IN THE TRANSVAAL

Stark in the morning sun's unwinking stare
  The naked hills lie agonised with shame,
Feeling their umber loins and shoulders bare
  Beneath the scorching insult of its flame,
Like exiled Adam, helplessly aware
  Of vanished Paradise, below the deep
Unmoving meadows of the ocean, where
  In hidden innocence they lay asleep.

But when the quiet evening comes, they seem
  Like exiles comforted, to take their ease,
Naked no longer then they lie and dream
  Girdled with shadow and the twilit trees,
Watching as in a mirror fade and gleam
  Their unforgotten Eden of the seas.

WINIFRED HOLTBY, 1926
Country Life, 1928

BETWEEN her first and second visits to Pretoria, Winifred had spent ten days in Johannesburg. She stayed there with Ethelreda Lewis, and reported a first impression of shops, miners, Jews, trams and traffic. In contrast to the driving activity of this cosmopolitan business centre, life in Pretoria seemed to have moved with a slow, measured dignity.

" If I had time, time, time," she wrote regretfully, " I could write down notes for a hundred novels and articles, but my days pass in a whirl."

On one of those days Mrs. Lewis took her to after-dinner coffee with Sarah Gertrude Millin, already the leading South African author though she had not yet written her notable biographies of Rhodes and Smuts. Winifred described her as " a lively, vivacious Jewess, dark, plump, very well waved and shingled — no side, no sentiment," and remained her friend and correspondent for the rest of her life. Upon Sarah — perhaps just because she was dark and Jewish, and saw so many dark-haired, dark-skinned people — Winifred left a permanent impression of glowing vivid fairness, " the gold-pale radiance " of which the poet Thomas Moult always speaks when he mentions her.

" You're such a golden person. I hate you not to be well," Sarah wrote affectionately to Winifred in 1932 after hearing of the first onset of her fatal illness.

Now, in March 1926, they sat in the pleasant book-lined living-room of the Millins' house, designed by the famous South African architect, Sir Herbert Baker, in a new avenue of Parktown West, and talked about South Africa. Besides Sarah Millin and Ethelreda Lewis, two or three other South African writers were present, as well as a pianist and a judge. Winifred described the scolding she had received from her fellow-passenger at Teneriffe, and Sarah Millin did not agree that first impressions were never to be trusted.

" There are two occasions," she maintained, " on which you can tell the truth about a country — when you have been there for twenty-four hours, and when you have lived there for twenty-four years."

Winifred assented. She could not hope, she said, to live in South Africa for twenty-four years, like Mrs. Millin, and write such a book as *The South Africans*, but though she had been in the city hardly more than twenty-four hours, she had already noticed four different worlds in Johannesburg. A week later, she wrote to me and described them.

The first world, she told me, was Sarah Millin's own. It was small and exquisite ; a world of witty, agreeable, intelligent and generous people whose like might be met in Chelsea, Vienna, New York, Paris or Rome. In Johannesburg their " centre of gravity " was Parktown, near the University. They were interested in books, writers, pictures and places ; in music, the theatre, marriage, religion and dreams. The impersonal sorrows that troubled them seemed unreal to the rest of Johannesburg, since they were not exclusively concerned with health, bank balances or domestic affections. Only those who wished to belong to it lived in this circle ; the few, like Professor W. M. Macmillan, Elsie Hall, the pianist, her husband Dr. Stohr, the psycho-analyst, who preferred " the quietly vivid conversation of a little Jewess with genius " and the society of Olive Schreiner's favourite nephew, Oliver, to " half-crown points, cocktails and printed ninon frocks of a morning."

The second world, wrote Winifred, was almost wholly feminine ; it was created by the leisured women who spent their time between the Country Club, the Automobile Club, the more fashionable tea-shops, and the gardens in Orange Grove.

" This is an easy country for white women," General Smuts told her when she met him afterwards in Cape Town. " They need not kill themselves by rough work as in Australia or the States. They have the natives to look after them."

But in spite of their leisure, and the wealth that purchased for them their armies of native servants, their long cars which glided through the hot sunlit streets, their luxurious luncheons which began with avocado pears and ended with Van der Hum, it did not seem to Winifred that the women of this second Johannesburg were happy, significant or secure. Their values, she felt, were vulgar ; " their fat jewelled fingers grasp ruthlessly at comfort ; they praise the achievement, not the effort to achieve ; the fame, and not the art which it rewards ; the political party, not the principles of government. Their enthusiasms are rapid as their quarrels, for they live in an unstable world, where Mrs. So-and-so who yesterday went to the Royal Garden Party to-morrow may travel second-class back into the Karoo." And, like all other women in South Africa, they had no vote, no political importance, no physical or psychological freedom — because of the native question.

" This is no country for white women," a capable middle-class mother told Winifred, in contradiction to General Smuts. " I wish my daughters could be sent to England. During the strike such dreadful things happened. I live in hourly terror of the natives."

Winifred discovered a third Johannesburg — the world of business men which supported and enriched the second. She went over the great mines where money was quickly made and still more quickly lost ; smooth-running lifts took her up and down the huge stone offices of a city with an over-stimulating electrical climate, six thousand feet above sea-level. At the Rotary Club where she spoke, the only woman amongst eighty men, she confronted the spectacled faces of Dutch, British and Jewish representatives, who cherished " high ideals of push, go, get, bounce, and other monosyllables of modern progress." Their politics were passionately controversial, but whatever their party, she found a curious consensus of opinion amongst these commercial experts of the Rand.

" They want," she wrote, " a white South Africa, strong, rich, successful, with her mines selling diamonds and gold at favourable prices to all the markets of the world ; they want a docile, healthy, useful black race, which knows its place and keeps in it, and provides sufficient labour for the fields and the mines and the factories, and the low-built delightful houses with their sunny verandas and inconvenient kitchens."

But there was another world in Johannesburg.

Not here only, but in every town that she visited, Winifred became keenly aware of a Fourth City, half hidden, menacing, aloof. At dawn its citizens poured from the locations into the mines and workshops ; they polished the parquet flooring in the Parktown bungalows ; they emptied the ash-bins and cleaned the streets ; they drove the carts drawn by limpid-eyed, softly treading donkeys. The roses and hibiscus and moon-flowers of the suburban gardens concealed little hovels from which, in the early morning, crept black " boys " and " girls " who

might be married men and women with families, to prepare
the tea and sweep the houses and cook the breakfasts of
their imperial employers. Right under the noses of the
white men and women, they led their own dark, mysterious
life.

Winifred was taken to the Bantu Social Centre in Johannesburg, where an American missionary arranged games and
lectures for the few urban natives fortunate enough to find
their way there. She stood in the hall of a native trade
union, a big room cleared for a Saturday evening dance,
hung with paper decorations and startling pictures drawn by
a native artist. At camp one night in the Transvaal, she
had heard two black servants teaching each other to read
from a child's exercise-book. But wherever she went, the
white people whom she met talked to her pessimistically
about the native question. They told her that higher
education was bad for natives and gave them ideas and
undermined their loyalty ; that political power was unsuited to natives, since they were not ready for it ; that
segregation and the Colour Bar and the disenfranchisement
of the black men in the Cape were necessary for the preserva-
tion of white civilisation and the safety of white women and
the happiness of the home.

Sometimes, as Winifred meditated on these statements,
they seemed to have a familiar ring. Suddenly, one day
in Pretoria, she realised why. In her mind she began
to substitute the noun " women " for the noun " natives,"
and found that these fiercely held, passionately declared
sentiments of white South Africa coincided almost word for
word with the old arguments in England against women's
enfranchisement, women's higher education, and women's
entry into skilled employment. She even perceived — as
Olive Schreiner had perceived before her — a close relationship between the two forms of subjection, for she knew
that every year since 1907 the Union Parliament of South
Africa had considered and rejected a bill for the enfranchisement of women, though it was lost by one vote only in 1923.
She believed then — and in spite of the debates, books and

government publications which she heard and read before
and after she left the country, she continued to believe —
that the future of South Africa depended upon its treatment of that fourth nation. Among the black peoples she
found a pathetic eagerness for education, and she felt
certain that they would not indefinitely rest content with
their status as labourers, segregated, exploited, despised.

It was this underworld of Johannesburg which joined
with the memory of the native compound at Kimberley to
rouse Winifred's compassionate indignant humanitarianism
to key-pitch, and eventually drove her to years of full-
time work for African natives. In her letters to me she
expressed her own view of "the native question" without
compunction.

"A man who was once a New York detective in the
Bowery says that nothing he saw there equalled the filth
and horror of this city," she wrote from Johannesburg
on March 8th. "There are common lodging-houses of
indescribable corruption, where men die of phthisis amid
the drunken bawling of their fellow-lodgers. Black prosti-
tutes spread syphilis from small evil hovels in the backyards
of those elegant houses where engineers' wives play bridge.
Fastidious Johannesburg will not tolerate the contamination
of black girls and men sleeping in white houses, so it shuts
them off into squalid yards . . . and professes complete and
horrified ignorance of the nightly occurrences that not unnaturally ensue. A respectable suburb recently forgot itself
at a ratepayers' meeting and cursed the Bishop because he
suggested using part of the rates for the erection of a native
girls' hostel in their quarter of the town, to prevent these
extemporised huts becoming brothels. The Cynthia
Stockley women are quite true to life. They live in the
exquisite houses built by 'Baker the architect outside
Johannesburg, shutting their eyes to the incredible filth and
danger of a city where a mixed population breeds a horror
of corruption."

Winifred understood now the bitterness of the racial conflict in which, without as yet fully realising it, she had already

ranged herself on the side of the oppressed. She was an honoured, fêted visitor from England — but she had seen elegant women in beautiful clothes holding up gloved hands in dismay because she had talked to " niggers." The South African Press, though unsentimental, she found more rational. A well-known editor whom she met spoke with bitter scorn of a government which, he asserted, said in effect to the natives : " Now we are all going to tackle your problem with real justice and equity. We will begin by depriving you of all legal rights. We will then shut you off from all industrial expansion. After that we will segregate you in those areas which are uninhabitable by us. And after that we will allow a few of you the privilege of performing the most disagreeable of our industrial occupations for starvation wages. Q.E.D."

The Nationalist Party, Winifred was told, might be crude and selfish in its conception of native policy, but the South African Party which so bitterly condemned it had enjoyed five years in office of almost complete inaction. As for the Labour Party, she reported, " it is simply a white workers' protection agency, with all the autocracy of trades unionism and little of its compensating security. . . . The real Socialist shrinks in horror from this blundering panic."

In Johannesburg she talked to Champion, the Zulu trades union leader, and spoke of the bitter early history of British trades unionism. She found him, in her own words, " reasonable, courteous, patient beyond description," but added that upon him rested the burden of millions of men, still uneducated, who had been brought into contact with western civilisation by the worst possible methods, taught the crudest elements of Communism " with a dash of militant Bolshevism," and then abandoned to find their own salvation.

On March 14th she wrote that she had also met Clements Kadalie, the leader of the Zulu Bolshevists, at the office of the Industrial and Commercial Workers' Union. This organisation was the only native trade union in South Africa, and its initials—I.C.U.—were soon to become as familiar to Winifred as her own name. She found its office headquarters a strange mixture of self-respect and squalor. Kadalie himself she thought vain, sensitive, suspicious, but according to his own standards sincere. He suspected the well-meant philanthropy of the Bantu Social Centre and similar white experiments in reconciliation, and refused to be associated with any of them.

At that period the Colour Bar Bill, which aimed at segregating all natives in reserved areas like those of Swaziland and Basutoland, was causing angry unrest among the black population. Winifred deplored the cleavage between the Bantu and all moderate sympathetic white opinion, which left an undiluted brand of vehement Communism free to impose itself upon native ignorance of history and economics. It was the reason, she believed, for the atmosphere of nervous tension which impressed her as the chief characteristic of South Africa. Five and a half million natives inhabited a Dominion where a million and a half white people dominated the country and owned seven-eighths of its land. Everywhere she met schoolmasters, farmers, and pleasant, kindly mothers of families, who dreaded the future for their children because of the natives' growing political consciousness. The shadow which derided, for her, the brilliant climate, which overhung the rich blossoming gardens and cast its sinister presence upon idle agreeable parties at country clubs, was the shadow of this fear.

"The situation here is quite terrible," she wrote. "A huge mass of absolutely helpless people ; a few half-educated black leaders, bewildered by modern industrial conditions and perplexed with an inbred inferiority complex when dealing with white men ; a huge indifferent or hostile white population, worried into the apprehension that may lead to extreme repressive action ; a Labour Party out to preserve white labour in the immediate present, with little thought for the future development of the country ; and a few really intelligent white people."

From the tiny minority which composed the last of

these groups, Etheldreda Lewis had organised a small band
of white experts to talk over racial problems at a series of
meetings in the Workers' Hall. Winifred went to one or
two of these meetings, and observed — as she was to observe
again later at Lovedale Native Mission — that the South
Africans who least feared the growing self-confidence of the
natives were those who habitually accepted their status as
human beings. Her own job, in relation to Mrs. Lewis's
experiment, she wrote me, was " to keep the Independent
Labour Party and *The New Leader* people informed of this
point of view. A curious little side-line."

This growing interest in native affairs, which she did not
attempt to conceal, was perhaps responsible for a strange
incident on her last night in Johannesburg. At the end of a
drawing-room meeting which she described as " petrifying "
because it included the Bishop and Dean of Johannesburg,
Philip and Sarah Millin, one or two professors from the
University and several members of the Schreiner family, a
small band of strangers in the audience seized her, blind-
folded her and carried her off in a car, mildly protesting, to
an address which — though she noted it — was supposed to
be unknown. There she was interviewed by half a dozen
masked men in black and white robes, the executive committee of a semi-secret, anti-Jewish society which she
described as an African version of the Ku Klux Klan.

Their numbers ran into five figures, they told her, and
among those present were " Members of Parliament and
people whose names would make me jump," but the
bourgeois little sitting-room with its embroidered table-
mats and vases of dyed grass mocked their ludicrous
attempts to be sensational. Watching the Honourable
Brethren endeavouring to drink tea through their inadequate
mouth-holes, Winifred was impressed only by the childish-
ness of her kidnappers and the possible effect of their anti-
Semitism in a racial atmosphere already dark with peril.
When they asked for her opinion of them, she gave it as
frankly as she expressed herself to me.

" I do find little patience," she concluded, " with these

semi-lawless, semi-secret organisations for the purpose of fanning all too easily aroused prejudice. South Africa probably is on the eve of a big crisis — but it will be a colour crisis, and for Gentiles and Jews to be thwacking at one another just now seems to me to be the height of irresponsibility."

During her three days at Bloemfontein in the middle of April, Winifred gave eleven lectures and took part in a public debate at the Town Hall.

Here, in the Orange Free State, she had penetrated to the heart of Dutch nationalism, and her advocacy of the League of Nations meant heavy work against the tide. The League, she found, was universally disliked by a population which regarded it as an instrument of the victorious Allies, and feared the supervision of native policy implied by a mandate system. Amongst them English was still a foreign tongue, and England herself an object of hatred.

" The Principal of the University Senate," she reported, " declared *me* to be imperialist British because in the course of a speech about disarmament and security I had not mentioned ' the menace of the British navy.' The intensity of the political feeling has to be experienced to be imagined."

She was taken outside the city to see one of the most moving and beautiful War memorials that she had ever beheld. A stark column rose above the dry thorn-bushes of the surrounding waste ; beneath it a flight of steps led to a low platform of warm brown stone. On the platform two sculptured women gazed out across the country with a poignant and splendid dignity, one holding on her knee the emaciated body of a dying child.

To-day we in England are apt to forget that concentration camps were not invented by Hitler. But South Africa does not forget. The Bloemfontein memorial which Winifred saw commemorates the 26,370 Dutch women and children who died in British internment camps during the Boer War. As long as their tragic indomitable figures stand there, that story of death and suffering will be remembered.

"But there is nothing," wrote Winifred in an article years afterwards, "to indicate the equally true story of the attempts made in the camps to save life and health; the sincere, if too impetuous attempt of Campbell-Bannerman and his friends, after the war, to secure reconciliation, and the gesture of abnegation by the victors with which the Act of Union was secured. The Dutch of Bloemfontein, looking at the silent witness of their magnificent memorial, remember; but they remember only half the truth, and that half does not help them to use their present ascendancy in South Africa with moderation. It is the same in Europe; unless memories are edited by wisdom, it would be almost better to forget."

Between her lectures Winifred had an interview with an enlightened Dutch lawyer, who occasionally acted for one or two prominent natives, and told her of a case then in his hands. Only the previous morning the leader of a native organisation, a cultured and intelligent man, had called at a local bank and asked to open an account. The cashier passed him on with an air of insolent indifference.

"Go to that baas over there."

"He's not my boss," expostulated the native.

The cashier flared up into a rage. "You dirty black swine, who are you talking to?" he cried.

The native replied quietly: "I was talking to you."

"Were you indeed!" the cashier shouted, and jumping over the counter he struck the native in the face. The native made no defence, but asked to be taken to the manager. This was refused, and he was bundled out of the building and left in the street.

He went straight to his lawyer, still self-contained and dignified, but burning with rage. The situation, as the lawyer realised, was acute. The previous year bad native riots had taken place in Bloemfontein, and only a week before a native strike had threatened their recurrence. The native leader had power and was respected by his colleagues; the story of the insult might lead to race-propaganda in the locations and serious trouble might grow.

Over the telephone in the middle of her interview, Winifred heard the Dutch lawyer patiently explaining these points to the bank manager. The manager was obstinate, but the lawyer at last persuaded him to see the native in his office next day, explain and apologise. The incident, Winifred gathered, was typical, and it led the lawyer into a passionate outburst on native character. He had worked with natives for years, he said, and, given equal opportunities, they were as intelligent as white men. They had a better physique, their minds were quick, and every year they were gaining in education and power.

She was beginning, wrote Winifred, to feel definitely negrophil ; she found the natives a gay, smiling people, who possessed the gift of laughter. When she wrote her letter I was in Washington, with its impressive memorials of Abraham Lincoln and the Civil War ; and though the unsolved problems of the South were discussed in America with pessimism, it seemed that South Africa had some distance to travel before she caught up with the United States.

At Bloemfontein a cable from England temporarily diverted Winifred's attention from politics ; it told her that Grace was the mother of a daughter. Here, too, in a conversation which lasted from the late evening until the early hours of the following morning, she heard domestic revelations about the stress of life in an isolated farm community which were, she wrote, " enough to fill a novel," and did, in fact, supply the theme for her next book, *The Land of Green Ginger*. " It embraced passion, tuberculosis, suicidal mania, neurasthenia, lack of sanitary accommodation and stifled creative desire — ' the healthy, sane life of God's out-of-doors,' " she commented ironically. Later, when we were both back in England, she told me that South Africa had taught her probably as much about marriage as the unmarried could learn.

" Things stand out more crudely," she said, " in that hot, dry atmosphere, where nerves are strung at tension point, and the reticence of women about their domestic affairs is broken by the greater loneliness."

At first, Winifred thought, she could not write this story owing to her scanty knowledge of the background, but eventually she solved her problem by putting the tale which originated in South Africa into a Yorkshire setting.

" I have a vague idea for a new novel germinating at the back of my mind," she wrote me from Grahamstown on May 2nd, " a newish notion for making use of any travel experiences I may have had without moving the scene from Yorkshire. . . . It all takes place at East Witton on the Wensleydale moors, but its vitality is to come from Hungary, Finland, South Africa and China ! It is the love-story of a woman, the daughter of a South African missionary, taken back to Yorkshire in infancy, with a passion for strange places . . . a person pining to get out of a shut-in valley farm. I want it to be crowded with colour and bizarre foreign effects, yet all to take place in one very remote district. It may be too mad."

By May 18th, when she was back in Cape Town, the title of the story had come to her.

" I have just thought," she announced excitedly, " of calling my new book *The Land of Green Ginger* after that lovely street in Hull." But a sentence in one of the note-books which accompanied her round South Africa gives a further explanation : " The Land of Green Ginger is about us and within us—like the Kingdom of God."

Just before she left South Africa, when she was in bed with influenza at Pretoria, she began actually to write this novel. Her heroine, she informed me, was called Joanna, and she had two friends. One, named Rachel, was appar-ently modelled partly on myself ; the other, Agnes, who lived in China, was inspired by Stella Benson.

" Joanna has a husband called Teddy, whom I hate, and two daughters, Pamela and Patricia, who are rather nice and excessively interested in theology. They live on the moors near East Witton, and Teddy has consumption, which he is always trying to prove attributable to his war service. Joanna falls in love with a Hungarian because he tells her Othello-like tales."

She had found, she said, a most appropriate quotation for the fly-leaf from her old friend William Blake, and she copied it out for me : " I know of no other Christianity and of no other Gospel than the liberty both of body and of mind to exercise the Divine Arts of Imagination — Imagination, the real and eternal world of which this Vegetable Universe is but a faint shadow." But when the book appeared in 1927, it was also prefaced by some lines from another favourite, Sir Walter Raleigh's *Manoa*, which had echoed in her mind throughout her travels in South Africa :

> . . . *Whilst my soul like quiet palmer*
> > *Travelleth towards the land of Heaven.*
> *Over the silver mountains*
> *Where spring the nectar fountains,*
> *There will I kiss the bowl of bliss*
> *And drink mine everlasting fill*
> *Upon every milken hill.*
> > *My soul will be adry before,*
> > *But after, it will thirst no more.*

Winifred's journey from Bloemfontein to Lovedale Native Mission in Cape Province marked another stage in her enslavement by the cause of the African native. She noticed immediately that the workers in the Mission Institute, surrounded by twenty thousand natives within a twelve miles radius, lived in ease of mind, slept on the ground floor with open doors and windows, walked alone, and talked with the negroes as she herself had often talked with countrymen in English rural lanes.

She was deeply impressed by the sane, serene atmosphere of the mission, compared with the apprehensive hatred everywhere else. Here, she thought, it was the church that seemed broad-minded, progressive and alert ; the laity who by their alarmed suspicion held back all advance in thought and statesmanship.

" The brooding fear that darkens most of this country has vanished, and the brilliance of the geraniums and kingfisher-starlings no longer seems ironically contrasted with the gloom of the white man's outlook," she wrote to me from her quiet mission bedroom. With its faded green carpet, high narrow windows, lace curtains, flowered wall-paper and photographs of clerical conferences, it was obviously imported straight from an English rectory, and she found it very restful after the harsh conflicts of Bloem-fontein. Among the seven hundred native students she felt : " These are my friends. Here I can speak as I really feel."

The opposite, she realised, was true of Grahamstown, the ultra-English city where even the monuments quoted Kipling, and the British traveller found himself in " Thomson Street " or " The Farmers' Rest " Hotel. It seemed to her, she explained, one of those " What do they know of England who only England know " places, where the population played at bridge, tennis, tea-parties and flirta-tions, and all the women wore smart evening dresses for dinner. Unfortunately, she admitted, her own garments were now much the worse for their exacting experiences. Her delphinium-blue bridesmaid's dress had steadily faded in the sunshine, and the newspaper descriptions of it in the various places where she had worn it had changed to corre-spond with its changing hue until the final comment re-ported : " Miss Holtby looked charming in opal-tinted crêpe-de-chine."

In comparison with Lovedale she was again oppressed by the intense political feeling of the country, and came to dread the approach of a hostess with the usual polite request : " Oh, do let me introduce Mr. X. He *so* much wants to talk to you." She knew that this meant the advance of a smiling fellow-guest who would forthwith tell her what she ought to think about the Dutch, the Natives or the Imperial Question, and expect her to agree. If she did not, she realised that the rumour would go round : " Oh, yes, Miss Holtby — only been in the country three months, and of course she thinks she knows everything."

Unconsciously, the fatigue of perpetual speaking, travel-ling and meeting strangers was beginning to affect her.

Though she stayed at a decorous women students' hostel belonging to Rhodes University College, she characteristically helped to nurse the sick husband of her hostess, returning from four and five lectures a day to the menial tasks learnt in her war-time nursing home. It was not surprising that she felt she was beating in vain against ignorance and prejudice which neither reason nor charity could conquer.

Back at Cape Town in May, she found herself among the mists and chilliness of approaching autumn. The oak trees were changing colour, the flowers disappearing from the gardens, though she noticed that arum lilies, " of the most Easter-wedding-funeral elegance," grew between the hovels of corrugated iron in any coloured slum. On May 11th, when she lectured at Huguenot University College, Wellington, her sense of depressed frustration was increased by the news of the General Strike in England. The difficulty of ascertaining the true economic issues beneath the crisis as presented by the South African capitalist Press — " which out-Northumberlands the *Morning Post*," she lamented — joined with anxiety about her family to increase her perturbation. One perpetual question at lectures and tea-parties — " And what about this strike in England ? " — now replaced the request for her opinion of South Africa, and finally drove her to a quite unusual outburst in one of her letters to me.

" Damn the Capitalist Press. Damn the contradictious imperfection of things, which presents no single clear issue for choice, allows no perfect cause, no uncomplicated loyalty, in this tedious, embittered world.   Damn. Damn. Damn."

Typically enough, the explosion was followed by an apology, and the gift of a sumptuous fan, made of white ostrich feathers; which she sent to London to await my return there in August.

" Sorry, my dear," she wrote. " You are the one person to whom I can pour out what froth of vexed emotions is spewed up from my inner consciousness, while my exterior, like the ' Companion for Elderly Lady ' in advertisements,

is ' cheerful and urbane.' " She was compensated, she
added, for her wrathful distresses by the memory of a
beautiful train journey from Port Elizabeth, where the
mountains with their flowering aloes and bushes of saffron-
yellow mimosa tumbled down to a dark-blue sea and white
dazzling sands.

" Oh, eyes are happy things — all that they see," she
concluded. " It is surprising that they keep company for
three score years and ten with our unquiet minds."

Throughout Cape Town in May 1926, an uproarious
controversy boiled round the problem of a flag for South
Africa. Competitors had been invited to send in designs,
and a certain English professor submitted four. Three of
these incorporated either the Union Jack or the Rose and
Crown ; the fourth, by means of a design showing a blue,
a green and a yellow stripe emerging from one red block,
tried to show how the four provinces had arisen out of the
Cape. This plan, known as the Vierkleur, was chosen, to the
fierce indignation of the South African Party. The choice
was said to be an insult to The Flag, and letters from " True
Briton " and " Old Die-Hard " filled the columns of the
newspapers.

One morning when the Flag Controversy was at its
height, Winifred escaped for a walk up Table Mountain.
As she scrambled down a steep, winding, sequestered path
on the lower slopes, she saw beneath her parks and gardens
with their green diligently watered lawns, strange trees with
silver leaves like scintillating chain armour, flaming patches
of cannas and watsonias, and beyond the gardens, Cape
Town splashed along the ragged coast like white spray cast
up by the vivid, restless sea. All round her grew aromatic
herbs and bushes, clicking with grasshoppers like the coastal
hills of Southern France, and above her shimmered the sea-
salted, sun-steeped air of the world's most exhilarating
climate.

Looking at the loveliness spread before her eyes, she
pictured again the varied scenes of her journeys through

this radiant, sinister land — the sloping vineyards, gracious colonial architecture and bare thorny Native reserves of Cape Province ; the rolling hills, reminiscent of Hungary, which surrounded the Orange Free State ; the silver mine dumps of the Rand ; the teeming locations of the industrial Transvaal ; the moist, semi-tropical Indian gardens along the rich Natal coast. She recalled conversations overheard in trains, restaurants, cafés frequented by students, the stoeps of private houses, the halls crowded with passionate amateur politicians ; and she remembered that all through those controversies and monologues one man's name had occurred, uttered with love, with loathing, with reverence, with execration. She could not avoid him ; his thought, his actions, his influence, permeated the convulsive, beautiful, violent and sunlit country. Soon she was to hear him speak in the House of Assembly on the Flag Bill dispute which was bitterly dividing the Dutch and British minority, and her still responsive mind thrilled with anticipation.

Suddenly, as she turned a corner, she came upon a man, stripped to the waist, brown, hard, muscular, playing with a dog which apparently wished to prevent him from re-placing his shirt after a sun-bathe. The man was laughing ; his bright, light eyes shone like the Pied Piper's in Browning's couplet :

> And green and blue his sharp eyes twinkled
> Like a candle flame where salt is sprinkled.

The short, stocky figure, trimmed beard, finely shaped head and youthful carriage were vaguely familiar to Winifred. She stood and watched the game with the dog, but the players did not see her. They vanished among the herbs and bushes, and she went on down the hill searching her memory for the likeness.

A day or two later she lunched at the House of Assembly — a substantial building of red brick faced with light stone standing in the middle of Cape Town — and went to hear the afternoon debate. She was swept into a small rustling circle, wives of members of the South African Party fulminat-

ing with patriotic fervour against the Dutch for daring to
suggest the exclusion of the Union Jack from the national
flag. They stood there waiting for General Smuts when
the editor of *Die Burger*, the Dutch nationalist daily paper
for the Cape, passed the group.

Winifred had interviewed the editor twice. Typically
remembering only that she had liked him, she sailed out of
the bevy of ladies with outstretched hand — and suddenly
felt the aghast silence of her hostesses burning a hole in
the back of her silk cape. What might have occurred she
could not imagine, had not General Smuts appeared at that
very moment to save her reputation.

Immediately she saw him, she recognised the man whom
she had seen striding down Table Mountain with a dog
at his heels. She knew that he was fifty-eight, but he
impressed her as so fit, so virile, so clearly marked out by
sheer animal vitality as a leader of men, that the difference
between youth and age became irrelevant. His slim, firm
hands, curiously white and fine for a farmer and a soldier,
reminded her of her father's, but the indefinable stimulus
given to her imagination by his dancing inexhaustible
energy recalled the most outstanding personalities of her
acquaintance — Bernard Shaw, Dame Ethel Smyth, Lloyd
George, H. G. Wells.

She recognised that here was a great man whose brain
had directed the nationalist Boer War ; laid the foundations
of Empire in the years succeeding it ; brought South Africa
in on the British side in 1914 ; helped to design the Covenant
of the League of Nations ; invented the mandate system ;
kept his country within the British Commonwealth and
achieved a fusion between the Dutch and British sections
of the white community. But she realised too that the clear
mind which spanned the world had blind spots in its vision ;
it could not perceive that when a man spoke of humanity,
he spoke of men with black and brown skins as well as
white. And she knew that these abrupt failures of the
imagination are among the world's most fruitful sources of
injustice, more common than sadism, more insidious than fear.

The ladies with Winifred in the House of Assembly closed round General Smuts, fluttering and flattering ; he was "Jannie" to one, "dear General" to another. Smilingly, delightfully, perhaps with his quick tongue in his cheek, he accepted their admiration and turned to Winifred.

"Miss Holtby, I have heard your fame from Bloemfontein to Pretoria."

"And I," responded Winifred, "have seen you in your shirt-sleeves on the mountain."

They both laughed, and the barrier of unfamiliarity was down.

"Come," said Smuts, "I must tell you about that dog. He wasn't mine, though I like dogs well enough. But he fastened himself to me and followed me — and then, at the top of the mountain I had a sun-bath. I tore off all my clothes and lay in the sun, and that poor dog — he did not know what to make of it ! Here was a man with whom he had climbed the mountain. He hadn't gone away. He smelled the same, but he didn't look the same. Sense of smell against sense of eye — what ? "

He was interested in that dog, thought Winifred, because he's interested in everything. He noticed the luncheon-table decorations of heaths from the mountain, and told her how the proteas and heaths that grew round Cape Town were indigenous to the great Antarctic continent, now lost except in South Australia and the Cape Peninsula. He was interested in the League of Nations Union in the provinces, in her idea of the Dutch being so much like Yorkshiremen, in the coal situation in England, in Hull, in his daughters.

"My daughters are creatures," he told her. "They saw through me when they were little bits of things. Clever ? I don't know. They are individuals. I could talk of my daughters all day."

"I understand," commented Winifred, "that Selma thinks of being an architect."

"No, no ! " he exclaimed, "she must not. She is to go to the University and take up politics. I want her as my secretary. I would always rather have a woman secretary. They are as intelligent as men and more adaptable. Men are full of their own ideas, so they do not grasp what is in your mind so quickly. The ideal secretary is a woman."

Someone mentioned his birthday, and he changed the subject immediately.

" Yes, I am getting old. But there are compensations. A leader of men — he must begin young, while he has physical strength, vitality. That's the great gift. But a young man cannot think. There are speeches I made in 1920 which to-day I blush for. My mind is only now beginning to develop. As we grow older, we cease to care so much for feelings. Power ? I wanted power. I had it. It is dust and ashes. There's nothing in it, I tell you. But one must keep fit. When I am up country I ride. Here — "

" There's a mountain handy. How fortunate ! "

" Yes. There's a mountain. And there are fifty different kinds of protea. The botany here is unique."

They spoke of the special March Assembly of the League of Nations, at which Germany should have been admitted and was not, and Winifred asked him to explain the catastrophic mismanagement of a beaten and still bitter enemy.

" The Assembly failed," he said, " because the big powers could not lay aside their little tricks. They could have got Germany in. It only meant cutting themselves off from their little games for a few moments. When one comes to a great work, then one must come in with clean hands, purged of the smaller interests. They did not."

" But if the smaller interests are promises made ? "

" Miss Holtby, when you are facing a great opportunity in political life, the only thing that matters is that you should not fail. The smaller things can be attended to afterwards. Now — it will be difficult. Germany will not be so ready. It has spoiled the gesture. But the League cannot fail. The idea is too big. It is too firmly rooted in people's minds. It will carry itself."

" But what about the mandate ? " Winifred inquired.
" Suppose Germany demands the restoration of some of her
colonial territories ? "

" She will demand," he said. " She wants German
East. She needs it for her material expansion. There will
be no peace without that — and there will be no trouble."

But even Winifred's limited experience could not accept
this. As Smuts talked, the impression grew of alert, amused
insincerity ; of a man saying what he thought would best
please the person to whom he was speaking. The Nationalists, as she knew, regarded the League as imperialist camouflage, a creation of the Allies for crushing Germany ; they
called it " another little stunt of Slim Jannie." She remembered hearing that Smuts was largely responsible for the
Bondelswart rebellion, which had done so much to discredit
the League in the eyes of South Africa ; that he had a
unique opportunity, when he returned from Europe after
the War, to carry his country with him in favour of international co-operation, but only addressed one meeting at
Johannesburg.

Evidently, she concluded with a mental shrug, a little
general optimism is what he believes to be good for League
of Nations Union lecturers. But when he asked her to stay
with him on his farm at Irene, she knew that, had she been
able to go, she would have found nothing more exhilarating
than two days of his society. He braced her like champagne,
like a frosty day, like brilliant sunshine on the water's surface.
Listening later in the debate to General Hertzog — spare,
grey, worn and quiet — she realised that there was only
one Smuts in South Africa.

Winifred's time in the country was approaching its end.
She had only one more long journey to make, for a final
engagement in Bloemfontein and a farewell visit to Jean
McWilliam in Pretoria. From the window of the train she
looked out on fierce, lovely moonlight, which turned to
silver the little white farms near the railway track. The
nights were cold now, wintry with strong winds and black

blowing cypresses; the South African moon, unlike the
tame, pale moons in England, was a brazen unvirginal
Jezebel, her face painted and her head tired with stars.

In Pretoria she went camping for the week-end with
young Pierneef, the rising South African artist whose pictures
were making the reputation which a few years afterwards
gained him an exhibition to himself in South Africa House.
At their camp twenty miles from Pretoria among rolling
hills covered with tawny gorse and green thorn-bushes, she
watched him painting golden willows and sunlight on tall
bulrushes.   Two pictures of his went back with her to
England : a woodcut of an anonymous tree with wild,
twisted branches, and a small oil seascape of a bay on the
east coast of Africa near Mombasa, painted in the vivid
blues and greens of a black opal. The oil-painting hung
for so long in the house which G. and I eventually shared
with Winifred that it seemed to become part of our home,
and when she died her family allowed us to purchase it. It
now hangs above the mantelpiece of our drawing-room in
Cheyne Walk.

The camping week-end was Winifred's last South African
adventure, for when she returned to Pretoria she was ill for
ten days with a severe attack of influenza. She had not
realised, she admitted, how completely the long series of
lectures, meetings, journeys and strangers had exhausted
her, for she always felt well in the splendid sunlight. But
now she lay in bed contentedly reading Tchekov's letters
and gratefully accepting Jean's concerned ministrations.

" I have neglected too much for the past ten years the
fascination of ill-health," she wrote me, pathetically
enough. " I appreciate so much the attention which it
secures and the flattery of a doctor's diagnosis."

When she recovered, Jean took her for a drive down a
yellow valley, between two sets of hills " like rollers sweeping
in from a brown frozen sea." The sky was a brilliant
turquoise ; the dark green leaves of the orange groves on
the back slopes of the hills looked glossy in the sunshine ; the
pink almond blossom coming out in the bare winter

gardens made a strange contrast with the baked terracotta earth.

It was her last vivid impression of South Africa. She was obliged to return to England, for she had now spent all her money ; her overwhelming lectures had mostly been voluntary, and though she had contributed innumerable articles to the South African papers, they could pay only low fees owing to their small circulations. Ten pounds for a picture and a loan of fifty which, true to character, she had impulsively offered to a distressed acquaintance, had left her with the price of her return ticket and thirty shillings.

At the end of June she said goodbye to Jean McWilliam, and sailed for England from Cape Town on the All-Third-Class steamer *Barrabool*.

CHAPTER XV

THE DARK CONTINENT AND ITS LENGTHENING SHADOW[1]

AVE, CAESAR !

" The Letter Killeth "

(Lines found written in her copy of *Back to Methuselah*)

Hail, Caesar ! We who are about to die
    Salute thee, and the law which thou dost give.
But were we now instead about to live,
    Hail, Christ, the Lord of Life, should be our cry.

In Caesar's country, laws envenom sin,
    From man to man is ignorance and strife,
But in the country of the Lord of Life
    The only law comes from the mind within.

Those who are bound so soon for death may keep
    From day to day the covenant of fools,
Fetter their passions with ignoble rules
    And stumble blindly to eternal sleep.

But we who seek the Kingdom of the Mind
    Know that our wills its liberties may give ;
Hail, Christ ! For we who are about to live
    Go now from hence, to seek until we find.

WINIFRED HOLTBY

WHEN WINIFRED began, in Johannesburg, to inform the Independent Labour Party of the progress made in the meetings between white people and natives organised by Etheldreda Lewis, she referred to this work as " a curious

[1] I am deeply indebted to Mr. A. Creech Jones, M.P., and Mr. W. G. Ballinger for much of the material upon which this chapter is based.

little side-line." Before many months were past, that " little side-line " was to overshadow her sky, taking her time, her energy, her money, involving many hours each week of letter-writing and speaking.

By the time that she left South Africa, Winifred felt that the comfort of its white population and the high standard of living attained by its white wage-earners were purchased at the expense of the native inhabitants, and she knew that those who enjoyed these advantages would fight to retain them. Her sense of justice urged her to protest, and even from far away, to help in resolving this conflict. She returned to England determined to rouse public opinion, and to urge those friends who shared her outlook to co-operate with the black people in a campaign for removing the cruelties and repressions which weighed so heavily on her conscience.

Among the men and women in South Africa who impressed upon her the gravity of economic and racial antagonisms was Mrs. Mabel Palmer, a lecturer in the Technical College at Durban. Mrs. Palmer, who had been an English university teacher and an executive member of the Fabian Society, introduced her to several leading non-Europeans, and discussed with her how the British trade unions could help them to solve their problems. In Johannesburg Mrs. Lewis had arranged for her to meet Margaret Hodgson, an Old Somervillian who was now Senior Lecturer in History at the University of the Witwatersrand. Margaret Hodgson was a year or two older than Winifred and had left Somerville before she arrived, but I remembered meeting her there myself when I first went up to Oxford in 1914. Dimly I recalled a short, strong-looking girl with sun-tanned skin and light brown hair, her face illumined by grey eyes vivid with sardonic intelligence. Her father, who knew the South Africa of pre-Boer War days, had been an Inspector of Schools, and she herself was brought from Scotland to Port Elizabeth as a child of ten. Now, as a highly qualified young woman with a sound training in history and economics, she, like her chief, Professor Macmillan, had become deeply concerned with the racial conflict which surrounded them like a wind always on the point of becoming a hurricane.

Winifred also met Howard Pim, a benevolent elderly Quaker who was head of a leading firm of South African accountants. Finally she had her interview with the black leader, Clements Kadalie, the General Secretary of the I.C.U. For the past year or two he had established his headquarters in Johannesburg, and was now vehemently stirring the black workers to an organised effort to improve their wages and working conditions throughout South Africa.

The I.C.U. had a remarkable history. Its origin is obscure, but the most likely story indicates that it started in Cape Town in 1917, not as a black union but as a white group composed mainly of radicals, who hoped to increase their strength by enrolling both African and " coloured " [1] workers. Their proposal slipped through, but when the European members realised that they were outnumbered by non-Europeans they took fright and resigned *en bloc*. Within a year Clements Kadalie emerged, and became secretary of the non-European remnant. By 1919, without money, experience or encouragement, he had organised the black and coloured workers into a presentable trade union.

Kadalie was a remarkable black African from Nyasaland, flamboyant and dramatic, with the demagogue's qualities of leadership. He claimed that his notion of a mass industrial union for Africans arose from reading the literature of the British Trade Union and Labour movements and the works of Henry George. The idea sprang to life when he was kicked off a Cape Town pavement by an irate white man who thought that pavements should be reserved for Europeans. One account relates that he was inspired by the Messianic complex which is the undoing of so many re-

---

[1] Always distinguished in South Africa from the black native races. Includes the offspring of the Cape Dutch-Hottentots and other half-caste peoples.

formers, and saw himself as the legendary "Black Man
from the North" who was ordained to save the black
people of the South from their white oppressors. Heaton
Nicholls, a Member of Parliament for a Durban Natal constituency, had used this story of the Black Man from the
North in a novel called *Bayete*, which is said to have
influenced Kadalie. He had been taught by the Living-
stonia Mission, and his reading was limited and disconnected.
As he spoke the Southern native language with difficulty, he
made his speeches in English.

In 1919, Kadalie took advantage of the long neglect of
native labour claims to organise a strike of native dock
workers. He brought off a great spectacular success, but
the few concrete results that followed vanished in a whirlwind of political verbosity. In 1923 he was charged, though
unsuccessfully, with a deficiency of £500 in the I.C.U. funds.
He decided to leave Cape Town for Johannesburg, the
centre of industry in South Africa. Here various repressive
measures, such as the Pass regulations and the Masters and
Servants Act, gave him plenty of material for an intelligent
survey of grievances, and his virulent tirades against the
Government stirred the natives to support him. Curiously
enough, the Government did not suppress these outbursts.
Smuts even expressed sympathy, and Hertzog, then in
opposition, sent a donation to the I.C.U. funds — a fact
effectively publicised by his opponents.

Kadalie decided on a sensational move. He defied the
Pass Laws by entering Natal without a "travelling pass,"
and was arrested and sentenced, but won his appeal to the
Supreme Court on the ground that the laws did not apply
to a native from outside the Union of South Africa. His
victory and the legend of "the Black Man from the North"
made him a heaven-sent leader in the eyes of the natives.
They came to his meetings in thousands and joined the
I.C.U. whenever he addressed a mass gathering, but they
had no idea of the necessity for regular trade union pay-
ments. Collections were taken in pails, which often came
back filled to overflowing with silver coins. Hastily im-

provised offices staffed by illiterate local officials could not
enrol the new members fast enough.   These offices housed
huge sums of loose cash which the officials did not know
how to bank, even if the banks would have accepted their
money.   Wholesale peculation and pilfering became the
habit of organisers recruited from the ranks of £4 a month
native teachers, whose mission-inspired Christianity enabled
them to perceive and place their own construction upon
the everyday negation of the Christian spirit by the white
races in South Africa.

The Zulu named Champion whom Winifred had also
interviewed in Johannesburg worked in association with
Kadalie as Natal secretary of the I.C.U. First a police
boy and then a native mine clerk, Champion encouraged
Kadalie to rouse the black workers, but was critical of his
power. He successfully fought many injustices in Durban
and by 1925 was in charge of a well-organised section of
the Union. Unfortunately for the I.C.U., some European-
inspired officials who wanted to smash the organisation
wrote a pamphlet accusing the Zulu secretary of mis-
appropriation of funds. An action for libel and defama-
tion followed, but Champion lost the case, and Justice
Tatham, who tried it, made severe strictures on the management of the I.C.U.   But the government took refuge
behind a clause in the so-called Industrial Conciliation
Act which stated that pass-bearing native workers' organisations could not be registered or recognised, and no action
followed.

In 1926–27 the income of the I.C.U. was estimated at
more than £12,000 per annum, and the membership was
over one hundred thousand. But corruption and mismanagement due to the ignorance, inexperience and
credulity of the members had begun to arouse general
criticism, and unprincipled lawyers were fastening on to the
Union to exploit opportunities created by the anti-native
Colour Bar and other forms of repression. To the white
sympathisers it seemed obvious that Kadalie required guidance, though they believed that if he could take advice he

might change the whole history of native policy. The I.C.U. had reached this stage of development when Winifred returned from South Africa.

About a month before Winifred came home, Mabel Palmer, on leave in England, called on several trade union officials amongst her friends. Among them was Mr. A. Creech Jones, now Labour M.P. for Shipley in Yorkshire. Mrs. Palmer suggested that he should meet Winifred on her return, and try with her to arrange for some expert committee in England to give sympathy and advice to the I.C.U. She also asked if he could put the black trade union in touch with the British and international trade union movement, and secure a platform for Kadalie at the International Labour Organisation at Geneva.

Creech Jones's knowledge of the I.C.U. was then negligible, but the plight of the black workers aroused his sympathy. A few weeks later he met Winifred at his office in Westminster, and together they made plans to help the I.C.U.

Winifred was then deeply concerned about the black workers' inexperience and the confusion in their organisation. It seemed clear to her that the Africans would receive little help and encouragement from the organised white workers in South Africa. They themselves, by their own efforts, must alleviate their misery and fight the discriminations practised against them.

Who would be free, himself must strike the blow.

Already Creech Jones had written to Kadalie about his problems, and he and Winifred discussed how to give help and publicity to the black union. They decided that it was then unnecessary to add one more to the long list of committees soliciting support for various causes; instead they appealed for sympathy and encouragement for the I.C.U. from the Trades Union Congress and the International Federation of Trade Unions. They also asked advice from the Independent Labour Party's Advisory

Committee on Imperial Affairs, since this included personalities with the experience of Charles Roden-Buxton, J. F.
Horrabin, H. N. Brailsford, James Maxton, Fenner Brockway
and Norman Leys.

During the next few years several of these men became
close friends of Winifred's, but Dr. Norman Leys was the
most intimate of them all. The author of a classic publication
on Kenya, Dr. Leys combined a country practice near Derby
with the fierce and practical defence of native peoples
exploited by imperial interests. Blown through life, as
Winifred expressed it, " by the high winds of idealism,"
he shared his ruthless sincerity with the martyrs and the
saints, and recognised in her the born crusader who fights
injustice without *arrière-pensée* of self-interest or cautious fear
of consequences. His honourable personality, which carried
passionate integrity to the limit of fanaticism, contributed
at least some ingredients to Winifred's portrait of Arthur
Rollitt, the uncompromising opponent of slavery and
profiteering in *Mandoa, Mandoa !*

In the early summer of 1927, Kadalie came to Europe.
He had readily agreed to a plan, suggested by Etheldreda
Lewis, that he should appear at that year's International
Labour Conference in Geneva as the unofficial champion of
the black races of South Africa. Winifred, with the officials
of the Independent Labour Party, met him at Waterloo.
Her difficulties in finding accommodation for him would
have defeated anyone less persistent ; for almost a day
she tramped vainly from one small hotel to another in
the Euston Road and similar neighbourhoods. I was then
expecting the birth of my son and could not tramp with her,
but we put through several telephone calls to hotels and
hostels, always with identical results. Eventually she discovered some rooms through the Society of Friends, but the
experience opened the eyes of us both to the notions of
hospitality entertained by the capital of a great empire
towards the native populations within its control.

In Geneva Kadalie was allowed to address the I.L.O.
Conference and meet groups of workers and other delegates.

Winifred received mixed reports which suggested that his advocacy of the black union's claims had roused some of the workers' delegates, but had failed to impress a calculating assembly of men and women trained to sift the grain of solid fact from the airy chaff of mob appeal. He returned to England and spoke at meetings in various parts of the country. Creech Jones, then a prominent trade union official, spent much time with him explaining trade union structure and practice, shaping statements of policy on the conduct of native affairs, and drafting a new constitution for the I.C.U.

Meanwhile a number of disturbing letters came from South Africa. Because of them Kadalie overstayed his leave, and spent much money on his expenses. His reception as a friend and equal by the Independent Labour Party and others over-elated him, and he was still too inexperienced to realise that the leader of a revolutionary movement must deny himself luxuries. Afterwards Norman Leys pointed out to Winifred how difficult it was for European standards of conduct to be accepted as elementary by a people with minds so starved as those of the Africans. The lack of it was responsible, he said, for the failure of most liberal movements among native populations, and there was little hope for the future until the Africans realised this for themselves.

" I'm afraid," he added, " there's no remedy for the cruelty and injustice that prevail in South Africa except the voluntary martyrdom of many, both black and white."

Characteristically enough, Kadalie did not reveal how his difficulties were increasing, nor explain the restrictions being placed on the advances for his European trip. He tried to arrange for an English secretary to return with him to South Africa, but Winifred and Creech Jones both felt that the person required was not a secretary but a trained and experienced trade union official. Mrs. Lewis had made the same suggestion, and Kadalie, increasingly worried, urged Creech Jones to obtain leave of absence and temporarily go out as I.C.U. adviser. The news spread in South Africa that he was coming, but as a National

Secretary of the Transport and General Workers Union and a Parliamentary candidate, he could not contemplate such a change. It became clear that some other official would have to be found.

In the early autumn Winifred and Creech Jones saw Kadalie off at Waterloo. He had a reserved seat in a compartment with white people returning to South Africa, but before the train left the station the compartment was his. As soon as he had gone, the search began for a trade union official with experience of labour organisation and the right political background. In the England of 1927 this was no light undertaking, for the British trade union movement was still recovering from the General Strike. At last George Aitken, the organiser of the Union of Democratic Control in Scotland, told Winifred that an insurance agent named William Ballinger from Motherwell, near Glasgow, was willing to have his name considered. His experience was more limited than Creech Jones was seeking, but he was Honorary Secretary of the Motherwell Trades Council and local secretary of his Union branch. He had also acted as Labour agent in several Parliamentary elections and had served for a few years on the Motherwell Town Council.

At Winifred's suggestion, Creech Jones interviewed William Ballinger in Manchester and explained to him how precarious was the job in South Africa. Kadalie had thought that the work might last for perhaps two years, but Ballinger felt that if he could only make himself indispensable to the native organisation the arrangement might be continued. He knew that he would have to break through the ostracism of the white people and gain the goodwill of the trade unions, but he felt that his sympathies were sound and his knowledge of the British working class movement sufficient. As urgent requests for an adviser were now coming from South Africa, Winifred and Creech Jones decided that if Ballinger could go he should leave immediately. He accepted the post, sold his insurance book, left Motherwell for good, came to London and met Winifred for the first time.

Winifred and G. and I were then occupying a maisonette at Nevern Place in Kensington, and it was here that Ballinger came to see her on the late afternoon of a dull day in early spring. He never forgot the small sitting-room which looked, and was, crowded; the firelight throwing shadows on the wall; the pleasant consciousness of the murky London twilight safely outside. Winifred sat on the rug before the fire, her feet tucked under her and her lips parted in eager expectation. She liked at sight the broad, muscular Scotsman with the open intelligent face and short-sighted, undaunted eyes behind large horn-rimmed spectacles.

They discussed South Africa; the War; the prospects of better international understanding. Obviously, thought Ballinger, she did not belong to the working class, but she had large human sympathies and there was no hint of patronage in her manner. She appeared rather to be deferring to superior authority.

" Are you really ready," she asked him, " to sacrifice the political opportunities which may be ahead of you, for an uncomfortable life in South Africa as a friend of the natives ? "

" Yes," said Ballinger. " It's a man's job. I'm willing to try it."

Quietly, but with deliberate intention, she persuaded him to speak of his early life; learnt that he was the eldest of a family of six left fatherless when he was fourteen; heard the tale of his entry into industry as a boy working at the coal " screes " of a colliery. When he was twelve, he told her, his father had taken him to see David Livingstone's birth-place at Blantyre, and he had never forgotten the story of Livingstone's life and death. In her turn Winifred described the strike at Rudston which had caused her to study the lives and conditions of farm labourers. They found another mutual bond in her mother's career on the East Riding County Council and Ballinger's as a parish and town councillor at Motherwell.

Ballinger did not leave London immediately, for the authorities were reluctant to endorse his passport. In South

Africa a good deal of publicity had been given to his appointment, and official apprehensions were wide awake. Persistently Winifred visited South Africa House, while Lord Olivier indignantly protested in the *New Statesman* against bureaucratic prejudice and hostility. At last the permit was granted. With an uneasy hope that a new chapter was about to begin for the black workers in Africa, Winifred, Creech Jones and the Rev. James Barr, M.P., saw Ballinger off at Waterloo. Winifred paid for his passage out of her own journalistic earnings, which were now considerable. She expected the amount to be refunded, as the I.C.U. had agreed to pay Ballinger's salary and expenses, but they were never to honour this arrangement. Neither she nor Creech Jones knew the real degree of confusion and disintegration which African efforts at industrial combination had reached during Kadalie's absence in Europe.

When Kadalie arrived back in South Africa, he found the I.C.U. threatened with chaos owing to the adverse judgment given by Justice Tatham in the Champion case. Already the branches were withholding funds and telling headquarters that members had ceased to pay contributions. The local officials thought that a visit from Kadalie and an account of his European experiences might revive enthusiasm. His reappearance did stir the waning interest of his followers, but it also gave them an opportunity for criticism.

" Kadalie, you went out black. Have you returned white ? " asked a buxom lady from Boksburg when Kadalie mentioned that he had thought of bringing a competent woman from England to act as his private secretary.

At the end of 1927 Kadalie attempted another spectacular expedient, designed to win European support. He called a conference, and by a large majority the I.C.U. carried a motion for the expulsion of an alleged Communist element which was actually clamouring for efficient administration. Champion broke away and formed a separate I.C.U. group in Natal. Then, for a time, the story that an important British trade union official was coming to South

Africa with funds to revive the I.C.U. stilled the vitupera-
tive raging of the various factions.

William Ballinger landed at Cape Town in June 1928.
He had found the peaceful voyage in the old *Kildonan
Castle* a pleasant change from the vexatious delays and cross-
questionings of officials who appeared to regard him as a
dangerous anarchist-communist with the deceptive appearance of a mild revolutionary socialist.   His arrival was less
agreeable.   Three days before landing, the information
greeted him : " Things won't be pleasant for you when we
dock at Cape Town."

Determined to know the worst as soon as possible, he
was among the first half-dozen to present his passport when
the immigration officers boarded the ship.   The effect was
electrical.   All the other passengers were cleared out of the
saloon, and he was told to regard himself as an " undesirable
alien " under detention.   After prolonged discussion he
finally received a temporary permit to land, renewable
every three months, and Kadalie came on board to greet
him.

" What a flashily-dressed, fine-looking black man ! "
thought Ballinger, for Clements Kadalie did not in the least
resemble the secretary of a struggling native organisation
in need of European advice.   Ballinger's first intimation of
trouble in the I.C.U. came when the secretary of the Cape
Town branch told him that they were not responsible for
inviting him to South Africa.

" You're not the first European to act as adviser to
Kadalie.   We want to know what's happened to our money."

When Ballinger reached Johannesburg, he learnt that
the I.C.U. was heavily in debt.   In the offices he found
a number of judgment orders and several summonses.
The officials had received neither wages nor expenses for
several months.   They were grievously disappointed when
Ballinger told them that he had not only brought them no
money, but his expenses had been advanced on the understanding that the I.C.U. would repay them.

Quarrels, peculation and desperation now plunged the

disintegrating Union into chaos. Two houses had been built
for two I.C.U. officials in Natal at a cost of £3000. A firm
of South African solicitors had received a large sum for appearing in court on behalf of I.C.U. members charged with pass
offences and drunkenness. Several thousands more were
expended on a company known as Vuka Afrika which had
gone bankrupt. Ballinger faced a situation of hopeless confusion and all but irretrievable disaster. His reports made
clear to Winifred, once and for all, that she was not supporting a flourishing black organisation in its struggle against
white injustice ; she was starting from zero in a campaign
in which the education of the native worker himself was
the first and by no means the simplest objective.

Typically enough, though she now faced the problems
of the Dark Continent in their portentous nakedness, she
was not dismayed. She realised that the I.C.U. would
neither refund the money she had advanced nor fulfil its
obligations to Ballinger, so she started energetically to raise
money for him amongst her friends. Ballinger received
a personal cheque from her for £25, with a letter urging
him to carry on, and to aim at becoming liaison officer
between the white and black workers in South Africa. The
money that she raised during his first year he shared with
the loyal officials, and from the time of his arrival maintained his resolve to champion native rights without becoming
a charge on the African workers.

Soon after Ballinger arrived in Johannesburg he met
Margaret Hodgson, who became his constant friend and
adviser. He also consulted Winifred and Creech Jones
about the malpractices of the I.C.U., and they both insisted
that it could only advance on a basis of complete financial
integrity. At home they collected books for the natives,
and constantly reminded the Dominions Office of native
needs and problems.

The numerous letters from Winifred which Creech Jones
has kept show how determined she was that Ballinger's
mission should not fail. She even wrote urgent letters to
Kadalie, but the little confidence that she had left in him

soon evaporated. In December 1928 he sent in his resignation as principal officer, took six months' leave of absence,
formed an independent and short-lived I.C.U. with headquarters at East London, and finally, a spent force, declined
into a tragic shadow of the self-appointed black Messiah who
had landed so confidently in England. The one encouraging event of that year occurred shortly after Ballinger's
arrival, when he inadvertently brought about a political
crisis in the Union of South Africa by out-manœuvring
Mr. Walker Madeley, the Minister for Posts and Telegraphs,
and causing the resignation of the Cabinet.

During the years that followed, Winifred made herself
responsible for keeping Ballinger independent of native
resources. She boldly collected subscriptions from such
eminent sympathisers as Bernard Shaw, H. G. Wells, Lady
Rhondda, Colonel Josiah Wedgwood, Lord Noel Buxton
and the Pethick-Lawrences, and sent these to Howard Pim
to administer and transfer to Ballinger so that the fund
should be beyond criticism. Working through the London
Group on African Affairs with the assistance of Mr. Livie
Noble, who had been a member of the Joint Committee of
Europeans and Africans in Johannesburg, she was a perpetual thorn in the flesh of Government complacency in
both England and South Africa.

Until his death in 1934 Howard Pim remained a friend
to Ballinger, often disagreeing with him but always ready
to give help and counsel. He visited England several times
and advised Winifred what policy to pursue. When he died,
and she had good reason to believe that she too might be
dying, she wrote to J. F. Horrabin a letter of which the
final sentence, whether it summarised Pim's attitude or not,
certainly expressed her own :

" We have lost, through the sudden death of Howard
Pim in Johannesburg, the best financial supporter and
strong friend of the movement there. Being ' respectable,'
a Quaker and a most successful chartered accountant, he
was able to stand by the co-operatives and trade unions in

a thousand ways. He really killed himself by continuing to work and take on all sorts of responsibilities after he had been warned not to, but I expect it was worth it."

Ballinger's friends in South Africa naturally included Etheldreda Lewis, who came to England frequently after the world-wide success of *Trader Horn*. Creech Jones also helped in raising funds, and persuaded the British Trades Union Congress to contribute. Winifred felt encouraged and rewarded when representative European trade unions began to recognise Ballinger's work, but the main responsibility continued to be hers. She described herself to Sarah Gertrude Millin as " Treasurer " of the Ballinger fund, but she contributed £100 a year to it from her own income, and wrote or dictated enormous numbers of letters in the effort to increase it. When she died I inherited, as her literary executor, dozens of files bursting with carbon copies of this vast correspondence.

" I must have written literally millions of words about Ballinger since 1927," she admitted to me in September 1934. " Perhaps they are the only words I have ever written which will deserve immortality. Well, well — better to be the willing scribe of one permanent movement for releasing the human spirit, than produce nothing but ephemeral if remunerative fiction."

She was ready to take on any task, any responsibility, which brought a contribution to Ballinger's work. When I offered, only half seriously, to give the fund ten per cent of the profits from my first American lecture tour if she would supervise my children and their German governess during my three months' absence, she accepted the obligation with alacrity. So long as international exchanges remained normal the fund just managed to provide Ballinger with a salary and travelling expenses, but when England went off the gold standard in 1931 its manipulation became a heart-breaking procedure. The money contributed lost about 6s. 8d. in every pound, and bank charges increased this loss to 7s. 6d. Automatically the minimum £600 which had to be collected rose to £800, and Winifred

felt as though she were perpetually rolling a Sisyphus stone
up a steep hill.

"I have now joined the 'Money Problemers'!" she
wrote to Phyllis Bentley on November 12th, 1932. "I was
informed casually that my African Fund is £300 : 4 : 6 in
debt yesterday, and they had 'kept it from me' till I was
'quite well.' Well, well. Let's all be ruined together.
Vera and I are going to the theatre to celebrate my bank-
ruptcy (more or less)."

Two months later, when the Macmillan Company of
New York promised her $750 advance on royalties for
the American edition of *Mandoa, Mandoa !*, she sent Phyllis
a cheerful postscript to this rueful confession : "This will
almost wipe out my share of the African debt."

Winifred's sense of obligation to the natives did not end
with the collection of money for Ballinger. Determined
to dramatise their cause until apathetic public opinion was
roused from its indifference, she wrote innumerable articles
and reviews dealing with South Africa in such journals as
Foreign Affairs, *The Nation*, *The New Leader* and *Time and Tide*.
She interviewed Ministers, Members of Parliament, Government officials and the secretaries of organisations, and
arranged committee meetings of African sympathisers at
our house in Chelsea. Amongst those who helped her most
at this time was Dr. (now Sir) T. Drummond Shiels, Under-
Secretary for the Dominions in the Labour Government
of 1929.

When African students came to England for a period
of training Winifred appointed herself their friend and
adviser, and paid for the education of one native student,
Hlubi, at Fircroft College in Birmingham. Her difficulties
in finding accommodation for Kadalie started her on a
persistent though vain endeavour to get a hostel for Africans
founded in London on the same lines as the Indian Students'
Hostel in Bloomsbury, and she wrote several Press appeals
for gifts of books to native workers. About 1929 she had an
idea of writing the history of the I.C.U. and began to collect the necessary material. Probably even the friends with

whom she worked on African problems would not now willingly substitute such a book for the novel *Mandoa, Mandoa !* in which her reflections on British Imperialism took final shape.

To anyone else this African campaign would have represented a full-time job. The number and extent of Winifred's enterprises, and the efficiency with which she carried them out, made her friends realise how little most people get through in a day. She seldom employed our joint private secretary for letters, having usually answered her large mail by hand before the secretary arrived. If anyone protested against the tax on her time and strength of this tremendous unremunerated labour, she always replied that South Africa had given her adequate compensation in experience. An expression of anxiety by Creech Jones brought a characteristic response :

" I do want you and Mr. Livie Noble to understand that I really do not exploit myself. If I choose to gamble on boys and girls instead of race-horses or bridge, that is my own little amusement, and I assure you that I never do without anything but things I am better without in order to do it."

In April 1935, five months before her death, when Creech Jones asked her to suggest names of liberal subscribers towards the education of a Nigerian, Ajayi of Reading, she replied by sending £25. He knew that she was working much harder than her state of health made advisable on the completion of *South Riding*, and returned some of the money. Her letter of thanks indicated how this was spent :

" What a pleasant surprise ! — But you really are all wrong about my ' generosity.' The point is that I am a childless spinster and can make with ease an income of £1000 a year if I *want* to make money. I was brought up economically and simply should not know how to spend all that on myself. At the moment, however, there is a good deal of family sickness up here in which all funds are welcome, and I am very glad indeed to have the £18 : 15 : 6 to help pay for an aunt's operation."

After the collapse of the I.C.U. and the reorganisation of his own position as friend and adviser to the natives, Ballinger investigated the social and economic problems of three High Commissioner's territories which were sources of labour supply for the Rand and the farms. Before each trip, Margaret Hodgson made detailed research into the administration of the territory. These studies were afterwards published, and Winifred helped to give them publicity in the British Press. But in 1931 Ballinger's health suddenly failed during a visit to Bechuanaland. Four years of overwork and anxiety had caused serious chest and lung trouble which made him an invalid for eighteen months.

Margaret Hodgson took him into her home and nursed him back to health. It was inevitable that these two — both of the same sterling Scottish origin, both inspired by similar humanitarian ideals and the same St. Francis-like indifference to physical comfort and worldly rewards, both starved of emotional satisfactions by years of hard unpopular work — should now, in their middle thirties, be falling in love.

By the time that Ballinger recovered, Winifred herself was struggling against the first attack of her fatal illness. His precarious position worried her and Creech Jones believed that it was retarding her recovery, which we all took for granted. The Independent Labour Party Imperial Committee had now broken up ; the London Group on African Affairs gave intermittent support but little practical help, and no other body showed signs of offering permanent assistance. For the time being Creech Jones undertook to act in Winifred's place as treasurer of the fund, and took as much off her shoulders as he could persuade her to abandon. Reluctant as Winifred felt in the early stages of her four years' struggle with death to admit that she was likely to die or even seriously ill, she confessed to him that " it is as well to have one's affairs tidy in such circumstances."

By 1934 she fully realised that the responsibility which she had carried for seven years would soon have to be assumed by others, and began detailed preparations for the continuation of Ballinger's work after her death. When he and Margaret Hodgson came to England that summer she arranged a reception for them at our house, and later helped to set up a permanent committee to support Ballinger's work. This committee became known as " The Friends of Africa," with Julius Lewin as secretary and the late Lord Sanderson as president. Winifred herself acted as the first chairman — a function taken over by Creech Jones after her death — and in spite of her growing physical weakness she immediately began a campaign for funds.

Before they returned to South Africa, William Ballinger and Margaret Hodgson were married. They had long wished to marry, but had feared the consequence, with its loss of income, which did in fact follow. Although she had held her History Lectureship at the Witwatersrand University for fifteen years and for eighteen months had acted as head of the department, Margaret Ballinger was dismissed from her post on the ground that married women could not serve on the staff. Winifred had now a feminist as well as a native cause to fight for in South Africa. In the articles and letters which she wrote on Mrs. Ballinger's behalf, she pointed out that two other married women had taught for several years at the Witwatersrand University. The real reason for Margaret Ballinger's dismissal was her marriage to a man whose native sympathies did not please an institution which derived financial support from various mining groups in the Rand.

On Christmas Day 1934, shortly after their marriage, Winifred wrote the Ballingers that she had a brilliant idea for a wedding present.

" Ten days ago I received from America an entirely unexpected cheque for £375. It is the result of continued sales of *Mandoa, Mandoa!* far beyond my expectations. £75 will go for taxation and American transfers and agents' fees. £100 I want to put by for emergencies. But the £200 is a completely unexpected gift from Heaven, as it were. I was going to send it to the Friends of Africa fund. . . . Then it struck me—why shouldn't you have it instead as a wedding present to buy your motor-car ? It would buy one, wouldn't it ? . . . Anyway, unless you would *prefer* me to hand it to the Fund, I very much want to write the cheque to you personally, as a token of my admiration and good wishes to your adventure together."

When the Ballingers returned to Africa, Winifred undertook to criticise and submit to editors the articles which they produced in the vain endeavour to compensate for Margaret Ballinger's lost income. From her own journalistic experience, she wrote them long letters suggesting how they should put their facts before a reluctant public. It was a thankless and difficult task which used up a great deal of Winifred's time, since most English magazine readers, like the magazine readers of every country, do not want information about South Africa and the political problems of our far-flung and far too complicated Empire, but only about their own clothes, cars, games, furniture and face-creams.

In the summer of 1935, the Trades Union Congress decided to send Ballinger, now a recognised champion and protector of native rights, as technical adviser to the International Labour Conference at Geneva, so that he could take part in framing a convention on the recruitment of native labour. It was also agreed that a Protectorate native should go with him, so Ballinger came to England accompanied by a huge and stalwart Swazi, Norman Nxumalo. They arrived in London with only a few hours to spare, and Nxumalo had no suitable outfit for the Conference. At that time Winifred was working desperately to finish *South Riding* and her play, *Take Back Your Freedom*, before she died, but as Ballinger was tired and had papers to prepare, she sent him to her room to rest, and rushed the Swazi round to " ready-to-wear " clothes shops.

" He is 6 ft. 5 and broad to correspond, and ready-made suits are not for that size here," Winifred wrote to Margaret Ballinger, who had remained in South Africa to carry on her husband's work. " We went from Chelsea to Victoria and Victoria to Regent Street, and ended up at Austin Reed's headquarters just on closing time ! However, we found something and went back to Stewart's to join the others. Everyone turned up but William and we were sure he had gone to sleep in my flat as he was very tired, so I told him to have a bath and rest ! So we rang up to wake him, but he had just started and did get to us in time to gulp a chop, and we all ran to the train and put them in. So we hope they got to Geneva all well this morning. But *what* a day for them ! "

She did not appear to regard the series of fatiguing obligations as " a day " for herself, but even over the hurried meal Ballinger noticed her pallor.

" Look here," he asked, " are you taking care of yourself properly ? "

She waved the question aside.

" I'm all right," she said. " It's you who have to take care of yourself. You're much more important than I am."

Later, on Ballinger's return, she gave him an account of herself which was nearer the truth, but when he had sailed she continued to appear at committee meetings of the Friends of Africa until a few weeks before her death. The last that she attended was held at Lord Sanderson's house near Sloane Square in the late summer of 1935. Creech Jones and Julius Lewin had now taken over full responsibility for the organisation, and through the arrangements that she had made with them, Winifred was assured that her work would go on. She and Creech Jones walked together down the King's Road, Chelsea, discussing his plans for the future. They were her plans no longer, but she knew she had given to South Africa a voice that would make articulate the needs and aspirations of African natives in the time to come.

Early in September she showed me a letter which Ballinger had written her on August 4th from the *Balmoral Castle* ; it told her that the " usual ostracism " had been tempered as far as Madeira by the presence on board of Naomi Mitchison and her husband and several of their friends.

" Dear William ! Dear Naomi ! " she commented appreciatively.

It was the last of Ballinger's letters that she was ever to read.

Eighteen months after Winifred's death, a group of native workers known as " The Eastern Circle of the Cape Province " nominated Margaret Ballinger, who had the necessary qualification by domicile for this district, as a candidate for the South African House of Assembly. Under the Native Representation Act of 1936, which then came into operation for the first time, the natives were to be represented in the House by three Members of Parliament. William Ballinger, unable to offer himself as a candidate, identified himself with his wife's campaign. Enthusiastically assisted by Etheldreda Lewis, he was responsible for obtaining the support of many African workers.

This first experiment in native representation had brought to the surface a number of candidates whose enthusiasm for the native cause had never before been conspicuous, and Margaret Ballinger found herself confronted by five male opponents. The enormous district which she had to canvass covered five hundred square miles, and the Ballingers took over a month to visit every part of the constituency. Travelling was difficult and inconveniently adventurous ; often they had to leave the main roads and find their way along veld tracks and washed-out rock-strewn paths to agricultural villages and native kraals. In spite of these obstacles they held nearly a hundred meetings, and drove three thousand miles in the car which was Winifred's wedding gift. Supporters of the Friends of Africa and several South African women's societies helped to finance the campaign.

As Margaret Ballinger was the first woman to be nominated by a native electorate for a Parliamentary contest, the opposition began by assuring the natives that it was against their tradition to be represented by a woman. But the native electors were less impressed by this propaganda than by Margaret Ballinger's eloquent, ringing honesty — " which," wrote Etheldreda Lewis, " even the most subtle of Natives is impressed by after his encounters with some of the candidates." Many electors suggested that a woman might restore to them the rights which had been stolen by men.

" It was the great White Queen who gave us the vote," they said. " Men have for years been gradually taking the vote from us. . . . Perhaps a woman will save the Bantu."

So on June 8th, 1937, they returned Margaret Ballinger to the House of Assembly for five years as one of the first native representatives of the Cape Province, with a majority of 157 votes over her four opponents.

" It is a magnificent outcome of Winifred's work," Mr. Creech Jones wrote to me a few days later. And to all of us who were supporting the Friends of Africa for love of her memory and in sure and certain hope of ultimate human justice, this simultaneous victory for her native policy and her faith in the powers of women seemed at last to justify the long campaign in which the social reformer had sacrificed so many of the books that the artist would have written.

Margaret Ballinger herself had already recognised Winifred's share in the political triumph which made her one of South Africa's leading women. When the first appeal was launched for the Memorial Fund which will perpetuate Winifred's work in South Africa by the foundation of a library for Johannesburg natives, she published a beautiful tribute to her in the *Johannesburg Star*.

" From the time," she wrote, " of her visit to South Africa in 1926, Winifred Holtby was firmly convinced that the last, because the most disastrous, challenge to the principles of justice and equality might come from this continent of Africa. She saw in the problem of the relationship of black and white the ultimate trial of our power to interpret and apply the doctrine of universal charity, involving in its failure the failure of our whole achievement. She recognised in South Africa the key to the situation, since here race contacts are oldest and natural conditions bring black and white into a closer and more permanent proximity than is possible elsewhere ; and with character and determination she set herself to assist in the fight to maintain what existed of the liberal principle here as a first step to its extension throughout the rest of the continent. . . . The Friends of Africa, conscious of all that they owe to her vision and energy, and knowing something of what she gave to Africa and Africans, feel that the most fitting tribute to her memory would be some recognition of this work of hers which epitomised all the greatness of her service in the cause of mankind."

CHAPTER XVI

"DIRECTOR, 'TIME AND TIDE'"

THE GRUDGING GHOST

Had I loved you more, you might
  Meetly rob my days of light.
Had we loved through steadfast years
  Gently then had flowed my tears.

But, unanswering heart to heart,
  Lived we all our days apart.
Love was nothing in our mind
  Save desire to be kind.

You are dead, and still I stand
  In the gold autumnal land.
Still I see the barley sheaves
  And the dance of fallen leaves.

You are dead, and still I meet
  Kindly faces in the street.
Laughter, music, talk and wine
  Still are sweet and still are mine.

Grudging ghost, why must you steal
  Joy from all these joys I feel?
Must you take from day to day
  Gaiety and youth away?

Must you still while seasons run
  Cast your shadow on the sun?
I have nothing more to give.
  Sleep, ah, sleep, and let me live.

WINIFRED HOLTBY
The Observer, 1928

ON JULY 17th, 1926, Winifred sat wrapped up in a rug
on the deck of the S.S. *Barrabool*, watching the leisurely

movement of the South Coast through a calm, silver afternoon. Folkestone, Dover, Deal and Broadstairs appeared as a dado of white cliffs and emerald grass ; France emerged as a pale violet haze gently stirred by the tranquil wind. The previous midnight she had stood on the boat deck and gazed upon the green and red lights of ships, like constellations on a dark sky, shaming the stars.

Only when she reached the peace of the slow-going third-class boat had she fully realised what a turmoil her tour had been, and how thoroughly exhausted she was. Not the least part of the strain had probably been due to something that she did not then appreciate — the effort of her youth to maintain its dignity and justify its convictions against older sceptics and critics who had tended, often unconsciously, to discredit her ideas because their exponent was immature. She had celebrated her twenty-eighth birthday just before she caught the boat.

" My real difficulty for the past six months has been my pseudo-lionism," she wrote to me ; " a sort of semi-respectful, semi-contemptuous, largely indifferent acquaintance. . . . I feel as though I had been buried in the provinces — and so I have, but provinces 6000 miles away and 300 years backwards."

The third-class ship, she told me, had been clean, adequate, austere as a hospital waiting-room, and not dissimilar in odour and appearance. There was nowhere to put her clothes, but then she had needed no clothes ; something cool for the tropics, something warm for the Bay, and there you were. The meals had satisfied her appetite without disturbing her digestion, and as a Yorkshire woman she had particularly appreciated high-tea at 5.30, with its banquet of herrings, corned-beef, pickles, jam and seed-buns. But the best meal of all was the bed-time snack of cheese and biscuits, supplemented by the passenger's own tea made in picnic-baskets, eaten on the hatches under the stars while the more sophisticated drank Vermouth at 3d. a glass and the more energetic danced to the gramophone.

As for the company, it couldn't have been livelier. Horse-dealers, boxers, shopkeepers, teachers, publicans, and fat comfortable ladies known to everyone as " Ma " — what more could you ask ? There was a giant Griqualand farmer called Bullocky, who danced with a wild elephantine splendour, and had once won a live bullock by eating a leg of mutton at a sitting, for a bet. Finally, she had conversed with a burglar known as Jock, who was being deported from Australia for illicit attentions to a safe. He was dark, with a romantic forelock, an agreeable voice and an engaging squint, but when she sat beside him at a ship's concert he snubbed her.

" Who's yer bit of skirt, Jock ? " the friend in the next seat had inquired.

Jock answered casually : " She's none o' mine. Too long i' the tooth for me."

Not even this disquieting episode had ended her adventures, for she and two shipboard friends — a Greek journalist and a Scandinavian stenographer — had nearly lost the boat after spending an agreeable afternoon on the Grand Canary, killing mosquitoes and inspecting a Bishop's heart pickled in spirits in the Cathedral crypt. As they ate ices in a tolerably clean restaurant, they heard from afar the shriek of a ship's siren.

" Dear me ! " exclaimed the Greek. " Does anyone know the time ? "

Looking from the verandah over the tossing water, they saw the *Barrabool* two miles away weighing anchor and puffing clouds of sinister smoke.

" The next P. and O.," the Greek observed, " calls here in about a week, I think. We'd better run ! "

They ran. On the quay a few Spaniards lounged in the sun, and to them the Greek explained — in French, German, English, Czech and Afrikaans, for Spanish was not one of his five languages — that they must have a boat. After several minutes wasted on misunderstandings, the boat arrived. It was a motor-boat, and the ferocious Spaniard with huge moustaches who steered it told them that their transport would cost £3. They had three shillings between them, but they promised the rest on a Cash-on-Delivery basis. The sea was rough, but Winifred, like other alarmed travellers, discovered that fear is the best remedy for sea-sickness. They caught the ship. They scrambled up the swinging ladder. How the Greek settled with the boatman Winifred never knew, for she had now only 15s. in her possession and he never allowed her to pay him back.

At Tilbury my mother met her, and she spent a night in Kensington before going on to Yorkshire. Amongst other accumulated documents, she found there a sheaf of letters from me. I was due back from the United States in mid-August, and as American publishers and editors had universally presented a barbed-wire entanglement of opposition to the literary offerings of an unknown English-woman, G. had agreed that I should spend the next half year in London to recover the lost contacts at home. Thanks to one of those idiotic misgivings which long separation provokes, I had found — Heaven knows how or where — some imaginary lack of response in Winifred's vivid, delight-ful letters, and had written suggesting a little sadly that perhaps she might not want to share the flat again during my six months in England.

She sought to dismiss these unworthy suspicions by an eager attempt to explain her own psychology.

"In one way I am self-sufficient; I can live; I can enjoy my life; see colours; hear music and voices; con-ceive ideas, taste new experiences, all with true zest and all alone ! . . . You must remember that, though superficially affectionate, my real nature is cold. I do not find demon-strative intimacy an easy thing. . . . This is probably a mean and ungenerous spirit which hesitates to surrender an iota of its selfish integrity. I do not excuse it. I am only trying to explain. But this inarticulateness, this inhibition against the expression of love, is always ready to rise up in me. . . . I wish that it were otherwise. I wish that I had not this subconscious desire to possess myself completely.

. . . I think that all love is gain. Only at times, an instinct beyond thought comes between me and the expression of love."

To her final reassurance, no word could have been added. " It is true that I love other people . . . that I find interest in almost every chance acquaintance — the people whom I met in Africa, or on the boat. But you are you. And because you are you, there is part of me with which, in Marguerite's words to Faust, ' I need thee every hour.' . . . Nothing could change me except your changing. Not your attitude towards me, I mean, but towards life. . . . I have gained more from your companionship than I shall ever tell or know. What you mean to me I can never make you see, for you are too humble beneath your thousand vanities."

Whether this was really true, I do not know ; I only record it because she said it. No one, least of all myself, is worth such pure rarity of devoted love. No treasure in heaven or earth can replace it, or atone for its loss.

A month later, Winifred went to Southampton to meet me on the *Majestic*. I was travelling alone, for G. had to attend a Conference in New Hampshire, and we were both anxious that I should pay my annual visit to Geneva. He was following by a later boat for a few weeks in England.

After the heavy, intense heat of New York in summer I was sallow and jaded ; my trousseau garments had become crushed and dishevelled with much packing, and as soon as I saw Winifred waving her hand beside my mother on the dock, I recalled the overwhelming consciousness of her vitality that I had felt when I first met her. The gladness and appreciation with which I now welcomed it was due not only to the friendship that we shared, but to the profound change in Winifred herself. At Oxford, for all her eager generosity, she had sometimes been crude, flamboyant, a little gauche, a little garrulous ; now she was poised and beautiful, confident and self-contained. In all essentials she might have been ten years older than the girl with whom I had taken Schools in 1921.

At my parents' flat that evening, I could not cease from watching her happy, mobile face. From America I had sent her as a birthday present a turquoise matrix necklace, with a pendant carved in strange symbolic flowers ; now, against her dinner dress of heavy black silk, its vivid colour enhanced the beauty of her blue eyes and her shining hair, made more radiantly golden by the South African sun. After dinner she showed me some carved wooden animals, the work of natives, which she had brought back from the Transvaal ; a slim, striped crocodile, a porcupine with spikes like sharpened matchsticks, a surprised-looking antelope, and a primitive horse which she had christened " Homer " because he was blind and very long.

In after years these animals had a too-adventurous history. When my children arrived and grew old enough to toddle, the grotesque creatures fascinated them irresistibly, and though I protested against their use as playthings, Winifred could never bear to restrain the eager, covetous fingers. Gradually the animals lost their tails, their ears, their feet, and ceased to be ornamental. The porcupine vanished altogether ; the others disappeared into cupboards. To-day only the long-tailed, blunt-nosed crocodile and two mutilated torsos survive to recall Winifred's exotic mantelpiece after her return from Africa.

On September 2nd, following her holiday in Yorkshire, we went to Geneva for ten days and saw Germany admitted to the League of Nations. Winifred sat in the Press gallery as representative of the *South African Women's Magazine* and the *South African Ladies' Pictorial*, and I found a seat near her on the strength of an article for *Time and Tide*. From these high vantage points in the *Salle de la Réformation* we looked down upon the bald head and flushed face of Gustav Stresemann, the much-enduring German statesman who had remarked that if the victorious Allies would make him only one substantial concession, he could save the peace of Europe for our generation. Like the rest of the world

Winifred and I were still living in the period of confidence. We believed that peace was saved when we saw Aristide Briand ascend the rostrum, hold out his arms to the German delegate, and cry in the golden voice of his superb oratory : " *C'est fini, la guerre entre nous !* "

When G. had returned to America after his brief visit to England, Winifred and I went back to the flat in Maida Vale. Though I missed him sadly, we both found it pleasant after the mingled stimulus and fatigue of constant travel to resume for a time the old shared life of regular writing and speaking. She was now excitedly at work on *The Land of Green Ginger*, but as each of us needed money we seized eagerly upon every journalistic commission that came in our direction.

Strangely enough, our months of absence—or perhaps the new experiences with which absence had provided us— appeared to have created a complete change of attitude on the part of several editors, and in a few weeks we both had as much work as we could fit into our crowded days. Three journals especially kept us constantly busy—the *Yorkshire Post*, the *Manchester Guardian*, and *Time and Tide*.

For Winifred the *Yorkshire Post* was an obvious contact. That autumn we came to know a member of its staff, Violet Scott-James, whose husband, R. A. Scott-James, was then a leader-writer on the *Daily Chronicle*, and afterwards edited the *London Mercury*. Winifred, with her East Riding background, soon became a valued contributor, and for the rest of her life continued to send the *Yorkshire Post* periodic articles and reviews. I wrote for the paper too, and in spite of its Conservatism and a long anti-feminist tradition, was invited to contribute some of its editorials during the summer of 1928 when several members of the regular staff were on holiday. It was one of the pleasantest and most courteous newspapers that we ever worked for, and we came to know very well several members of its London office in Fleet Street.

The *Manchester Guardian*, with its international reputation and high journalistic standards, had proved in the early nineteen-twenties quite impervious to the onslaughts of two optimistic beginners, but now the barriers suddenly fell, and the magazine editor, Madeleine Linford, sent us agreeable, encouraging letters. It was particularly satisfying to write for the *Guardian* since on most questions our opinions were similar to its own, and the magazine page became our favourite — and apparently favoured — stamping ground when we had anything special to say. For eight years I wrote regularly for this page, and Winifred, though less frequently, for almost as long ; she also contributed stories and travel articles to the miscellany column.

With Lady Rhondda and *Time and Tide* Winifred was already in close contact before she went to South Africa. I also received kindly encouragement from the paper at the time when I most needed it, and for two or three years wrote fiction reviews and occasional articles on current problems or the position of women. These regular contributions ended after 1930, and gradually grew more and more sporadic until they ceased altogether. But for Winifred *Time and Tide* became, like her work for Africa, one of those lifelong major activities which filled her thoughts and dominated her sky.

Immediately Winifred returned to England, Lady Rhondda invited her to become a Director of the paper. She accepted with humble, astonished enthusiasm, and was appointed the youngest member of its distinguished Board. Her eager youthful delight in attending the regular Board dinners at Lady Rhondda's flat was quite unconcealed ; everybody wore their best clothes, and she bought one or two new evening dresses in which to enjoy the still awe-inspiring society of Cicely Hamilton, E. M. Delafield, Professor Winifred Cullis and Rebecca West. To the end of her life Winifred enjoyed these functions, and when serious illness permitted only occasional late nights, she reserved her energies specially for Board dinners. Her new official position continued to fill her with pride and amazement. When the paper moved from a small Fleet Street office to

a house in Bloomsbury Street, she had some cards specially
printed which she used at public functions :

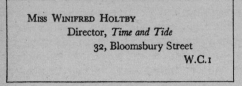

Miss Winifred Holtby
Director, *Time and Tide*
32, Bloomsbury Street
W.C.1

Her work as Director soon became inseparable from her
growing friendship with Lady Rhondda.

" She liked me," Winifred confessed candidly, " because
I was a farmer's daughter with a racy tongue, a fund of
not-too-vulgar tales, a certain knack for writing useful stuff,
and because I neither embarrassed her nor she me."

As Lady Rhondda frankly admitted in a series of articles,
" Some Letters from Winifred Holtby," published in April
1936, many subjects which interested Winifred deeply made
no special appeal to her.   Despite her appreciation of north-
country raciness, the agricultural background of the
Yorkshire yeomen-farmers was outside her experience,
which perhaps explained her indifference to Winifred's
early novels.   Nor did she share Winifred's interest in African
natives, though from affection for her she contributed nobly
to the Ballinger Fund.   She and Winifred had also been
brought up on totally different economic levels.   Their
standards with regard to comfort, food, houses, furnishing
and travel accommodation were, and remained, completely
dissimilar, since increasing success had no effect whatsoever
upon Winifred's methods of living and working and her
habit of giving nearly all her money away.   Winifred
once told me with amusement that after they had lunched
together at restaurants on *Time and Tide* press days for several
years, Lady Rhondda remarked, " I can't think why your
bill always comes to so much less than mine," and learnt
to her astonishment that from sheer force of habit Winifred
always chose the cheapest dish on the menu whether she
liked it or not.

But in the working life of London the two of them had almost everything in common. Both were dynamically interested in books, in politics, in getting things done, in social philosophy, and in people — above all, in people ; in the writers, scientists, politicians and leaders of contemporary movements who counted most in the England of the nineteen-twenties and thirties. Perhaps more than anyone else on the staff of *Time and Tide*, Winifred shared the desire " to find, to test and to spread the customs and the ideas that would be health-giving and life-saving," with which Lady Rhondda had founded the paper.

Lady Rhondda regarded Winifred as a brilliant journalist and an excellent satirist, but never believed that the novel was her medium until the publication of *South Riding*. She thought that Winifred was wasting her time writing fiction, and would be better employed in working entirely for *Time and Tide* and one or two of the other journals which soon clamoured for her articles.

" I did not think she had it in her to become a novelist," she confesses in her article on Winifred's letters.

When *South Riding* appeared she reversed her judgment, realising that Winifred, like all writers who possess the quality of greatness, had learned her trade slowly, and with her last novel was reaching only the beginning of a career that might have placed her high among the creators of permanent literature.

Winifred was damped but not intimidated by Lady Rhondda's verdict on her novels. The fact that a few people whose judgment she also respected — Edward Garnett, Stella Benson, St. John Ervine, Phyllis Bentley, Violet Scott-James — thought her books had merit was sufficient encouragement. She would, I am convinced, have gone on writing novels if none of us had believed in them at all.

Apart from her books, she found more pleasure and stimulus in her work for *Time and Tide* than in any other single activity. It kept her in touch with the surge and sweep of current happenings ; it gave her the satisfaction of a worth-while job well done ; and it brought her into con-

tact with famous men and women whose work and significance she humbly believed to be infinitely greater than her
own. During her periods of convalescence after 1931, her
refusal to give up *Time and Tide* was at least as adamant as her
determination to go on living in Chelsea. She felt that
without the paper she would be cut off from the main currents
of life, an isolated exile, dead before her time. Sometimes,
in the moods of fatigue and depression produced by ill-
health, she found in journalism the temptation that ephemeral
work always offers to the person who does it supremely well
without effort, but must labour slowly and with pain to
produce literature of lasting value.

" Oh, but I could so easily become just your lieutenant,"
she wrote to Lady Rhondda after her first attack of illness
in 1931. " You don't know how often I've been on the
brink of suggesting it. If I could concentrate entirely on
Time and Tide I could, I know, be more than a little use.
And it's work I love. I enjoy it so. You strike sparks out
of me.

" I could get well and come to town, and, without the
perpetual drag of trying to do my own work, that would be
easy. It wouldn't tire me. What is tiring, I know, is this
perpetually divided state — the private nunnery of the mind
into which I must go to do anything creative, and the
incessant call of the passing moment which makes the good
journalist — and the good friend and the good political
plotter. I was trying to be all at once."

The squib-like vivacity of Winifred's regular reviews and
articles gave *Time and Tide* a quality peculiar to itself.
It was largely this which earned her the description of " the
most brilliant journalist in London," and any editor might
well have imagined that her true work lay here. The
vitality of these contributions was only equalled by the speed
and verve with which she tossed them off. If we turn back
the pages of the paper, we can still feel tears of laughter and
pain fill our eyes when we find her telling us, after describing a mistake in the identity of a town, that " there is no
need to stumble blindly about the Midlands " and recom-

mending a new series of guide-books to England's less exhilarating cities ; or come across her grave assurance, in reviewing an experimental publication by Sir Oswald Mosley, that "even a somersault is Action."

The tragedy of journalism lies in its impermanence ; the very topicality which gives it brilliance condemns it to an early death. Too often it is a process of flinging bright balloons in the path of the hurricane, a casting of priceless petals upon the rushing surface of a stream. So, at least, thought Violet Scott-James, who became, from 1926 onwards, one of Winifred's most devoted friends. Intelligent, cultured, fastidious, she believed beyond all else in the value of artistic integrity and the contemplative life, and never, perhaps, wholly understood the vehement passion for reform which every example of conspicuous injustice produced in Winifred.

Amongst Violet's friends was Edward Garnett, then the chief reader for Jonathan Cape. He shared with her his own view of Winifred's promise, and after *The Land of Green Ginger* was published Violet became interested in Winifred's novels and in these alone. She soon ceased to press the claims of the *Yorkshire Post*, for she believed that Winifred's gifts as a literary artist would soon achieve recognition if she would only step out of the turmoil and give her time and thoughts exclusively to her books. Again and again — in conversations, in letters, even in the long obituary notice which she wrote for *The Times* — she deplored the dissipation of Winifred's energies, though she came at last to realise that the responsibility lay with a concourse of claimants rather than with Winifred herself.

"People don't realise the *importance* of Winifred," she once said sadly to me after some unusually prolonged period of politics, journalism and domesticity had prevented Winifred from completing the novel of the moment. But even Violet, who perhaps understood more clearly than any of Winifred's friends that her unselfishness was the greatest enemy of her creative power, learnt when her own private problems afflicted her how difficult it was to refrain from leaning upon Winifred's understanding and practical sympathy. To Violet, as to all of us, Winifred's ready gift of generous co-operation was presented almost before she realised how deeply she needed it. Many people who in Winifred's eyes were, unlike Violet, merely acquaintances, regarded her as one of their special friends owing to the interested concentration upon their affairs of which she was capable whilst in their company.

In relation to the general public and the various journals with which she was connected, Winifred's apparently eternal patience invested her with the part of perpetual " go-between." Her files were filled with letters from enthusiasts asking her to put an article or a paragraph into one newspaper or another on subjects ranging from the Lytton Commission to legalised abortion.

" Can you get Lady Rhondda to consider noticing it in the editorial notes," runs a typical request, " or get in a letter *in your most gently persuasive vein, yourself* ? "

Publishers and their budding authors wrote to her continually, imploring her to " call attention " to the latest work of genius in the columns of *Time and Tide*, the *Yorkshire Post*, the *Nation*, or, in later years, the *News Chronicle* or *Good Housekeeping*. She replied to them all with friendly, encouraging letters which went a long way towards compensating her eager correspondents for the frequent inevitable failure to report their cherished achievement in note, letter or review.

Since Winifred died, many people have wondered where exactly her genius for friendship lay. It came, I think, from an instinctive skill in the art of human relationship which most of us acquire only after years of blunder and quarrelsome pain. St. John Ervine has said that she saw her radiance in other people, and this is undoubtedly true. But it is also true that few individuals are jet black or even neutral grey ; most of them possess their own radiance, their peculiar glamour, if the beholder's eye is benevolent enough to discern it. Winifred realised that the desire to

" be good " is a fundamental part of each normal person's make-up. It may be overlaid by pessimism, camouflaged by cynicism, transformed by bitterness, but the observer who perceives it beneath the trappings can usually count on a gracious response.

Winifred had an infallible consciousness of the other person's standpoint ; usually she put her friends' wishes first and her own second. When she wrote letters she invariably began by referring to her correspondents' interests and problems. If she answered the telephone she always replied, however disastrously the call had interrupted her, as though the speaker at the other end were the one person whom she wanted to hear. In conversation she seldom discussed her own troubles ; she encouraged other people to talk about theirs. She was never offended ; she seemed to be quite without the apparatus of sensitive pride and vulnerable dignity used by the person who lacks confidence to defend his ego against a world of which he is deeply suspicious. Meanness and irrationality were the only qualities that she feared, and she always took for granted that people were generous and rational until they had proved beyond doubt that her trust was misplaced.

When, very occasionally, someone did her a service, she promptly expressed her delighted appreciation ; her very surprise (for she was not without her own brand of cynicism) added to its spontaneous sincerity. Although, especially in her last years, she had a marked capacity for trenchant criticism, she seldom criticised individuals for their conduct, and only then after the most thorough search for extenuating circumstances. She never committed the deadly sin of undermining another person's self-confidence, for she knew that self-confidence takes half a lifetime to build up but can be destroyed in half an hour.

The result was a gracious magnanimity, a never-failing charity, which evoked love by the warmth and generosity of the love that it gave. A recent volume of popular psychology puts to its readers, as a test of their ability to win affection : " If you died to-morrow, how many people would come to your funeral ? " In Winifred's case, we know the answer. Midday on Tuesday in London is a busy hour and St. Martin-in-the-Fields is a large church, but at Winifred's funeral service it was crowded to the doors. Half the congregation were people who hardly knew her, but many of them wept as bitterly as though they were mourning the best friend they had ever lost. Probably very few reflected that if they had wept less and ! ft her alone more, she might, even in her short life, have produced a larger quantity of the permanent literary work which embodied her dearest aspirations.

At the end of March 1927, I returned to America for a few months, and Winifred came to Southampton to see me off.

" I shan't miss you because I shall be too busy," she wrote the day after I sailed. " But I think about you a great deal, and with continual love and joy. The thought of you is a pleasure to me which has no overshadowing of pain. Utter confidence and tenderness in another brings rest and joy alone. There is no pain, as in passion. Be happy."

She had heard, she told me, from Sarah Gertrude Millin, upon whom had fallen the task of arranging the future of her mother and her two young brothers after her father's death.

" It is rather consoling," Winifred confessed, " to know that even the great and the ' arrived ' are not immune from domestic complications—and yet infuriating to reflect how the efficient must always be handicapped by other people's dependence upon their efficiency."

Her solitary life was again full of work and obligations. The prospect of votes for women at twenty-one was coming so near that politicians now began seriously to compete for the support of the " under thirties." At a meeting of the Equal Political Rights Campaign Committee, where she represented Lady Rhondda, Winifred was persuaded, as one of the unenfranchised, to organise a series of open-air meetings in Hyde Park. She sat on hard seats through interminable speeches, harangued amused, sympathetic crowds from collapsible platforms, lobbied Members of Parliament in the House of Commons, talked to policemen, walked in poster parades, and always regretted that she was enfranchised by nature ten days before the Royal Assent made the Equal Franchise Bill law in July 1928. Her knowledge of women's organisations was intimate, their use of her services frequently excessive, and in spite of her deep sympathy with their aims, she described them in her fourth novel, *Poor Caroline*, with a satiric candour which left some of them gasping.

That year which marked the end of the decade following the War gave no hint of the European setback to women's liberties that was to come five years afterwards. Few surviving records read so forlornly as the Bills and resolutions of a past epoch, but the agendas of committees on which Winifred served, and the printed copies of measures for which she pressed, at least provoke the reflection that all this effort is now embodied in legislation which, in spite of recent reaction, has altered the whole complexion of life for millions of men and women. Some understanding of this achievement by our period of history came to Winifred and myself when we attended the All Night Watch Service for Mrs. Pankhurst in June 1928, and together kept part of the vigil beside her coffin in St. John's Church, Smith Square. To us, grown to maturity after the suffrage campaign, she had existed mainly as a legend, but a sense of obligation for our heritage of comparative freedom and equality brought us through the midnight streets of Westminster to the shadowed church where her body was lying in state.

In April 1927, Winifred wrote me that she had just interviewed Storm Jameson, whom she had not previously met, for the " Women of the Day " series in the *Yorkshire Post*. In my reply from America, I enclosed for *Time and Tide* a review of Storm Jameson's new novel, *The Lovely Ship*. I added that I was probably going to have a baby.

Winifred can hardly have welcomed the prospect of a

new disturbance in her domestic arrangements, but she wrote me an affectionate letter characteristically describing the prospective infant as a " sauce of joy." When G. decided to change his American professorship to a half-time post so that our family could be born and reared in England, she suggested joining the household from which he would so often be absent. The Maida Vale flat, we agreed, would certainly be too small when a baby and its equipment were added to our accumulating books, so even before our return in June she began tentatively house-hunting.

In September we moved to an upper maisonnette in Nevern Place off the Earl's Court Road, where a climb up an appalling flight of dark linoleum-covered stairs led to several pleasant rooms with south-facing windows. Winifred was doomed that year to the nervously exacting society of pregnant women, for Grace, with whom she spent a summer holiday in Scotland, also expected a companion for the baby Anne.

During the autumn Jonathan Cape published *The Land of Green Ginger* — a story of which a correspondent wrote to Winifred seven years afterwards : " It is, I think, the kind of book that one reads without realising how deep it is going, and finds oneself remembering even details of it long afterwards."

After rejecting *The Runners*, John Lane had refused this book also the previous April. As Winifred's literary agent had warned her, they disliked its realistic descriptions of tuberculosis. Feeling especially sympathetic because I had been unable to find a publisher for a small travel book of my own, I wrote her from the United States : " It is very queer how our fortunes run together — we both got two novels off in the days when no one would look at our articles, and now that people actually demand our articles, no one will take our books ! "

But she was luckier than I, for Jonathan Cape's acceptance soon followed, and the firm of McBride published the book in America. I had suggested that she should modify her graphic descriptions of illness, but even this proved to be unnecessary. Cape gave her an advance of £30 on the day of publication ; it was not yet a spectacular sum, but we had grown so accustomed to expecting no profits from our books that the amount quite impressed us.

Like *The Crowded Street*, *The Land of Green Ginger* had only modest sales, but the setting of the story, being divided between Hull and the North Riding, did create some interest among literary specialists in Yorkshire. One of these, the deputy chief librarian at Bradford, who lectured on Yorkshire authors, asked Winifred for biographical information about herself and her stories. In reply she sent him a complete list of place names distinguishing between real and imaginary localities in her Yorkshire novels.

For the light that it throws on her personality and the continual conflict of her thoughts, this novel is among the most illuminating of Winifred's works. As she had foreseen in South Africa, the story gathers up her travel experiences into a series of beautifully designed pictures with all irrelevancies omitted. The natural verbosity which tormented her at Oxford had at last proved an asset by making her dissatisfied until her work was purged of every superfluous excrescence.

To the heroine of the story, Joanna Leigh, Winifred gave her own character and imagination unsharpened by her intellect. From beginning to end the book sparkles with tiny flashes of self-knowledge. Like Winifred, Joanna possesses an inexhaustible capacity for exhilaration by small colourful pleasures ; she also shares Winifred's gay freedom from the social tyranny which labels cheerful, unconventional actions as " not done." But perhaps her most remarkable asset is the buoyant inability to be offended, which once caused Winifred in a review to quote appreciatively a remark by Lord Balfour : " I am quite unable to harbour resentment for long, because I always forget the reason why I was originally angry."

Unlike most of us, Winifred and her heroine faced the fact that to be supersensitive, easily hurt and constantly in need of comfort, is not evidence of superior quality, but merely an exacting form of anti-social egotism.

One or two reviewers criticised the sequence of catastrophes piled upon Joanna's undaunted shoulders, but Winifred knew that she did not exaggerate the cruelty of life. Through the experiences of friends in South Africa, she had vicariously confronted the multiplication of disasters, the raining of storm after storm from ceaselessly threatening skies. Before long, her family and her own fate were to repeat the story.

Winifred dedicated *The Land of Green Ginger* to " A Philosopher in Peshawar who said that he wanted something to read," for Bill had now fulfilled his often-repeated intention of joining the Air Force. In South Africa the fascination of work and travel — like all similar preoccupations — had relegated him to the background of her mind, and she returned to find that he had gone to India, sharing both the voyage and the humble position of aircraftsman with his squadron companion, T. E. Lawrence.

Though the book was dedicated to Bill, its gay, vivid, tragic, undaunted theme has less to say of love than of death. Winifred was still a girl under thirty when the story was completed, yet the consciousness that death is always near and means the final relinquishment of every desired contest is conveyed with a strange haunting clarity. As though she knew that she herself was to be cheated of the long years which she coveted and would have filled with joy and creation, she faced the problem of human mortality and found everlasting life only in the fecundity of the imperfect flesh.

" The dead lie in their graves, Joanna thought. They who desired life and conquest and activity have sleep at last, perhaps, and calm decay. Life moved on, away from Teddy, away from the struggles which had been so real and so intense to him. Life made her, who had been his friend, his companion, his lover, inheritor of his immortality."

On the shortest day of that year, the child was born whom Winifred had thought of as "beloved" even before she knew that his existence was probable. The evening before his birth, I wrote an article for the *Manchester Guardian* which I left unrevised on my desk when I went to the nursing-home early next morning. Finding it there Winifred revised and typed it for me, much distressed by a doctor's discouraging but mistaken report which suggested to her imagination that I might never return to type it for myself.

That evening, when the boy was two hours old, G. came to see me. Winifred, who had accompanied him through the frosty streets, was allowed into my room afterwards by some oversight of the matron, who to my intense exasperation excluded her for the next four days. Dizzy as I still felt, the sight of her radiant face cheered me like a tonic.

"Oh darling! you are *clever*!" she cried with excited relief when she learnt that the business of producing the baby had been executed without disastrous consequences, and she and G. walked back arm in arm to Nevern Place to celebrate John Edward's arrival.

On her next visit she picked up the human atom in her arms and examined him with fascinated curiosity; he was the youngest thing that she had ever handled.

"His head's just like a pussy-willow," she observed dispassionately, and from that moment she became his discreet but devoted slave.

No "childless spinster" was ever better acquainted with babies than Winifred; in addition to the nursery atmosphere which she sampled during the next few years in London, domestic crises at home frequently called her to Yorkshire to help with the care of Grace's two little girls. Yet she seemed quite deliberately to seek — though not always to enjoy — the society of the very young, recognising that their presence brings a knowledge of facts both hard and tender, and destroys many sentimental illusions. She believed that not only the women but the men who had no contact with children lived in an artificial world which lacked an essential part of experience.

" Babies are a nuisance, of course," she wrote me at the end of 1926 when I was making up my mind to embark on a family. " But so does everything seem to be that is worth while — husbands and books and committees and being loved and everything. We have to choose between barren ease and rich unrest — or rather, one does not choose. Life somehow chooses. If I were you, I would be rich. Even if it ultimately kills you, you'll have been alive and we all have to die, even those who never lived."

This confidence that motherhood was worth-while even for women who had much else to live for, sprang from no sentimental theorising. Long before John Edward was born, Margaret de Coundouroff and Grace's Anne had taught Winifred that pink toes and golden curls are not the most conspicuous aspects of babyhood for those in charge of it. When a friend came to our flat shortly before her marriage, Winifred exhorted her with realistic earnestness.

" Take my advice. If you ever find you're going to have a baby — Buy a Mangle ! "

Often the habits of babies bored her, as — if we are honest — they bore us all, but with John she never appeared impatient, and judging by her letters she never was. Of the five babies, beginning with Margaret and ending with my daughter Shirley, whom Winifred knew from birth, John was the only boy. He became an attractive child, with large dark eyes and a mop of nut-brown curls, and the rarity value of his sex perhaps inspired her deep affection for him.

" John Edward, the little boy, is a radiant joy to me. He is so beautiful and intelligent," she wrote to Jean McWilliam when she took charge of the children in 1934; and to me in America : " Shirley is a darling, of course, but my sweet John ! "

Often she commandeered him on the nurse's half-day, or took him on clinic afternoons to the Chelsea Babies' Club, which was so largely responsible for the good health of both my children. One picture that will live with me always is a memory of Winifred pushing John along the Cromwell Road to Kensington Gardens on a summer afternoon. Dressed in a thin garment of light blue crêpe and a white hat over her golden hair, she strode up the long sunny street as though she were steering the perambulator across the Yorkshire wolds. John, aged eighteen months, wore a blue and white cotton overall and a linen hat. The swift swinging movement excited him ; with his back to Winifred he jumped joyfully up and down as each new curb of the pavement was successfully negotiated. Blue, white and gold, the fairy-like cavalcade soon vanished into the warm shadowy distance.

Winifred had at least the satisfaction of inspiring a reciprocal affection — and few things are more rewarding than a child's open uncalculating devotion. She was the best-loved figure of John's early years ; I can still hear his voice ecstatically crying " Oh — *Auntie* ! " when she returned home after her first period of illness in 1931, still see his unsteady feet tumbling over each other as he rushed along the passage to greet her. Her death when he was seven was the type of blow that parents would give their lives to spare a small sensitive child. For weeks his half-concealed heart-break made him silent and miserable. To-day, at eleven, he remembers her vividly, but still cannot speak of her.

The joys of motherhood are not excessively apparent during the first few weeks of a baby's life. Many times during the early part of 1928, I was moved by an unworthy envy of Winifred's success, popularity, freedom, and the glowing confidence of manner that they gave her. In the autumn, when I stole ten days from John Edward for a brief holiday in Monte Carlo, a friend of the Smeterlins mentioned the impression that Winifred had made while visiting them in the summer ; she had come into their room like a fresh breeze from the country, sparkling with health and beauty and gaiety. No one seemed further from mortal sickness and early death, though the latent trouble was already at work. Her zest for life had a physical as well as a spiritual quality; in the end it kept her alive and mentally alert long after a less vital woman would have died or existed with a clouded mind.

As first lieutenant on *Time and Tide*, Winifred found her social contacts changing in both quality and quantity. Tied as I was to a child, and depressed by the sense of frustration and fatigue which is an after-effect of childbirth, I probably exaggerated the extent to which she was being " taken up " by the famous. Just as I now have recurrent dreams that she is not dead but has decided, for a reason that differs with each nightmare, to live permanently out of my reach, so I began to dream that we were both back at college, but when I suggested sharing a flat she was hesitant and haughty. Anxiously she ridiculed these illusions of ill-health, for though she was excited — as any young woman making her way in the world would be — by the enlargement of experience involved in meeting the owners of international reputations, she was incapable of realising that in a few years' time her books would have enabled her to know these personalities in her own right and on an equal footing.

She did her best to share with me such few acquaintances as she dared to invite to the humble maisonnette in Earl's Court, and the crowded little sitting-room managed to hold quite a number of memorable week-end parties. Incongruously enough, it was there that Rebecca West met her husband, Henry Andrews, whom she married in 1930. Among the *Time and Tide* directors, Winifred found Rebecca both the most fascinating and the most alarming. Henry Andrews, a New College friend and contemporary of G.'s, had long been an admirer of Rebecca's books, and after Winifred went on the Board of *Time and Tide* he persistently urged us to arrange a meeting. Tentatively we invited Rebecca to the maisonnette. She came, and Henry spent the evening on a cushion at her feet.

When the party broke up, we apologised for his uninterrupted attentions, anxiously afraid that Rebecca had been bored. But she only laughed.

"Really, I quite enjoyed it," she said gaily. "It was just like listening to a publisher's blurb!"

Henry helped her down the long flight of dark precipitous stairs, and when they reached the street he asked if he might take her home. The rest is a pleasant chapter of literary history.

Winifred's eager interest in such encounters and her animated description of them in letters (" I do love meeting important people," she wrote to Jean before she had been to South Africa and realised that one can meet too many), has occasionally led to misjudgments of her values. In his *Daily Telegraph* review of *Letters to a Friend*, Harold Nicolson wrote scornfully of " this girl who cared so much about second-rate celebrities." No doubt it is difficult for the Harold Nicolsons of this world, born in the purple and inheriting without conscious effort a perpetual sequence of life's most stimulating experiences, to realise that for the few who rise from the dead-level of provincial complacency — a background infinitely more destructive to mind and spirit than the life of the slums—the newly-acquired friendship of the famous awakens an emotion which is quite unrelated to snobbery.

The famous, after all, do lead more interesting lives, and are therefore more attractive companions, than the sons and daughters of universal suburbia (which is not a locality but a state of mind). For an intelligent young woman the stimulus of a conversation with, for example, Harold Nicolson himself, exceeds beyond any valid basis of comparison that of listening to a monologue on her querulous obsessions by a bridge-playing, servant-preoccupied matron from Marshington-on-Mud. It is only their fortunate ignorance of Marshington's suffocating mental atmosphere which prevents the Harold Nicolsons from understanding that eminent companions, for those unaccustomed to them, may be not merely a method of measuring progress but a spiritual and intellectual tonic.

But even this tonic has only a proportionate value, and Winifred, being a hard-headed Yorkshirewoman, was quick to perceive that the society of the famous has its own variety of tedium. All too soon, many celebrities lose their simplicity ; they become contemptuous of the undistinguished, impatient (sometimes excusably) with the constant supplications of the humble. A few fall into a softness of living which demands luxuries unattainable by ninety-nine per cent of the population.

When a measure of fame began to come to her, Winifred remained one of the exceptions. She realised that the obscure, if less stimulating than the famous, are more varied and infinitely more restful. She perceived that those who can afford to delegate every humble duty and are never compelled to wash up, push perambulators or even answer their own letters, grow spoiled, censorious and detached from reality. The more distinguished her public engagements became, the more obstinately her perception of fame's threat to normal decent compassion led her to share the commonplace burdens of others less fortunate. She would travel to an editorial conference direct from performing the humblest services for a sick relative ; she would hurry late to *Time and Tide* Board dinners after helping me to bath the babies and put them to bed.

Keenly as she enjoyed the brilliant gaiety of holidays on the Riviera, another mood led her to prefer the unostentatious peace of seaside lodgings in Yorkshire or Devon. The luxurious comfort of a first-class sleeper on the Blue Train never gave her the same appreciative thrill as the journey from Cape Town on the *Barrabool*. To the end of her life she was as ready to give up an evening to the African negro whom she was helping to educate or the enterprising little milliner whom she had first met as an elementary school-child in Bethnal Green, as to men and women whose names were household words.

During her final years, sorrows which she had once remorsefully regarded as the exclusive misfortunes of others came in bitter sequence to counterbalance her friendships, her achievements and her enjoyment of life.

In the early spring of 1928, an epidemic of influenza

broke out in Yorkshire. Grace's second baby was due about mid-April, but at the beginning of March, when Edith de Coundouroff was staying with us at Nevern Place, Winifred was surprised by a telegram announcing the birth of another daughter.

A letter followed to say that Grace was ill with influenza : her persistent coughing had caused the premature birth of the child. Shortly afterwards a second letter announced that the influenza had turned to pneumonia. It was succeeded almost immediately by a laconic telegram : " Better come."

Winifred and Edith went up to a Yorkshire in which roads and railway tracks were blocked by heavy falls of frozen snow. The specialist hurriedly summoned to Grace had to leave his car in a ditch and walk nine miles through the blinding storm.

He arrived too late to save her life. She had not enough resilience to fight the combined effects of pneumonia and childbirth, and at 2.30 in the morning of March 11th she died. Winifred had sat with her throughout the previous afternoon and evening ; then she returned to Cottingham and her father while her mother remained at Bridlington.

" She was slightly better last night," Winifred wrote to me. " She knew me when I was there, but ironically true to our relationship I irritated her even by going into the room, and her last words to me, when I went up for the second time with a message to the nurse, were ' Don't stare. You make me tired.' "

Next day the tiny premature baby, weighing less than six pounds, was baptised in Grace's room with her mother lying dead. The scrap of humanity seemed to Winifred so fragile and so sweet that her one preoccupation during the mournful little ceremony was the fear that it would catch cold. After Grace's funeral in the bitter March wind, she stayed in Yorkshire for two or three weeks, going through her sister's possessions and making them tidy for her nieces to inherit.

Late in the spring she came back to town, tired and

dispirited but glad to escape from the aftermath of domestic sorrow. Almost immediately, an invitation arrived from Stella Benson, again home from China, asking Winifred to go on a motor tour in Ireland with herself and her husband. I urged her to accept ; she had not seen Stella for two years, and the trip would be a change from the atmosphere of mourning and regret.

At first Winifred sent a note of refusal. She couldn't possibly take a holiday in Ireland now ; there was an accumulation of correspondence ; she had already let *Time and Tide* down for several weeks ; complications were increasing in Africa ; her parents would expect her to be available if they came to London. Then, like a sudden gale, reaction against the crippling negations of grief and remorse swept down upon her.

" Damn it !" she exclaimed, " I *will* go !"

And she tore up her letter, and went.

That motor tour and Stella's society acted like balm upon an aching wound. Winifred wrote afterwards of the wild coast and rugged hills ; the green amazing days which brought forgetfulness ; the arum lilies growing beside the Irish cabins as she had seen them grow outside the Kaffir kraals. But Grace's ghost continued to haunt her. When the late summer brought the brilliant society of the Riviera, and in Yorkshire the yellow corn stood ripe for reaping, she distilled into a poem called *The Grudging Ghost* her perpetual sense of guilt because she was still alive to enjoy the beautiful autumnal world, while Grace — who had infinitely less capacity for happiness, but would have loved her children — lay dead in her grave beside the North Sea.

Winifred herself lived only just long enough to realise that by dying Grace had perhaps served her daughters best. Brought up by their father and their grandmother, and later by an affectionate step-mother who cared for them with an energy of which their mother had never been capable, they grew into responsive, intelligent girls whose existence justified Grace's short life with its brief series of golden days.

CHAPTER XVII

THE PEAK ABOVE THE PRECIPICE

HOUSE ON FIRE

This house was built for grief.
   Sorrow alone,
Sorrow without relief
   Could make it strong,
Stiffen the crumbling clay with frequent tears,
Set firm the stone.
Impregnable throughout the weary years,
It would last long.

But since with perilous joy
   I reckless dwell,
Happiness will destroy
   Both roof and wall,
Set the tall thatch and oaken door alight,
   Till, blazing well,
Conspicuous as a torch in the dark night,
   My house will fall.

WINIFRED HOLTBY
Time and Tide, 1932

IF WINIFRED could come back to-day and be asked whether she would willingly re-live her short life with its final years of pain, I think she would reply that, intensely as she had enjoyed it all, the years 1929 and 1930 in themselves made that life worth while. Never before, in spite of periods of sorrow, had she lived so swiftly, so vehemently, so gaily. Never again was she to be capable of so large a total sum of achievement, or to enjoy, with a sense of perfect well-being unshadowed by fear, so many short but zestful holidays in pleasant sunny places.

One of the first of these holidays was a short trip to
Paris in the company of Dot McCalman and Jean McWilliam
during the Easter vacation of 1929. Dot, who had put in
three years of sound work at Somerville and finished her
course with a good Second in 1925, was now History mistress
at a school in Tonbridge ; Jean had come over for one of
her periodic holidays in England. The three of them went
for long walks together in the woods at St. Remy de
Chevreuse, where the brilliant sun through the wintry
branches gleamed gold upon the snowy clusters of anemones
in the short wet grass.

They travelled to Paris with Lady Rhondda, who had
a speaking engagement at the American Women's Club.
After leaving Calais, they began to discuss the usually artificial character of happy endings in novels.

" All you have to do," maintained Winifred, " is to keep
silence after one point of time. Any story is happy somewhere, though all really end with death."

And lightly, to prove her argument, she wrote the verses
called *Happy Ending*, which now appear the most intuitively
prophetic of her poems. In an alternative version transcribed in one of her notebooks, these verses were re-
entitled *Cynic's Song*.

She returned to find England working itself up for the
General Election of May 1929, which put the second Labour
Government into office. Throughout this election both she
and I spoke for Monica Whately, Labour candidate for
the St. Albans division of Hertfordshire. We had left
the Liberal Party for the Labour Party four years earlier,
and now discovered, like many other amateur politicians,
that there is nothing so effective as one's own speeches for
converting one to a cause. During the last ten days of the
campaign the weather turned warm and benign, with
azure skies and a light dancing wind. Canvassing in the
Hertfordshire lanes through a calm season of lovely weather
gave us a different view of active politics from the dreary
November elections in Bethnal Green during 1922 and 1923.
Like the majority of women Labour candidates, who are

given Die-hard cathedral cities and Tory agricultural areas
to fight as constituencies, Monica Whately did not win, but
the final victory of the Party was a fair compensation for
books and articles laid aside.

In the autumn of 1928, Winifred had contributed a
volume called *Eutychus or the Future of the Pulpit* to the To-day
and To-morrow Series, an edition of small half-crown
booklets which the publishers Kegan Paul were then running
with conspicuous success. She described her little essay in
satire as " A Short Treatise in the form of a Plain Dialogue,
suggested as a possible epilogue to Fénelon's *Dialogues sur
l'Éloquence.*" Its three characters, Fénelon himself, Anthony,
a young man about Bloomsbury, and Eutychus, who represents the plain man with his infinite capacity for boredom
by long discourses, debate the topic that it takes three to
make a sermon — the preacher, his authority, and the congregation. They finally agree that the authority of the
pulpit is passing to the public platform. The dialogue
sparkles with the firework-like epigrams and satiric humour
characteristic of the series, but it dates, like all pamphlets,
in its topical references.

Shortly before the General Election, Winifred brought
out another booklet entitled *A New Voter's Guide to Party
Programmes*. She designed it to answer, again in dialogue
form, the questions which a newly enfranchised young
woman voter might put to the canvassers of all three political
parties. The dialogue necessarily covered the topical issues
of the day — the Locarno treaties, British troops on the
Rhine, the reduction of armaments, reparations and international debts, the Safeguarding Duties, the raising of the
school-leaving age. This model of impartial electioneering
was based upon a wide and rapid reading of political books,
pamphlets and speeches ; the impressive list of titles in the
footnotes testifies to the thoroughness of its preparation.

Now, the election and its controversies over, Winifred
turned thankfully back to her true medium of fiction. For
some little time the theme of her fourth novel, *Poor Caroline*,
had been shaping itself in her mind, but before she began

to write it in earnest, Jan and Edith Smeterlin carried her off for another August holiday at their villa in Monte Carlo. Here, for once, she did no work, but occupied a lazy twelve-hour day in eating, sleeping, swimming, and sending me animated descriptions of temperamental Riviera society.

" People here are the most hair-raising gossipers I ever heard. Their love-affairs are recounted in detail, and probably without any accuracy at all. Tenors quarrel and threaten suicide, swear they will have each other's heart out, and are next seen going off to supper arm-in-arm. . . . On their own job, most of these musical people are thrilling. Off it, their ideas are almost exclusively confined to cannibalism. They eat each other's characters and reputations daily — a Black Mass. Edith and Jan are different — both so intelligent and sweet. . . . When women here rave about their lap-dogs, I think of John Edward and giggle. The more I see of dogs, the more I like children."

One evening the Smeterlins took her to dine with Sam Barlow, the American composer, and his wife at their ninth-century house in the fortress-village of Eze, two thousand years old. I had given her a gold-embroidered evening coat for her birthday, and she wore it that night, looking more golden than ever. She found the Barlows' house built into the cliff and furnished with tapestries, ikons, crucifixes and giant oak chests, so that its past seemed to live again. They dined on an outdoor terrace from which she could see the whole Riviera coast from Nice to Bordighera.

" The clouds," she related, " were *below* us, the moon above and the stars. When the clouds broke we saw the lights in the towns along the coast like other constellations, and a moon again in the sea. Jan played Chopin, and Barlow played his own music, and it was all so lovely that I went into the dining-room by myself and wept. It was stupid, but so unbearably lovely, and no one saw except perhaps John van Druten, who sat next me at dinner and is a perfectly charming, unspoilt boy. I don't know if he saw me weeping, but he came and stood by me — sheltered me from the people until I had repowdered my red nose and he said that he had just arrived that day and felt *ébloui* too. He taught at Aberystwyth and loves teaching, but likes being successful better. He still finds it great fun to be rich and live among lovely things. Everyone else here takes it for granted."

At the end of August she came back from the Riviera, and took charge of John Edward and his nurse while G. and I spent ten days in Vevey and Geneva. At a small house lent to me on the Surrey Downs, she wrote *Poor Caroline* and played at intervals with the twenty-months-old baby. Her reports, sent to me almost daily, showed that her preference of children to lap-dogs was not impaired by close proximity.

" He runs for intervals," she wrote, " and talks all the time, to flowers and quite imaginary bow-wows, and to Mummie and Daddy and Nannie, whom he seems to see like the Presence of God in every Burning Bush ! He is gloriously well, brown in most parts and eating like a tiger, and seems full of a perfectly enchanting happiness that I never saw in any other child. I *do* love this place. The Downs grow more enchanting with every hatching bramble."

That autumn a sadder form of vigilance had to accompany the writing of her novel. Her father had never been robust, and now, when he was nearing seventy, he became seriously ill with angina and recurrent pneumonia which continued until his death four years later. Since Grace was dead, Winifred could not endure the thought of her mother carrying this burden without a daughter's help. Though Edith de Coundouroff still lived at Cottingham and for years regarded the care of David Holtby as her special task, Winifred made constant journeys to Yorkshire on Saturday mornings, sometimes sat up with her father half the night, came back to London by the early train on Monday and rushed immediately to *Time and Tide* office.

At that time the paper went to press early in the week, and required its leading articles and notes by the first post on Tuesday morning. Winifred usually came back in the late afternoon with a leader and several notes to write, which had to be posted by midnight. Practically all her week-ends passed in this way for two or three years, and, according to her doctors, probably contributed by their strain and fatigue to the early onset of her final illness. But even when she knew their cost, she refused to regret them.

" It was all interesting and somehow *real*," she wrote to Sarah Millin of her father's illness after a year of her own. " Wrestling with sickness is like a real fight. I wouldn't *not* have been partly trained as a nurse, I wouldn't *not* have sat up nights tense with the feeling of defying death, for anything."

In November 1929, while Winifred was away nursing her father, I began to write, as an autobiography, the book called *Testament of Youth* which had been struggling for more than ten years to find expression. I had not worked on it for three weeks when I discovered that I was going to have another child. As our combined library was steadily growing, and John Edward and his possessions now filled every corner that our books and papers did not occupy, this meant yet another move. All three of us were now making quite respectable incomes, so we decided to find a house where we could remain for more than two or three years. Manageable houses were then at a premium, and between us we inspected seventy-six in the Chelsea and Kensington neighbourhoods before we found what we wanted in Glebe Place, Chelsea. It stood in a row of tall moderate-sized houses built in one of London's worst architectural periods, but it gave us the number of rooms that we wanted and a long, narrow back garden for the children to play in. By the conversion of the attic to a top-floor library, it also provided accommodation for our books.

Long before the cleaning and decorating were finished G. had left for his annual visit to America, so Winifred and I moved into the house without his aid in the spring of 1930. The move did not lack its incidents, for our " lady " housekeeper, disgruntled at the prospect of working in an ordinary kitchen, walked out the day after the furniture was delivered, leaving us with no help but that of a daily maid in her 'teens.

Winifred was then suffering considerable pain from inflammation in one of her ears and my new baby was due in three months, so neither of us was ideally situated for arranging books and moving furniture. My mother had fortunately taken John Edward and his nurse until the house was in order, so we tackled the job as best we could, starting at the top and working downwards. On the attic floor I sat for hours among unsteady pyramids of books which the furniture removers had poured helter-skelter from their packing-cases, and handed them up to Winifred, who by standing on a pair of low steps could just reach with her long arms both the top shelves and me. It was the most fatiguing fortnight we had ever spent, but we both agreed that the result was worth it.

With its babies, its books, its toys, its friends, and the companionship of both G. and Winifred, the household in Glebe Place was the nearest thing to complete happiness that I have ever known or ever hope to know. I believe that Winifred felt the same. Even her last illness, which never destroyed her capacity for enjoyment, did not quench the gaiety of our shared home. The golden illumination of love, of friendship, of complete mutual compatibility, continued to shine over it until she was gone, when the place became intolerable with its constant reminders of " happier things." Never have I understood so clearly as at Glebe Place, from the time of Winifred's death until G. and I moved to Cheyne Walk in 1937, the truth of Dante's sorrowful lament :

> *Nessun maggior dolore*
> *Che ricordarsi del tempo felice*
> *Nella miseria.*

The unusual domestic arrangement which suited us so well gave rise, I was assured, to a plentiful crop of rumours. Chelsea is notoriously the home of the unconventional, but if most of its myths have as innocent an origin as those circulated about ourselves they are indeed tales told by an idiot, full of sound and fury. Our friends at any rate, appeared to be singularly unaffected by our local "reputation." Visitors were always in and out, ranging from Names such as Norman Angell and E. M. Delafield to members of the Chelsea Labour Party and Winifred's native students from Africa. We began to arrange small but ambitious dinner-parties for which our limited dining-room accommodation was hardly adapted; the problem was always how to fit the big hired chairs round the large family table and still leave room for the serving to take place without the server's hindquarters being painfully scorched by the gas-fire.

"We give a dinner-party to-night," ran a typical letter from Winifred to Phyllis Bentley in September 1933; "Vernon Bartlett, Hungarians called Palyi, the literary editor of the *Sunday Times* called Lakin. Frantic borrowing of glass and silver from paternal mansion ! Also buying of more chairs. Accommodation not intended for large tables ! "

Besides the dinner-parties we lightly organised At Homes to which we invited crowds of a hundred and more, only to find that the sprinkling of celebrities who accepted were usually just the ones who wanted to be kept apart. In our small rooms this was not an easy problem, especially as, however propitious the date, wind and rain invariably made it impossible to use the garden. Oddly enough, in spite of these disadvantages, our parties were usually a success.

One summer evening when William Ballinger and Margaret Hodgson were in England, we gave an African party for natives in London and their British sympathisers. To the intense interest of the artists in the surrounding studios, an exotic crowd of mixed races and nationalities streamed in at our front door. For once the night was warm and fine, so the party was able to migrate into the back garden, where huge Jamaican negroes and smaller students from Cape Town mingled with Colonel Josiah Wedgwood and Ellen Wilkinson.

Winifred had frequent native visitors to tea ; amongst them occasional unfortunates found her lovely ethereal fairness irresistible. One, who appeared to be a man of substance, made her a passionate declaration of love in his Maida Vale flat while the gramophone played " No Rose in All the World." Later he served a term of imprisonment at Wormwood Scrubbs for embezzlement.

Each time a coloured visitor came through the front gate, the children stood at their nursery door wide-eyed and enraptured. When G. or I came in, the exciting information would be conveyed in a tense whisper : " Daddy ! Mummie ! Auntie's got an *African* in her room ! " John Edward called his cherished golliwog " H'lubi " after the native student whom Winifred had befriended, and for several years " Mr. Ginns the King of Africa " — a half-naked black gentleman with highly coloured accoutrements — figured prominently in his drawings.

Whenever we were not working, or entertaining, or visiting friends, or consoling relatives, Winifred and I went for walks in Battersea Park or along Chelsea Embankment. For the first year or two we also struggled with the garden, conscientiously sowing seeds, tugging the heavy roller or planting cuttings brought by Winifred from Cottingham. But try as we would the flowers refused to grow, and thanks to cats, slugs, small active feet and the marks of toy wheel-barrows and perambulators, the oblong of tussocky grass resisted all our efforts to turn it into a lawn. In the end we gave it up and, like other Chelsea and Battersea residents, adopted the Old English Garden in Battersea Park as our private Elysium. Whenever we were tired or sought peace from interrupters we ran to it across the suspension bridge, and it always consoled us. Each time we saw it we felt inclined to cry : " But this is the best yet ! "

In May, the flame and crimson of giant tulips blazed from the scented shadow of lavender-blue lilac and snow-white hawthorn. In October, enormous dahlias in sulphur, crimson, magenta and scarlet made a wild clamour of audacious colour against shoulder-high Michaelmas daisies

in every shade of mauve from royal purple to the faintest
off-white. Even in winter the garden possessed its gusty
exhilaration of wind, sea-birds, flying petals and scuttling
leaves. On summer Sundays the fountain played, the
bronze goldfish slid like flaming quicksilver beneath the pink-
petalled, golden-hearted water-lilies, and poor but exuberant
Chelsea lovers shared the spectacle with overworked Battersea
mothers as proudly as if they were exhibiting their own
garden. Watching them crowd down the narrow gravelled
path to the crazy paving between the flower-beds, and
observing on every face the same shock of surprised delight
in the glory of this communal treasure, we would whisper
triumphantly to each other : " The Revolution has come ! "

When Winifred was in London we walked in the garden
three or four times a week. I went alone too, but it was
not the same as going with her. I go alone still, but it is
even less the same, for whenever I am there I seem to see a
tall fair ghost standing against the clipped yews to feast her
eyes upon the luxuriant vividness of asters and chrysanthemums, or kneeling on the paved path to catch the exquisite
faint perfume from the triangular beds of mauve violas
and pink dwarf roses.

As soon as the house in Glebe Place was fit to inhabit
and my mother's cook had come to replace the lost " lady "
until the baby arrived, Winifred settled down to write two
plays and finish *Poor Caroline*. Play-writing was the least
successful form of literary work that she ever undertook ;
throughout her life it brought her neither money nor
recognition. But had she survived for a few more years, the
creative zeal which had performed exuberant dramas in
the Rudston kitchen, produced *Espionage* at school, and
given vitality to two Somerville Going Down Plays, would
certainly have found its place on the stage. Her ambitions
in the theatre were almost as definite as her aspirations in
fiction, and to the end of her life she wrote specimen scenes,
filled note-books with scraps of dialogue, and drafted plots
on the back of postcards.

Her first play, *Judgment Voice*, begun about 1929, turned on the story of a scientist who invented an instrument for listening-in to the past. It was a product of the fascinated interest in broadcasting which inspired her articles in the *Radio Times* and *The Listener*. She was sadly disappointed when the British Broadcasting Corporation tested her voice and found it unsuitable for the wireless. (" They said it sounded too patronising — of all things ! " she told me disgustedly when she returned from the test.)

Judgment Voice scintillated with ideas and vitality, but the dialogue " stuck " in places ; it showed evidence of an amateurishness largely overcome in her recently-published last play, *Take Back Your Freedom*. In 1931, when Leon M. Lion rejected it in spite of approving "the brilliant inventive-ness of the plot, the keen characterisation and the always lucid and interesting dialogue," she turned the play into a short story, *The Voice of God*, which was published during 1934 in the volume *Truth Is Not Sober*.

Meanwhile she had begun a light comedy of women in business, *Efficiency First*, written with all the *élan* of that peak period in her progress. This trifle represents Winifred in her lightest, gayest mood ; the plot is so amusing, the dialogue so delicious, the marks of the amateur so easy to remove, that I still wonder why no manager perceived its possibilities. Judging by the uncompromising realism of her dialogue, the able heroine, Sarah Terrans, appears to have been first cousin to Lady Rhondda :

Sarah : . . . Rupert, I am unpopular. They think I'm a hard, grasping, aggressive disagreeable woman.
Rupert : Everyone who has power has enemies.

In July, Winifred put this play aside in the hope of finishing *Poor Caroline* before the impending addition to our household arrived. With the nurse in residence and the next-to-the-top floor a welter of cot-blankets and " Simple Garments," the race between the novel and the infant finished, by a narrow margin, in favour of the former.

T.F.—L

"I'm as empty as a sucked grapeskin," Winifred wrote to Phyllis Bentley on July 22nd. "Working till about 1.0 every morning with masses of correspondence about native affairs, trying to draft a new play, and expecting Vera's baby hourly!"

My daughter was born on July 27th, inconsiderately arriving at 4 A.M. I learnt the next day that Winifred had stayed up all night to help the nurse and our recently acquired woman doctor. She had always wanted, she said, to witness the birth of a baby; it would come in so useful if she had to describe it in a novel. I did not know until a fortnight later that all through this period she had been racked with anxiety and grief, or that four days after the birth of Shirley, Dorothy McCalman had died.

Soon after her holiday with Winifred in Paris the previous year, Dot had been appointed tutor at the Oxford Training College. She was one of those rare individuals who are gifted with a passion and genius for teaching; now, fully equipped with an Honours Degree and a teacher's certificate, her new position as a trainer of teachers represented the climax of a heroic adventure. After less than a year at the College, her health suddenly began to fail. A local doctor diagnosed latent appendicitis, but when the summer term ended and she had taken a short rest, she seemed so much better that he thought she would benefit by a holiday with her sisters in Cornwall. She had hardly reached the country when a critical attack developed. Rushed to the best Cornish hospital available, she collapsed after the second of two urgent operations.

Winifred suppressed both this information and her sorrow, but I discovered the one by subsequently finding, amongst the previous week's copies of *The Times*, the obituary notice of Dot McCalman contributed to its columns by Winifred herself. The extent of her grief I never knew until, going through her correspondence after her death, I read a letter which she had written to Edith de Coundouroff:

"I wish I could see you and talk about Dot. I have missed you so much over this, because of course here I had to pretend that it was all all right, because I didn't want to distress anyone. I feel if I could have cried just once, I should have felt better. . . . Nothing I ever did for Dot could be anything like the pleasure she gave me. Her lovely character was beyond praise. . . . I feel that a cloud has moved across the sun."

Like so much of the knowledge which Winifred hid from her friends for their own sake, this discovery came too late for me to ask her forgiveness for the pain caused by my inability to share her mourning. Only the other day I re-read her memorial notice of Dot McCalman. Though the column which Violet Scott-James wrote of Winifred in *The Times* of September 30th, 1935, was beautiful and appreciative and just, it seems to me now that Winifred's own words were still more appropriate, and even truer of herself, than of the valiant and generous woman of whom she wrote :

"Those who had followed her career from the beginning felt that her true work had just begun. Still young in years . . . she was younger yet in spirit, in love with life, with youth, and with the satisfaction of learning. As a teacher she was gifted with eloquence, humour, gaiety, and a vivid and scholarly sense of the living past. As a friend her selfless generosity, her capacity for enjoyment, her devotion and loyalty were unique. What she might have accomplished had she lived is beyond prophecy ; but though her death cut short the promise of a brilliant career, it cannot destroy the radiance of her triumphant life."

In the middle of August, Winifred left London for a holiday with Lady Rhondda at Agay in the South of France. For the first time she travelled by aeroplane to Paris. I was still in bed when she came to say goodbye, and remembered afterwards the exaggerated casualness of her farewell. She made this flight just after the air disaster at Meopham in which Lady Ednam and several other well-known travellers perished ; the newspapers had been full of gruesome details, and Winifred's last few nights before her journey were broken by grim apprehensive dreams. As usual, she did not communicate these fears, and I could not understand her telegram announcing a safe trip nor John Edward's triumphant repetition of the tidings " Auntie caught a parrot " — his own version of her adventure — until G. told me that she had gone to Paris by air.

I also did not learn until some years afterwards that, on her journey south after the aeroplane flight, she was suddenly smitten with the first of the severe headaches, due to high blood-pressure, with which we were to become so anxiously familiar in the near future. By the time that she arrived she was almost speechless with pain, but characteristically she crushed it down and said nothing to any of the party at Agay.

Although Lady Rhondda gallantly endeavoured to abolish the inequality between herself and Winifred created by her wealth, her fifteen years' seniority and the conspicuous part that she played in the world, it was impossible for anyone with Winifred's humility and sense of proportion to forget it. For her Lady Rhondda was the leader and editor as well as the beloved friend, and she never quite outgrew the sense of affectionate reverence once expressed in the comment : " I always feel I ought to stand up when she comes into the room." Above all she was determined that a distinguished woman who carried a heavy burden of responsibility without herself possessing the advantage of robust health should be spared the tiresome inconvenience of other people's ailments.

Nobody's achievements ever suffered more cruelly than Winifred's from vicarious catastrophes ; nobody realised more clearly than she how heavily the burden of the unfit lies upon the overworked fit.

" Everybody's tragedy is somebody's nuisance," she once remarked to me with the ruthless realism which so seldom escaped outside her thoughts.

She knew that the work of women, however important, is traditionally liable to this form of interruption. All the more, therefore, because Lady Rhondda was a woman, she would not, and never did, ask her to share her secret pain. So as soon as she could escape she threw off her travelling clothes and went for a swim round the red rocks of the Mediterranean coast. Unaccountably, the headache disappeared as suddenly as it had come.

Having no physical courage myself, I was filled with admiration by the news of Winifred's flying and diving exploits on that holiday. Had we but known, both were probably the worst possible activities for someone whose blood-pressure must already have been high. For a few days after her headache she suffered from a *malaise* which she could not explain, but ascribed to the depression caused by Dot's death. The thought of Dot, of her lost work and happiness and the ease with which her life might have been saved, haunted Winifred throughout that holiday. Only recently I found in a notebook dated September 1930 a long poetic experiment — the study for a poem rather than the poem itself — which reveals how her grief for Dot mingled in Winifred's memory with her aeroplane flight. This study opens with a section called " The Aeroplane." The second part, under the heading " Notre Dame," contains three lines of invocation which will recall to the lovers of *South Riding* the beautiful chapter entitled " Miss Sigglesthwaite Sees the Lambs of God," and the poignant passage beginning " Oh, time betrays us ! " :

> *Oh, time is death,*
> *Come, cypress-candled death,*
> *Take us before time kills our life . . .*

Death was to answer Winifred's prayer. She at least, like Dot McCalman, had to fight no losing battle with time. Those whom she loved are left to face in their turn that bitter challenge, but she was of the company whom age shall not weary nor the years condemn.

Winifred went on from Agay to Geneva to join some members of the Six Point Group who were working with an organisation known as the Equal Rights International for an Equal Rights Treaty. There they shared a shop and an office with the American National Women's Party outside the Assembly Hall in the Place Neuve. A few of them, including Winifred and Alice Paul, the founder of the Women's Party, lunched with Dr. Beneš, who won their hearts by sending a huge bouquet of pink roses to bless their campaign.

"The Pension de Peyraud," wrote Winifred, "is a small whirlpool in which unwary English, American, Swiss and Chilean women are caught swirling, and scattered to interview delegates, queue for Press tickets, or pacify Alice Paul. The last-named takes the most doing. That woman seems to be a little marvel of obstinacy, gentleness and self-confidence. . . . To-day I am still in a dressing-gown in my room, for I feel that if I get dressed, I shall be swept out to interview the Irish Free State or Bolivia !"

As the vigorous baby girl whom I was nursing with the expert help of the Chelsea Babies' Club made a holiday impossible for me, I decided to spare Winifred additional work by taking over her correspondence. We had then no secretary, so I opened and answered it as it came. I found that it consisted mainly of requests to speak, write, read manuscripts and perform many other unremunerated services ; letters from Africans ; "fan mail" about her articles ; multitudinous press-cuttings ; and a number of cheques from periodicals. Familiar as I was with the extent and persistence of the claimants on her time, their confident appeals to her benevolence revealed the diverse services which she managed to perform for individuals of whom each apparently believed that he or she was the only one :

"Look here, I want you to keep an eye on my book while it's going through the Press. . . ."

"Darling, can you meet me on Saturday afternoon ? I'm afraid X. is going to lose his job after all, and the cook left yesterday. I want your advice. . . ."

" I rely on *you* to look after things in my absence. If it wasn't for you I couldn't go at all. . . ."

" Dearest Winifred, could you possibly lead our deputation to the Home Secretary on Monday? Z. has fallen out; she had to go to a nursing-home last night. . . ."

" Dear, I'm counting on you to run over next week-end. P. and Q. are laid up again, with two nurses, and they're *both* asking for you. . . ."

" The A.s can't keep Mrs. B. with them any longer. She upsets the children and the servants are threatening to give notice. It means a boarding-house or lodgings, I'm afraid. Do you think you *could* look out some inexpensive rooms for her on your next free afternoon — quiet, because of her nerves, with a good-tempered landlady?"

If these are not actual quotations, they are interchangeable with many which occur, for fifteen years, all through her correspondence. No wonder that she wrote to Lady Rhondda early in 1931: " Illness, other people's illness, invariably scares me, because I have felt it all my life to be the enemy of my work and freedom," and added in another letter at the end of the year:

" It's just as well that I am going into the country. It is quite true that when I am interrupted sixteen times a morning by the telephone ringing, as I am in London, all with requests for me to do something, I shall never be able to tackle a concentrated piece of work. I believe that is why my short things have hitherto been best. I can get them done at nights and week-ends. But this London life, which I love so much, where refusals and saying ' No ' are just as much interrupting and distracting as saying ' Yes,' may really be impossible as a background of big solid work. One's mind is always darting off into new problems, new ideas. Even reading the newspaper is a distraction which for me can fill almost a complete morning—for one newspaper sends me to another newspaper, and that to ring someone up to confirm something, and that to jot down ideas for an article. . . .

" Oh, Margaret, why haven't we seventy lives ? One is no use."

After Winifred's death, I went through over thirty note-books of various dates which testify to the ceaseless fertility of the ideas that she mentioned. How many similar books she threw away, it is impossible to guess. The ones that survive show that no scrap of her time was ever willingly wasted. Their pages are crowded with paragraphs for stories ; suggestions for articles, notes and editorials ; descriptions of people and places scribbled in trains or buses as she passed by ; jottings for speeches ; lists of books to read or review ; schemes for lectures and classes ; observations on schools visited ; summaries of Bills to be put through Parliament ; little vignettes of travels abroad. Many of these are interspersed with experiments in gay doggerel rhymes under such cheerful titles as " The Cosmopolitan Cock " and " The Pertinacious Pig." Her mind was like a spring-tide in full flood ; rich, shining, vigorous, and capable of infinite variety.

At this time her reputation as a journalist was at its height. Not only was she writing regularly for *Time and Tide* and continuing her articles for the *Yorkshire Post* and the *Manchester Guardian* ; she was now doing weekly novel reviews for the book page of the *News Chronicle*, and contributing long and frequent stories and essays to the *Radio Times*, *The Clarion*, *The Realist*, *Good Housekeeping*, *Woman's Journal* and a dozen other periodicals. Sometimes, from this period almost until her death, she would have several contributions in one weekly issue of *Time and Tide* alone — an unsigned leading article, two or three unsigned notes, a signed essay or story, a book review inscribed " W. H.," and even, for about a year between 1929 and 1930, dramatic criticisms under the pseudonym of " Corbin H. Wood." But even these terrific obligations might have been, for a writer of her energy, compatible with a larger output of enduring work, if relatives, friends, lovers, acquaintances and strangers had mitigated their unceasing demands upon her magnanimity.

Her tragedy lay in the responsiveness of her generous temperament, her disastrous willingness to put aside her permanent interests for the temporary convenience of others, her humble readiness to estimate all those for whom she worked as her superiors. It is only too easy to understand how the sensitive artist who could re-create a countryside, people it with living men and women, and convey to the reader all that was most real and lasting in their spiritual conflicts, came to be judged by her external armour of superb co-operative efficiency as a brilliant journalist and nothing more.

Poor Caroline, Winifred's fourth novel, was published in January 1931. It tells the ironical story of the Christian Cinema Company, its grotesque elderly founder and secretary, Caroline Denton-Smyth, and the way in which both affected the fortunes of a small group of miscellaneous people temporarily drawn into their orbit by a series of haphazard adventures.

The book went into a second edition, received a large number of enthusiastic reviews, and was by far the most successful that Winifred had written, but one or two of her intimate friends, such as G. and Lady Rhondda, objected to it strongly. G. maintained that it revealed " an unwholesome pity-complex " in Winifred, and Lady Rhondda disliked it for a similar reason. She thought that it showed signs of an underlying fear, and as it was published so close to Winifred's first serious breakdown, she suggested later that the fear was provoked by a subconscious knowledge of approaching fate.

But though *Poor Caroline* appeared at the beginning of the year which was to end in catastrophe, it had actually been completed the previous July, and was written during 1928 and 1929 at the very peak of Winifred's triumphant vitality. The story's intention was perhaps misunderstood owing to an incomplete knowledge of its origin.

Winifred's family circle included a large number of outlying acquaintances, distantly related to old friends or

" in-laws," who in the course of years had become self-constituted claimants to hospitality, loans and advice. Amongst these pensioners was an elderly eccentric named Mary Horne, the aunt of one of Winifred's early governesses. Like Caroline Denton-Smyth in Winifred's story, Mary Horne subsisted largely on hope ; she invented or participated in numerous commercial projects, all of which were designed to make her fortune and that of the shareholders if only sufficient money could be raised. Various " loans " were coaxed out of Alice Holtby for the development of these schemes. The last, an early experiment in cellophane paper, might actually have justified Mary Horne's enthusiasm had she survived long enough to carry it through.

A small, plump, fantastic-looking woman with a fondness for cheap highly-coloured clothes and long dangling chains, Mary Horne must have been in the near-seventies when Winifred returned from South Africa. Repudiated by contemporaries weary of her importunities, she fastened with joy upon a young, strong and flourishing member of the philanthropic Holtby family, and compelled her to play the same charitable and exacting rôle as the young South African girl, Eleanor de la Roux, fulfils in *Poor Caroline*. How much money Winifred actually gave her I do not know, but she probably managed to extract a substantial sum.

For the next two or three years, Mary Horne became one of Winifred's most persistent *attachées*, writing letters, demanding sympathy, expecting attention. Finally, on the way to Early Service at the beginning of 1928, she fell under a 'bus, fractured her thigh, and eventually died in a North Kensington municipal hospital. Winifred felt obliged to visit the hospital and run innumerable errands for the querulous invalid, who wanted to be moved to a nursing-home for which she had no money to pay. When she died, Winifred was compelled to attend the inquest and arrange the funeral.

Coming back from the inquest, an unwonted feeling of bitterness oppressed her. She had spent her time, her youth, and her energy upon this crazy old egoist, and had

received nothing in return but further demands. She knew
that she was now in the main current of national events,
where she could create and influence public opinion, yet
she had been involved, to the detriment of more important
claims, in the vast, sordid irrelevance of infirmaries, inquests,
cheap undertakers and censorious coroners.

Poor Mary Horne ! she thought. To live so vainly and
die so forlornly, her extravagant speculations bringing her,
at the last, nothing better than a pauper's bed in a Poor
Law hospital ! And yet . . . had she, from her own point
of view, lived so vainly after all ? Those grotesque dreams,
those glittering though baseless " certainties," that feeling
of self-importance, that confidence of success only just round
the corner—were they not, in a sense, their own reward ?
Was not Mary Horne yet another of the privileged company
who knew that somewhere, just beyond the commonplace realities of life, lay the perfect party, the silver mountains, the Land of Green Ginger—" the real and eternal
world of which this Vegetable Universe is but a faint
shadow " ?

Before she reached home, Winifred realised that Mary
Horne had repaid her with the richest gift that any friend
could bestow. She had given her the missing theme for
her new novel. Within the next few weeks she began to
write *Poor Caroline*. Its opening words were those of the
dedication : " *In Piam Memoriam*, M. C. H."

On its own limited scale I regard this book as one of
Winifred's best—though Naomi Royde Smith, reviewing it
just after publication, remarked that it represented " Notes
for a masterpiece " rather than the masterpiece itself. Com-
menting ruefully on the " rush and clamour " of Winifred's
life as described in the biographical note on the dust-cover,
she concluded : " *Poor Caroline* is a novel only potentially
great. . . . It provides evidence that if life should allow the
time and provide the impulse, Miss Holtby may very well
be the author of a completed masterpiece before her career
as a novelist is over."

After Winifred's death, Naomi Royde Smith was

challenged by another novelist, John Brophy, for remarking that Winifred had lacked the " consecrated egoism " of the true artist. *South Riding*, the " completed masterpiece " predicted four years earlier, had not then appeared. But if the function of the artist is to observe and re-create with imagination and insight, then *Poor Caroline* is a work of art. The fact that the chief person observed is a self-deceived optimist with an unbalanced devotion to hopeless projects does not mitigate the value of the observation or reduce the authenticity of the art. Winifred did her utmost to get inside Mary Horne's remembered personality as a method of atoning to the dead enthusiast for the impatience which she had secretly felt towards her schemes and borrowings, her preposterous claims and untimely mishaps. To Winifred's natural compassion, Mary Horne's final defeat by igno-minious death was a tragedy for which, in its long-range results, she wanted to find compensation.

" Caroline is not a symbol of me," she assured Lady Rhondda, " but an expression of herself, and I did not mean it to be a depressed nor dead-sea-applish impression either. I meant to leave the impression of someone silly but vital, directly futile but indirectly triumphant, a person who—as Eleanor realised, standing by her grave—had in the end been able to give to those she wished to benefit their heart's desire."

She added, still repudiating the imputation of fear : " I love life. I love my work. I love London. I love the multifarious activities which go to make the kind of life I lead. So far as I remember, all unhappinesses I have ever had have arisen from—

(*a*) Religion.

(*b*) Fear for other people whom I love.

(*c*) My work not being good enough — that most of all, I think — and all the consequences coming from that.

" There may have been more, but I can't think of them. If only all the people in the world would keep well and happy. I ask nothing more of life, except that I should be a great artist. Amen. Amen."

In the spring of 1931, Winifred again changed her publisher. The success of *Poor Caroline* brought her an offer, too financially advantageous to be rejected, from the firm of William Collins, so she left her friend and admirer Jonathan Cape and signed a new three-novel contract. It was largely on the substantial advance for her next novel, *Mandoa, Mandoa!*, that she lived when the beginning of her illness temporarily reduced her working hours to one or two a day.

On Collins' part the arrangement was both profitable and perspicacious. The sales of *South Riding*, which have now reached 70,000, more than rewarded their foresight, but Winifred was never a remunerative author in her lifetime. Many of the struggling writers who appealed to her for advice and envied her literary success would have been astonished to learn the modesty of her earnings apart from journalism. In England, *Mandoa, Mandoa!* has barely yet made its £350 advance ; even the cheap edition sold only 1303 copies in the first six months. The sales of the collected short stories, *Truth Is Not Sober*, amounted to no more than 2838 during the first half-year after its publication in 1934, and the satirical narrative, *The Astonishing Island,* sold less than five hundred copies.

Winifred first lunched with her new publishers during the political crisis of 1931, which gave the National Government its long term of office. The head of the firm, Sir Godfrey Collins, was about to become Secretary of State for Scotland, and as I was then abroad she wrote to describe their meeting.

" The Collins lunch was very amiable. The young man rather sweet . . . and most flatteringly deferential. Old Sir Godfrey, the Complete Business Man, regarding the output of books as an Industry, subject to all modern methods of Mass Production, Rationalisation, etc. etc. Rather disconcerted when I told him that I had *no* intention of turning out two a year regularly and doubted if I should do one. But when ne decided that my views on literature were utterly incomprehensible, he turned round and gave me instead a lecture upon how he had prophesied precisely this political situation in letters to *The Times*."

During Winifred's holiday in Brittany that summer she made no progress towards providing Collins with even one novel, for the manuscript that she took with her was not fiction at all, but a critical study of the work of Virginia Woolf.

At that time Winifred's Derbyshire contemporary, the poet and novelist Thomas Moult, was editing a series of "Modern Writers on Modern Writers." When he invited her to contribute a volume and choose her own author, she selected Virginia Woolf, whose novels she had always admired, as a deliberate exercise in intellectual discipline.

"I took my courage and curiosity in both hands," she wrote to Sarah Millin in 1932, "and chose the writer whose art seemed most of all removed from anything I could ever attempt, and whose experience was most alien to my own . . . I found it the most enthralling adventure — to enter, even at second-hand, that world of purely aesthetic and intellectual interests, was to me as strange an exploration as it would have been for Virginia Woolf to sit beside my mother's pie and hear my uncles talk fat-stock prices and cub-hunting. I felt that I was learning and learning with every fibre of such brain as I have. To submit oneself to another person's mental attitudes, to sink oneself into their experience — it's almost like bathing in a strange sea. . . .

"I know I am not a good critic. My own taste is far from impeccable. . . . But I do find adventure and enlightenment in the intensive study of any mind better than my own — the more alien, perhaps, the better. I feel that it enlarges my own too narrow horizons, and helps to extend my lamentably limited knowledge of the art which is (even if I sandwich all practice of it between political meetings and domestic chores) my social medium."

Winifred did not know Virginia Woolf at all when she began to write her book, so with conscientious humility she wisely limited her subject's life-story to a brief introductory chapter. Realising also that contemporary biography depends for its truth upon inside knowledge, she wrote for advice, even on this chapter, to the composer, Dame Ethel Smyth, whose friendship with Virginia Woolf was of many years' standing.

In February of that·year, Dame Ethel's new Choral Symphony, *The Prison*, in memory of her friend H. B. Brewster, had been performed in Edinburgh and London. Winifred wrote an appreciative article on the Symphony in *Time and Tide*, and later defended Dame Ethel against attacks by male music critics who found it difficult to appreciate a woman's composition. Dame Ethel, now over seventy, was touched by this ardent support from a conspicuous member of a younger generation. She wrote Winifred several letters in her racy, inimitable style, and persuaded Virginia Woolf to send her some facts which could not be obtained from libraries. Finally, when the biographical chapter was finished, she read and criticised it, filling the margin with corrections and suggestions.

" I wish I could employ her as a secretary ! " wrote Winifred, adding with truth, " It is extraordinary with what consistency the biggest and busiest people do most promptly and thoroughly any little job."

Dame Ethel remained a benevolent friend for the rest of Winifred's life. In October 1933 we both spent an afternoon with her at her house in Woking, and on January 6th, 1934, went together to her Festival Concert at the Albert Hall, given on her seventy-fifth birthday and attended by Queen Mary. After spending most of the afternoon in the Royal Box, Dame Ethel, by way of an entertaining contrast, invited some of her friends to a tea-party at Lyons in the Brompton Road. Winifred and I were included.

It was one of the funniest afternoons that I ever remember. Walking from the Albert Hall to the Brompton Road, we found some of the most highly publicised " names " in music and Mayfair gleefully scrambling up Lyons' staircase to their reserved tables in the first-floor restaurant. Dame Ethel, with Sir Thomas Beecham, Sir Hugh Allen and Lady Diana Cooper, took possession of a conspicuous corner, to the excited mystification of the normal *habitués* and the embarrassed confusion of the attendants. One aristocratic guest, surveying the scene through her lorgnettes, took a horrified glance at the mixed and noisy crowd, and then, with the expression of a sufferer from bad stomach-ache, hurried down the stairs at twice the rate that she had come up.

Staying with Lady Rhondda at St. Lunaire, Winifred worked on her critical study for seven hours a day. When she showed her the first draft of the earlier pages, Lady Rhondda did not approve ; they read, she commented, " as if written in extreme fatigue " — as they doubtless were. But Winifred was not conscious of overwork, for in spite of the cold rainy evenings and the cold windy sea of that miserable summer, her writing was combined with a careful programme of bathing, meals and moonlit walks among privet hedges and pines and glow-worms, ending with ten o'clock chocolate at a café opposite the Casino.

This routine should have restored her vigour, but somehow it did not.

Early in August she went on to a hotel at Abondance, in the Haute Savoie, to look after Violet Scott-James's young daughter Marie, who was convalescing at the top of a mountain after a long illness. Here Winifred had a sequence of headaches similar to the one which had followed her aeroplane flight ; in both cases the high altitude was probably the cause. As drugs were unobtainable in the isolated hotel far from civilisation, she tried to cure herself with brandy and soda — the worst expedient that she could have chosen.

Directly she left the mountains for a few days with the Smeterlins at Cap Ferrat, the headaches again disappeared. She visited the new Beach Casino at Monte Carlo — " a real Grand Babylon full of celebrities and champagne " — watched Somerset Maugham losing at *chemin de fer*, met Peggy Joyce, the original stage heroine in *Gentlemen Prefer Blondes* who was staying at the Smeterlins' villa, and wrote me that twenty-four hours of the Mediterranean had made up for all the previous rain, fatigue and discomfort. Her spirits recovered immediately. One evening after the first thunder-rumbles of the coming political *débâcle* had begun in England, she saw Sir Oswald Mosley — who had " prophesied Crisis " and " counselled Action " — still at the gaming tables in the new Casino. A day or two later she sent in an exuberant lampoon entitled *Crisis* to *Time and Tide*.

" After all," it asked in conclusion,

> *Is there much difference*
> *Between the new Casino at Monte Carlo*
> *And the new International Bank at Basle ?*
> *Do bankers know much more*
> *About the rise and fall of Credit*
> *Than croupiers know*
> *About the next resting-place of their spinning ball ?*
> *Is not Roulette*
> *As important to those who play it*
> *As Politics ?*
> *And almost as expensive ?*
> *And what the Hell is Reality, anyway,*
> *Especially in a wet August ?*

While Winifred was travelling round France, I took John and Shirley to a furnished cottage at Rustington on the Sussex coast, which for the sake of economy we shared with two acquaintances and their small daughter. The children were too young to travel far and too noisy for hotels or lodgings, but the closer my acquaintance with that cottage became, the less attractive its habits appeared. The stoves would not heat, the fires would not burn, and outside the sun would not shine ; the rain which deluged Brittany had even less mercy upon Sussex, and we spent the greater part of each day watching the few warm clothes we had brought steam lugubriously round a smouldering kitchen range. After contending with the housekeeping, doing half the housework, and periodically pacifying the two nurses who quarrelled continually, I returned to London in a very bad temper.

Never, it seemed, had the contrast between Winifred's fortunes and my own been so overwhelming. She, at the proud summit of her career, went everywhere, met everyone and did everything, while I spent nearly all the time at home, looking after two energetic and exhausting babies, and trying to overcome a daily sequence of vexatious domestic problems in time to get an hour or two's work each evening on my autobiography. True, Winifred's literary achievements, apart from her journalism, had been comparatively modest, but I, in the mid-thirties, had never achieved anything worth mentioning at all. Not realising how much of her own holiday had gone on solicitude for others, or ever dreaming that she had visited the Riviera for the last time, I was again ungracious enough to envy her. Although I tried to camouflage the failure of our holiday by graphic descriptions of its more ludicrous discomforts, my envious exasperation crept into my letters, and she came home determined that I too should visit the Mediterranean that summer.

Almost before I realised what was happening, I found myself with G. at St. Raphaël while she took charge of the nurse and children. A night or two after we had left England, she went to a Beethoven Promenade Concert and listened to Jelly d'Aranyi, the Hungarian violinist, playing the concerto which my brother Edward had so often performed. As she listened, enraptured and relaxed, she found herself thinking of Edward, and the words " I am his deputy " came into her head. Suddenly she realised that tears were running down her cheeks, to the consternation of the amiable young man in the next seat. How deaf and dumb, she thought, is my appreciation of this beauty compared with what Edward's would have been ! How strange it is that he should haunt me whenever I hear music, though I never knew him ! Perhaps this is the effect of seeing his grave on the Asiago Plateau — that grey, sinister, extraordinarily moving place.

All the next day she tried to get her feeling about him into a poem which she called *Symphony Concert*. At last she wrote and sent it to me with a letter asking: "Does it really mean that de la Mare's 'Look thy last on all things lovely' is literal truth? Does it mean that to love certain beauties intensely means to leave some of your spirit behind in them? Or does it simply mean that the story of Edward, his appearance, his aloofness, his talent and his death, are naturally associated in my mind with music, so that when I hear music, I think of him?"

I opened her letter sitting in the sunshine at a table outside a small St. Raphaël tea-shop. After looking at the letter, I read the poem:

For me to-night they build these frozen towers,
These battlements of music, these supreme
Pinnacles carven, garlanded with flowers,
Enchanted architecture of a dream.
Yet, entering, I know that all I see
Of loveliness was never planned for me.

My footsteps stumble at the open door,
I grope along the halls with outstretched hand,
Seeing a little, and forgetting more,
Admiring where I cannot understand,
A gaping stranger, idly loitering
Round the deserted throne-room of a king.

These were your palaces; you loved and knew
The terraced garden to its farthest ends,
The empty corridors I wander through
Were crowded with your memories, your friends,
And not a fountain, not a cup, was wrought,
But drew fresh beauty from your mastering thought.

I am your deputy. Ah, pardon then
This dull perception, these untutored ears.
How should I hear as well as other men
Who, under every song, for thirteen years,
Have heard re-echo that last sound you knew—
The shrapnel splintering before it slew?

In spite of Winifred's generosity, our holiday was short-lived. For some time G. had thought of standing for Parliament ; the deepening crisis brought the certainty of a General Election, and we had not been away a week before a letter arrived at home asking him to offer himself as Labour candidate for a West London constituency, Brentford and Chiswick. Winifred telegraphed the invitation, and he returned immediately. A day or two later he wired that he had been selected and I followed him back to London, to support him for several weeks by speaking and canvassing against the rising tide of reaction and fear.

Winifred flung herself with her usual enthusiasm into the General Election, whipping up energies which were failing with a rapidity which her excitement did not allow her to realise. The house at Glebe Place became a whirlwind of politics. She laid aside *Virginia Woolf*, and I, perforce, *Testament of Youth*. While I remained in Chiswick she rushed up to the north to support Charles Roden Buxton, and down to the south to speak for Monica Whately. When I lost my voice she took my place in Brentford, and held a sequence of meetings until G. appeared.

On the night of the Election, she accompanied Lady Rhondda to the champagne party on the top floor of Selfridge's which she afterwards described in *Mandoa, Mandoa !* and heard the results announced to a cheering audience of jubilant Conservatives. At Chiswick, through a rolling curtain of sulphur-coloured fog, G., less disastrously defeated than many of the Labour ministers, addressed an invisible crowd from the balcony of the Town Hall. The fog, thickening hourly, imprisoned us in the constituency, and we spent the night at the house of the previous Labour candidate, Dr. Stella Churchill. At 2 A.M. I rang up Glebe Place. Winifred had just returned. She told me that almost the whole Labour Cabinet, from Arthur Henderson downwards, had vanished like a house of cards before a whirlwind, and popular panic had swept a National Government into power with an overwhelming majority.

Three mornings afterwards Winifred did not appear at

breakfast. She was often late, answering her letters, and
I thought nothing of her absence till the meal was over.
Going to her room, I found that she had been ill all night,
and was now endeavouring, with a violent headache, to
dress for an interview fixed at eleven o'clock with Sir Norman
Angell.

I looked at her more closely. There were dark circles
under her eyes, and her face was pale with the ominous
yellowish pallor which was to become so familiar during
the next four years.

"Look here," I said, "don't you think you'd better lie
down instead of going to see Norman Angell? I'll ring up
his secretary and say you can't come."

To my secret dismay—for it was her habit to disregard
minor illnesses when anything of interest was about to
happen — she answered immediately : "Yes, please ring
up. I'm afraid I can't go."

CHAPTER XVIII

THE ABYSMAL HOUR

FOR THE GHOST OF ELINOR WYLIE

1. *Escort*

Not when you glittered, royally attended,
    Gallant and debonaire,
By brilliant words and dancing mirth befriended
    I was not with you there.

But roused by pain, in the abysmal hour
    When angry pulses leap,
And black blood lashes its frustrated power
    Against tall cliffs of sleep.

Then, when the hounds of fear sprang from the shadows,
    In horror's hue and cry
Hot on your heels, through the grey morning meadows
    Hunting you down to die ;

Then, when you thought that there was none beside you,
    No prince nor poet near,
Only the silver sunrise to deride you
    And your pulsating fear ;

Then, when you turned, by livid moonlight sickened,
    Seeking the hidden sign—
My breath it was upon your breath that quickened ;
    The fear, the pain, were mine.

WINIFRED HOLTBY
Time and Tide, 1932

At first nobody took Winifred's illness very seriously.
Our doctor attributed her collapse to overwork, and recommended a few days' rest in bed ; her family wrote cheerfully, advising her not to overdo things and take life quietly

for a bit. Clare Leighton, her friend since the end of our college days, invited her for a brief convalescence to her week-end cottage at Monks Risborough in Buckinghamshire. Lady Rhondda, in collaboration with the doctor, developed a minor malady which required a Christmas holiday in Tunis, and invited Winifred to go with her as her guest. Preparations for this journey to the sunshine were already in progress when Winifred struggled out of bed and went down to Monks Risborough on November 7th.

She returned, officially recovered, on November 13th, and wondered why her lecture on Virginia Woolf to the National Liberal Club that evening seemed so terrific an effort. Next day she travelled to Cottingham for the week-end, and returned to town on the Monday to resume her ordinary life. She met friends for meals, worked at *Time and Tide* office, attended a Board Meeting on November 19th, and on November 22nd went to a ceremonial dinner for Cicely Hamilton which she had largely organised. Early the next morning I found her in a state of collapse, with sickness and a violent headache, precisely similar to the first occasion.

I shall remember the persistent irony of that day until I die. At midday G. and I had to attend the Surrey funeral of my late headmistress, a close family friend, and I was obliged to leave Winifred for two hours in the care of the household staff. The first attack had passed off after a few hours' rest and, still accepting the doctor's explanation of overwork, I expected the second to follow the same course. But when I returned from the funeral, the children's nurse was waiting on the doorstep to tell me that Winifred was still very ill. I summoned the doctor immediately ; puzzled and perturbed, she suggested that Winifred should go to a nursing-home for closer investigation.

Somehow I dressed her, packed her suitcase, and took her there. She struggled bravely, but was hardly able to help herself at all. The short journey from Chelsea to the Earl's Court nursing-home seemed like hours of purgatory owing to her continuous sickness. Even the case-hardened matron looked distressed at the sight of her exhausted face. " She does want a rest, poor thing ! " she exclaimed.

Going back to Chelsea, I fought against the same intuitive fear that I had felt when Winifred was first taken ill. Cold and persistent, it dominated the rest of that day's incongruous programme, which compelled me to make an encouraging speech and receive a presentation bouquet at a post-election Labour "Social" in Chiswick, and to complete an urgent article for *Home Chat*, entitled " Has the Pleasantness gone out of Life ? ", in which my function was to maintain that it hadn't.

Winifred stayed in the nursing-home until after Christmas. Her mother, distressed, came to London to see her ; various doctors made various tests ; a specialist examined her eyes for a possible brain-tumour. No satisfactory explanation of the headaches and sickness emerged, though her blood pressure was found to be abnormally high. At length the doctors concluded that overwork had produced some obscure toxic condition. They advised absolute quiet for five or six weeks, and forbade visitors and letters.

It was then that we discovered the value of a long and close friendship which had made our minds and outlooks virtually interchangeable. I found that I could answer her voluminous correspondence to her satisfaction without consulting her ; I could correct the proofs of her articles and stories as though they were my own. During the next two months the number of proofs I corrected, requests I refused, and engagements I cancelled for her were a small indication of the amount that she had tried to do.

Because she really had been tired, the rest, superficially, did her good. Early in January, the doctors suggested a few weeks' convalescence in a mild seaside climate. Friends living in Exeter found a small convalescent home on the cliffs above Sidmouth, in South Devon, and on January 5th, 1932, I took her down there. I fully expected a similar trip to the journey in the taxi, but we arrived without disaster. As G. was not yet due in America and could supervise the children — who for once co-operated without having accidents or developing diseases — I was able to stay for ten days at an hotel on the Esplanade to make sure that the change had not upset her.

They were days of huge gales and roaring seas. Every morning we took a short gusty walk through the white rain of spray on the water's edge. Every afternoon, as she was now allowed to write a little, we sat together over the fire in her small sitting-room, working at *Mandoa, Mandoa !* and *Testament of Youth*. Evening after evening as darkness gathered, the wind howled and the rain beat against the windows. To reach my hotel, I had to scramble down a steep cliff path through a wood to the Esplanade. The wood was pitch black on those January evenings, and when I reached the bridge across the Sid at the bottom, the waves from the high tides were often breaking over it. Winifred used to light me to the path with her electric torch, and then stand holding it above the cliff till she saw me on the empty promenade. Every night I looked back and waved to her from the bridge as she stood with the tiny bulb of the torch still glowing to give me a sense of direction through the wood, just as the glow of her personality gave me a sense of direction through life.

After I had gone she ventured one day on a 'bus-ride to Seaton, the next town eastwards along the coast, to visit the St. John Ervines in their recently-acquired new home. St. John was then working on *God's Soldier*, his biography of General Booth. He showed her his small pagoda-like study overflowing with books, which looked over the long hill running down to Seaton Bay, and took her round the sloping terraced garden where crimson gladioli and scarlet oaks imported from America would glow in the autumn. At the end of January, she felt ready to come home and work again.

" I want to be quiet and domestic and lazy," she wrote, " and sit about with you and the dear silly children."

So John Edward and I met her at Waterloo. She seemed cured, but a week later another small collapse indicated that she was not. Once again the doctors conferred, and

suggested a few months in some country place where life
moved quietly. Angry with herself for feeling no better
and with the state of the world for its unsatisfactoriness, she
began by resisting.

" C. P. Scott dead," she wrote dejectedly to Lady
Rhondda. " William Graham dead. Manchuria. The
arrest of Gandhi. The Disarmament Conference farce. My
God, what a world ! Roll on ruin. Or perhaps not. But
God forbid that I should ever live in the country and play
bridge with colonels ! "

Nevertheless she went, though not to play bridge, for
continued high blood pressure and headache eventually
conquered her determination to stay in London. Clare
Leighton and Noel Brailsford found rooms for her in a rural
cottage in Monks Risborough where they could keep an
eye on her, and once again she departed in the vain search
for health.

I had intended to go down to Monks Risborough every
few days, but though Winifred had perhaps never needed
me more, I did not see her for over a month. Early in
February John Edward developed chicken-pox ; ten days
later I caught it from him, and being somewhat mature for
the disease took it very badly. Winifred, supervised by a local
doctor, was now allowed to get up only for the middle of
the day. At the local hotel she made friends with Mr.
Ernest Rhys, the editor of *Everyman's Library*, who was living
there.

" A darling," she wrote. " Over seventy, knew Swinburne. And lovely manners."

He told her of other friendships, with Havelock Ellis,
with Olive Schreiner. She found him kind, considerate
and tactful, one of the most delightful companions she had
met. Sometimes, in the late winter afternoons, he escorted
her home from the hotel over the darkening fields, reciting
his own poems aloud " in a lovely rolling voice."

Forbidden to work at her novel for more than an hour
or two each day, she lay in bed every evening looking out

at the fields sloping up to the starlit Downs and listening to concerts on her portable wireless set. One Saturday night she heard Sir Henry Wood's orchestra perform the work of Bela Bartok, the Hungarian composer; turning off the light, she followed the wild, lovely rhythms until the Downs and the music and the starlight seemed all to be one, and she was not sure whether she was looking at harmonies or listening to stars.

But there were other nights when even music was too exhausting. Overwhelmed by the drugs with which the doctors were trying to reduce her blood pressure, she lay in the lonely darkness thinking sorrowfully about the hampering interrelation of man's imperfect body and his aspiring soul.

" Put all the miseries that man is subject to together, sickness is more than all," she quoted to herself from John Donne's Sermons. " In poverty I lack but other things, in banishment I lack but other men. In sickness I lack myself."

Her control of that interrelation during her last few years was to be her greatest problem, its success her most magnificent achievement. But at first her inability to adapt her physical weakness to her mental vigour distressed her greatly, and she discussed it in many letters with Lady Rhondda and myself.

" I still find it hard to believe," she wrote Lady Rhondda, " that that feeling of extraordinary physical exhilaration, which makes me want everyone else to drink champagne at parties in order to get near my own plane of natural stimulus, was simply the symptom of a disease. . . . I have doubts sometimes whether *my* blood pressure, which made me feel so enormously alive and so avid of experience, is not the proper one and this poor half-stupefied condition to which they are reducing me may be a disease. . . . I warn you that if I find myself when back in the normal world one of those half-alive people for whom I used to be so sorry, I'll run myself back to my old state of stimulus and live fully or bust."

Often these evenings passed into long nights of pain and terror when she lay sleepless, worrying over her family or her work. Her father was now seriously ill again, and she suffered constant anxiety for her mother, yet the thought of going north to help and perhaps collapsing again when she arrived there was more, for the moment, than she was able to face. Both books and articles disturbed her mind ; the series for which she had written *Virginia Woolf* had suddenly failed, and now Faber & Faber, to whom her agents had sent it, had turned it down. The editor of one journal which frequently published her articles complained that her latest series had "lost its sparkle " ; he apologised for making her write when she was ill, and alarm seized her lest she should produce second-rate work without realising how bad it was.

Sometimes, unsleeping, she watched the relentless interminable moonlight vanish, and the grey sky turn to dawn. One night she started up in terror at the sound of phantom horses galloping through the village street ; suddenly she realised that the galloping was in her own head, the throb of her over-stimulated blood through her brain. Sympathising with my predicament at home she said nothing of these experiences in her letters, and I, submerged in chicken-pox, with both children now ill, realised them only dimly. Since I was not available she turned for comfort to a ghost — the ghost of Elinor Wylie, the American poet and novelist, whose work she admired. Only recently, Elinor Wylie had died from high blood pressure at the age of forty-two, and in her sympathy with the imagined suffering which she believed must have been still more acute, Winifred sought the courage to endure her own.

Her headaches and their incalculable appearances brought her an unfamiliar sense of insecurity. As she wrote about this time in *Mandoa, Mandoa !*, life seemed " a very precarious affair, a delicate treading over brittle ice that might at any moment break and plunge one down into black, ice-cold water, beyond the reach of any human solicitude or indifference." Like Lily Sawdon in *South Riding*, she began to feel that the pain which intermittently attacked her had a personality of its own ; she even apostrophised it in the sketch for a poem *To Pain*, found in a notebook of this date :

> *Constant companion of my wakeful days*
> *And uninvited bridegroom of my bed,*
> *Withdraw a little and thy hand upraise*
> *From my tormented head.*

In this crisis of her spirit her thoughts turned to St. John Ervine, whom she had seen so recently ; his affirmative, pugilistic defiance of the continual suffering caused him by the loss of a leg in the War had long aroused her admiration, and at one time she even thought of asking for his help.

" When I was in almost constant pain," she confessed to him in a letter written on February 25th, 1935, " I nearly came once to ask you what one did about it, and especially of the fear that one would soon not be able to keep up appearances. . . . Then I thought that asking or conversation was quite unnecessary. I had only to remember just how you did behave and that ought to be enough."

This recollection of his undefeated fortitude perhaps inspired the further tentative lines which testified to Winifred's conquest over a momentary self-pity never again indulged in, and expressed her realisation that suffering is an essential part of experience, without which life would be mediocre, colourless, incomplete.

> *The weariness will pass ; the pain is mortal.*
> *The loneliness by night, the fear by day*
> *Fall back defeated at the grave's dark portal*
> *And, like a sun-crossed shadow, fade away.*
>
> *But these will live : the angry word unspoken,*
> *The gift forgotten and the hard race run,*
> *The heart unconquered and the faith unbroken. . . .*

The unfinished verse was confused, but she was obviously calculating that courage and benevolence achieved in spite of physical anguish were worth the struggle because they carried their own immortality. She was right ; her distress has vanished now save in its dim reflection in our memories, but the words and works which she wrested triumphantly from her suffering remain, and in them the stabilising quality of her presence which makes the rest of us seem so small and unreliable.

In the end it was neither Elinor Wylie nor even St. John Ervine, but the young lambs of that bitter early spring, which completed Winifred's spiritual victory over pain and fear and death. During February the severe weather had kept the lambs under the shelters, and on March 2nd seven degrees of frost still held the Buckinghamshire country in an iron grip.

" I am sitting up in bed having had breakfast," Winifred wrote me next morning. " The hills are bathed in a silvery haze. A man is leading three beautiful horses along the road, and the birds are singing, singing. . . . The lambs have pink transparent ears, like flower-petals. They are so sweet."

All through February and March, the graceful charm of the lambs seemed to possess her mind with a curious comforting tenderness. She mentioned them in nearly every letter from Monks Risborough, and wrote me shortly before Easter that just as the music of Bach's St. Matthew Passion, relayed one afternoon from York Minster, had reached the words : " Who is he that betrayeth Me ? " she saw " all the little lambs of God come skipping over the hill." Evidently at that moment was born the chapter on Miss Sigglesthwaite and the lambs which contains some of the loveliest passages in *South Riding*.

On one of the coldest mornings of that spring, after she had learnt from a London specialist that she might not have more than two years to live, she went for a walk past Clare Leighton's cottage to a farm further up the hill. She felt tired and dejected ; her mind, still vigorously alive in her slow, impaired body, rebelled bitterly against her fate. Why, she wondered, should she, at thirty-three, not yet in the fullness of her developing powers, be singled out for this cruel unforeseen blow ? She knew, for the constant demands of her friends had made it clear to her, that her life was infinitely valuable to others. She thought of all the half-dead people who " put in time," as though time were not the greatest gift in the universe, while she, who could use it so superbly, was soon to be deprived of it for ever ; and she felt that her mind could hardly contain the rising anguish of that realisation.

Just then she found herself standing by a trough outside the farmyard ; the water in it was frozen and a number of young lambs were struggling beside it vainly trying to drink. She broke the ice for them with her stick, and as she did so she heard a voice within her saying : " Having nothing, yet possessing all things." It was so distinct that she looked round, startled, but she was alone with the lambs on the top of the hill. Suddenly, in a flash, the grief, the bitterness, the sense of frustration disappeared ; all desire to possess power and glory for herself vanished away, and never came back. She walked down the hill with the exhilaration which, says Storm Jameson in *Civil Journey*, " springs from the sense of having lost everything. It is a feeling like no other, a curious form of spiritual intoxication, perhaps not repeatable."

Winifred never told me of this incident nor of the sentence of death passed upon her, until June 1935, when she had only three months to live. By that time she thought —or, as I now suspect, allowed me to believe that she thought—that she had outwitted the doctors. The moment of " conversion " on the hill at Monks Risborough, she said with tears in her eyes, was the supreme spiritual experience of her life. She always associated it afterwards with the words of Bernard Bosanquet on Salvation·:

" And now we are saved absolutely, we need not say from what, we are at home in the universe, and, in principle and in the main, feeble and timid creatures as we are, there is nothing anywhere within the world or without it that can make us afraid."

Throughout March, before Winifred went up to the specialist, numerous friends and acquaintances came to Monks Risborough to see her. She appreciated the kindness of their intention, but often found it almost unbearable to listen to the solicitous advice which inevitably communicated to her the burden of their own anxiety.

" When, when, when, shall you be able to come ? " she wrote to me with unwonted impatience. " My thoughts only dwell on you with such rest and gladness. . . . I *must* get on with my book. You are the only person I know in the world who does not prevent one working."

She meant, of course, that after the years we had worked in each other's company she could tell me to be quiet if I was interrupting her, with a frank directness which those less habituated to her moods might misunderstand. It was work—our mutual coachings with Mr. Cruttwell—which had first brought us together ; work which united us long before the deeper ties of affection forged our minds and spirits into a partnership indissoluble even by death. In Bloomsbury and in Maida Vale we had fought with combined vigour for leisure and privacy in which to write our books against a constant barrage of requests to make speeches, sit on committees, attend deputations, send letters to the papers and act as Press secretaries to innumerable organisations. After my marriage Winifred had joined in my struggle for time to write in spite of the claims of husband, household and children—not out of pure altruism, but because she knew that the integrity of the artist depends, if the artist happens to be a woman, upon fighting successfully against the tradition that domesticity must be the first preoccupation of a wife and mother.

Now, confidently, she turned to me to help her fight the equally cramping tradition that an invalid's first preoccupation must be his illness. She knew I should understand that for her, even more than before, the most important thing in life was to write books which would enshrine some permanent quality of truth and beauty,

simply because this had always been the most important
thing in life for myself.

Her appeal seemed too urgent for the conscientious
observance of quarantine, and I did go down for the day
on March 11th, nobly driven by Monica Whately because
I was not yet sufficiently free from infection to travel by
train. Winifred looked to me no better, and the village,
which I had not seen before, appeared as a bleak vignette
of frozen downs and bare tossing woods. Half-way back
to London, a heavy snowstorm turned to a crawl our journey
home along the Uxbridge Road.

But before I went to see her, Winifred had already
received the unexpected intimation of another visitor. Bill,
she knew, was due back from India after his six years'
service ; amid the poems and miscellaneous writings which
he sent her in the hope that she could place them, he had
remembered to mention his impending return. Since her
illness she had had no communication from him, but now,
suddenly, he wrote that he was coming to see her.

In her depressed condition she dreaded lest he should
make any emotional demands upon her, though she hardly
expected it after so many years ; she realised that he had
never needed her—though God knew what it was that he
needed. On his return from India he had refused two tolerable posts on the ground that " civilisation was on the eve
of a crash "—a situation in which civilisation was to remain
poised for so many years that those who demanded security
as a condition of work were liable to become permanently
unemployed. Was he, Winifred asked herself interminably, a
genius who preferred the rôle of an inglorious if far from
mute Milton to one of triumphant attainment, or a war
casualty whose capacity for achievement remained perpetually impaired ?

There seems little doubt that it was Winifred's loving,
reliable loyalty which tempted Bill perversely to demonstrate
the opposite qualities and deliberately turn himself into her
beloved vagabond, a recurring decimal of emotion which
appeared and reappeared with a persistent incalculability

that kept her constantly on tenterhooks. Whether he was practising a sedulous technique or merely following the will-o'-the-wisp impulses of a wayward disposition, he created throughout Winifred's life a situation utterly different from the one imagined by the scandalmongers who invented for her a lurid series of homosexual relationships, usually associated with Lady Rhondda or myself.

Bill came in the middle of March, and stayed for two or three days. After six years he and Winifred met as though they had parted the previous week, and she found him kind, amusing and sympathetic.

" Bill leaves to-morrow," she wrote me on March 17th. " I have thoroughly enjoyed him. He is ridiculous and quite irresponsible, and won't or can't take the future seriously, but he is charming, considerate and funny, makes me laugh, gets on with all the neighbours, and has done me a great deal of good instead of tiring me."

By the end of March, Winifred's blood pressure had become higher than ever and its cause was still undetected. It seems strange to-day that the real nature of her illness was not discovered sooner, but I am told that Bright's Disease is normally an ailment of later life, which seldom attacks the young and is usually fatal when it does. I had now become thoroughly alarmed ; no treatment given her seemed to have been effective and I wrote urging inquiries by G. in America, and by the Smeterlins in Paris, Berlin or Vienna. I didn't feel prepared, I told her, to accept the prospect of her living permanently as a semi-invalid, under the threat of a blood pressure liable to rush up at any moment.

" We must and will tackle this enemy at its root," I insisted ; " you shan't go on just temporising."

About this time her brother-in-law suggested a visit to a renal specialist, while Clare Leighton recommended Dr. O., an Austrian bio-chemist who had a unique knowledge of glandular and circulatory functioning. Winifred, as determined as we were to get herself back to normal, agreed to go up to London and see them both.

"Dear love," she wrote to me encouragingly, cheered by the prospect of a cure at last, "I'm not at all devastated" (she spelt it "deverstated"). "I'm enjoying it all. I'm so egotistic that I am enchanted at all this egocentric concentration on my symptoms! I've never felt so important in my life!"

Early in April, Clare drove her up to town, and I met her, with our doctor, at her specialist's consulting-rooms. In *South Riding* Winifred draws his portrait as the cancer specialist who interviewed Lily Sawdon at Kingsport — a transposition which gave a number of readers the mistaken impression that she had suffered from cancer herself. But it was in a *Good Housekeeping* article on "How to Enjoy Bad Health"[1] that she quoted the remarks with which he prefaced his announcement that she could not hope to live for more than two years.

"Well, perhaps it's not so much a question of getting better, as of adjusting. If we can help you to adjust. . . . Of course, I don't say it isn't possible . . . ahem, ahem. . . ."

I stayed behind in the waiting-room, reading a favourable review in *Punch* of Phyllis Bentley's newly published novel, *Inheritance*, which Winifred had voted "magnificent," and never dreamed that sentence of death was being passed upon her behind the closed door. When she came out her cheerful expression was unaltered. She exchanged a ribald joke with our doctor, went on for a further examination by Dr. O. at another address, and at lunch-time told me gaily that the two specialists wanted her to return to the nursing-home for "lots of tests." I took her back there in the afternoon, imagining that she would go straight to bed.

Instead, she rang up H. G. Wells, whom she knew slightly through *Time and Tide*, and invited herself to tea. She had just learned, she told him, that her days were numbered, and as she had always wanted to meet him, she would consider it a definite stain upon her courage if she allowed herself to die without doing so. He happened to be in,

[1] Republished in *Pavements at Anderby* as "Machiavelli in the Sick-Room."

and, astonished but benevolent, asked her to come along. She found him alone, and for two hours they talked *tête-à-tête*. He lived up completely to her idea of him, she told me afterwards, and she had never enjoyed herself more in her life.

After another brief visit to Monks Risborough Winifred returned to London permanently, and remained in the nursing-home for several weeks, enduring tests made by the specialists in the hope of prolonging her life. Even she admitted that some of these made her " wildly ill," but she only once hinted to me of her peril.

" If I'm not put really right now, there's a danger of my getting Bright's Disease or something foul like that. To stop it and make me a hundred per cent well, they say I must be under trained observation the whole time."

She was full of apologies for having to spend so much money on her illness, and begged to be allowed to contribute her usual share to the housekeeping expenses at Glebe Place. This, of course, we could not permit, and as though she had not repaid us a hundred times by her constant generosity, she wrote with eager affection : " One day I'll try to pay you back for all this trouble and expense — though I can never repay your patience and your sweet bright darling face round the door. Bless you."

Actually, I did not go to the nursing-home as often as I wished, since I usually found somebody with her. Even during her last illness, she had an unbroken succession of visitors until the final days.

" My room's like Piccadilly Circus," she remarked to me about a week before she died.

When her malady was thought to be temporary and she could not escape, as in health, to work or an appointment, the temptation to use her as a safety-valve for their troubles was more than some of her friends could resist. On several occasions I failed to resist it myself.

For the remainder of her life, wherever Winifred went and whatever she did, Dr. O. kept her under observation for a ludicrous fee — because, he said, he learnt so much from her case. He was the least " professional " specialist that I have ever seen ; the only time he visited our house he wore tennis shoes and an informal jacket which looked like a blazer. But, unlike the owners of " bedside manners," he treated Winifred with great respect for her intelligence, avoiding so far as he could any drugs which might impair her creative powers. He never deceived her by representing his attempts to arrest the progress of her disease as more than experiments, but, recognising the value of her congenital optimism, he always insisted that if he did succeed she might live for years.

His treatment involved a careful diet, long nights of sleep, a complicated series of drugs and hypodermic injections, a careful choice of exercise, and the limitation of her work as far as possible to quiet writing and journalism. This programme would seriously have interfered with the activities of most human beings, but Winifred took it in her stride and still achieved more in a day than anyone I have met. Actually, Dr. O.'s prescriptions added to her life the extra two years which enabled her to write *South Riding*. Since her literary reputation will rest mainly upon this, the world of letters as well as her own prestige owes a considerable debt to Dr. O.'s skill and understanding.

Once her routine of treatment was established, Winifred was allowed to return to Glebe Place. Several of her friends, and for a time we ourselves, questioned the wisdom of this decision ; there were, we knew, other households where she would be welcome which would give her greater comfort and spare her the constant noise of the children. But in her own eyes, apparently, there was no second choice. She did not want luxury or silence, but a home in which she could be completely *déboutonnée*. This was possible in mine, not because she loved me more than others, but owing to the long familiarity which alone permits of thorough relaxation. The nursing experience of my war-time years, which the care of the children had revived, was an additional source of reassurance. Too many people — men, women

and children — had, she was aware, been ill in my presence
for one more to rouse any reaction but sympathy and a desire
to function with maximum competence. She knew that
her attacks of pain might distress but would never agitate
me ; she was confident that I should not interfere with her
management of her life even though her way of living meant
an earlier end.

A final consideration was, undoubtedly, the devoted
loyalty of the young married couple, Amy and Charles
Burnett, who had managed for so many years the domestic
side of our household. When illness descended upon her,
Winifred, who had made demands on nobody, dreaded to
find herself at the mercy of servants who would grudge bringing her meals to her bedroom and look with disfavour on
the late rising and early bedtime so often made necessary
by sleepless nights. She had joined with G. and myself
in making it possible for the Burnetts to get married ;
she had attended their wedding and helped to provide the
honeymoon which was our household gift, and she knew
that they would respond to her needs with the unconventional
adaptability of those who have graduated from servants to
family friends. During her last four years, their affectionate
co-operation was of incalculable assistance in enabling her
to lead the life that she wished. She got up and went to
bed when she liked, and had the special meals she required,
without the nagging fear of a resentful domestic " atmosphere " which makes so many women tackle the daily
round when they ought to be resting.

When Winifred finally returned from the nursing-home
she appeared, to those who only knew her superficially,
to be the same gay, exuberant individual whom ill-health
had struck down at the height of her powers. But gradually,
like other intimate friends, I noticed a subtle difference.
The strange religious experience beside the lambs' trough
at Monks Risborough had fortified her with the power to
face the bleak truth of her future, yet keep her own counsel
even amongst those who loved her best ; but at times the
knowledge caused her to appear withdrawn into herself

and a little detached from the rest of us, as the *Prédestinés* are withdrawn.   Like Dr. Bleriot's dying wife in *Mandoa, Mandoa !*, " she dwelt apart in a shadowed country where those who are young and doomed can know only each other."

Did she who loved life so deeply that she endured indescribable pain and discomfort in order to give herself a few more months of it, perhaps reflect that there are worse things than dying young and beloved, with one's mind consciously in tune with all that is best in the life of one's time ?   Did she remember that it is sadder still to grow old and lonely, to watch the friends of a lifetime vanish like lighted candles blown out one after another by the breath of an unseen presence ; and saddest of all to reach the stage of crying doom upon one's epoch, condemning its youth and deploring that which is new and experimental because one's mind has died before one's body ?

At any rate she knew, with Jean Stanbury who loved Bill Durrant in the story of Mandoa, that " in life nothing is ever finally settled ; that the dilemmas recur, and the decisions have to be re-made again and again, and that only in death is finality."   Perhaps, like Jean herself, " soothed by the thought of that final rest from criticism, from judgment, and from choice, she slept."

CHAPTER XIX

LIFE OVER DEATH

THE AEROPLANE

(Lines in Memory of Dorothy McCalman)

This is the thought of man
Molten into steel, woven into silk.
This is the thought and the will and the courage of man
Which swings me
Above the small beloved and chequered isle,
The green isle.
The island you peopled with cavalcades
Of knights riding to war
And kings that died.
The isle that is rich with the people of your thought.
This is your steely sea, dappled with cloud,
Flecked with white cuckoo-spit,
These are your little tossing boats like water beetles
Scurrying hither and thither.
I too have left the earth,
I too will follow.

My silver wings careen toward the field,
My swooping wings scoop up the stubbled hill ;
The form of the field lies plastic to my will,
I mould the hills and hollow the valleys, I—
I have left the earth. I have sought the heavenly sky.
This is better than life, and if this, this is to die,
Then I will follow you, I—
I, too, will die.

WINIFRED HOLTBY, September 1930

FOR SEVERAL WEEKS during the summer of 1932,
Phyllis Bentley stayed with us at Glebe Place to enjoy the
agreeable aftermath of her success with *Inheritance*.

Perhaps because they were all Yorkshire women as well

334

as writers, Winifred's friendships with Phyllis Bentley and
Storm Jameson made less demands upon her than many
others. She could talk to them without fear of misunderstanding though all detailed explanation was withheld.
They understood Yorkshire reticences, Yorkshire dignity,
Yorkshire inhibitions, because they not only shared them,
but experienced, like Winifred, secret moods in which the
inhabitants of the rest of England appeared shallow, fussy
and unreliable.

Winifred's numerous letters to Phyllis, whom she had
known as a fellow Yorkshire writer since 1927, show a
freedom from effort, a confidence that everything she says
will be taken at its intended value, which is not characteristic of all her correspondence. To Storm Jameson, with
whom she became friendly after their original interview,
she wrote less frequently, but their meetings were always
easy and pleasant, with explanations of manners and motives
" taken as read."

Saved now from envy of the benefits, forbidden to her,
which others possessed, Winifred genuinely enjoyed Phyllis's
astonished delight in being fêted and entertained after a
long uphill struggle for literary success. On the few evenings
that she had no engagements the three of us talked together
in the garden, or wandered slowly along the Embankment,
while sky and river were touched to flame by the magnificent
sunsets of that golden June. When the lightly massed clouds
behind Chelsea Old Church had deepened from orange and
crimson to fuchsia and purple, we sat at the pavement
tables of the little Lombard café—one of the two oldest
cottages in Chelsea—drinking coffee and watching the
passers-by. Amongst them, arm-in-arm, walked Charles
Morgan and his wife, Hilda Vaughan, who then lived in a
flat overlooking the river.

The cottages have now been pulled down and Winifred
is dead, but the pleasant ghosts of 1932 still linger about
their desolate site. Winifred never allowed the shadow
which lay across her life to spoil that enchanted summer
for Phyllis. Perhaps it was not spoiled even for her, for she

has told us in her short story, *Sentence of Life*,[1] that the glories of this earth are only truly valued by those about to lose them. It may be that the shades of death gathering in the distance added a brighter beauty to the flaming clouds, a deeper tenderness to the translucent sky.

Before the summer holidays Winifred received, as usual, an invitation to join the *Time and Tide* group at Agay, but she knew that she could not face the long journey to the South of France. As she had felt so much better at Sidmouth than at any other place since her illness, I took the children there for their holiday and she joined us. Later in the autumn we went together again, visiting the St. John Ervines at Seaton and E. M. Delafield at Cullompton. Winifred was now correcting the proofs of *Mandoa, Mandoa!* and working on a short new satire, *The Astonishing Island*, based upon a series of articles published in the *Radio Times*. The fate of *Virginia Woolf* also was now satisfactorily settled, for Wishart & Wishart had accepted the book on July 28th.

With us to Devonshire, on both occasions, went the unwieldy manuscript of *Testament of Youth*, now nearing the end of its third year of writing. While Winifred had completed *Poor Caroline*, *Virginia Woolf* and *Mandoa, Mandoa!*, this autobiography had plodded interminably along, the testament not only of youth but of an undistinguished and retarded literary career. Again and again, convinced that the reading public would never be interested in the story of an obscure free-lance writer, I was tempted to abandon it, but periodically Winifred read what I had written and urged me to go on.

"Never mind how long it's taking," she would say. "It's got a quality of some kind. Really, I do know this. I haven't reviewed literally hundreds of books without learning to recognise something worth-while when I see it." She would add with Yorkshire directness : "You wait. You'll wipe all our noses ! "

So I laboured on. Many times I did so only because she insisted.

[1] In *Truth Is Not Sober*.

Between the two visits to Sidmouth, Winifred had gone to Cottingham for the first time since her illness. At the end of August she spent what she called " a pre-war evening." With her parents she motored through Rudston and called on some of their old employees ; these included an aged woman who wept and kissed her mother, and an elderly labourer who reminded her that she used to do " a bit o' thrashin' " with him. At Driffield, as on hundreds of market days, they had supper with an aunt and cousin in a house where even the carpets were unchanged. Driving home through the twilight over roads so familiar that part of her, she said, seemed " to fit into their hills and hollows as one does into a familiar and well-hollowed bed," they passed a lane where a schoolboy and a schoolgirl had walked together long ago. Suddenly they saw a familiar figure striding along, and Bill came up to them and stopped the car.

" It was all too extraordinary," she wrote. " Hardly a detail out of order. Imagine yourself at Buxton doing something precisely as you did it in 1913 — and feeling no older, no different, just as much ' inside ' as ever."

On October 7th, Winifred's study of Virginia Woolf appeared. It had sold five hundred copies by the end of the year, a very fair number for a purely literary publication of its type.

In some respects this little work of criticism is the profoundest of Winifred's books. It is rich in understanding and appreciation, yet dominated by a respect for integrity and a philosophic valuation of truth not always characteristic of propagandists and social reformers, admirable as these practical contributors to life may be. The critics who hold that Winifred was "not an artist" because she wrote *Time and Tide* leaders and lectured for the League of Nations Union, should re-read *Virginia Woolf*.

In spite of her deep respect for her subject, Winifred did not allow admiration to blind her judgments. While emphasising how completely the occupations followed by

Virginia Woolf's fiction characters contrast with those of the Yorkshire provincials amongst whom she herself grew up, Winifred reveals the extent to which Virginia Woolf lacks her own supreme gift of understanding the forlorn, the pretentious, the stupid, and the half-educated. Virginia Woolf's men and women write, paint, lecture, teach, edit the classics and read in the British Museum ; they inhabit a specialised mental planet having no remote contact with the crude everyday world in which Rachel Hammond of *The Crowded Street*, Joseph Isenbaum of *Poor Caroline*, and Annie Holly of *South Riding* could be multiplied ten thousand times.

The description of Virginia Woolf's development amid the woman suffrage campaign and other political pressures of the early twentieth century enabled Winifred to state her own basic problem — the conflict between means and ends, between practical measures for bringing the good life nearer, and the creation of enduring beauty which is part of the good life itself. The book is one prolonged analysis of the meaning of true art and the method of its attainment. Winifred also understood how cruelly irrelevant may be the obstacles standing in the way. Her own suffering gave her a knowledge, which her vitality might otherwise have withheld, of the problems confronting an author who writes under the perpetual menace of serious illness. Another quality which she and Virginia Woolf shared was their inability to be shocked — a form of toleration which originated, for Virginia Woolf, in the freedom of her father's large library, and for Winifred in the primitive realities of life on a farm.

Through the study of Mrs. Woolf's books, she came to formulate more clearly her own philosophy of life and death. Of the flashes of insight that come to some of the characters in the novels, she writes :

"These are the moments of revelation which compensate for the chaos, the discomfort, the toil of living. The crown of life is neither happiness nor annihilation ; it is understanding. The artist's intuitive vision ; the

thinker's slow, laborious approach to truth ; the knowledge that comes to the raw girl, to the unawakened
woman — this is life, this is love. These are the moments
in which all the disorder of life assumes a pattern ; we
see ; we understand ; and immediately the intolerable
burden becomes tolerable ; we stand for a moment on
the slopes of that great mountain from the summit of
which we can see truth, and thus enjoy the greatest
felicity of which we are capable."

Analysing *Jacob's Room* — Virginia Woolf's only " war
book " — Winifred realised that each person dwells not only
in himself, but in the mirror made by the eyes of his friends
who regard him. Did she, before she finished revising her
study, think of the " room " that she herself occupied, the
large part that she filled in the mirror-consciousness of many
people, and acknowledge how soon that room was to be
empty ? If so, she accepted its coming emptiness as part
of the cruelty of living which death alone can resolve. As
the little volume moves towards its concluding analysis of
The Waves, it becomes a vehicle for Winifred's thoughts on
mortality. She sees death not merely as a tragedy, but as
something which illustrates the meaning of life. What
matters is the ebb and flow of human existence, its events,
its changes, rather than the relationship of any individual
to those changes and events. She perceives that when she
herself is the individual, this continuity is of more significance, even to her, than the termination of her consciousness
that death will bring.

" Life," she writes, " flows on over death as water closes
over a stone dropped into a pool. . . . Fate is certain ;
death is certain ; but the courage and nobility of men and
women matter more than these."

And she makes her final chapter, which she added late,
embody her own triumphant challenge to man's mortality.
Like the last years of her short life, it is a cry — the cry of
Virginia Woolf at the end of *The Waves* : " Against you I
will fling myself, unvanquished and unyielding, O Death ! "

By the end of the year, though she still suffered from occasional violent headaches, Winifred was sufficiently recovered to take part once more in the typical days of the children's typical babyhood. A letter to Sarah Gertrude Millin, written on December 11th, 1932, indicates that she had also resumed her typical habit of stepping into the breach :

" This letter is written incoherently, I fear, for Shirley, aged 2½, is playing here, and about every three lines I have to rush and rescue her from the retaliations of the cat, whom she is teasing, or from her own alpine hazards on the arm of a chair, or to blow her nose, as she is confined to the house with a cold. Vera is in bed with acute gastritis — the result of a chill taken while exploring the Brontë country a fortnight ago — and yesterday, ' to cap all,' as we say in Yorkshire, the housemaid was taken ill with bronchitis and Shirley sick on the nursery floor. This household tosses about on its little domestic storms of sickness and whatnot, but it is, I think, an unusually amusing and human one. I could not leave it and live in refined isolation with the arts for anything ! "

That year's long purgatory had not destroyed her eager interest in small, unusual things. One cold afternoon, walking past the School of Engineering in South Kensington, she bought a sprig of white heather from a flower-seller who told her that he was an ex-florist. Thin and ill, but still dignified, he told her his history. He had lost his job the previous year through economy cuts in his firm ; one illness after another had taken his savings, and with them his final hopes had gone.

" If I had five pounds behind me, I should feel a different man," he said. He did not expect Winifred to give him five pounds ; he was merely explaining the exaggerated value which money acquires for those who have none.

The heather-seller's personality and story captured Winifred's imagination, and she related the incident in the " Notes on the Way " which she wrote shortly afterwards in four numbers of *Time and Tide*. A business woman in the

City, reading these Notes, sent Winifred five pounds with which to put the ex-florist on his feet. The problem now was to find him; he had only been a wandering street-seller, and she knew neither his name nor his address. Eventually, after much fruitless investigation, she appealed for help to the taxi-drivers near the School of Engineering. One of them remembered the man and promised to send him to our house if he reappeared. A few days later the ex-florist called at Glebe Place and with incredulous gratitude received his five pounds.

Winifred meant to keep in touch with him, but an unsatisfactory visit from Bill, who dined with us just after Christmas, drove other people's problems from her mind. All at once, like the spirit blowing where it listeth, something else entered it instead.

" Three nights ago," she wrote to Phyllis Bentley, " after a rather depressing evening spent with my-young-man-who-never-will-be-more-than-my-young-man, I suddenly knew what my next novel was going to be about — quite, quite irrelevant. But it came just like . . . that, when I was getting rather desperately undressed for bed. I've felt like a prince ever since. You know."

This story was *South Riding*. But nearly another year was to pass before, exuberantly, she told Lady Rhondda : " I've got a new novel all bubbling and boiling in my head. It's all about local government and aldermen and county councillors — a romance ! "

The beginning of 1933 found her often in moods of gay exhilaration — not the wild, hysterical gaiety of those who must eat, drink and be merry because to-morrow they die, but the genuine gaiety of one who seems to have said to herself : " I've always found life amusing. Now that so little of it is left, I'm going to see just how amusing it can be."

People have often said to me that Winifred's last years must have been " very sorrowful." They were tragic, courageous, magnificent, perhaps, but I am sure that she herself would never have regarded sorrow as their keynote. Her response to the knowledge that she was doomed was

the vivid and glorious satire which makes *Mandoa, Mandoa !*
unique amongst her books. Even in the darkest hours of
January 1932 she could let off tiny farcical squibs such as
the little essay " Let's Abolish the Dear Animals," published
that month in *Time and Tide.*

One January day in 1933, she went to interview Leonard
Woolf at the Hogarth Press about new sources of help for
the Ballinger Fund. At the end of the interview she had
an hour to occupy before another appointment, and decided
to use it in communicating to her friend Creech Jones the
information that she had just gathered. She realised that
she was passing a large hotel in Russell Square; it
seemed a convenient place in which to write a letter, so she
walked in.

" Has Mr. Graham arrived here yet ? " she asked the
office clerk. The clerk replied that Mr. Graham was in his
room. Inwardly chiding herself for choosing so ordinary a
name, Winifred added hastily : " I mean Mr. Graham of
Cottingham." A search was made. When it not unnaturally failed to reveal Mr. Graham of Cottingham, she
observed sadly : " I was *afraid* he mightn't come. . . . Do
you mind if I go to the writing-room and leave him a
note ? "

The clerk, by this time much intrigued, gave her permission, and she passed an hour comfortably writing her
letter to Creech Jones. Then, going up to the desk, she
asked again for Mr. Graham, and was told sympathetically
that he had not yet appeared.

" I've decided not to write after all," she said tragically.
" Please tell Mr. Graham when he comes that Miss Briggs
has called."

And she hurried away to her appointment, leaving the
clerk and the hall-porter romantically certain that they had
witnessed a scene of rejected love.

For all the surface absurdities with which she amused
herself, Winifred was too responsible to ignore the obligation
to leave her affairs in order that her illness laid upon her.
Her new concern for the Ballinger Fund arose from the

need to make it independent of her own contributions, and she realised that she ought also to make her Will. An old acquaintance whom we all loved — Ada Moore, the eldest sister of Eva and Decima Moore, and Honorary Secretary of the Six Point Group — had recently died from cerebral haemorrhage following a period of high blood pressure. As a teacher of elocution Ada Moore had lived a long and active life, whereas Winifred was still young, but she knew that her smaller total of years did not reduce the danger. So she made her Will, naming me as her literary executor, and on some unspecified date of 1933 wrote me a letter which she enclosed with it.

I read this letter just after her death. It showed me that two years earlier she had imagined that her end would come in a similar manner to Ada Moore's. The fear that she expressed in it of being a " nuisance " dominated her throughout her illness. However great her pain, she determined that neither my work nor anyone else's should suffer as her own had done from the physical afflictions of relatives and friends. So she kept Dr. O.'s reports to herself, purchased and used her drugs as he directed, and learnt how to give herself injections. I understood this resolution, and never attempted to shake it. In one sense it made her companionship, as she intended, no more exacting than that of a normal person ; had she chosen she could have lain with the whole weight of invalidism upon those who shared her life, and been wholly justified. But her method had its difficulties. It meant that persons closely associated with her must watch carefully for symptoms which she never admitted until they were impossible to conceal. Because she would not acknowledge her need of them it was difficult to offer her services which the sick normally require, and more than one of us accumulated a bitter heritage of self-reproach for requests made to her at moments when, unknown to us, she was unfit to fulfil them.

My Very Dear [ran her·letter],

I suppose that there is one chance in a thousand that I

might die quite suddenly if any accident happened to send up my blood-pressure. If this did happen, I want you to have as little trouble as possible. . . , I have left you my literary executor. I think there should be no confusion. I have no saleable MSS. hidden anywhere. . . . My short stories might make a volume but I doubt it. . . ."

After giving me various detailed instructions about letters and papers, she concluded :

> I have been very happy. I have had a lovely life. I am not in the least afraid of anything but being a nusance [*sic*]   If by any chance you should read this because I have had a stroke and am paralysed completely like Ada Moore, please, if you can, see that I am not allowed to live on and be a burden. That is the only terror I have.
>   I love you always.
>   WINIFRED

This letter was written before she had even begun *South Riding*. Though ample evidence exists that she knew that she might not live to see its publication, she added no request concerning it. She knew that I was competent to undertake, as I had so often undertaken, the correction of her typescript and proofs, and, apart from these minor alterations, she evidently trusted me to publish her book exactly as she left it. This was done.

At the end of January, Winifred went to the first evening party that she had been able to attend since Election Night at Selfridge's. The party was given at Claridge's Hotel by Harold Latham of the New York Macmillan Company, and Winifred attended it, with Phyllis Bentley, as an author whose novel *Mandoa, Mandoa !* had just been accepted by Macmillan with enthusiasm. The firm was so pleased with the story that they made it one of their " featured " autumn books, and, after the comparative failure of her two previous novels in America, Winifred knew that her future there — supposing only that she had one — was satisfactorily assured. Between

September 1933 and May 1934 the American sales of
Mandoa, Mandoa ! amounted to nearly nine thousand copies.

In England the novel had just been published with
considerable *éclat* by Collins. Neither they nor its American
publishers had any conception of the indescribable difficulties to which its ribald and often savage humour had been a
determined challenge. While writing it at Monks Risborough, at Sidmouth and in the Earl's Court nursing-
home, Winifred had often been half-doped with drugs
which affected her body but left her mind abnormally
clear.

" I've come to the conclusion that one's health has little
effect on the *quality* of what one writes," she told Sarah
Millin two years afterwards. " It affects the ease with which
one writes, which is different. . . . I know that some of the
most gay and vital stuff that I have written I wrote in such
pain that I used to cry over the paper."

Certainly the story shows no trace of invalidism. It
required an unusual amount of research and Winifred could
not then visit libraries, so she used the intelligent help of a
Somerville contemporary, Katie Gilchrist, who was herself
recovering from an operation and could only do sedentary
work. Nevertheless she suffered from perpetual qualms
about the quality of her book.

" My publisher will hate my new novel, poor lamb, if
ever I contrive to write it," she lamented to Lady Rhondda
in December 1931. " Sometimes I have nightmares about
it — £100 taken and spent for a novel that will hardly be
a novel — a work of fiction, yes — but a sort of satirical
symposium of empire-building . . . and he is hoping for
a nice love-story. Oh, dear, what a mess. And I know I
could do what he wants well enough to satisfy him — and
I am not at all sure that I can do what I want, to satisfy
me. I've had five shots at it — got over 100 pages done
three times — and all abortive. None will do. My brain
thinks satirically and realistically, but my pen will run away
into romance. If ever I write quickly, I write soft romantic
stuff — and I want to do something hard, muscular, com-

pact, very little emotional, and then the emotion hammered into the style. Metal-work, not water-colour."

Winifred's story of an attempt by an enterprising travel agency to advertise an isolated principality in Central Africa sprang from a double origin. In composing this remarkable small chapter of imaginary international history in which love, ambition, jealousy, courage and a variety of other human emotions were inextricably entangled, she re-lived the impulses, opinions and impressions which had sent her straight from South Africa to begin her campaign for the natives.

" I really care a good deal about our monstrous behaviour in breaking faith with ignorant Africans," she confessed to St. John Ervine when he accused her of writing an over-intellectual novel in order " to make old girls sit up." " When my forebears weren't farming, they went out to Uganda and places and I'm a passionate imperialist by instinct."

But the final inspiration came, as the best ideas for most books do come, straight out of the blue. One evening in 1931, we invited Monica Whately to supper at Glebe Place. During the meal she entertained us with an account of the Abyssinian Emperor's coronation, given to her by an American friend then staying at her flat. Though Monica had never been to Abyssinia and her story was second-hand, she related it with characteristic racy vividness, calling up exciting scenes and highly-coloured pictures. The narrative started in Winifred's mind a train of thought which suggested how she might embody her views on imperialism in a novel, without covering the now familiar ground all over again.

Unfortunately for Winifred the novelist Evelyn Waugh, who had actually been to the Abyssinian coronation as a spectator, was simultaneously at work on a book entitled *Black Mischief*. Being unhandicapped by illness, he published his novel first. It was a Book Society choice, and *Mandoa, Mandoa !* therefore had no choice of being selected.

Winifred suffered from another chronological misfortune in the fact that her book appeared two years before the

Abyssinian War. Addis Ababa had not yet become a household name when she mentioned it in her second chapter. Had the publication of *Mandoa, Mandoa!* coincided with Mussolini's first adventure in imperialism, the sudden universal sympathy for all things Ethiopian might have made it a best-seller in two continents. I still wonder that, during this period of excited militarism, no enterprising screen producer perceived the story's possibilities as a film. In the summer of 1935, a few weeks before her death, Winifred received a letter from May Lamberton Becker of the *New York Herald-Tribune* " Books."

" I am going to call attention in this department," it ran, " to the fact that the most informing — and upsetting — book to read to-day on the Abyssinian crisis is *Mandoa, Mandoa!* I wrote the review in *Books* ; this summer I bought the English edition to re-read in the light of present events. Heavens, how well it stood the test ! "

Winifred dedicated the book to myself — as she said, " irrelevantly." Perhaps she decided to do so in the belief that the story might be her last. She had never dedicated a book to me, and wanted to be sure that she gave me one. But she knew too that I should agree with her ideas, sympathise with her conclusions, and perceive the significance of her leading characters. Especially was she aware that I should understand and fully appreciate her treatment of Bill Durrant.

Mandoa, Mandoa! has much to give to the lovers of Winifred's books but even more to the admirers of her personality, for it explains the secret history of her emotional life. In it she reveals the hidden love, the suppressed exasperation, the mingled pity and respect for the man contemptuous of feathering his own nest, aroused in her by the only individual whom, for two tantalising decades, she ever contemplated or desired as a husband.

The Bill Durrant of the novel makes his first appearance in a street at " North Donnington," characteristically wearing the colours of his Conservative brother's opponent during the General Election of 1931.

" Bill was there, standing against a lamp-post, hatless, his longish brown hair blowing across his forehead, the Socialist colours of red and yellow pinned to his coat, his arm round the shoulders of a young woman who waved in her free hand a small wooden rattle. He looked ill, shabby, dissipated, yet Maurice knew that the irony of family likeness had given to both brothers the same tall, wiry figure, the same finely-drawn features, the same light, curving smile. He could watch, as though in a mirror, his own expression on his brother's face down in the crowd. As he had smiled at the unsportsmanlike antics of the mob, so Bill smiled now at the victor's complacent rhetoric."

On page 233, another description of the fictitious Bill Durrant, as seen through the eyes of Jean Stanbury, shows that the heroine of *Mandoa, Mandoa!* shared Winifred's painful, realistic freedom from love's romantic blindness.

. . . " He had exploited her shamelessly, shamelessly . . . feeding upon her, demanding from her, yet always remaining just sufficiently detached to give her nothing in return, to place upon her all initiative for greater intimacy. He had interrupted her evenings, eaten her suppers, borrowed her vitality. And though she had not sent him away, she could never yield completely. Always, even while lending him her knowledge and her practical sense, she had felt the unsleeping clock of criticism beat in her brain, tick, tock, tick, tock, marking his faults, her withdrawals, the time that both were wasting, the energy they spilled."

But though this portrait suggested characteristics belonging both to Bill Durrant, the representative of Prince's Tours who went to Central Africa to investigate Mandoa, and to the real Bill who wandered unattached about the Yorkshire wolds, it was not the whole truth about either of them, and nobody knew this better than Winifred.

Throughout the story of Mandoa, Bill Durrant is the only character who despises neither the " downs and outs " of English society nor the " lower races " of British Imperialism ; who approaches every situation with an open, unprejudiced mind ; who is completely free from self-consciousness, and humorously incapable of being shocked by any human quality. Bill is as much at home with the coloured slaves of Mandoa as amongst the unemployed at the North Donnington Labour Exchange ; he has no " superiority complex " except towards those who cultivate their own interests at the expense of the poor, the helpless, the oppressed. His sympathetic understanding of human hopes, griefs, motives, misdemeanours and limitations is deep and intuitive ; he alone perceives the baffling direction of psychological undercurrents in the minds of both black and white ; he withholds his compassion only from the uncompassionate, his co-operation from the " top dogs " intolerantly accustomed to sycophantic service.

Two months after Winifred's death, the real Bill went north to help one of her closest friends who was standing as a Labour candidate in a depressed industrial area. There, for three weeks, he lived with his colleague at the local hotel, and but for certain unimportant geographical distinctions, his functions and occupations closely resembled those which Winifred had allocated to Bill Durrant in Book Two, Chapter VIII, of *Mandoa, Mandoa !* :

" He wandered about the streets, inspecting alterations, or he dined with different families, teaching young sprigs of nobility how to play the gramophone. Or he sat on his verandah dispensing cocktails to whichever members of the staff cared to visit him. Because, after his first panic, he was really interested in people, they became interesting. He learned not only about Jordan's gastric disabilities, but about the shop assistant with social aspirations whom he had carelessly married when he was a student. He knew the secret disappointment of Cooper's soul, and the religious foundation from which sprang Nicholson's eternal optimism.

"It did not occur to him that anyone could think him supernumerary, for it seemed as though his work was as important as any. He had so many people to keep in a good temper, so many crises of misunderstanding to evade, that though he spent most of his time in having a drink, first with Mandoans in a stockaded courtyard, and then with Europeans in the Rest House or hotel, his activities seemed indispensable to the Mandoan renaissance."

Bill's original was equally indispensable to the Socialist cause in a vast constituency. Just as Bill Durrant had perceived the consequences of Mandoan corruption, so the real Bill understood the results of British industrial depression and knew instinctively how to contend with both cynicism and pessimism. In that next-to-the-most disastrous General Election for Labour since 1918, he could not ride his candidate home, but if anyone had been able to push him to victory, Bill would have done so. His resourcefulness was unfailing, his memory phenomenal, his patience inexhaustible, and though, unlike the fictitious Bill, he had never voted Labour, his loyalty was beyond all question.

Friends began to speculate hopefully. Was Bill really pulling himself together ? Perhaps Winifred's death had changed him ? But a later experiment, in quite another quarter, proved conclusively that Bill was once more his old self, cheerfully contemptuous of powerful efficiency, and sublimely free from any puritanical impulse to become an orthodox character.

Just when some brilliantly appreciative reviews of *Mandoa, Mandoa !* were raising Winifred's spirits to sunlit heights unattained since her breakdown, the now familiar cloud of family disaster appeared on the horizon. She was summoned to Yorkshire ; her father, long slowly dying of angina, had become ill with pneumonia and bronchitis. They all knew that the end could not be long delayed.

That February in Yorkshire was a month of deep white snow and brilliant sun, with huge pale clouds leaping up in a clear cobalt sky. The weather recalled the March of Grace's death, yet Winifred, struggling to complete *The Astonishing Island* by her dying father's bedside, could nevertheless write : " I still feel that it is somehow better, more fruitful, more enriching, to be bound up v'th the exasperating complications of people and things rather than to enjoy a dry rootless immunity."

At home, taking care of two children suffering from whooping-cough, and alone because G. was now in America, I awaited Victor Gollancz's verdict on *Testament of Youth*. Thanks to Winifred and Phyllis Bentley, who had jointly mentioned it to Harold Latham, the still incomplete manuscript had been accepted, to my incredulous astonishment, by the Macmillan Company of New York for publication in America. Since they wanted to know its English publisher I had sent it on to Gollancz, who had heard of it through Phyllis and asked for the first refusal. I could not believe that Macmillan's acceptance was more than some inexplicable accident, and the period of waiting, combined with the children's persistent coughing and the sad daily bulletins of Winifred's father, became a prolonged nightmare of suspense.

On the morning of February 21st, the long expected letter lay on the breakfast table. Fortified by the absurd omen that the bath water, which was invariably cold in the mornings, had for once been hot, I tore open the envelope and read the incredible contents, which ended with the words : " I shall be very proud to publish it." Hardly knowing what I did, since Winifred was not there to be told that she had been right after all, I got up from the table and went down to the river.

It was one of those brilliant early spring days which rival the fairest mornings in June. Along the Embankment the pale flawless blue of the sky seemed to mingle with the azure shadows on the river's surface, and the sun turned the edges of its tiny ruffled waves to a brightness too dazzling

for human eyes. Still under the spell of temporary stupe-
faction, I walked on to Battersea bridge and gazed at the shining stream with the dim consciousness of a Rubicon crossed,
a battle lasting half a lifetime ended, until the strain and the
tension and the bitter disappointments of the past seemed
to melt into the molten gold of the radiant water.

Suddenly remembering the debt that I could never repay,
I ran to the post office to telegraph to Winifred, and on to
a favourite flower shop in Sloane Street to send her a box
of white lilac and blue irises and pale pink tulips with folded
glistening petals. This change of fortune was her doing, her
achievement ; it was she who had made me go on again
and again when despair had prevailed. It seemed incon-
siderate to feel so happy when she, an invalid herself, was
at home watching her father die, but she had once said that
what mattered was the existence of happiness, the golden
day, in the world, and not who experienced it. She had
never grudged joy to another ; she would be glad, I believed,
to know her critical judgment endorsed, pleased with the
brave and gay spring flowers.

And she was. She telegraphed back excitedly ; she
wrote me that evening as jubilantly as though the long-
delayed reward had been her own :

" It's so lovely to know that even if driven between
Shirley and revision and maids and chores and coping,
you are facing happiness rather than care. I have become
so much accustomed to feeling you part of me that every
line of happiness in your letter . . . lights up the candles
on my Christmas tree. I am so glad because *my* judgment
is justified too. I know now that all my hopes for what
you may do with the book are going to be justified. It
will be the instrument to give you that power you need to
work for the things you care about and fulfil your destiny
and yourself. That is the only security and the only
happiness."

She now sat, she told me, for several hours a day beside
her father, entertained her mother at meal-times, and lived
in a detached world of books, reviews and ideas. Gradually

South Riding was taking shape in her mind, and everything that happened subconsciously became part of it. One morning, in Bridlington, after a heavy snowfall, she saw a completely white snow-covered shore, a black furious sea white-flecked by foam, a sky piled with angry reddish-purple clouds, and fourteen great merchant ships from the North Sea at anchor sheltering in the bay. The scene went into the chapter of *South Riding* which describes the great Yorkshire storm.

At the beginning of March, she came to Glebe Place for an interval of rest. Together we went to see the film of *Cavalcade*, and she wept all through it from reaction and fatigue. It wasn't the war part really, she said, but " those poignantly silly tunes that did it, after reading your book and feeling the force of all that accumulating disaster upon those innocent people."

She returned to Cottingham, after a difficult and tiring journey, to find her father very close to death.

" He's been ill so long," she wrote to Phyllis, " and is so tired and in such distress of weariness, one can only wish for the end to come quickly and quietly. . . . I've been held up for $1\frac{1}{2}$ hours in snow and one hour in flood and am quite alive, only tired at times beyond words — so I've not done so badly."

David Holtby died peacefully on March 9th, at five o'clock in the evening. Winifred and her mother were both beside him. He was buried at Bridlington on a brilliant day, followed by a crowd of mourners in which the old farm servants from Rudston joined. The choir, wrote Winifred, sang the *Nunc dimittis* as the bearers carried the coffin between banks of flowers into the spring sunlight.

Immediately the funeral was over, the inevitable exhausting aftermath of death descended upon the house at Cottingham. Visitors thronged it from morning till night ; " a chorus," as she described it, " of relatives, lawyers, friends, undertakers and inquirers — a sort of factory of post-mortem activity." Letters poured in and, to spare her mother, she answered three hundred and fifty by hand in less than a week. She also acknowledged all the flowers, and wrote reports for the local papers.

On the day of her father's death, her " Notes on the Way " describing *Cavalcade* appeared in *Time and Tide*. Though written during the strain of his last hours, they read as freshly as if she had composed them in the sunshine at Monte Carlo.

" I congratulate Noel Coward," she wrote, " for so successfully exploiting those memories that now, after so many years, release the tears we could not shed when they were part of our lives." Gaily she lampooned the film, *Round the Empire*, which had preceded *Cavalcade*. She quoted with wry enjoyment the narrator whose cultured voice proclaimed regretfully that " Africa is, even now, predominantly native," and described the Vision Splendid of battleships steaming against a sunset to the tune of " Rule, Britannia!" In conclusion she spoke of " the Next War " which had entered so deeply into her imagination, though she was to be spared the horrid prolonged rehearsal ending in dire calamity which the rest of us have now lived to see.

" It is all part of the atmosphere of our generation," she commented, " the thing that enters uninvited into our thoughts."

The next series of " Notes " were written sitting up in bed on a Sunday morning ; no other time was available in that harassed household. Had Lady Rhondda been at *Time and Tide* office, Winifred would probably have been spared this additional self-imposed obligation. But Lady Rhondda had gone away for five months, to recuperate in Greece, Egypt and Palestine from a long period of indifferent health, and the new assistant editor, left in charge of the paper, wanted someone upon whom she could rely in a crisis.

" Winifred . . . was the obvious person to turn to," Lady Rhondda wrote in *Time and Tide* after Winifred's death. " True, she had only a few months before partially recovered from her first bad breakdown. But we all hoped there would not be too many crises. Light-heartedly but with a very full sense of responsibility, she took on the extra burden. I need not say that there were far more crises than we anticipated — there always are."

Looking back upon the intensified catastrophes at home added to the unforeseen crises on the paper, it seems a miracle that Winifred survived that spring at all. In the middle of March she took her mother to Scarborough to escape from the army of painters, electricians, upholsterers and charwomen which had now invaded their house. Amongst her books was Lady Rhondda's newly published autobiography, *This Was My World*, which Winifred had read in manuscript, criticised and helped to see through the Press. Though slight, she wrote me, the book was vigorous, courageous, vital, and "splendidly free from bunk." I replied agreeing with her judgment of its quality.

Completely exhausted, Winifred had not the energy to read anything more ; she only wanted, she said, to sit on the cliff and watch the great waves, in curves three miles broad, sweeping into the bay. But even here the procession of daily callers never ceased. They finally provoked her, in her next letter, to an outburst of candour.

"I should enjoy running anything from a Charity Ball to a Crown Colony, but to be the tactful go-between, never to be able to say *just* what one thinks, to compromise between conflicting interests (for neither of which I really care a damn, concerning matters which seem to me quite unimportant), to talk to relatives with whom I have not one thought in common, to write letters to people who are vague names to me — all this, combined with a blind, streaming cold, a small succession of quite trivial headaches, and the knowledge that if the heavens fall my *Schoolmistress*, *News Chronicle* and *Notes on the Way* articles must be got off to time — have left me no ounce of energy for personal feelings. I have been an institution, not a person — never alone except in bed — writing usually in a room full of people so that I can be on the spot if needed. And the effect is a little dulling to all the apprehensions. . . . Some time, when all this is over, I am going away quite by myself somewhere for a few days, where no one will ask me a question to which I only vaguely know the answer."

She would like, she said, to find a quiet place in Yorkshire where she could plan her new book in the appropriate atmosphere. Her visits to Withernsea and Hornsea in 1934 and 1935 were the consequence of this resolve.

In spite of a spring as grim, in its different fashion, as the previous one, she was back in town early in April, and writing, at Victor Gollancz's request, the beautiful description of *Testament of Youth* which appeared on the dust-cover of the first edition. Though far too generous to the book, it was one of her finest pieces of writing, full of emotion and power. Undoubtedly it was largely responsible for the initial interest of the reading public.

When she composed this summary I was away at the sea with the now convalescent children. She told me afterwards that she had spent a whole Sunday on it in a white heat of excitement.

" I'd give almost anything I possess," she wrote, " to do this so well that everyone in Europe for generations to come would want to read your book . . . but oh, what a lame and halting version it is of what I feel I could write. I re-read much of it and wept again, but I feel that the tears have been singularly barren of results. Oh, damnation ! "

She enclosed a copy of her précis, and when I read it I felt like crying too. I could only write her a letter of gratitude which could have been repeated a hundred times during the sixteen years of our friendship, and was, in effect, an acknowledgment of all that her life had meant to me.

" What a joy, what a love, what a genius of insight and intelligence you are ! With what complete and comfortable confidence one can leave everything, however delicate and difficult it is, in your hands ! What supreme piece of good fortune gave me, I wonder, the miracle of your friendship — a miracle that I've done nothing to deserve ? Darling, do live for ever. When ever I think of you I am reminded of the little phrase (whose was it ?) ' There is none like her, none.' "

Later Victor Gollancz wrote that he liked her description " enormously." He approved of it, indeed, so much, that he offered her a £700 advance on royalties if she would give him a novel. When she said that her novels were promised to Collins, he asked if she would write her auto- biography for him instead, and she agreed to consider the proposition.

Unfortunately her generosity to me did not purchase her freedom from the troubles in Yorkshire. She returned there later in April to find a new series of disasters. An aunt had been smitten with a stroke ; Grace's elder daughter was gravely ill with pneumonia ; and so many neighbours and friends were sick or dying that life in Cottingham resembled her short story, *The Casualty List*.[1]

" It goes on until one almost feels as though a war were on, the unending war of mortality against man's brittle life — and I keep remembering those words from ' 'Tis pity she's a whore ' that Forde wrote and Virginia Woolf quotes :

> *O, my lords,*
> *I but deceived your eyes with antic gesture*
> *When straight one news comes huddling on another*
> *Of death and death and death. Still I danced forward.*

And we do dance forward. The whole house is still ripped up by workmen and spring-cleaners and a young woman demonstrating the new electric washer, and the manager of the electrical works came for breakfast, and Tumpty is having kittens in the conservatory among the goldfish and budgerigars ! . . . Bless you, my dear, my safety-valve, my incomparable companion."

She had now, at least, more than one safety-valve. Not only to me, but to Phyllis Bentley and Stella Benson, she poured out in her vivid, incomparable letters the sorrows,

[1] Originally written for *The Heaton Review* (a Bradford publication) in 1932, and later republished in *Truth Is Not Sober*.

humours and exasperations of those desperate weeks. In writing to Phyllis, who knew every implication of Yorkshire, she did not report the typical family visits or the easily imagined conversations ; she discussed books, and moonlight walks, and the illustrations which Batt had done for *The Astonishing Island.*

" After your father died," she inquired, " did you, I wonder, go through a period of externally cheerful dryness, in which you could do any amount of uncreative work, write perfectly coherent answers to letters and so on, but find no reason really for writing to anyone and nothing to say ? I expect it's a form of fatigue or shock or something."

But to Stella, who did not know her surroundings, she described the relatives who descended on the house like locusts, and their conversations about current events ; she had bought, she said, a very large and complicated tablecloth to embroider while listening. This symbol of dutiful womanhood, which was still incomplete when she died, became known to her family as The Five Years' Plan.

" Here," she told Stella, " no one talks of anything but the British Engineers in Russia, their Brutal Trial, and the Belated British Embargo. . . . You might think from the tone of conversation last week that Metro-Vickers were Saintly Missionaries sending forth Noble Martyrs whose torture and persecution is an unprecedented form of savagery."

But long before her letter finished its journey she learnt that Stella Benson was seriously ill in South China, and continued the correspondence in deep concern.

" Oh my dear Stella. . . . To be ill in South China . . . sounds comfortless in the extreme and I hate it for you. You have an amazing spirit. I love the way you launch off into the wilds ignoring the dilapidations of the body, but I know enough of illness to realise that the resolution which prompts action is poor comfort in nights and early mornings when nothing seems of any importance except one's infernal pains and miseries. . . . I still sometimes wake

early in the morning with my head s....... o an iron
nut and my pulses pounding wildly with ...... excitements ; but this form of illness ha. its ...... ide.
I always feel rather collapsed after the episode ; but while
it lasts I feel curiously exalted . . . and I cherish vain
but encouraging hopes that one day I may, in such a frenzy,
compose a really Great Work." Typically she concluded :
" The lilacs are just beginning to burst, the beech buds are
swelling, the asparagus is showing above its manure, and
here is a cowslip."

But the last and now the most comforting of her
alleviations was Bill. With the half-buried instinct for
service which had prompted the religious aspirations of
his early youth, he appeared at his best in family crises.
He made Winifred play bagatelle, ran errands for her,
stamped her enormous correspondence, and finally took her
to Beverley to visit some friends.

She describes that day as " exquisite — the sort of thing
one only expects in youth." At Beverley, where they arrived
too early, Bill took her to look at the carvings in the Minster,
and told her absurd stories of the carver's thoughts. They
had tea over a big open fire in a book-lined room ; they
went for a walk to an oak wood full of anemones, and stayed
there talking nonsense till the moon rose.

" A lovely and happy time," she told me, " perfectly at
ease_ and Bill completely himself. . . . I feel so extraordinarily at rest when he is here — as though something
about him were a support and a stay."

In June Winifred and I escaped together for a week at
Painswick in the Cotswolds, staying at the village hotel
opposite the grey stone church with its thick screen of yews.
Near the steep road through Bull's Cross we rambled among
summer meadows filled with buttercups and long luxuriant
grasses, or walked in deep woods where the paths were
fringed with mauve wild orchis, cone-shaped and tall. It
was a pleasant interlude of peace, not spoiled even by the
news that the Book Society had rejected *Testament of Youth*

as its choice for September, or by the dilatory progress of *The Astonishing Island*, published on May 1st.

This attempt to imagine how England would look to an uninstructed visitor from Tristan da Cunha who took nothing for granted had moments of real wit, but it was the least effective of all Winifred's books. Again, as with *Mandoa, Mandoa !*, ill-luck pursued her, for the previous publication of A. G. Macdonell's brilliant *England, Their England* undermined such success as the book might have had. The last three thousand words, she told me, were written two days before her father's death, in the midst of answering twenty telephone calls and attending to visitors. Though ironical enough in itself, the situation was hardly ideal for the composition of satire.

Towards the end of the summer, though she still could not manage the journey to the Riviera, Winifred decided that she would risk a holiday with us in France. We chose Hardelot, seven miles from Boulogne on the Pas de Calais coast, where a speedy return home could be arranged if necessary. As the children were now old enough for a nursery boarding-school, G. and I took Winifred to Hardelot, and Violet Scott-James joined us there. Winifred found that she could walk for two or three miles through the warm resinous pinewoods or across the vast open stretch of hard brown sand, so we boldly decided to revisit the battlefields and the Base camps which we had not seen since 1921.

On the nineteenth anniversary of the War, we stood together in front of the great memorial at Thiepval to the Missing of the Somme, and saw, upon the huge arch which framed the golden harvest meadows, the names of the 73,367 men who, on one battlefield alone, had never been found or never identified. Above that grim record of the mutilated and unrecognisable dead, we read their memorial inscription :

" Here are recorded names of officers and men of the British Armies who fell on the Somme battlefields July 1915 to February 1918, but to whom the fortune of war denied the known and honoured burial given to their comrades in death."

There were 35,000 similar names, our guide told us, on the Memorial at Arras, and later we found nearly 15,000 more carved between the pillars of the colonnaded cemetery at Pozières. What had happened, we asked ourselves, to the mortal remnants of those slaughtered thousands? Were they collected in vast gruesome pits of skulls and bones, or had they been ploughed, exploded and steam-rollered into the soil? Was our car, passing along the wide new roads, driving over them all the time? We learned only that each year, when the beet harvest was over in the Valley of the Ancre, the peasants working there still discovered five bodies a week. No wonder, we reflected, that for many years the French had refused to live in this deceptively beautiful countryside which covered a charnel-house.

As we left the memorial on Thiepval Ridge, we walked between flower-beds fragrant with violas and delicately petalled roses. Everywhere larks were singing, and the sweet, warm scent of cut grass filled the mild air. Before us lay the Somme country, miles upon misty miles of verdant undulating land, rolling in gentle curves towards the blue-grey horizon. Somewhere beyond the verge were hidden the spires of Amiens, where, in a hotel close to the Cathedral, we had spent the previous night.

In 1921, when Winifred and I had visited Amiens Cathedral on our way home from Italy, we had noticed the boarded-up windows resentfully bearing witness to the German shells which had smashed the stained glass, and wondered how long the memory of that hatred would continue. Now — alone in the Cathedral at twilight because Winifred had decided to recover from our journey sitting quietly in the flower-bordered square beside the hotel — I saw that the windows were boarded-up still. Standing in the deep cobalt shadows beneath the intense violet-blue of the great rose window, I realised that all too often, when hatred ceases to be an emotion, it becomes a policy. High up in the gathering darkness of the roof flapped the pigeons, like enormous bats heralding, as harbingers of evil, the tense animosities of the coming decade.

After leaving Thiepval on that 4th of August, we moved from memorial to memorial through an immense open-air museum. Only the small German cemeteries, tended by the French in areas once occupied by the British, still contained the humble black crosses which bore the names of their half-forgotten dead. At Albert we lunched at a new hotel, optimistically named *Hôtel de la Paix*, beneath the shining golden Virgin on the top of the restored Basilica. Outside the town, we found homely hens pecking peacefully and placid cows munching the rough grass at the edge of the huge mine craters of La Boiselle. As we drove through Aveluy Wood we saw that between the new trees were rust-red gaps of barren earth where the first gas shells of the War had destroyed the productiveness of the soil. Yet the Tynesiders' Memorial beside the Albert-Bapaume Road contentedly exhorted us : " Think not that the struggle and the sacrifice were in vain."

Where, indeed, we mentally inquired, was vanity to be found, if not in the legacy of hatred by which one war prepared the way for the next ? What a cheating and a camouflage was this combined effort of man and nature to create the impression that war was glorious, just because its aftermath could wear an appearance of beauty and dignity when fifteen years of uneasy peace had passed over mankind ! How was the new generation to be persuaded that the lies which drove men to destroy one another were not made into hallowed truths by the fact that they had echoed for centuries down the long corridors of time ? Not, it seemed, by these monumental miles of illusion on the Somme.

A week later, we visited the site of Winifred's W.A.A.C. camp at Camiers, and the desolate fields at Étaples where I had once nursed German prisoners. In the main street of Camiers, the coloured tents and painted horses of a village circus gave her the idea for one of her finest short stories,

So Handy for the Fun Fair.[1] Walking together down the switchback road to Étaples, we saw that notice-boards marked " *Danger. Défense d'entrer* " were erected at intervals among the humped mounds covered with ragwort where the hospital tents had stood, and wondered whether the danger came from tetanus or the possibility of unexploded bombs overlooked after air raids.

Leaving the road, we spent an hour in the great military cemetery where many of my former patients lay buried. In contrast to the small cemeteries on the Somme it looked enormous, spreading like a huge open fan from the pinewoods on the top of the hill down to the flat marshy ground which surrounds the railway line. The top windows of the Royal Picardy Hotel at Le Touquet, we observed, looked directly on to the cemetery, and we wondered how many of the wealthy guests ever noticed it, or remembered. Searching for the German graves, still marked by their wooden crosses, we discovered most of them amongst the headstones dedicated to Indians and other members of native regiments.

" All the outcasts together," remarked Winifred cryptically.

But in the Visitors' Book for 1933, enclosed with the registers of the graves in the cemetery wall, some of the spontaneous comments which accompanied the names showed that with the peoples of the world, and with them alone, lay the initiative of which their governments appeared incapable.

" *Que tous les peuples prennent exemple,*" ran one anonymous message. " *Les Anglais, Portugais, Canadiens, Indiens, Allemands, tous sont unis dans une paix éternelle. Puissent-ils tous reposer en paix.*"

Turning a page we found, in one brief inscription, the sad evidence of the new militarism which was already rising from the ashes of the old : " *5 Réfugiés allemands, 10.8.33.*" We too inscribed our names, and in the firm belief that faith is indeed the substance of things hoped for, we wrote beneath our signatures the words : " No More War."

[1] In *Truth Is Not Sober.*

Throughout that autumn in London, Winifred worked at her books and articles with returning confidence. For a brief interval her health improved ; she was able to write to Dr. O. the following year that his treatment had given her four months' respite from pain.

Submerged in the rising flood of letters, lectures and speeches which had followed the publication of *Testament of Youth*, I was often away from home during those months, and she wrote me several letters mentioning her " Farm and School novel " which had not yet acquired its title. Encouraged by the temporary return of her vitality, she accepted, in succession to Clemence Dane, the large but lucrative task of monthly three-thousand-word book-reviews in *Good Housekeeping*. St. John Ervine, a frequent contributor, had urged her appointment, but for several years she had written miscellaneous articles for the magazine, and in 1932 had been mentioned by the editor to her literary agent as one of those authors who never let her down.

Although, superficially, this job might appear to be just another tentacle of the journalistic octopus, it gave her perhaps more scope for her distinctively literary qualities than any work she had yet done for newspapers and magazines. She had always been a rapid, voracious reader, and somehow managed to assimilate on 'bus and train journeys, or during breakfast in bed, the twenty or thirty novels to be covered by each review. Thanks to the wisdom of editorial latitude, these articles are still fascinating to read quite apart from the mostly ephemeral books round which they were built. Not only did they enable Winifred to use those perceptive critical qualities which gave distinction to her monograph on Virginia Woolf; they left her imagination free, and thus contain much of her philosophy of life.

At the end of the year, breaking in upon this contented oasis of time, a new sorrow came to her which was none the less grievous because it had not been wholly unexpected. On the morning of December 8th, a telephone call came to Winifred from our literary agent. It told her that Stella Benson had died of pneumonia the previous day while visiting, with her husband, the French Colony at Tonkin. She was only forty-one, but it was remarkable, her mother wrote to Winifred, that her fragile body had reached even that age. Stunned and pale, Winifred came into my study and told me the news.

" Oh, Stella ! " she whispered, hiding her face. No longer, now, was she the conscience-stricken possessor of immunity ; she understood the meaning of bereavement, of pain, of sorrow and of death as fully as even the most sorely smitten of her friends had understood it. Grace and her father had gone before her, Dot McCalman and now Stella Benson. Soon, soon, she knew that she must join them ; she, too, would die.

But at least she could talk to me of Stella as she had felt that she must not talk of Dot McCalman. We spoke of the poet's " exquisite and excited vision " which had given its white fire to her lovely ruthless novels, and recalled how we had watched her the previous year — a small remote figure in dark blue, prim and precise, making a decorous little speech in a husky, inaudible voice — receive the *Femina Vie-Heureuse* prize for *Tobit Transplanted*. It seemed strange that the sharp candle-flame of her mind — so much brighter than most which are extolled in our time — should have burnt itself out in that remote corner of the earth.

On December 15th, I went with Winifred to Stella's memorial service at St. Mary Abbott's Church in Kensington, where she had been married twelve years earlier. Apart from her family, only a small gathering of writers was there — Rebecca West, Cicely Hamilton, G. B. Stern, E. M. Delafield, and her future biographer, R. Ellis Roberts. Less than two years before her own funeral, Winifred heard — as we were to hear then — the singing of " Crossing the Bar," and listened to the Lesson from the Book of Wisdom which Dick Sheppard was to read over her coffin : " But the souls of the righteous are in the hands of God, and there shall no torment touch them. . . . For though they be punished in the sight of man, yet is their hope full of immortality."

CHAPTER XX

RESPITE

THE SHIPBUILDER

If all my ships put out to sea
And never came again to me,
And I should watch from 'ay to day
The empty waste of waters grey—
Then I would fashion one ship more
Of broken driftwood from the shore,
And build it up with toil and pain
And send it out to sea again.
With this last ship upon the sea
I'd turn and laugh right merrily.

WINIFRED HOLTBY, 1920

DURING March, April and May, 1934, Winifred carried out the resolve that she had made just after her father's death to find some quiet place in Yorkshire where she could work on her new book in solitude.

In December she advertised in the Hull *Daily Mail* for a small furnished cottage on the Yorkshire coast. A few days later, exactly the house that she wanted was offered to her in a row of workmen's cottages close to the sea front at Withernsea, on the coast of Yorkshire a few miles east of Hull. It had three rooms, electric light, and a bath in the scullery. The rent, clear of rates, was 10s. a week. She took it jubilantly, and arranged with the mother of seven daughters across the road to "do" for her daily. On March 14th she went up to Hull and moved in.

Never had she known a period of such peace and happiness. The living-room, with its large kitchen range and big bow window which caught the sun, had a pleasant

atmosphere of friendliness and freedom. On the wide ledge
of the window-sill, she arranged her *Good Housekeeping* review
books in their scarlet, emerald and canary-coloured covers.
Friends coming to visit her knew, from the moment that
they entered the unpretentious seaside road, which of the
little uniform grey houses was Winifred's cottage.

The previous month, her collected volume of short
stories, *Truth Is Not Sober*, had been published by Collins,
and was soon to appear in America — where, wrote Phyllis
Bentley, who was over on a lecture tour, the booksellers
asked about Winifred wherever she went and wanted to
know her future plans. Many of the stories had appeared
in *Time and Tide*, as Winifred acknowledged when she wrote
her dedication :

> For Viscountess Rhondda
> To the leader, with homage
> To the editor, with gratitude
> To the friend, with love.

A number, however, had appeared in other journals of
various types, such as the *Radio Times*, the *New Statesman*,
the *Manchester Guardian*, *The New Leader* and *The Bystander*.
So she divided them into four categories — " Satiric,"
" Exotic," " Bucolic " and " Domestic."

" Bucolic " includes the tale, *So Handy for the Fun Fair*,
which Winifred described later to St. John Ervine as " my
only ' war ' story ", and acknowledged as her favourite.
But as a category, " Satiric " perhaps contains the largest
number of characteristic stories and sketches. Gently, with
delicate malice but without bitterness or anger, she ridi-
cules political movements, national possessiveness, religious
fanaticism, garden villages, anthropologists, model mothers,
the heroic detachment of scholars from subjects of popular
interest, and the domination of the world by men. The
publicity methods of the Press — a favourite subject for
satire which had already enlivened the later pages of
Mandoa, Mandoa ! — receive their full measure of sardonic
attention. *The Celebrity Who Failed*, which narrates the

water-walking exploits of a young woman called Amelia who was annihilated by the newspapers, originally appeared in the *Nation* soon after Amy Johnson's first flight to Australia. *The Voice of God*, on the same theme of listening-in to the past as the play *Judgment Voice*, innocently describes the consternation of newspaper proprietors who discover that the Message from Galilee which they have bought the exclusive right to broadcast is not delivered in English.

This last story made its ironic appeal to the British Broadcasting Corporation, and in April Winifred listened to Felix Aylmer, the actor, reading it over the wireless. Later it caused a small Press sensation owing to the use of a similar topic by Canon H. R. L. Sheppard and Howard Marshall for a novel which obtained the record advance of £1000. When Winifred received a bundle of press-cuttings in which this sensational though unconscious plagiarism was fully exploited, she sent Dick Sheppard a copy of *Truth Is Not Sober* and a letter remarking how natural it was that new ideas based on contemporary inventions should occur simultaneously to different people. At first, thinking that the book had come from a publisher, Canon Sheppard did not discover the letter, but eventually he found it, and wrote a charming, apologetic reply.

Truth Is Not Sober went into three editions and brought Winifred much praise from reviewers.

" Miss Holtby does not laugh at things or people," wrote R. Ellis Roberts in a typical notice ; " she shows us how life, or God, if you like, laughs at them. There is something medieval in the simplicity of her satire, in the directness of her vision. She has the rare gift of being naturally unembarrassed in the presence of truth."

Encouraged and happy, Winifred embraced her solitude with ecstasy.

" I love every minute of this life," she wrote me. " I taste it and roll it over and over on my tongue."

The little house fulfilled all the longing for peace, for leisure to think, for time to be alone and create without constant disturbance, which comes to be the strongest passion of beset and interrupted lives such as hers. No one who has never been the centre of perpetual demands related to other people's interests knows what joy can lie in quietness and solitude.

Day after day she seemed to be getting better in that strong bracing air of the small town built on reclaimed coast land — " eight miles out to sea an' should grow coral," as the inhabitants described it. Soon she found herself able to walk several miles a day and to sleep ten hours a night without pounding and aching in every pulse. During the warm spring mornings she sat on the sands making notes for *South Riding* ; all afternoon she wrote in the sunshine pouring into the south window of her cottage bedroom. On nights of bright sharp moonlight she left her leaping fire and strolled along the coast, watching the jewelled glitter of the moon on the sea while ideas and sentences sprang to life in her brain. One of her loveliest allegories, *The Comforter*,[1] came to her during a late night walk after she had heard a broadcast of her beloved St. Matthew Passion, which runs like an underlying theme through much of *South Riding*.

Ugly as the little town might seem by normal aesthetic standards, she discovered with the late flowering of the Yorkshire spring that it had beauties of its own.

" Yesterday morning," she wrote me on May 13th, " was hot, windy, radiantly clear. . . . I walked about three miles southward towards Spun Point. The tide goes out nearly half a mile, leaving an enormous stretch of sand and sky, a thin rim of sea on the horizon, and the warm red of the shallow cliffs. . . . I found a little stream that came down and broke into the cliff with a rich daisy-and-buttercup meadow beside it, and actually a few cowslips and purple orchises. This is not at all a flowery part of the world. . . . The weather broke last night with squalls, a blazing sunset, and a rainbow ringing the town. . . . I have never before seen a rainbow in twilight. The town was half dark, the

[1] Published in *Pavements at Anderby*.

lighthouse lit ; but the setting sun caught the deep greenish-tawny clouds and made a complete rainbow."

Early in April Winifred reported that *South Riding* was taking shape in her mind. Much of her time was now passed in reading the local newspapers for background and material. She felt well and happy, she said — " just loving every minute." A letter of mine written on April 9th comments on her title, and adds : " I do hope (and Violet Scott-James, with whom I had tea on Saturday, also hopes) that you'll make it a *big* book."

But even at Withernsea, she could not give all her time to this novel. The previous year John Lane had invited her to contribute a volume entitled *Women and a Changing Civilisation* to their topical series, The Twentieth Century Library. The proposition was not lucrative and she cared more for her novel than for any cause in the world, but the subject was so important that she felt she must not refuse lest the task should fall into the wrong hands. By March she had the book completely in draft but there were still many facts to verify, which seemed a burdensome task when all her thoughts were bound up with *South Riding*.

Another project arose from a peace symposium called *Challenge to Death*, which Storm Jameson was editing for Constable. The book originated in a dinner given on February 7th for Lord Cecil — who was then still regarded as the peace leader *in excelsis* — and Winifred and I had both agreed to contribute. Her chapter, which she called " Apology for Armourers," explained with gentle ironic benevolence that armaments manufacturers were not saints who could be expected to resist the law of supply and demand. Realising how badly the public needed information on the traffic in arms she had again felt that she must not refuse, and now she had to wrestle with the copious material sent her by Dorothy Woodman, the indefatigable secretary of the Union of Democratic Control. At the beginning of May she wrote that she had not touched her cherished book for a fortnight, thanks to this chapter and the page proofs of a small monograph called *Race and Economics in South Africa* which she was correcting for William Ballinger. Her services to his study did not end here, for she spent ten pounds on its publication and distribution.

Winifred had not been able to keep her address a complete secret, and, too soon, everybody found it out. Her brother-in-law brought his little daughters over for a day on the sands ; letters pursued her and she told me ruefully that she never had less than eleven to write each morning. The organisers of numerous good causes also bombarded her, assuming that now she was " all right again " she would be delighted to speak for them. When the local clergyman asked her to address a children's rally, she sent me in desperation a letter of refusal to post in London. Once she left Yorkshire she knew that she would have no chance to work on her book at all, " as *Time and Tide* wants lots of me, and Ballinger is coming to England, and Howard Pim, who supported our funds in South Africa, is dead. And life altogether is going to be full of Africans and Armaments ! "

Nationally it was a disturbing spring. Various strong emotions had been stirred by the Hunger Marchers' gathering in Hyde Park on February 25th, and by the publication of the proposed " Sedition Bill " with its threat to civil liberties. Encouraged by twelve months of Nazi success in Germany, the Fascist forces in England seemed to be gathering their strength. The threat which roused every political organisation to active vigilance inspired Winifred to write, that autumn, her anti-dictator play, *Take Back Your Freedom*. It started her speaking again in the summer, and later sent her, as an " observer " for the Council of Civil Liberties, to the Blackshirt Rally immortalised by the cartoonist, David Low, as " The Pest Match." There, as she wrote Lady Rhondda, " Blackshirts like prize bullocks at an agricultural show marched round and round inside the police ring snorting. Communists outside, like barrackers at a football match."

In spite of the claims of *South Riding*, her keen sense of the Fascist menace even sent her to a Blackshirt meeting in Yorkshire. Here, as the audience emerged, she distributed anti-Fascist pamphlets issued by the Union of Democratic Control. She was so terrified by the prospect, she admitted, that she lost two days of good work through sheer fright, but when the day came she fulfilled her function with admirable aplomb. Dressed up in a fur coat and white kid gloves, she handed out externally innocuous leaflets with so imposing an air that the Blackshirt steward beside her took her support for granted.

" *Very* impressive meeting from the stage management point of view," she related. " Forty imported Blackshirts stood at attention throughout a speech so bad that I yearned to get up and make it for the poor man. . . . Extremely handsome, perfect male figure, nervous, charming, mentally defective ; Adonis of face and fourth-form boy in ideas. I don't know if he or I did any good or harm. Withernsea prefers the new Pierrots, who are *very* good."

Although she grudged every moment stolen from her book, Winifred's correspondence reveals that even during this period she still found time to help acquaintances whom she hardly knew. One long series of letters contained her advice to a school contemporary, Doris Burnett, who wanted to use her experiences as a racing motorist in articles and a novel. Another embodied her attempts to help Mary Gaunt, an author many years her senior, to publish her autobiography.

One or two of her interruptions were as welcome as solitude. On March 18th, at Beverley, the East Riding County Council elected her mother as their first woman Alderman ; the election was unanimous and received with acclamation. Far prouder than she had ever been of any triumph of her own, Winifred shared in Alice Holtby's interview with the reporter and photographer who motored over from Leeds. The photograph, one of the best that she ever had taken, shows her sitting, fragile but happy, at her mother's feet.

After her death Miss Amy Durham, the journalist who interviewed them, wrote to me from the *Yorkshire Evening Post* recalling the warm welcome that they gave her beside the sitting-room fire at Bainesse on that bitter March afternoon. She remembered the old-fashioned tea comfortably spread on the big table, and Winifred sitting on the hearth-rug afterwards, in a navy blue frock trimmed with large green buttons, laughing and affectionately teasing her mother, " like a pale flame that shone constantly." There seemed, the guest remarked, to be a rare love and sympathy between mother and daughter. This interview, she wrote, was the happiest that she could remember ; it had helped her through many others with " celebrities " who despised the Press but dared not defy it.

During the third week in March, I had four speeches to make on one day in Hull. After addressing the Luncheon Club, the City Library, a girls' school and an appeal tea-party, I spent the evening at Cottingham talking to Winifred, who came over from Withernsea. The week-end that we had planned there together was postponed by a long attack of measles on the part of the children, who always staged their infectious diseases when I was most fully occupied, but I managed to visit the friendly grey cottage with its book-lined window-sill just before Winifred left early in June.

From time to time, she told me, Bill had been over to see her there. He appeared to enjoy her society, but always she was conscious that her gifts and her growing fame caused the perpetual gulf between them to widen. She had typed some short descriptive articles that he had written, and placed one for him in the *Manchester Guardian.* His visits, as usual, were unannounced and capricious ; she never knew when he would come, how long he would stay, or just what he would expect of her. Long before I went to Withernsea he had vanished for some days and, inexplicably, reappeared in Cornwall.

Winifred returned to a London summer which almost achieved the hectic normality of her pre-invalid days. She attended *Time and Tide* Board dinners, went to the office on press days, held committee meetings of African sympathisers at Glebe Place, and even, once more, ventured on platforms.

Her first effort after nearly two years was discouraging and quite untypical. In June a women's organisation which specialised in imperial problems invited her to speak on the Colour Bar at their annual conference. Many officials and visitors from South Africa were to be present, and she felt, as always, that she ought not to refuse. Into the first sentence of her speech she introduced the phrase : " Of course, I'm only a journalist " — not meaning to disparage journalism, which she regarded as the finest of professions, but merely to indicate that she was not a colonial expert in the same sense as the officials, civil servants and overseas doctors in the audience.

But a self-conscious group of journalists in the gallery regarded her remark as belittling their profession, and hissed it vigorously. Utterly taken aback, for nothing of the kind had ever happened to her before and she did not understand the reason for it, she carried on with her speech in spite of being a sick person, and as unpractised as every speaker becomes who avoids public platforms for more than a year. But she came home exhausted, depressed and quite unlike herself ; her head ached and her eyes were swollen as though she had been crying.

" They *hissed* me ! " she kept on repeating incredulously.

But the next experiment completely restored her self-confidence, for she was asked — the first woman ever invited — to make the Speech Day address and give away the prizes on July 30th at Bridlington School. Like so many events of her last two years, this visit contributed to that strange rounding-off of experience which gave so unusual an appearance of completion to her short and crowded life.

Her old friend and teacher, Mr. Robert Horspool, was present on that day to greet Winifred and her mother. Recently, when I visited him in Bridlington, he told me that he had attended thirty-eight school Speech Days, and of

three outstanding addresses he thought Winifred's the best.
One or two of the older masters, he said, had viewed the
prospect of a woman speaking to the boys with some
trepidation, but from her opening words she had complete
control over her large mixed audience, and received rousing
applause at the end. Even the smallest boys were attentive,
because they heard something worth remembering.

Winifred began by referring to herself as an " Old
Boy," and spoke of the early connection between the school
and Rudston. She recalled her " art " lessons and the
distractions which adorned them, not forgetting the game
of throwing lumps of sugar into cups of tea. After describing
the schools that she had visited in South Africa and other
countries, she concluded with another memory which that
summer's gathering threat of European catastrophe made
all too relevant.

" Twenty years ago," she said, " in August 1914, the
Officers' Training Corps from the schools all over England
went away after their summer term. But the senior boys,
instead of going back to school or to the university, passed
on into the Great War, which to those of you here to-day as
students must seem as a tale that is told. I remember
many of those boys, and some were my friends. The names
of some of those who did not come back are on your walls
and in your honours list. There were many millions of
men killed in the four years which followed that summer-time
twenty years ago. Those young men who died would now
have been between forty and forty-five years of age. They
were our natural leaders, not only in religion, but as artists,
scientists and teachers. They were the people who in the
ordinary way would now be in offices, on farms and in
workshops, or in local government and teaching in our
schools. They were men who would have given the stability
and balance that we need to-day. It is because they are not
here that your generation — especially those who are just
stepping out into the wider world — have so hard a task
before you. I wish you well in your great adventure."

The intuition of coming international disaster which

caused her to refer at Bridlington to the Great War impelled her, that autumn, to revive her speeches for the League of Nations Union. She ought, she felt, to work for the Peace Ballot ; to oppose, with all the diminishing strength of her handicapped body, the rising tide of reaction and intolerance.

" The voice of passion is a loud, exciting voice," she wrote in a review of Norman Angell's *Preface to Peace.* " Like the Heavenly Anthem it is capable of drowning all music but its own ; yet it is rarely of Heaven that it speaks. It cries with wild, exhilarating, blood-warming disturbance that the Jews shall perish, that Ireland shall be free, that France shall march on, march on, till foul blood waters the furrows of her fields, that Hungary will never submit to the humiliation of her peace treaties, no, no, never, or that Britons never, never, never will be slaves."

Because she understood the need for those quieter voices which quote facts and revive memories, and realised how few are the detached minds which in times of growing crisis have the courage to find out and tell the truth, she drove herself forth to a series of meetings round London and in Yorkshire. It was now no light undertaking for her to make a speech. " I can manage a half-hour's lecture if I rest before and after," she confessed, " but that's my limit. Alas ! no American tour for me, I can see."

On October 17th she took part in a " Youth demands Peace " demonstration at the Kingsway Hall ; on November 3rd she led a rally at Hessle, near Withernsea, to encourage some of the Union's village branches ; on November 4th she gave an address from the pulpit of Cottingham Parish Church, where throughout five centuries no woman had spoken. The following week she appeared in Rudston and Bridlington. Armistice Day, the last that she was to know, found her addressing a crowded hall at Harrow.

" I cannot bear that there should be another war," she wrote on July 1st to John Brophy, who had sent her a copy of his war book, *The World Went Mad*, in which she shared the dedication. " And I don't know what to do about it, except to go on — as Tagore said — ' trundling the little wheelbarrow of propaganda across the world.' "

After her death, in her League of Nations Union file for that year, I came across a typed copy which she had made of *Poem, 1933* by Richard Goodman :

> *Huge images of death lurk in my brain*
> *and track me where I go ;*
> *here in this city, here in Summer's plain,*
> *I am smothered under shadow.*
>
> *Not being with friends nor even this tall day*
> *where the light sings*
> *brings peace, release from these ; I cannot play*
> *nor find my joys in things.*
>
> *They are my thoughts of war and war's disease ;*
> *I move with men*
> *and watch an equal dark behind each face*
> *striking them iron.*
>
> *Over my love and breaking on my joy*
> *this fear descends :*
> *I see guns shatter and slow fog destroy*
> *my friends, my lovely friends.*

In our day of calamity, we, her friends, can at least thank God that by passing through the waters before us she was spared this experience.

In mid-September G. and I went together to America, he for his usual half-year of teaching and I for a lecture tour. Throughout that summer I had suffered from misgivings about this rash arrangement, but Winifred consistently urged me to go. My life, she said, contained so many invalids and dependent people to whom a plethora of disasters might happen that the only course was to disregard them all and take the plunge. Did she, I have often wondered, include herself among those to be disregarded ? Did she realise that she might not survive until my return ?

At Southampton she saw us off by the *Berengaria*, and found, to her amused astonishment, a patch of mustard and cress — evidently sown by some scattered seed from a cargo — growing between the railway lines on the dock. To make sure that she was right she picked and nibbled it, then gathered a bunch and put it in her button-hole to convince other people that the surprising fact was true. A passenger leaning over the gleaming cliff of the liner felt sorry that anyone should be content with such meagre luxuries, and threw down a pink carnation for her to wear. She pinned it to her coat ; and returned to London reading the 1349 closely-typed pages of St. John Ervine's recently completed biography of General Booth, *God's Soldier*.

" St. John's rapscallion vitality is just right for this history of Blood and Fire," she commented to me, and four days later sent him her criticism :

" It is really superb. Warmest congratulations. I wept several times — the ' fried bread ' incident for some reason being entirely disrupting. I can't judge the complete rightness of your appendix, of course. And I had previously read Catherine Bramwell Booth's account, which takes necessarily the same attitude (or rather, you are sympathetic to hers). But it *reads* convincingly. If there was obstinacy and lack of judgment on Bramwell's side, there was charity and rare courage. . . . Thank you for a grand book. . . . If you'd never written another line nor done another thing, you'd have done a good life's work there."

She went home to a domestic existence dominated by children, including her new god-daughter Belinda Hardy, the younger child of Sylvia Garstang of Leeds whom we had known at Somerville. Realising that she could hardly hope to survive until the baby girl grew up, Winifred left for the small Belinda a letter to be opened on her fifteenth birthday.

" By that time," she wrote me, " its admirable advice

may seem very stuffy and old-fashioned ; but I have given her £5 in her own cheque book, so that may counterbalance everything."

It is clear to me now that, even in the interests of the Ballinger Fund, I should never have allowed Winifred to add the supervision of John and Shirley to the other obligations of that autumn. This new responsibility was mitigated only by the fact that she loved them dearly. Her affection for them, always warm-hearted, appeared to grow after her doctors had told her that if she married she could never hope to have children, since the attempt would destroy her. In each new tragedy she seemed to look for its constructive application, and after 1931 she lavished upon my son and daughter all the understanding devotion and lively imaginative sympathy that she would normally have given to children of her own. Her stories entertained them for hours ; her choice of small amusing presents was a perpetual solace for minor injuries and temporary disappointments. She invariably treated them both with courtesy, and therefore received, as a matter of course, spontaneous politeness and loving obedience in return.

The children were actually cared for that autumn by their gentle German governess and my friendly domestic staff, but from choice as well as conscientiousness Winifred saw them frequently. Her letters to me were filled with small affectionate details about their toys, their parties, their baths, their ridiculous conversations, their loveliness when asleep, and their very occasional tantrums. John, dark-haired and dark-eyed, had always been very close to her heart. Shirley, with her large blue eyes and pale gold head, might easily have been Winifred's child rather than mine. In addition to a vigorous intellect and a sturdy freedom from inhibitions, the winds of chance had even endowed her with a fearless passion for horses and other farm animals.

" She's caught her hair from me," Winifred once remarked amusedly as she cuddled the flaxen-headed infant against her shoulder.

On October 15th, a long letter reporting progress went off to New York.

"John," it concluded, "to-day observed : ' When are you going to get rid of that cold, Auntie ? ' (I've had a sniffle for some days, so have only been seeing the children at close quarters when out of doors.) I replied 'As soon as I can.' John, contemplatively : ' Wouldn't it go quicker if you didn't talk so much ? ' (Screams of joyous laughter from Shirley ; John continues to look bright and helpful.) . . . I love this dear household and its lovely children."

When I wrote in November, perturbed by the slow progress of her book, she characteristically assured me that the children were not the cause. Five South Africans had arrived simultaneously in London, and their problems demanded her constant attention ; other coloured visitors from overseas must have parties arranged for them and meet only those with whom they could feel at ease. Before the end of the year she had resigned from a favourite club where she often lunched because it would not admit her friend, Amiya Chakravarty, the gifted Bengali poet who had come to England for research work at Balliol College, Oxford.

"We certainly behave," she commented afterwards in *Time and Tide*, "rather oddly in the capital of an Empire consisting of some 430 million ' coloured ' races and a minority of 70 million ' white.' "

One afternoon an incongruous quartette gathered in her study for tea : Eric Walrond, a negro poet from New York ; Una Masen, a Jamaican dramatist who was writing *The Autobiography of a Brown Girl* for Victor Gollancz ; Winifred's cousin, Daisy Pickering ; and the vivacious cosmopolitan writer, Madame Odette Keun.

"Would you say that party would mix ? " she asked me. "What time do you think the last departed ? 9.45 ! Was I tired ? But it was interesting. Discussed the colour question, miscegenation, birth control and race prejudice inside out."

Unhappily for her work, not all her visitors appeared by arrangement. Apart from the bevy of inquiring South

Africans, friends " dropped in " for a few moments and stayed for three hours, consuming afternoons intended for the revision of a chapter or the completion of a review.

" By 5.30," she wrote of a day taken up by three such casual callers, " I had not been out. It still poured with rain ; so I deserted the children, put on a mackintosh and ran to the English Garden. The lowering sky was a heavy sort of lavender colour, reflected in the Michaelmas daisies — great clouds of them, taller than I, and in the foreground all round them, dahlias of crimson, puce, orange, scarlet, flame, lemon and white. I never saw it so royally gorgeous — the rain dancing on the lily pond, churning the paths to mud and bringing down the sodden leaves from the trees."

On October 5th, Winifred's short study, *Women and a Changing Civilisation*, was published. She had again left some of the research work to Katie Gilchrist, who co-operated gladly ; it was a comfort, she said, in a harsh world to contemplate Winifred's " wise and kind existence." Many of the older feminists who had worked for years in the suffrage movement also helped her with material ; they felt deeply indebted to her for carrying on their fight in its many new manifestations.

" You are one of the people one can joyously differ from," wrote Mrs. H. M. Swanwick. " There is so much left to applaud and to love."

Winifred dedicated her book to two of those veteran campaigners, Dame Ethel Smyth and Cicely Hamilton, " who did more than write *The March of the Women*." The idea of inscribing a book to them had come to her in 1930, when we went to Westminster with Cicely Hamilton to see Stanley Baldwin unveil the statue of Mrs. Pankhurst in Victoria Tower Gardens. That morning's *pièce de résistance* had undoubtedly been, not Mr. Baldwin, but Dame Ethel Smyth in the grey and scarlet robes of a Doctor of Music, conducting the band of the Metropolitan Police Force in her own rendering of " The March of the Women," written to Cicely Hamilton's words. At least half the audience in the crowded enclosure remembered that Dame Ethel, on one of the many occasions that the police arrested her, had first conducted the March with a toothbrush from a window of Holloway Jail.

Women and a Changing Civilisation is a brief and exceedingly competent account of woman's position throughout the ages, and especially of her developing status in the twentieth century, with its far-reaching epic changes. It describes the triumphant climax of the woman's movement on its political side in the decade following the War, and faces the new threat to freedom made by the economic slump and the anti-feminist doctrines of the totalitarian states. Because Winifred wrote the book, its style sparkles with an epigrammatic freshness too seldom characteristic of social histories. Repeatedly she brings the jewels of her pictorial imagination to adorn her main thesis that the history of woman is not the record of her relationship to man, but the story of her place in the universe. Since the common humanity of men and women is far more important than their sexual differences, the only adequate history of women would be a history of mankind and its adventures upon a changing globe. The qualities, Winifred maintains, of candid comradeship, spirited courage and brave self-reliance fostered to-day in women's education have always existed, but have only been recognised during the past few years as more desirable than feckless ignorance, elegant idleness and squeamish sensibility.

In conclusion, she emphasises, as in many lectures and articles, that the inequality of the sexes mainly arises from " the deep subconscious belief that women have less right to be at work than men." No one knew better than she, with her divided conscience, the exasperating sense of guilt that assails the professional woman who continues her work when her household is suffering from some minor inconvenience which any of its members could put right if they chose. No one was more vividly aware that this traditional obligation presses with greater weight upon the woman artist, whose work can be laid aside, than upon the woman doctor, dentist, solicitor or civil servant protected by an office and an engagement book safely filled with professional appointments. Only, Winifred believed, by the training of a younger generation in a new set of values could the work of women be secured against the constant external interruption which had harassed her own.

"The old excuse 'I'm *only* a woman' is still heard in the land," she wrote in a Silver Jubilee article published by *The Queen* the following spring, "but its power is waning. This is the foundation of all future achievement — to have faith in one's self and one's capacity. All art, all leadership is impossible without that confidence, and it is confidence which the past achievement of women, limited as it may have been, has made possible. 'I'm a woman and proud of it,' is the more modern cry. To-morrow, perhaps, we shall hear less of both, and more of 'I'm a human being, and so it is my responsibility to do such and such.' And then it will matter less whether there has, or has not, been a woman Shakespeare. It will matter only that humanity achieves great art, great statesmanship, great science and great sanctity ; that one sex is not shut off from such achievement and that both rejoice in what humanity at its best can be."

Winifred's book received between sixty and seventy reviews, nearly all long and enthusiastic. The one, perhaps, which surprised her most was a full appreciative column in the *Daily Sketch* on the day of publication. After going through several editions, the book was republished at 5s. in July 1939. During the months which followed its first appearance, a large collection of odd, interesting and tragic letters arrived from Winifred's readers, and she received more invitations to speak than she could have fulfilled in a lifetime.

"I feel sometimes," she confessed to Lady Rhondda, "that I shall die of *embarras de richesses* — an odd complaint and doubtless a temporary one, and perhaps not deadly."

Three days after the publication of *Women*, chance brought Winifred into contact with a formidable anti-feminist whose potential hostility she transformed into friendly admiration. On October 8th, she spoke at one of the now celebrated Literary Luncheons arranged by Christina Foyle, the enterprising young daughter of the well-known bookseller. Sir Josiah Stamp, the economist, was also due to speak, but owing to his illness, James Agate, the literary and dramatic critic, took his place. In the chair sat old Sir Harry Preston, *bon viveur* and popular proprietor of the Royal Albion Hotel at Brighton. His memory was beginning to fail, wrote Winifred ; " he mixed me up completely with Lady Noel Curtis-Bennett, called me ' My lady ' and said that whenever I was in Brighton I must come and see him and his wife and bring my husband. So I said that whenever I was in Brighton with my husband, I would."

After the luncheon, James Agate sent Winifred a special request to take the chair for him when he spoke the following month at the *Sunday Times* Book Exhibition. Winifred was much intrigued, for Mr. Agate had long been one of our theoretical " hates." When *Testament of Youth* was published, he had done his ferocious best to make mincemeat of its four-day reputation in a savage review which surged over three or four columns of the *Daily Express*. Later, when I met him in Winifred's presence, he commented with sardonic amusement on the " Christ-like spirit " in which I had accepted this singular service. Winifred was fully aware that cowardly timidity had been more responsible than Christian forgiveness for my meek failure to protest, and she appeared at the *Sunday Times* Exhibition intending to lash our enemy with the most scurrilous sentences from his own review. But the neuralgia which handicapped his speech disarmed her ; she could never, she lamented, " retain a good hate."

Instead, when *Ego*, the first volume of James Agate's diary, was published in January 1935, she reviewed it with amused enjoyment in *Time and Tide*, justly describing its author as " irascible, buoyant, affectionate, exacting,

unintimidated and unsatisfied — more French than English."
In February she actually persuaded him to debate with
her in aid of the Six Point Group on the promising motion
"That women should be suppressed." She decided to be
the proposer herself and let James Agate spend half an hour
in refuting his own anti-feminism. Appreciating the irony
of the situation he accepted, and the three of us dined
together beforehand at the Café Royal.

The evening was a triumph for Winifred. Wearing one
of the most beautiful dresses that she ever chose — a long
black velvet with a bodice of gold tissue and a vivid scarlet
sash — she spent a brilliant forty minutes arraigning
ministering angels, modern girls, mothers-in-law, censorious
spinsters and mature females who squandered their emotions
on Pekinese.

James Agate was too shrewd to attempt a reply. He
side-tracked the motion in a masterly series of anecdotes,
but Winifred had given him a new conception of at least
one "blue-stocking." When she died, he added to the
obituary notice in *The Times* a footnote expressing genuine
grief and respect.

Winifred saw little of Bill that autumn, but a paragraph
in a letter to America describing a friend's sorrow for her
lover showed that he was unforgotten.

"J. T.'s man has died. Poor J. He has been the centre
of her life for years. Yet lucky J. — she could do something
for him. . . . I seem to beat with all my energy against a
barrier of despair. . . . It is like loving the dead whom you
can't touch or help."

When I returned from America on John's birthday,
four days before Christmas, Bill's troubles were temporarily
eclipsed for Winifred by the excited writing of her play,
Take Back Your Freedom, and by Christmas preparations.
Thanks to memories of feudal philanthropy which reached
its height at "festive seasons," Winifred had developed, as
she once admitted to Sarah Millin, "such a ferocious, persistent, irrational and maniacal detestation of Christmas,

that I always forget until it is right on top of me that the damnable season is due." But for this last Christmas, as for all the others, she made a long list of presents which omitted not even the least of her acquaintances, and went home to share three days of exhausting celebrations with her mother, her nieces, innumerable relatives, and the annual contingent of retainers from Rudston.

She returned to three weeks of enforced imprisonment. Just before I landed from America, John had come home from school with a mild attack of mumps. Now, with his usual habit of passing on germs which hardly affected him to adults in whom they assumed their most virulent form, he inflicted Winifred with a new source of miserable discomfort. She did not complain, for the compulsory avoidance of everyone but myself enabled her to make progress with *South Riding* during her convalescence, but the ignominious affliction left her more abysmally depressed than her own habitual handicaps.

Since this new visitation did not call for a specialist I summoned the children's doctor, who was greatly perturbed by his routine test of her blood pressure. When I explained that this condition was now chronic and she had permanent treatment for it, he only said gravely : " It kills in the end, you know."

Even then my mind refused to accept the warning so clearly offered to it. Like most of Winifred's friends I was tempted — with a self-deceiving optimism that she herself encouraged — to regard her as a " special case," and to feel confident that Dr. O., who had kept her alive and active for so long, could go on working the miracle that he had undoubtedly performed. We resembled Robert Carne of *South Riding* visiting his invalid wife in the Harrogate nursing-home — " after his reason ceased to believe, his heart still hoped."

During the last February of Winifred's life, when she wrote from Hornsea to say that her latest medical tests showed a remarkable improvement, I was still blind enough to send her an excitedly hopeful response :

" It sounds unbelievable that you could actually have improved in spite of all the work you do — almost perhaps as though you were still young enough for part of the lost tissue to be re-endowed with life. You are such a pathological eccentricity anyway, that almost anything seems possible. This is quite the best news I have had for ages. I don't deliberately worry you about your health more than I can help or discuss it with you, because I know this would only irritate you and would do no good ; but I think about it constantly. Not only on your account, but for the most selfish possible reasons. . . . I don't believe even my work would give me much pleasure now if I hadn't you to share its success or failure with. But this is all selfish. The real point is what you can do with your own work if you only have time. You *must* have time — and if only you take reasonable care of yourself, there seems to be, now, no reason why you shouldn't have. It's marvellous to be as you are after such a complete smash-up only three years ago."

CHAPTER XXI

THE FACE OF THE WATERS

RESURRECTION

He had been free.
He had looked into the clear face of death and known salvation.
As a bather strips before diving he had stripped
Himself of desire, memory and sorrow.
He had stood poised above the lucid water,
The sea of oblivion spread itself before him,
The kingdoms of the world fell back behind him
Like a grey shadow, like a small wraith of smoke,
Their hopes, their powers, their pleasures, their excitement.

WINIFRED HOLTBY, 1935
Time and Tide, 1938

In the middle of February 1935, Winifred went to
Hornsea, another small Yorkshire town about fifteen miles
north of Withernsea on the East Riding coast, in the hope
of repeating the progress made the previous spring with her
now half-finished novel.

Unable to find another cottage, she took lodgings in a
modest house kept by three sisters. Her sitting-room, facing
south down a long strip of garden, showed her unpretentious surroundings very similar to Withernsea, but the
town had more trees, and a bird-haunted mere surrounded
by tall bulrushes. She could see black lambs skipping in
a paddock, and the ground beneath the dark shrubbery
already brindled white and yellow with snowdrops and
aconites.

Again, as at Withernsea, she rejoiced incredulously in
her solitude. She went for long walks beside the foaming
sea on mornings of gleaming sunshine ; she climbed the

steep cliffs and saw the huge curve of Bridlington Bay, dominated by Flamborough Head, stretch widely before her. To obtain local colour for her novel, she attended meetings held in the Floral Hall to discuss the Silver Jubilee celebrations. Like Bridlington and Withernsea, Hornsea made its contribution to the composite " Kiplington " of *South Riding*, but the place gave her less peace, less freedom from interruption, than she had found at Withernsea the year before.

All day as she worked, the practising aeroplanes from a local squadron dipped and roared, catching the light on their silver wings, climbing into the blustery sky, graceful as seagulls. When she walked along the coast, seaplanes zoomed over the town, and bombers dropped their depth-charges into the North Sea. As they soared up into the gale, puffs of white smoke rose from the water and a dull boom shook the windy air. Rehearsal for pandemonium, thought Winifred, and the girl at the bakery, selling her a loaf, echoed the perpetual uneasy dread which these mock battles had revived.

" It's all right when you forget what they're really after."

The constant sinister sounds began to torment her, destroying the concentration of her thoughts.

" All the time," she wrote me, " the news in the paper is so disturbing that I feel I ought not to be sitting here comfortably writing a novel. I ought to be stumping the country against rearmament. . . . Life is so short. The menace of horror is over us all so completely, that to waste time on self-pity seems extremely unintelligent. . . . A war may be coming, but I find it difficult to finish my book among sounds that make me imagine that it has started already."

The bombing aeroplanes were by no means her only source of interruption. Even though her father was dead, the inexorable visiting of aged and invalid relatives went on. It was expected of her ; it was part of the ruthless north country family tradition in which she had been reared, and though she wept with fatigue and mourned the lost hours which rendered even more precarious her race with death to finish *South Riding*, she never dreamed of shirking her obligations by protesting that she was the greatest invalid of them all. Afternoons vanished upon exhausting visits to the aged uncle inaccessibly dying of cancer amid the decaying splendours of Dowthorpe Hall ; week-ends were devoted to an elderly second cousin suffering from the same disease in a small Harrogate house. Nothing could have illustrated more clearly than the last months of Winifred's life May Sinclair's lament that great women, unlike great men, can never get rid of their relatives.

" Wild horses won't drag me south till May," Winifred told Phyllis Bentley. " I have nine lectures up here, any way, and three sick-beds to visit, all in different places, and spend hours in buses. . . . I think my book is morbid and trivial. Blast."

The new outbreak of meetings, like the visits to invalids, involved the very type of running round that was most dangerous for Winifred's health. Before she even settled in Hornsea, she addressed the National Union of Women Teachers at the Free Trade Hall in Manchester on " Equal Pay." In the same fortnight of March, she visited Hull, Leeds, Stalybridge, Harrogate and Ashton-under-Lyme. Her lecture at Hull University College was crowded ; a Hull League of Nations Union meeting which the disturbing aeroplanes compelled her to accept was packed in every corridor with people who stood motionless through two hours of speeches and questions. At the Open Door Council Conference in Ashton-under-Lyme, she met Froken Anna Westergaard, the second head of the Danish State Railways, as well as the veteran feminist, Margaret Ashton — " a little beaky-nosed, red-faced, sweet woman." Her own speech so much impressed the audience that ten months later a member of it wrote to me, recalling her appearance and describing her dress trimmed with sparkling coloured sequins which caught the light as she moved.

Finally, in April, she lectured amid bursts of delighted laughter to the National Union of Teachers at Scarborough

on " Woman in the Modern World " ; and spoke, persuaded
by local expectations, to a " Purity and Social Welfare "
meeting at a Wesleyan School in Driffield. Here she wore
a bunch of red roses given her the previous day in Hornsea
by Bill.

" That, at least," she commented to me, " I owe my
sense of humour."

From the beginning of March Bill had been periodically
in evidence, never leaving her quite free, yet offering
neither certainty nor satisfaction.

" I had a very disturbing week-end," she wrote me
early that month. " I returned to find a letter from Bill
inviting himself down for the day on Thursday. I never
asked him. I want and don't want him. I want to WORK.
. . . I took myself vigorously in hand that evening, and
decided that if I could not have what I wanted, I would
want what I could have. It is undignified and ridiculous
to regret or complain, and I am damned if I won't enjoy
everything. . . . I must go and meet Bill's bus. The sun
shines. The air is full of a fierce frosty brightness. I have
written across my heart : ' I will not be dismayed.' And
the curious result is that, at the moment, I am not. After
all, it is loving and not being loved which is the vitalising
experience. I will give him everything that he is prepared
to take, though I think that is very little, and be thankful
that at least I have known what it is to love."

That afternoon, because it was the first warm day of
spring and she was with him, she succeeded in walking
eleven miles. They sat and smoked on a rifle-range, watching the ubiquitous aeroplanes bombing a target in the sea.
For a moment she imagined that she was back with him in
the War twenty years ago — a child whose half-developed
imagination had not yet learned to respond to a boy's
romantic courtship. . . .

He announced that he was going to Spain; went to
Worcestershire instead ; sent her a card in April to say that
he was back, planting sunflowers, and would like to cycle
over.

" Oh, to hell with all heartache and disturbance ! " she cried, but as usual she wrote telling him to come. He came, and took her to the Tivoli in Hull, where he introduced her to two of his friends — a barmaid aged fifty-seven, and the assistant manager of a third-rate music hall. The next day, divided between amused appreciation and rueful regret, she sent me the last letter that I ever received from her on their strange, unresolved, yet indestructible relationship.

" Bill went off this morning. I am a fool to want more than I get from him. What I have is so gay, foolish and charming — something everyone needs — a frivolity, an enchantment, a relaxation. Then, in his black moods, he revolts both against and towards me — does and does not want me. Is not going to Spain. Is going to Norway. May, he says, come to Wimereux if he makes enough money. . . . Well, I have got out of the episode a red rose and another scene for *South Riding* and a further understanding of how people behave in bars after a football match (which is, after all, something). I can't pretend I don't owe him far more than he owes me. I love every tone of his voice, every movement of his hands. And I wouldn't *not* love him for anything. But it is, I suppose, a humiliating and ridiculous situation for a woman of my age, intelligence and interests. . . .

" My long and often painful experience has taught me this — that passion can become friendship. I don't say without heartache — yes, and a *physical* ache. But then one never expects life to be without heartache, and I personally have never known it to be without some humiliation. . . . I assure you that one need allow it only to affect a very small area of one's consciousness, and it need not affect the relationship to the person involved at all."

At the end of April, Winifred left Yorkshire and joined me for an Easter holiday in Tenby, on the south coast of Pembrokeshire. We were alone together, for G. had travelled east four weeks earlier to spend the spring in

exploring Russia. She was racing ahead with *South Riding*,
I beginning my long novel, *Honourable Estate*. In the intervals of writing, we walked over the crisp empty sands,
immense like the sands at Hardelot, but pale yellow instead of
reddish brown. From the high indented cliffs on the way
to Manorbier we looked across the blue bay to Caldy
Island, where the white Cistercian monastery faced us on the
long green shore — " a shining focus," wrote Winifred afterwards, " to that pale and cloudy land lit by the western sun."

At Hornsea, when she left, the spring had barely begun,
and she was enraptured by the woods and fields filled with
violets and primroses, the deep lanes scented and warm
as in Devon. That spring was one of the loveliest that I
remember ; I was glad afterwards to recall its beauty,
since it was to be her last. The luxuriant riot of flowers
seemed to defy all the laws of natural history ; blackthorn
and roses bloomed together ; celandines still jewelled the
grass though the sweet-peas were shoulder high ; the
swamps gleamed golden with kingcups and yellow irises ;
in the woods the aconites, not yet dead, raised their frilled
cups between magenta orchis and creamy primroses.

By way of light relief our comfortable hotel, which Lady
Rhondda had recommended, provided us with a Gentleman.
(That, Winifred felt sure, was what he would have wished
us to call him.) He was a middle-aged business man who
travelled daily to London from his house in Essex, took
Turkish Baths in order to Keep Fit, never ate white bread,
and thought Low's cartoons " perverted." For Winifred
his attitude towards " Ladies " was so reminiscent of the
behaviour of Empire Builders towards Natives, that she
urged me to pay it special attention.

During a Sunday afternoon expedition — on which, to our
dismay, he resolutely accompanied us, causing Winifred to
walk much further than she should have done — he insisted
upon paying for our tea, because he was a Gentleman, and
presented each of us with packets of inexpensive cigarettes
because " Ladies like smoking." Later in the evening he
completely wasted three valuable hours in which Winifred

was trying to compose her " Notes on the Way," a capable
financial expert from *Time and Tide*, who had joined us for
a few days, was pursuing the fortunes of her stocks and
shares through the financial columns of *The Times*, and I
was endeavouring to write my novel. Since concentration
became impossible, Winifred took down his conversation as
"copy" for her Notes. It certainly was too good to be wasted.

Ladies, he informed us, looking disapprovingly at the
occupation of our *Time and Tide* friend, should be forbidden
such papers as the *Financial Times*. It was too strong meat
for them. He knew that some Ladies who had had a few
hundreds given to them by Gentlemen liked to follow the
progress of their stocks and shares in the papers, but he
wasn't sure that it was altogether *wise*. Too upsetting for
their nerves. Ladies, he suggested, were safer with Culture,
and he gave us a little lecture on the National Gallery.
Then, to be sure, there was Chess. Some Ladies played
that — not so well as men, of course, but they did *try*. We
listened tolerantly ; perhaps too tolerantly. At any rate,
the Gentleman never guessed from our conversation, our
appearance or our names — which he did not learn, since
he never troubled to inquire them — that one of us managed
the business side of a London journal, another was the
author of an autobiography which had already brought
in a good deal more than the " few hundreds " that he
thought suitable for Ladies, while the third was just completing a Yorkshire novel which was to earn, in terms of
royalties and film rights, over £7000.

Before we left Tenby, Winifred had an acute attack of
headache and sickness, and I felt guiltily that I should never
have allowed her to make the long journey from Hornsea
to South Wales. It seemed puzzling and perturbing that
she had just accepted an invitation from Liberia, issued
on the strength of *Mandoa, Mandoa!*, to be the guest of its
Government that winter and write them a confidential report.

Winifred had long been interested in this Negro Republic
on the West Coast of Africa. Though it had not yet succeeded in impressing its dignity upon the civilised world,

she knew that the Liberians had faced every problem of climate, pests, primitive tribes and rival imperialisms common to colonists in tropical regions — with two added complications. No one, because they were Africans, expected them to succeed ; and every European power hoped to be the residuary legatee of their inevitable failure. She longed to see the country because it was a portent, a symbol of African independence, and a challenge to Negroes to work out their own political destiny.

" I want to go to West Africa in the winter," she wrote to Phyllis on May 27th, " and it is the one place to which O. seems reconciled to my going as everything happens very slowly there. . . . So I am going to the Gold Coast and Nigeria first to study conditions for comparative purposes. I am supposed to start in November."

During the summer she investigated, at the School of Tropical Medicine, chemical safeguards against tropical diseases, and answered perturbed letters from Dr. Norman Leys pointing out the special dangers for herself of a country where medical knowledge was primitive. As late as September 6th, she arranged with the President of the New York Macmillan Company for an immediate advance on *South Riding* to cover the expenses of her tour.

After her death this projected journey troubled the imagination of her friends. Was it one more example of her unconquerable optimism, or a deliberate challenge to fate ? Did she, who had sat by so many death-beds and attended so many funerals, realise how near to death she was, and determine to escape from the paraphernalia which surrounded it ? Had she calculated the suffering that she might have to face in a land as yet unreached by the merciful alleviations of science ?

The letters and documents of 1935 shed no further light upon these bewildering questions, to which we shall now never know the replies.

Winifred and I returned to London in time for the May-Day Rally in Hyde Park which preceded King George the

Fifth's Silver Jubilee. *South Riding* was now complete except for revision and the final chapter. For this Winifred required the Silver Jubilee as background, and therefore could not begin it until the national festivities were over. Since we took John and Shirley to watch the procession from the window of a large bank in Queen Victoria Street our own experience was hardly relevant to her novel, but she knew that the description of local functions in the Yorkshire newspapers would give her what she wanted.

On May-Day Sunday, being unable to find our political colleagues from Chelsea, we joined the Battersea Women's Labour Party at Hyde Park Corner and marched to a peaceful rally of good-tempered citizens singing " The Red Flag " a little out of tune. In the wake of the procession the usual banners, souvenir-sellers, bands, babies and bicycles appeared, but there were few spectators ; the small crowd that gathered seemed more interested in the red, white and blue flagpoles which supported the Jubilee decorations, than in the remote prospect of a Revolution. The Park was as hot as midsummer ; serene groups of picnickers on the grass removed their hats and shoes, fed their babies from bottles, and ate their hard-boiled egg sandwiches out of paper bags. Nobody appeared impressed by an angry pamphlet called *Twenty-five Years of War and Starvation*, which a shock-headed young man did his best to distribute. It was the most English of May Days — cheerful, tolerant, amused, and quite unexcited by conscientious ferocity.

" This," I remarked to Winifred, surveying the placid bourgeois scene, " explains why we have been able to preserve such a stable monarchy."

She agreed. " Yes, and it also explains the difficulty of getting social reform in this country. People don't want it badly enough — or rather, they don't know that they do. All the same," she added, " we've done pretty well in the past twenty-five years," and she told me that she had refused, the previous day, to sign a resolution sent her by a left-wing organisation protesting against the Jubilee celebrations.

" I told them," she said, " that whatever he may have

thought of us himself, the King's reign has been the most
propitious that English women have ever known. I've seen
a woman Cabinet Minister walking through the lobby of
the House of Commons and a woman architect chosen to
design the Shakespeare Memorial Theatre. I've heard my
own mother applauded by a County Council as its first
woman alderman ; I've been heckled as an agitator for
demanding the Vote in the Equal Franchise Campaign of
1928, yet I've been enfranchised and I've voted. And I
know that those people who say the world's no better off
since women were let loose in it, simply don't know what
they're talking about."

She was to speak, I knew, as the representative of the
younger feminists at the Jubilee dinner of the Women's
Freedom League the following week. When the evening
came she paid tribute to the work of the older campaigners
in a speech so gracious that it is still remembered by those
who were present, and, anti-imperialist though South Africa
had made her, she joined in the message of congratulation
sent from the Freedom League to the King.

"But it's not only the women," she said, as we left
our contented fellow-Socialists in the Park and walked
slowly home to Chelsea. "What really stopped me from
signing that document was my memories of Rudston. I
remember a village with no artificial light, no telephone, no
telegraph, no health insurance system, no means of transport
except our own pony-trap and the weekly carrier's cart,
with its slow horse which took an hour and a half to get to
the nearest shops. I remember the alarms of sickness at
night, the long painful hours of waiting for the doctor, the
babies that died unnecessarily, and the rigid class divisions.
I remember my father — so gentle that his beloved memory
is already a legend in the village — opposing the Saturday
half-day for his farm labourers. I remember the village
idiots too ; in my childhood they were a recognised feature
of every countryside. And then I think of to-day's raised
wages, the improved housing, health services, buses, women's
institutes, the regulated hours of work, the wireless, the

young farmers' clubs, the playing-fields, the well-run
homes for mentally defective children, the rural community
councils. . . . No, no, no ! As a countrywoman I can't
protest against Jubilee celebrations."

When the last function was over, Winifred took a single-
roomed flat in one of the many new blocks rising up round
the King's Road, Chelsea, in order to have an office of
her own. She had no intention of leaving Glebe Place, but
her writing and her many semi-official interviews now
required more privacy than any household could give.
From this flat she went, later in May, to meet John Brophy
for lunch in the West End.

The two had been friendly since they first met at a
ceremonial luncheon given for H. W. Nevinson in 1933.
John had many contacts with theatres and producers ;
he made several attempts to place *Take Back Your Freedom*,
and it was indirectly through him that Mr. Tyrone Guthrie,
now the producer at the Old Vic, ultimately took out an
option on the play. But an almost stronger link was John's
friendship, dating from his wartime service in the East,
with Lawrence of Arabia.

From the time that Winifred and Edith de Coundouroff
saw a film of Lawrence's adventures at a Hull picture-house
soon after the War, " T. E." had exercised a compelling
fascination over Winifred's mind. Bill's contact with him
in the Air Force at Peshawar had revived this interest, and
she read and usually reviewed every Lawrence publication
produced by himself or his various biographers. John
Brophy believed that he could arrange for them to meet,
and the luncheon had been booked to discuss this plan.

But when John saw Winifred he greeted her gravely.
On the way to the restaurant he had read in an early
evening paper of Lawrence's motor-bicycle accident. He
rang up Captain Liddell Hart, and learned that " T. E."
would almost certainly die. This sorrowful information,
instead of a project for their meeting, was the news that he
had to give Winifred.

After her death, John told me that he had booked the

same table at the same restaurant for another lunch with
her on the day that she finally went into the nursing-home.
The ill-fortune which haunted this particular table seems as
uncanny as the story of Lawrence related to me by Mrs.
Thomas Hardy at Dorchester in 1936. Lawrence, she said,
had been one of their greatest friends, and often came over
on his motor-cycle to see her. On his last visit, shortly
before his death, he seemed nervous and depressed. When
she urged him to tell her the reason he finally admitted that
he had been disturbed throughout one night by a bird
tapping restlessly at his window-pane. Although he constantly drove it away, it always came back.

When *Seven Pillars of Wisdom* appeared at the end of
July 1935, Winifred reviewed it in *Time and Tide*. There is
a curious coincidence in the fact that her last important
book review centred upon the man whose own recent death
had prevented their long-desired meeting just when it seemed
to become a possibility. In her review she described
Lawrence as the divided man, unsure of himself, shamed by
duplicity ; the lifelong victim of the peace treaties " which
destroyed his plans, broke his promises, and brought upon
him that doom of dishonour, the fear of which darkens the
tale of his stewardship."

But perhaps her most appropriate comment on the end
of Lawrence's tormented life had been made the previous
year in a review of Liddell Hart's *T. E. Lawrence in Arabia
and After*. She concluded this criticism by quoting a verse
from the Oxyrhynchus Sayings of Jesus, found in 1903
and translated by the Rev. Charles Taylor :

> *Saith Jesus,*
> *Let him not cease that seeketh Wisdom until*
> *He find, and when he has found let him marvel, and*
> *Having marvelled he shall reign, and reigning*
> *He shall rest.*

The only memorable article that Winifred wrote after
her review of *The Seven Pillars of Wisdom* was a dramatic

criticism of Shaw's new play, *The Simpleton of the Unexpected Isles*, which she saw at the Malvern Festival in the last week of July. She went with Lady Rhondda and they stayed at the same hotel as the Shaws — who lived, Winifred wrote, in a whirl of reporters, visitors and rehearsals.

On his seventy-ninth birthday, Shaw called Lady Rhondda and Winifred on to the balcony to be photographed with him. The picture appeared in several illustrated newspapers, and, despite the softening effect of print, reveals the strain of Winifred's face and pose. In a letter to me, she admitted that she " felt rotten the first three days." Though she loved the calm lush country, she found watching the plays and tramping over the Malvern hills almost more of an ordeal than she could bear.

Throughout her visit she suffered from the same pain and sickness which had seized her at Tenby. This time she concealed it so successfully that her companions did not even guess that she was ill, but a letter written me late in 1935 by a visitor to Malvern who met her at the Festival reveals how seriously her fragile appearance impressed a stranger unaccustomed to the fatigue which now so often appeared in her face and gait. From Malvern onwards, with one short interval, she was a person so sick that anyone else would have been in bed with day and night nurses in attendance. Yet she went to the first night of *The Simpleton*, and immediately afterwards sat up until the early hours writing her notice so that the sub-editor of *Time and Tide* could take it to London by the breakfast train. The superhuman effort and the lost sleep left her, she confessed, " rather jaded," yet her article is as keenly critical and intellectually appreciative as a reviewer in the best of health could have written.

" Seeing," she concluded, in words which were so soon to be truer of herself than of Shaw, " with the eyes of a poet and prophet what might be made of this human experiment, he stands before us in his challenging courage and ends this vision of Judgment with the cry : ' All hail, then, the life to come ! ' "

She returned to London on August 1st, to continue doggedly the revision of *South Riding* now that the Silver Jubilee chapter was complete. In spite of the unalleviated pain which she had permitted to spoil no one's enjoyment, she could still write to me : " Malvern was lovely. Especially yesterday when we walked over those bland, serene and lovely hills in the sunset with the Shaws. I am more fascinated by G. B. S. than ever. Unfortunately I had the same sort of sick attack I had the last days at Tenby and simply could not walk about much. But I've consulted O. since I came back, and apparently it's only a question of taking more padutin when I feel like that."

The growing inability of padutin to support her was soon made clear by an overwhelming series of domestic disasters. At the end of July, I took the children and their governess to Wimereux for their first holiday in France. Winifred was to join us when she had finished her book, and G. after a series of engagements in Cambridge, but Edith de Coundouroff and Margaret, now sixteen, went with me to the same small hotel close to the shore.

Three days after we left, my father died suddenly and tragically in London. The following morning, as we were starting lunch, Winifred appeared unexpectedly in the lounge. Although I had assured her for years that my war-time horror of telegrams was outgrown, she had never quite believed it. Now, with the instinctive consideration which counted no cost on behalf of those whom she loved, she had crossed the Channel to spare me the shock of an abrupt disclosure and to fetch me home.

John, always keenly alive to her presence, was the first to notice her arrival.

" Look ! " he exclaimed excitedly. " There's Auntie ! "

The moment that I saw her standing there, without luggage, in her check tweed travelling coat, I knew that some major disaster had occurred. Leaving the others in the dining-room, I went to her at once.

" Something's happened. Is it G. ? "

" No," she replied. " It's your father " ; and she gave

me the news of his death. But her confidence in her capacity
to endure the hurried journey was now far in advance of
her powers. She had hardly spoken when she became so
ill that my distress for my father was eclipsed by perturbation
for her. Why, oh why, had she come herself? Edith and I
anxiously asked each other. I knew that I could have
sustained the blow, for blows had not been uncommon, but
if sympathy suggested that someone must take the long
journey, could she not have gone to my mother while G.
came over to France? Only later did I realise that she must
have known herself too near to death to endure the prospect
of remaining in its atmosphere.

All that afternoon Winifred lay on my bed while I
hurriedly repacked my suitcases. There was no time to
make new arrangements for the children, so I left them
in France with Edith while I returned to my mother.
Winifred's condition, we agreed, was so serious that it was
unsafe for her to be long out of London ; somehow or other,
I must get her back to Glebe Place and the drugs which
sustained her. We made her take some food, and unexpectedly, with a new effort of her astonishing recuperative
powers, she rallied. On the boat, until sea-sickness compelled her to lie down, she stayed with me on the upper
deck, looking into a flaming sunset which mocked with its
remorseless beauty the sorrowful story of human mortality.
Grief for my father and the anxious pain of leaving the
children in a country strange to them, gave way before the
fear that she would again collapse a long way from home.

Our train was due in London at 11 P.M., but owing to
the August Bank Holiday excursion trains which crowded
the line, we did not arrive at Victoria until after midnight.
G. had waited for me on the platform for an hour and a
half ; I was about to let him hurry me away when I
remembered that the staff at Glebe Place were on holiday,
and Winifred, ill and exhausted, would have to return to
an empty house.

"Don't worry about me," she urged, at once perceiving
the cruel dilemma. " Your mother needs you. I shall be

all right when I get to my medicine-chest."

In the dark, nightmare-like confusion of the crowded station her determination prevailed, and I went to Kensington. When I saw her the next morning she seemed, as so often, almost recovered ; she would fulfil, she announced, that week's original plan of lecturing to the Liberal Summer School at Cambridge, spending a day with the Norman Leys in Derbyshire, and taking her mother to Harrogate. She did in fact carry out her programme ; but knowing, as I now do, how swiftly her end was approaching, I still find unforgivable my failure to save her from passing that night alone.

From Derbyshire she wrote to me of my father — " I shall always think of that gay, handsome, kindly man I first knew, who was always so sweet to me " — and went on to relate another tragedy encountered on August Monday.

" Driving back from Derby last evening Norman and I came upon a man and woman who had been thrown from a motor cycle. She was sitting weeping by the road with a badly cut and bruised face, but he, a big young fellow, had a fractured skull and Norman . . . said he was not likely to recover. They were young, and probably lovers, and it had been, I expect, a lovely holiday."

She had decided, she said, that as she had been going to France later in any case, she would finish revising her book over there, and help Edith to take charge of John and Shirley. Winifred had become so much their second mother that she knew I should be happier if she were over in France, and it would be better to keep the children for a few days longer out of the atmosphere of family chaos and sorrow. Torn between compunction for her, anxiety for them, and the exacting aftermath of sudden death, I made no serious effort to alter this plan. She invited Hilda Reid to join her, and within a week of my departure the two of them arrived in Wimereux.

The " few days " lengthened into weeks, for we had hardly left my father in his grave at Richmond when G.

became seriously ill with an obscure form of septicaemia which might, the doctor thought, have been caused by a germ picked up in Russia. His illness was catastrophic, for he had recently been elected a Labour candidate for Sunderland. Rumours of a General Election had already begun ; he should have been in the North exploring his constituency, and an avalanche of political correspondence was already descending upon us. The need to deal with it promptly and in constant collaboration made a nursing-home impossible ; we were neither of us in the mood for a stranger's perpetual presence, so I opened the house, brought the staff back from their holiday, and for three weeks nursed G. under the doctor's instructions. But I could not manage John and Shirley too, and Winifred, cheerfully co-operative as ever, announced that she would gladly keep them in France. She felt much better, she said, and was getting on with her book, and really resting.

Already she had written most tenderly of the children, whom she had found asleep when she and Hilda arrived late at Wimereux.

" I went in to see them and darling Shirley was lying on her side, her clothes right off, her little brown legs all bare. She is gloriously brown. This morning they both came bounding into my room, Shirley ecstatic because I remembered to bring her pink bear. . . . I wish I could do more for you than boil water and write letters, and keep an eye on dear John's blue behind, as he gets pails full of sea for his pool ! John actually put his arms round my neck and kissed me. I felt so flattered. . . . I *love* the children," she adds later. " They warm my heart and refresh my spirit, and who knows what sort of an academic busybody I might be without them ! "

All day she wrote in the watered garden of the small white hotel, where even in that torrid summer the grass remained green, and the flame-coloured nasturtiums ad-mired their reflected beauty in the oblong, brick-lined pool. When the revision of *South Riding* palled, she wrote an article on the constant intrusion of politics into a French seaside holiday during those months of crisis. The word, at that time, had not yet become habitual ; Winifred was never to know the long twilight of apprehension described by a Left-wing journal as " crisisteria." But already the French fashions were crisis-conscious ; in a chic little dress-shop vivid with striped awnings, she saw a tailored suit marked " *Mode de demain. Soie d'Abyssinie.*" Her article, the last that she ever wrote, appeared in the *Yorkshire Post* on August 26th. Even her journalism, like her novels, ended in the county of her birth.

She wrote at last to tell me that she had finished *South Riding*, and was spending the last few days of her holiday in a delicious idleness which gave her time to send me longer letters and a final instalment of her brave philosophy.

" I do no work. Read novels, walk a little, play beggar-my-neighbour at night, and hope that this determined lethargy will pay itself back in energy for the rest of the year. I really was rather a rag by the end of the summer. . . . It's no use pretending I don't need constant holidays more than a normal person does."

When she returned, she said, I must take a holiday myself to recover from the family afflictions.

" I can do anything at all to help — quite different from the worm who went to France. . . . It's not strange or neurotic at all to think you hear your father's voice. One does. I used to hear Father in his room at Bainesse. I think we all have our fears of ' tics ' and madness to fight. Mine isn't madness exactly, but I know that in times of crisis my body always panics. Before I was ill I was a natural coward ; but now I have completely lost all confidence in myself ; I have a haunting terror of complete panic and collapse — and it has good reason behind it too. Much better reason than your fear of heredity. . . . I think it is no use pandering to our phobias. I suspect everyone with imagination goes through life with some secret dread or shame. We have to get along as best we can with the constitutions fate has given us, as with the face or talents. But sometimes it is comforting to know that we are not alone in our fears and self-distrusts."

In the evenings, now that she need no longer compel herself to write, she joined the others at the Café d'Atlantique on the sea front and consumed innocuous coloured *sirop* while they drank *crème de menthe*. Looking from the grey cliffs at the broken after-glow of the sunset with mackerel clouds dappled across the fading turquoise sky, she watched the wheeling arcs of the lighthouses begin to glimmer over the darkening water, and the bright eyes of the Kentish coast wink at her from the beloved land which she had at last described to her own satisfaction.

She had completed *South Riding*, that novel in which the artist and the social reformer had met and mingled in final co-operation. When she began her story two years earlier, the possibility that she might never live to end it had been faced and accepted. But now the book was finished, and she knew that it was good.

No one who is not a writer can even imagine the mood of exhilaration and relief which this consciousness of completion brings. There is nothing comparable to it except the sublime thankfulness of a mother when, against all the chances of illness and accident, her child at last is born. But the self-ordained apprehension caused by an unfinished book can be, and usually is, worse than the automatic process of waiting for the birth of a baby. Physical pregnancy is limited to nine months ; intellectual pregnancy may last for any period from a week to a lifetime. Only those who have experienced them know the increasing moments of panic when a book which has been two or three years in the making reaches its final months. The risk that ideas which have potential immortality may be for ever entombed in their mortal prison then becomes intolerable, forcing a man to be a coward about his body in order to preserve the treasures of his mind.

It is bitter not to see an important book published, and to miss, as Winifred missed, the sweet consolations of material reward and enduring fame. But what really matters to the writer is to get his work out of his vulnerable brain on to the paper which man has endowed, like so many of his inventions, with a higher capacity for survival than his own. Once this process is finished he can look, as Winifred looked, into the face of the waters, and know himself free from fear.

CHAPTER XXII

"SOUTH RIDING"

FOR THE GHOST OF ELINOR WYLIE

II. Coronation

Must you have roses for your coronation?
  Orchids like butterflies,
Exotic lilies, and the clove carnation
  That bleeds before it dies?

I have made you a wreath that is not of the laurel.
  No laurels nor bays are mine.
My flowers are bindweed and the rusty sorrel,
  Mallow and eglantine.

I have twisted my traveller's joy above your portal,
  For traveller's joy is rest;
I have plucked for you thyme, since now you are immortal,
  Quick-fading time's a jest.

And out of these I have woven a wreath and crowned you.
  Below your delicate feet
I have spread my feathery grasses, and all around you
  My wild wold flowers smell sweet.

My herbs are plain; but their stems are all the stronger.
  And look! I offer you
Poppies, to make your quiet sleep last longer,
  Mandragora, and rue.

WINIFRED HOLTBY
Time and Tide, 1932

THE SUCCESS of *South Riding* and its international fame
make it a book which cannot be treated as merely one event
amongst others in Winifred's complicated life.

Her only novel that comes near to it in stature is *Mandoa,*

Mandoa ! but except for those who know its hidden springs the earlier story belongs to a more intellectual and less broadly human category, and has therefore a less universal appeal.

From the moment that *South Riding* appeared, critics and public alike acclaimed it as a masterpiece, a classic, a picture of England which, as the novelist Helen Simpson suggested in her broadcast review, may well stand as Winifred's monument.

By the time that Winifred had finished this last and greatest novel, she knew her own work too well to be wholly unaware of her achievement. But her innate scepticism about her ability to capture a large public prevented her from counting upon even one of the many triumphs, won by the book, which came too late to reward her.

South Riding was the choice of the English Book Society in the month of its publication, March 1936. Of the original 8s. English edition over forty thousand copies were sold ; of the American between ten and twenty thousand. The following year Edinburgh University awarded the book its annual James Tait Black Memorial Prize for the best novel of 1936. Soon after its publication it was issued in the Albatross Continental edition, and has already been translated into Dutch, Danish, Swedish and Czech. Directly it appeared Victor Saville, the screen producer, bought the film rights ; he was looking for a typical English picture, and the critics selected his production as one of the best British films of 1938.

The title *South Riding* was kept in the screen version, as well as the sub-title, *An English Landscape*, for Winifred, as Victor Saville perceived, had created a whole countryside for the reader's delight. Though the land of her story was old and historic, with all the colour and glamour of tradition, it was also newly imagined through the ingenious reconstructions of her creative artistry. Winifred was not the first English novelist to remake local geography. Just as Arnold Bennett, in writing of the Staffordshire Potteries, saw Five Towns where the map records six, so Winifred added a fourth Riding to a county which only possesses three.

Many of her readers, unaware that " Riding " is derived from the Saxon word " thriding," which means " the third part," began to inquire why " the administrative County of York " should have possessed a North, West and East Riding, but never a South. Already her " South Riding " shows signs of becoming as well-known a literary district as Thomas Hardy's " Wessex." Only recently one Yorkshire local authority, inspired by Winifred's novel, seriously discussed whether the existence of a South Riding, however etymologically incorrect, might not simplify the process of Yorkshire administration.

South Riding was the work — and probably the first typical work — of Winifred's maturity. Amongst her writings it represents both an end and a beginning. It is an end in the sense that, when compared with her first novel, *Anderby Wold*, it gives an uncanny appearance of completion to her literary cycle. It is a beginning because it clearly indicates what she could and would have done had she survived even for another decade. From its pages we can estimate the real measure of her quality.

When *Letters to a Friend* was published in 1937, some of Winifred's more disparaging critics spoke of her " immaturity " as scornfully as though she were a case of arrested development. Actually, judging by the masters whose complete records we possess, she was reaching her full stature at about the same age as some of the greatest writers, who are usually slow growers. How many of England's best-known novelists and dramatists would be famous if they had died at thirty-seven? George Eliot, at that age, had published nothing but articles and translations. *Scenes of Clerical Life* appeared when she was thirty-nine. At thirty-nine also, Galsworthy published the first volume of *The Forsyte Saga* ; Arnold Bennett at thirty-seven had written only *Anna of the Five Towns* ; Bernard Shaw was forty-two before his plays began to appear.

Even when Winifred wrote *South Riding*, her radiant life had not reached its prime nor her vital work its zenith.

Not only her friends but all lovers of English literature have reason to regret that she will produce no more novels, create no more men and women in the likeness of our human frailties, our superb loyalties, our brave and pathetic aspirations.

Long before she actually began *South Riding*, Winifred had wanted to write another Yorkshire novel. One of the friends most interested in its progress was St. John Ervine, who lamented the fact that she had apparently abandoned her own locality after publishing *The Land of Green Ginger*. When he suggested that she should dedicate the successor of *Mandoa, Mandoa !* to him, ·it was in the belief that this would be the Yorkshire story which they had often discussed. Instead, she perversely inscribed *The Astonishing Island* " To St. John Ervine, who asked for it." By way of apology, she wrote him, in January 1933, a long letter to explain the delay in the appearance of *South Riding*.

" For about three years I've been trying to get another Yorkshire book, but there are difficulties. My father retired from farming in 1919 when I was twenty-one and I've never been on our farm since. Every time I go to Yorkshire I go to Cottingham, which is a suburb of Hull and more remote from farming than Chelsea is. I can't go and stay with my other relatives. They suspect me as a writing freak. I can't stay with anyone else in the East Riding because it would hurt my parents' feelings, and they have been so amazingly good to me that I should feel a swine. I can't write about the old pre-war conditions that I knew in every fibre of me, because the moment I try, my consciousness of the present farming tragedy blocks it all out. I have made false start after false start, and am always checked by the feeling that I must get back to the East Riding to-day.

" I have now got almost a whole novel planned, but don't seem able to get to work on it till I get better into the atmosphere of the agricultural slump. It's *awful* what is happening in the East Riding. And I daren't tackle it till I am certain that I understand just what I am doing and can be just and real. I suppose that I shall eventually produce something, but not until I feel ready to do it. I can't get out of my head the really tragic things that are happening. I mind the ruin of the land itself as much as I mind the financial ruin of the farmers, who, in many cases, asked for it by trying to live like squires. I can't go back to the old pre-war days. I said all I knew then in *Anderby Wold*. I don't know quite where and when I can tackle Yorkshire. I can only wait till it ' comes.' "

Nine months later the book had " come " sufficiently for her to believe — incorrectly — that he would probably dislike it. In a letter characteristically acknowledging the frequency of their friendly but vigorous controversies, she told him so.

" You are quite one of the kindest people I know. For all that I shall probably quarrel periodically with you for ever.

> *I did but see him passing by,*
> *Yet I must fight him till I die. . . .*

" You'll probably hate my book. But if you do, at least know that even when I annoy you, I love you. And if I wrote a book simply to please one other person, however nice or wise or worth while pleasing, instead of writing the book I feel I have to write, it wouldn't be much of a book, would it ? "

Between these letters she had been steadily filling two large note-books and several folders with suggestions and material.

" The town v. the country," runs a typical comment. " Changing the world. *Anderby Wold* theme post-war, but active, not passive." This is followed by a description of her chief male character, Robert Carne, as she first conceived him. " Councillor Carne is a farmer—about 55 — tough, grizzled, a suspicion of side-whisker, clever, shrewd, stubborn, passionate."

Both note-books and folders would repay a careful study by any young writer anxious to discover how an experienced

craftsman sets to work. The note-books reveal the thoroughness of Winifred's observations ; they contain graphic
detailed descriptions of people and places, animals and
flowers, the different varieties of grasses on the salt marshes
near the Humber, the behaviour of lambs and human
beings in a typical English scene on a March evening :

" The sun behind the little farm house. The outline of
tiled roof and chimneys softened as though of velvet. The
odd straws on the old thrashed stack like silver — like glass
needles, colourless, gleaming. The ewe with her triplets
lolloping off into the field — they dance on black legs.
Their breath comes like smoke in the very clear cold air.
The soft grey distance — trees like smoky wraiths on the
horizon — not a cloud in the sky. Faint grey .steeple
$4\frac{1}{2}$ miles away. Old, old man feeding hens in little garden.
The woman at the line — the little socks — her glance
flashing constantly towards the house as though she were a
marionette jerked by a string towards where her children
were."

In the folders are details — many surreptitiously gleaned
from her mother's waste-paper basket — of County Council
administration, its minutes, resolutions and agenda ;
medical officers' reports ; copies of Mental Deficiency
Acts ; outlines of Labour Party policy ; village handbooks ;
circulars on local government ; clauses from Acts providing
against such forms of corruption as the experiments with the
building sites on " Leame Ferry Waste " which caused the
downfall of Councillor Huggins :

" If a member of a local authority has any pecuniary
interest, direct or indirect, in any contract or proposed
contract or other matter, and is present at a meeting of
the local authorty at which the contract or other matter is
the subject of consideration, he shall at the meeting, as
soon as practicable after the commencement thereof,
disclose the fact, and shall not take part in the consideration or discussion of, or vote on any question with respect
to, the contract or other matter."

Finally there is a detailed map of the "South Riding" which shows that both North and East Ridings have lent their crashing seas and sweeping wolds to give sound and colour to Winifred's fictitious Yorkshire. The industrial, smoke-blackened West Riding of Phyllis Bentley's novels forms no part of her "English Landscape." Certain places on the map follow the geographical sketch given to the Bradford librarian. "Hardrascliffe" here seems identical with Bridlington, situated within the fold of Hardra's (Flamborough) Head; "Kiplington" is geographically nearer to Withernsea than to Hornsea; "Flintonbridge" represents Beverley; "Kingsport" is, as usual, Hull, and the "River Leame" the Humber.

These records contain nothing which explains just how and why the theme of *South Riding* came to Winifred — "like that," as she put it to Phyllis — after an unsatisfactory December evening with Bill in London. But it was undoubtedly the work of her beloved and admired mother on the East Riding County Council which gave her the idea of a novel showing how local government, with its apparently impersonal decisions, affects the human histories of men and women in every community. Here again, the strange rounding-off of Winifred's life becomes apparent in the interaction of her literary work and her personal relationships. Her mother had published the child's first booklet of immature verses; it was to her mother that the mature woman dedicated the last and best of her novels.

"I admit," she confesses in her Prefatory Letter to Alderman Mrs. Holtby, "that it was through listening to your descriptions of your work that the drama of English local government first captured my imagination. What fascinated me was the discovery that apparently academic and impersonal resolutions passed in a county council were daily revolutionising the lives of those men and women whom they affected. The complex tangle of motives prompting public decisions, the unforeseen consequences of their enactment on private lives, appeared

to me as part of the unseen pattern of the English landscape.
" What I have tried to do in *South Riding* is to trace
that pattern."

This theme meant far more to Winifred than the choice
of a new subject for a novel. It represented the reconciliation, at long last, of the artist and the social reformer who
had wrestled for so many years within her personality.
Thanks to the wisdom of growing maturity, she realised
that for her there could be no final victory of the one over
the other, so she found material for literature in those preoccupations which had hitherto dragged her away from it.
In *South Riding* she threw down a challenge to pity, the
deadly and recognised enemy of her achievement, and pity
itself, captured, enthroned and crowned, became the
apotheosis of her art.

The result was a story which, for all its differences of
time and place, bears a close family likeness to Ibsen's play,
An Enemy of the People. Would the clever literary critics
who maintain that the political and social themes of
Winifred's novels put her outside the ranks of the artists
take, I wonder, the same view of Ibsen ? To mirror universal values in local or personal experience is surely a
major function of art ; and in this Winifred superbly succeeded. Travelling over England in the four years since
her death, I have met men and women in more than a
hundred cities and towns who have said to me of *South
Riding* : " This might have been our own Council. These
are our ideals for our community."

For a long time the title of *South Riding* remained un-
decided. Winifred's original suggestions, as indicated by
her note-books, were *Councillor Carne of Maythorpe* and *The
Teacher and the Alderman.* At a later stage *Take What You
Want* (the beginning of the Spanish proverb quoted on the
title-page : " Take what you want, said God. Take it —
and pay for it ") was discussed as an alternative, and all but
chosen in America. But finally, and fortunately, the shorter

and more beautiful title appeared on the book in both
countries. The idea of it first occurred to Winifred in April
1934.

" I have at last begun to think of my own novel," she
wrote me from Withernsea on April 5th. " I think I shall
call it *South Riding* — it's a pretty name and ambiguous and
rather romantic."

I told her that I liked it, and she replied on April 10th
saying how glad she was that I approved.

" As I see it now it's going to be an immense spread
book. In time occupies only from July 1932–July 1934 "
(this was extended later to make the period of the Epilogue
coincide with the Silver Jubilee) " and in space only a few
score square miles ; but every possible kind of family comes
in. All the county councillors and all the parents of the
children at the high school. The headmistress of the high
school and the most conspicuous conservative councillors
are still the chief protagonists ; but the whole comedy-
tragedy of local government comes in, and each part is
called by the title of a committee of the council. . . . And
each part treats of some aspect of administration as it affects
a human life — or several human lives, while all the time
a fight is going on between the people who want to plan
and change things by deliberate will, and the people who
just want to ' let things happen.' (It's a more profound
cleavage than between mere Conservatism and Socialism,
to my way of thinking.) "

Many incidents of the story, recognisable by correspondents to whom Winifred wrote regularly, arose out of her
own life in Withernsea and Hornsea. One night in March
1934, she heard a handsome and popular preacher " with
an atrocious delivery " give a really entertaining sermon
at a local Wesleyan chapel on the text " Can the reed grow
without wind ? " He supplied, perhaps, the model for
Alfred Ezekiel Huggins, whom Winifred, with typical irony,
made not only the weak brother among the Councillors but
the local lay preacher.

A forlorn ex-servicemen's settlement ten miles from

Withernsea provided the inspiration for "Cold Harbour Colony," where Winifred's fictitious war victims struggled against poverty and despair amid the drains and dykes of reclaimed land in the slime of the "Leame Estuary." Wandering alone one day over the miles of brownish-purple mud where the Humber looks across to Lincolnshire and the Grimsby water-tower, she met an old man whose conversation suggested the discovery of Carne's body by the Holly children on the banks of the Leame. He told her of the flotsam and jetsam thrown up on the sand from the ships riding by, and the corpses washed to the foot of the breakwater along the dam.

"But," he added, "it's finding bones by lamplight does for me."

The dreary hotel where Winifred stayed in Manchester when she spoke in February 1935 for the National Union of Women Teachers, supplied a pattern for the similar hotel in which Sarah Burton, the school-teacher, is prevented by Carne's last-moment attack of angina from becoming his mistress. The programme for a "Grand Variety Concert" at the Floral Hall in Withernsea gave a model for the colourful performance of "Madame Hubbard and her talented pupils." The troubles of a Yorkshire shopkeeper who wept because his wife had refused to sleep with him since the birth of their eight-year-old son were reflected in the "lost home comforts" of Councillor Huggins. She longed, Winifred wrote, to recommend the publications of Dr. Marie Stopes, but hesitated.

"Surely," she commented, "he must have heard of birth-control at his age. What would you have done, leaning over a counter with your arms full of rhubarb? Mother was scolding me again at the week-end for making my books too 'lewd.' I should hate that, but life is a little lewd."

The book, continued her letter, which she had meant to be a satirical comedy, tended to turn into so depressing a tragedy that she ran round and round looking for comic relief.

"Whenever I approach these people and find their hidden lives, I find sorrow and loss and cancer and debts and fear of old age or penury. However, meanwhile there are the fried fish-and-chip shops, the pierrots and small babies who appear, in this part of the world, to be regarded as undiluted entertainment, taken round from house to house, tossed into the air, chucked under the chin, wheeled home at all hours ; every rule of the Chelsea Club broken — and they are adored ! "

From time to time she was seized by periodic misgivings that her work was " anaemic and poor to the tenth degree." It had become, she wrote to Phyllis, " so sad, sad, sad — all about cancer and the Means Test and scholarships sacrificed to families . . . that I doubt if anyone will want to read it." But from Hornsea, when the greater part of the writing was done, she wrote recording a deep affection for the people whom she had created and a growing — though still intermittent — sense of confidence in their future.

" I have a feeling that if I can only do what I want to do, it might be good. But I know I can't do half what I want to do, not through lack of opportunity but through lack of power."

For those who can read it, Winifred wrote her auto-biography in *South Riding* as clearly as she had once written it in *Anderby Wold*, and far more profoundly.

Her book is not only an achievement of the mind ; it is a triumph of personality, a testament of its author's undaunted philosophy. Suffering and resolution, endurance beyond calculation, the brave gaiety of the unconquered spirit, held Winifred back from the grave and went to its making. Seed-time and harvest, love and birth, decay and resurrection are the immemorial stuff of which it has been created. In it lie both the intuitive and the conscious knowledge of imminent death. Its lovely country scenes go back to the earliest memories of the Yorkshire child who, only thirteen years before she died, had come as a brilliant

Oxford graduate to London. Her unconcealed passion for the fields and wolds of her childhood suggests that she returned with relief to her beginning because she knew that, beyond the brave struggle for life and for time, the inevitable end was near. On the flyleaf of her novel she quoted from V. Sackville-West's pastoral poem, *The Land*, a verse which testified to her abiding sense of the Yorkshire that made her :

> *I tell the things I know, the things I knew*
> *Before I knew them, immemorially ;*
> *And as the fieldsman with unhurrying tread*
> *Trudges with steady and unchanging pace,*
> *Being born to clays that in the winter hold,*
> *So my pedestrian measure gravely plods*
> *Telling a loutish life.*

But there is more of Winifred's experience in her book than her background, all-embracing as that was. Though the love-story of Robert Carne and Sarah Burton is less her own than the story of Bill Durrant and Jean Stanbury in *Mandoa, Mandoa !* it contains the same element of frustration and loss, the same conviction that even the pain of being left unsatisfied may be turned, by those who will learn from it, into the beginning of wisdom. In her last years Winifred not only knew the meaning of love ; she possessed the art to make her knowledge articulate. The " cold as the north pole " quality which J. B. Priestley denounced in *The Crowded Street* had long melted in the poignant consciousness of unavailing devotion. Sarah's love for Carne, Carne's hopeless passion for his demented wife, are revealed with a convincing intensity which sometimes becomes too real for endurance.

But if, in *South Riding*, Winifred's lifelong loyalty to Bill is transformed and camouflaged, the beauty and tenderness of her relationship to her mother, triumphant over all distinctions of age, education and values, appears undiminished. In the Prefatory Letter, which contains her final tribute to this relationship, Winifred states that Alderman Mrs.

Beddows is not Alderman Mrs. Holtby. The statement is true. No character drawn by a creative author remains the photographic reproduction of a human model ; whoever may first suggest the fictitious personality, it speedily develops its own characteristics and ends as a remote relative of the original. But, as Winifred herself admitted, there were certain qualities peculiar to Alderman Mrs. Holtby which she could not allow Alderman Mrs. Beddows to disown.

" I confess," she writes, " I have borrowed a few sayings for her from your racy tongue, and when I described Sarah's vision of her in the final paragraph, it was you upon whom, in that moment, my thoughts were resting."

She might have added that in the moving scene between Alderman Mrs. Beddows and Sarah Burton, when the two women are discussing the death of Carne and Sarah at last acknowledges her love for him, the philosophy which shames, comforts and reinvigorates the grief-stricken schoolteacher is that mingling of compassion, common sense and wisdom born of a long life's experience, which represented the philosophy of Alderman Mrs. Holtby :

" Who are you to think you could get through life without pain ? Did you expect never to be ashamed of yourself. . . . You've just got to get along as best you can with all your shames and sorrows and humiliations. Maybe in the end it's those things are most use to you. . . . When there's no hope and no remedy, then you can begin to learn and to teach what you've learned. The strongest things in life are without triumph. The costliest things you buy are those for which you can't even pay yourself. It's only when you're in debt and a pauper, when you have nothing, not even the pride of sorrow, that you begin to understand a little."

Winifred thought of Sarah Burton as herself, though she made her heroine small and red-haired, with the appearance of Ellen Wilkinson, M.P., whom she had always liked and admired. She identified herself with the things which are new and progressive, while perceiving clearly their strident crudity and occasional vulgarity. But she acknowledged that the old, the mellow, the traditional — that side of life which Robert Carne represented and against which she, like Sarah, had always fought — still claimed from her the emotional loyalty which does not invariably accompany intellectual allegiance.

In *Anderby Wold*, that first novel from which *South Riding* marks the full circle of her development, her best-loved character was the young man who typified the future. In *South Riding* it is the middle-aged farmer, the " big heavy handsome unhappy-looking man " fighting his lost battle to save those doomed dignities which Winifred and her kind had helped to destroy, who wins and retains the reader's affection. As Winifred herself grew older, she realised that memory and tradition become dearer with time ; the fight against them is over and won, and the conqueror can perceive with detached eyes the virtues which were invisible to the fervent belligerent.

In portraying the numerous minor characters of her story, Winifred's lifelong endeavour to understand other people's emotions in the light of her own experience approaches a superhuman wisdom and clarity. She was drawing so close to the border-line between life and death that she saw men and women as the God of Mercy sees them, with infinite pity and loving comprehension.

From her own part in the constantly thwarted struggle for international peace, she realised " the deep fatigue of those whose impersonal hopes do not march with history." From the loss of George de Coundouroff and other childhood friends in war, from the deaths of Stella Benson, Dot McCalman, her sister and her father, she knew that " the dead are most needed, not when they are mourned, but in a world robbed of their stabilising presence." It is her own perpetual interruption by the demands of the elderly and the ailing which cries aloud with the voice of the unhappy science teacher, Agnes Sigglesthwaite :

" Oh, time betrays us. Time is the great enemy !
Time crowns us with thorns, exposes us to mockery,
crucifies our bodies, defeats our laborious endeavours.
The old prey upon the young — Mother upon me and I
upon the children. . . . Must the young, the free, the
hopeful, always be sacrificed to the old, the bound, the
helpless ?   Is this the final treachery of time, that the old
become a burden upon the young ? "

But *South Riding* is perhaps most clearly and poignantly
autobiographical in its attitude towards suffering and death.
The knowledge, the fear, the grief which Winifred withheld
from her friends lives in every page of this book ; she
endowed her characters with her own pain and confronted
them with her personal disasters in order that, finding
compensation for them, she might console herself.

" All her work was — partly subconsciously, I imagine
— for the past few years, full of references to her own death —
if one had the key," Lady Rhondda wrote to me at the
beginning of 1936 ; and this is truer of Winifred's last novel
than of anything else that she wrote.   Within the framework
of the main theme, one subsidiary story after another
develops round the pride and the isolation of coming death
secretly realised and accepted.   With intimate awareness
Winifred describes the effect of pain upon mind and body ;
the consequences of terror, of defeated hope, of perpetual
endurance.   She understands the eager appreciation of
each simple pleasure, each conspicuous moment, tasted
by those about to die ; she acknowledges the discomfort
and humiliation which illness causes to all lovers of beauty,
health and intelligence.

Though *South Riding* is a hopeful and lovely book, never
morbid, and often vital with gay satiric humour, several of
its leading personalities are faced with disease and premature
death.   Robert Carne perpetually dreads a fatal attack of
angina ; Lily Sawdon, the innkeeper's wife, suffers from
cancer ; Joe Astell, the Socialist Councillor, who bears so
close a resemblance to William Ballinger, sees his work

for humanity doomed by tuberculosis. Hereditary insanity threatens Carne's young daughter Midge; the fear of death in childbirth hangs over Mrs. Holly, struggling to rear her large family in the comfortless squalor of The Shacks. All Winifred's creatures feel the burden of their mortality; they defend themselves only by their own courage against the sentences passed upon them by fate.

Through Joe Astell and Lily Sawdon, Winifred admits her readers into the secret of her own mental and physical fight. She divides her stricken personality between them; Astell embodies the threat of illness to the mind, Lily the shrinking of the vulnerable body from pain.

"Astell," she writes, looking back upon her own experience, "was not afraid of death. He was afraid of a haemorrhage, of a sanitorium, of the survival of his restless mind imprisoned within a helpless body. . . . He had thought himself inexhaustible, if ever he thought of himself at all, until the week when he had collapsed, after a speaking tour. . . . From that time he had been a stranger to himself, constantly ailing, unable to be sure that he could keep an appointment or fulfil a promise, horrified by his own unreliability, ashamed of impotence. . . . There were days when he could not work at all, nights when he lay in terror waiting for the cough which tore his body, dawns when he woke with racing pulses, hunted down corridors of dreams by hounds of fancy."

Lily Sawdon, dying of cancer, does not fear death either; nor has she, like Astell, a self-appointed service to perform for mankind which will cease with her life. Her only terror is that of becoming unable, through the loss of alleviating drugs, to conceal her pain and its significance from the kindly cheerful husband whom she loves.

"She had not yielded yet. Morning after morning she had crept, livid with pain, to her secret store, her most intolerable nightmare that she should one day find

it bare. That fear pursued her far into her dreams. . . .
It aroused her early in the mornings, haunted by a panic
that was of the body rather than the mind, the panic
that even this remedy should fail her, that she would be
left at the mercy of her pain, disarmed, defenceless."

When at last she does make confession to Tom Sawdon,
acknowledging the temporary insanity of her shame and
distrust, the scene is all but unbearable until we recall the
previous chapter in which Lily passes the Kiplington
Hospital — floodlit as Winifred had once seen the London
Cancer Hospital in the Fulham Road — and perceives in
it the gateway to the final release for man " pushing his way
from dark to dark."

It is this gradual acceptance of death as a friend which
gives their poignant yet luminous atmosphere to the final
chapters of *South Riding*. With the clear enlightenment
born of her own peril, Winifred understands the men and
women who already belong to those dim regions where the
living walk as strangers, yet who hide from their friends
their consciousness of encroaching doom. She realises that
the death which swoops down from the sky or roars upward
from the sea may sometimes appear a mercy and a relief ;
she knows the reassurance brought to the soul tormented
with griefs and problems by the certainty that life is not
perpetual nor sorrow everlasting.

Already, in her study of Virginia Woolf, she had expressed
a similar idea in a comment on *Jacob's Room* :

" The world, with all its beauty and adventure, its
richness and variety, is darkened by cruelty. Death, if
it ends the loveliness, the adventure, ends also that.
Death balances the picture. It completes the pattern.
It makes even cruelty fall into place. It is completion."

Now, in the Epilogue to *South Riding* which coincided
with the closing weeks of her own short life, she faces the
fact of death through the eyes of Sarah Burton who has
just escaped annihilation in an aeroplane accident, and finds

consolation for the years that she will miss in the same undaunted philosophy :

" She had been shaken out of sorrow. She had looked into the clear face of death and known her lover. She would fear no longer, not even Carne's sad ghost. She would live out her time and finish the task before her, because she knew that even the burden of living was not endless. Comforted by death, she faced the future."

CHAPTER XXIII

"SINCE JOURNEYS END . . ."

HAPPY ENDING

Ah, close the chapter on this hour !
The grass so green, the air so sweet,
All springtime burning in a flower,
All summer blossoming at our feet.

If what's to come be past our mending,
All that has been has led to this ;
Then give the tale a happy ending
And close the chapter with a kiss.

What if estrangements follow greetings ?
What if our lovely loves grow cold ?
Since journeys end in lovers' meetings
Keep silence now ; this tale is told.

WINIFRED HOLTBY, 1929
Observer, 1935

WHEN WINIFRED died, one final question continued to trouble her friends. How far, they asked, had she realised the certain fatality of her illness ? Did she know in the summer of 1935 that death was so near ?

These doubts can never be wholly dispelled, for, like all individuals of great courage, Winifred kept her counsel to the end. Partly for their own sakes, partly because she feared that their anxiety might limit her freedom, she was deeply concerned to spare most those whom she loved best. But apart from the clear testimony provided by *South Riding*, there is sufficient evidence to show that death found her prepared and unafraid.

With me, as with other intimate friends, she was always

deliberately vague about her own prospects of survival. She came nearest, perhaps, to telling me the truth one afternoon when we had tea together in the courtyard of a small Chelsea restaurant the spring before she died. We were discussing some plan of future work, when she remarked quite casually : " But, of course, I mayn't be able to do it. I shan't live to be old, you know. I'm damned and doomed."

When I asked her, alarmed, whether her illness had entered upon some new phase, she answered calmly : " Oh, no, I didn't mean that. I'm quite all right. But Dr. O. said I couldn't expect to live — well, as long as Mother. That's why I make the most of my time ! "

Remembering now that last year of our friendship, I believe that my blindness, like that of others, was cultivated with subconscious deliberation. I did not really want to know how ill she was, because I could not picture life without her. Perhaps the most realistic of us all was Jean McWilliam, who saw Winifred for the last time when she visited England early in 1935. From their conversation she gathered, and accepted, the impression that Winifred never expected to see her again. In her Introduction to *Letters to a Friend*, she has related how, as her train moved out of the station, Winifred drew herself erect, beautiful and glowing, and gave her the W.A.A.C. salute.

Besides Jean McWilliam there were two other friends — both of them, like Jean, about to go very far from England — to whom Winifred told the truth. One of these was Isabel Brett, the wife of our American publisher, who visited England three months before Winifred died. Shortly before sailing, Mrs. Brett told her that she ought to arrange an American lecture tour, and invited her to stay at their house. Winifred replied that she would never see America ; she was too ill, now, to think of a tour and could not hope to live much longer. In accordance with her own request, this conversation was never reported to me until I stayed with the Bretts during my second American tour in the autumn of 1937.

The other friend was William Ballinger. To him, as to Creech Jones, Winifred appears to have spoken quite frankly. Financial transactions and the future of the African campaign were involved ; she could not allow those friends who shared her responsibility to indulge in comfortable illusions.

William Ballinger relates that when he came to Europe in June 1935, Winifred's pallor troubled him greatly. He determined to speak to her about it on his return from Geneva. The opportunity arose on his last Sunday, at the end of July. Winifred had arranged for him to write his report at her Chelsea flat, and when he arrived she was waiting there for him. Soon after he appeared she collapsed, sick and faint, on her divan, but she assured him that nothing was wrong but a slight dizziness. Later, when they had lunched, she took him for a walk across the Albert Bridge into Battersea Park. In the Old English Garden he mentioned his anxiety about her health, and urged her to take a rest. She told him that rests were no longer of any use to her. She had a novel to complete, and a play which she hoped might be produced in the autumn, and then she would be finished.

" My work's ending and my life's ending," she said quietly. " There isn't much time."

She expressed her concern that his work should go on, her anxiety lest funds should prove insufficient. Ballinger tried to cheer her with the information that he had only been given six weeks to live during the illness contracted in Bechuanaland. But she insisted with gentle certainty that she really could not hope for more than a few weeks of life.

"Promise me," she added, "that you won't alarm Vera or any of our friends."

He promised gravely to keep his knowledge to himself.

" It all seemed so unreal," he wrote to me two years afterwards. " The lovely gardens in the heart of London — a great woman speaking quietly of the end. The African scene seemed impossible, even grotesque, without Winifred."

When Winifred returned from France with John and Shirley, she appeared superficially sunburned and well. By that time G. was recovering from his illness, and I discussed with her my plan to take him to Monte Carlo for his convalescence. He could not hope, our doctor told me, to get through the General Election without a good holiday.

In the end he fought, lost and survived it without any holiday at all.

As soon as she had returned the children safely to me, Winifred went home to spend a few days with her mother. Early in September she came back, perhaps aware that she had bidden Yorkshire good-bye. On September 4th Mr. Tyrone Guthrie booked a luncheon engagement with her to discuss her play, *Take Back Your Freedom*. Without waiting to return to Chelsea, she telephoned me excitedly that he had promised to produce it.

The following day we both had a business interview with the Society of Authors, and I realised that the long discussion had tired her beyond endurance. At her own request we walked home through Hyde Park, but she seemed unable to hold herself erect, and too exhausted to speak distinctly. The effect of her holiday had already vanished and she decided to consult her doctor. He thought that she might be suffering from an overdose of arsenic in one of her injections, and advised a few days' rest.

Before she could take it, a new series of family afflictions crowded upon her. Alice Holtby wrote in agitation that Grace's husband, without warning her, had married again, and she feared — as time was to prove, quite without cause — that the stepmother might not be kind to her grandchildren. Immediately afterwards two members of the older generation died in Yorkshire, and Winifred knew that her mother, who had endured so many funerals, would not wish to attend these alone.

But this time her body, so often over-driven, refused to respond to her will. She could not, she realised at last, compel herself to travel north again. Instead she lay on her bed wearily correcting the recently completed typescript of *South Riding*. How unfit she was to revise it at all and to perceive minor errors, I discovered when I went through the typescript afterwards to prepare it for publication.

On the evening of September 9th she became worse, and was ill throughout that night. Still stupefied with the shock of my father's death and the fatigue of nursing G., I fell fitfully asleep though I tried to keep awake, and have never since been able to forget that I did less for her in those hours of darkness than I could and should have done. Next morning it became clear that the skill of an amateur was no longer sufficient, and as she had never used a general practitioner, in desperation I rang up her specialist.

Though he normally saw Winifred only at his consulting-room, he came to the house and ordered her into a Devonshire Street nursing-home for a week's intensive treatment. To G. and myself he spoke quite frankly.

" She's got a fifty-fifty chance," he said. " When I saw her in the spring of 1932 I didn't think she could last two years. But since she's defeated my calculations there's no knowing what she may do. This new attack of illness may mean anything or nothing."

That afternoon I went again through the process, now so sadly familiar, of packing her suitcase and helping her to dress. When I took her to the nursing-home in a taxi she feared that she might be ill all the time as in 1931; but she managed to arrive there without disaster. As I paid the driver she walked erect up the steps of the nursing-home, rang the bell, and went in bravely.

I can still see her in the clothes that she wore that day — a black silk dress with a blue pleated frill, a long black cape, and a halo hat, the fashion of the moment, against which her soft fair hair glowed like an aureole. Anxious though I was, I did not dream that I should never see her dressed again, or realise that she had left for ever the home which we had shared for so many years. Her nurse allowed me to stay with her for a time in the large quiet room which Dr. O. had chosen. I unpacked her case and arranged on the dressing-table the bunch of crimson roses which I had bought for her that morning.

For the first few days, Winifred endeavoured to lead her normal life. Our secretary went daily to the nursing-home with her letters, and she dictated the replies. But gradually, owing to increasing headache and sickness, she was obliged to give up the attempt. Night after night she could not sleep. For the first time the fears that she had expressed through Lily Sawdon were fulfilled, and the injections which had so long sustained her failed to bring any relief. The thought of leaving her and going to Monte Carlo became intolerable ; we abandoned our plans, and I arranged instead to take G. to Brighton, the most accessible place where he could hope to recover his strength. We did not want even to go there, but Dr. O. urged us to leave lest Winifred should become alarmed. In her case, he said, such psychological factors as her energy and her optimism had counted so heavily that the certain knowledge of imminent peril might retard her recovery.

When we went I felt more unhappy than ever. The previous day Winifred had seemed, for the first time, really disheartened ; her eyes were swollen as though from tears, and I realised that she had hardly eaten, drunk or slept during her ten days in the home. She implored me to talk of books, of politics, of anything that would take her mind from her illness. The light hurt her eyes, so I drew down the blinds, and for two hours sat beside her talking quietly in the darkness. We spoke of *Time and Tide*, of the Abyssinian crisis, of the arrangements made in America for the publication of *South Riding*. And, at the last, she mentioned Bill.

" I wish he'd come to London and see me," she said wistfully.

But it was Edith de Coundouroff, loyal, loving and faithful, who came to London to take care of Winifred while G. and I were in Brighton. Of that strange, garish, heavy-hearted week-end I remember only the sunset of violet clouds and golden palaces on the evening of our arrival, and a telephone call from Edith on the Sunday night to say that Winifred seemed worse and she was greatly troubled.

I couldn't stay at Brighton any longer, I told G. desperately, and I promised Edith to return to London on Monday morning. That night I went to bed with a dull overwhelming sense of being back in the War with doom close at hand.

Next morning, as I was packing my suitcase before breakfast in the lovely sunlight of a perfect autumn day, a porter told me that I was wanted on the telephone. The message was from Edith, to say that Winifred's illness had suddenly become acute, and she had telegraphed for her mother. A moment later a second call came for me from the nursing-home : " Miss Holtby is unconscious and her condition is critical."

G. and I pushed the rest of our possessions into our cases, threw on our clothes and rushed to the station to catch the first available train. As we left the hotel a page-boy gave me a letter. At first I did not recognise the handwriting ; then I realised that the almost illegible scrawl was Winifred's. Even during that week-end of pain and weakness, she had replied to a description which I had written her on our first evening of the Regency atmosphere of our hotel.

" Darling," ran those last lines, " why not move to the Metropole if plush bores you? Had lovely supper last night, two chicken sandwiches and slept all night and O. says I can have tomato-juice cocktails and biscuits every morning. Sorry to be so gastronomic but this is news for *me* ! Do have a holiday. I am *much* better. Overwhelmed by offers of visits. Edith will do everything. Give G. my love. I wish you both shared my passion for the Pavilion. Funniest institution in the world, I think. Love. W."

At the nursing-home Edith met me ; a sudden change, she said, had come during the night, and in the early morning Winifred had relapsed into coma. Some " Factor X " unforeseen by the doctors had caused it, and they knew now that there could be no hope.

We stood on either side of her bed as she lay quiet and fair and pale against the pillows. She looked so young that the years since we were together at college seemed to have fallen away. I realised, with the slight shock of irrelevant discovery, that the sophisticated cosmetics which we now all used made the faces that they adorned appear older, not younger. Her eyes were failing, but she recognised my voice as I knelt beside her.

" But I thought . . . Brighton . . . " she whispered.

" Shirley had a cold and I had to come back," I said, inventively exaggerating the truth.

Winifred smiled weakly. " She . . . *would* ! "

Outside her room I told Edith what Winifred had said to me of Bill. Would a summons provoke his contra-suggestiveness and cause him to stay away, we wondered ? But there was no time to lose, so together we concocted a telegram.

" Winifred critically ill, still recognises people. Has asked for you. Come if you wish."

In the afternoon a reply came announcing his arrival in the early hours, and the next morning he appeared at Chelsea.

We had feared that Winifred might not live through the night, but unexpectedly a course of injections had restored her to full consciousness. She spoke to me cheerfully, telling me that all her pain and discomfort were gone.

" It's so lovely to be free from it again. Do you know, I was beginning to get frightened. . . . I wanted St. John. St. John would have understood. He knows what it's like when pain frightens you. . . ."

The Press had now received the news of Winifred's illness, and daily bulletins appeared in *The Times* and else-where. Throughout that final week of her life, a procession of visitors streamed through the nursing-home like a pageant of her past. They came and went, while a few of us — her mother, Edith, Lady Rhondda, Hilda Reid, Violet Scott-James, G. and myself — remained there lest any sudden change should occur.

" I've never had such a lovely twenty-four-hours as this,"
she told her doctor on September 24th. " When I get better
I shall have a terrible character after all this flattery. It's
worth having a headache because it's so lovely when you
don't — like the man who knocked his head against the
wall because it was so perfectly heavenly when the pain
stopped."

Bill's coming, in itself, had brought her a motive for
holding on to life. No longer absorbed in the inspiration
of writing or the stimulus of political controversy, her
dying mind fastened upon the fundamental love and
loyalty which her journey from childhood to maturity,
from insignificance to fame, had left unchanged. There
couldn't be many people, she said, who had loved the same
man for thirty years and not married him in the end. . . .
She asked for Bill continually. After she had woken one
night in sudden terror and found no one beside her, he
volunteered to sit up with her. Any one of us would have
done the same, but she wanted no one else.

Did she know? Did she know? We asked ourselves
that question as though all our future happiness depended
on the reply. She spoke continually of getting better ;
was this, as usual, to spare us, or did a doubt exist in her
mind ? If it did, I believe that she was determined to fight
it ; to cheat the doctors again and snatch from life whatever
period of respite courage could win.

One afternoon towards the end of that week I sat
alone beside her. Roses, carnations, lilies of the valley,
filled the room with a royal glory ; their exotic scent
delighted her though she could no longer see them.

" Are we by ourselves ? " she suddenly inquired, and
when I assured her that we were, she began to put me a
question.

" Vera, do you think . . . ? "

But if, as I imagined, she intended to ask me whether
she was dying, she suddenly changed her mind.

" It's so strange," she continued instead. " Life seems

to be rounding itself off in such a queer way. . . . I used to want the things I did want so badly, but now I don't any more. . . . All impatience gone. . . . Whatever I may do, remember that I love you dearly. I'm intensely grateful to you. . . . Often when I've been all tangled up and haven't known how to get through, you've said to me : ' But this is the end — this is how to get out.' "

I was to give John and Shirley a present from her, she insisted.

" I've got so many flowers. Choose two of the nicest roses and take them to my two darlings. . . . You know, when I was in France with them, I *prayed* that I might bring them back to you safely. Perhaps it was silly, but I wasn't taking any chances."

Two days before she died, a final blood test made by the specialist showed that the last hope had vanished. Winifred herself felt no worse ; did I think, she inquired, that if she spent her convalescence in a country cottage, Bill would look after her ? But perhaps it wouldn't be fair to marry when she couldn't have children.

" Vera," she pleaded, " you wouldn't let me do anything ignoble, would you . . . ? "

As I left the nursing-home that evening a newspaper placard confronted me : " ABYSSINIA MOBILISES." Everything that Winifred and I had worked for — peace, justice, compassion—seemed at that bitter moment to be gone. G. told me afterwards that two days earlier she had described to him a questionnaire which she had seen in the *Daily Mail*, asking its readers to say what their last wish would be if they had only two days to live.

" What would you have said ? " he inquired, for she evidently wanted to tell him.

" A decided British policy," she answered promptly, and added : " But I don't intend to clear out yet."

When the doctor had given his final verdict, G. and Bill went home together. Now, at last, Bill realised that the moment towards which his plans had vaguely converged was about to escape him. Could he grasp it before it was

gone for ever ? He'd always really thought, he said, that he
and Winifred would marry in the end, but their positions were
so unequal, and there seemed to be plenty of time before
them both. . . . Now that she was dying, the success which
had set her apart from him was a barrier no longer. . . .

On Saturday morning, September 28th, I went early to
the nursing-home. When I left Winifred, the astonishing
lucidity of her mind seemed for the first time a little clouded ;
thoughts that she was chasing eluded her, and she begged
me to return later and help her to capture them.

" Don't bother about the rest of to-day," she said. " But
will you come back last thing at night, after everyone else
has gone, and straighten out the tangles in my mind ? "

Of course I would, I told her. As a nurse came in with
some tea and I rose to leave the room, she repeated her
request.

" You'll come back to-night, won't you ? "

I promised faithfully that I would, kissed her and left
her. Not knowing that she had spoken to me for the last
time, I joined G. outside the nursing-home. We walked
down Marylebone High Street to St. James's, Spanish Place,
where Winifred had been my bridesmaid ten years before.
As we went into the church, the lovely organ which had
played our wedding march began to roll triumphantly from
the vaulted roof. Kneeling in the dim light beneath the
tall windows, we seemed to see the ghosts of ourselves
standing together in front of the altar, and Winifred behind
us in her blue dress, golden, Madonna-like, reassuring. . . .

While we stayed there listening to the organ, Bill sat
with Winifred in the nursing-home. There was still just time
for their strange, erratic story, constantly broken and as
often resumed, to end in as much of contentment as most
of us are destined to know.

When Alice Holtby came later in the morning she found
Winifred eagerly awaiting her, vital and glowing as though
it were not death but life that lay ahead.

" Mummie," she said, " when I'm better, Bill and I are
going to get married. It's just an understanding between

us — not really an engagement. You don't mind, do you, darling ? "

And Winifred's mother, on the point of losing, at seventy-seven, the last of those who had made up her life, responded gallantly : " Mind ? Why, I'm delighted ! I've just lost one son-in-law, and now I've got another instead."

Reassured, Winifred repeated happily : " Not an engagement — just an understanding," as the doctor came into the room.

To her, the last injection that he gave her was simply another of the many that she had endured in the past four years. Only a few of us realised that it contained morphia, administered lest the valiant mind which had remained so resolutely clear and gay through suffering should be violently impaired by the shock of joy. She closed her eyes upon the belief that the elusive happiness which had so often mocked her was to be hers at last, and never knew that I came back at night in fulfilment of my promise, and sat beside her through the silent hours while she drifted across the borderland.

She died in her sleep just as dawn was breaking over London. It was the last Sunday in September, and a gentle, radiant morning.

EPILOGUE

FOR THE GHOST OF ELINOR WYLIE

III. Peace

Put up your bright sword ; you have done with fighting.
  Your enemies are fled.
There's no more need for mirth, nor joy's requiting
  Among the quiet dead.

The wounds are healed now and the wrongs are mended ;
  The feud is buried deep.
Now, the brave battle of your laughter ended,
  You, if you will, may weep.

Your terraced garden, your fantastic palaces
  Were all too high, too cold ;
Bitter the wine you drank from crystal chalices,
  Heavy the carven gold.

Your glass and silver were too faery brittle,
  Your silk brocades too thin.
Come, you may warm yourself down here a little,
  With a shroud to shelter in.

Here are dreams, to give you rest in the night season,
  Silence to ease your pain,
And in the grave you'll find sufficient reason
  To turn and sleep again.

WINIFRED HOLTBY
Time and Tide, 1932

AT RUDSTON on October 2nd, 1935, a silent gathering of friends and villagers followed Winifred's coffin down the sloping churchyard to its grave lined with ivy and clematis.

The crowd was as large as the throng of writers, publishers, journalists and politicians which had come the previous day to hear Dick Sheppard conduct her memorial service at St. Martin-in-the-Fields, but except for a few friends from London, it was utterly different. These were her people ; it was here that she belonged.

The morning had been brilliant with sunshine, and now, at noonday, though the sun had vanished, the air was still bright. As the coffin with its cross of violets was lowered into the flower-lined earth, we tried vainly to realise that now she was gone, quite gone ; soon, like the deep waters of the sea, the flood of our trivial occupations, interests, emergencies, would close over her, engulfing her once so lovely image.

Across the long autumn grass as we left the churchyard, a little leaping wind carried to us the exquisite perfume of the flowers heaped beside the upturned soil. Wreath upon wreath and cross upon cross of roses, chrysanthemums, lilies, carnations, dahlias, gladioli and forget-me-nots, they made such a bank of scent and colour as the village had never known. A journalist who had attended many famous funerals wrote later that only at the burial of Ellen Terry — who lived to be more than twice Winifred's age — had she seen so many flowers sent in honour of a distinguished woman.

"She has come home," said one Rudston dweller, "bringing her laurels with her."

But after her death and burial — as always with those who have been exceptionally gallant and beloved — there were some who set out to destroy the legend which they alleged that her friends had created. The reviews of her posthumous books — not even excluding *South Riding* — began to strike a captious and disparaging note. Pretentious young critics triumphantly unearthed the old complaint that Winifred was "not an artist" ; they deplored what they described as attempts to make her a "literary figure" ; they dismissed her compassionate studies of human needs and problems as "documentary." One supercilious novelist, reviewing *Letters to a Friend*, described their author with unperceptive contempt as "an enthusiastic Martha."

What these commentators were really deploring, though

they did not know it, was the fact that Winifred had always been a typical product of her age ; an age of perpetual and intensive propaganda by screen, wireless and Press, in which it is less possible than it has ever been for a writer to live in serene detachment from the controversies of his time. As Winifred herself had realised in her biographical chapter on Virginia Woolf, the problem of the twentieth-century woman, artist there analysed was precisely her own. The conflict which throughout her life divided her mind and spirit was not peculiar to herself.

"At certain moments — and this is one of them," writes Winifred's Yorkshire contemporary, Storm Jameson, " all writers who can claim to be called ' living ' must be political in a sense. They must have what the Quakers call a concern to understand what is happening in the world, and must engage themselves, in their writing, to promote no comfortable lies, of the sort which people will pay well to be told rather than the truth at these times. A care for justice, a detestation of cruelty, are no more than one expects of an honest writer. He can sometimes — if he has taken care to be born into a more fortunate age — leave thinking directly of them. But not this day. Not this day, with us."

Like most debunking campaigns, the superficial and ignorant judgments passed upon Winifred — in some instances by writers whom she had encouraged when her assignments on *Good Housekeeping* and *Time and Tide* gave her power over their future — were not only unworthy but untrue. Winifred was not a Martha but a saint — with the sensitive social conscience of sainthood and its noble, deplorable exploitability. Moreover, she was a young saint. Inevitably, she spent a great deal of time serving many persons much older than herself, who felt — as senior people so often feel — that youth can easily afford to squander its generous vitality, and who could not or would not realise that her time in the world was to be shorter than theirs. No one was ever more passionately desirous of sitting still in the house ; no one was ever more ruthlessly compelled by relatives, friends, acquaintances, readers, fanatics and propagandists to be careful and troubled about many things.

It is, I believe, impossible to over-estimate what the achievements of her imagination would have been when full maturity had taught her the wisdom of withholding her eager, conscience-smitten compassion, and she had learnt that one's self, and not the demanding, exploiting world, is the rightful judge of how one's time should be spent. The best books are seldom written — though *South Riding* proves that they sometimes can be — in odd moments left over from promoting the interests of others. That is why the artist must be jealous and fierce for himself, and why we, if we are wise and far-seeing, will be jealous and fierce on his behalf. The enormous, unlimited selfishness of mankind, so pitiless and yet so pitiable in its ruthless blindness, has always extinguished much noble work that should have been cherished in the treasure-house of literature, music and art. But it has deprived itself of few things better worth having than Winifred Holtby's unwritten books.

No one is especially blameworthy, for the simple reason that all of us, whether seniors or contemporaries, were cruelly and intolerably to blame. We all exploited her. She had so much to give ; she gave it with both hands, and we all took — thereby emphasising her own deeply-implanted social tendency to destroy both her life and her literary reputation. According to our different standings and in our various ways, we, her most intimate and devoted admirers, made use of her magnanimity to further our personal ends. We laid our domestic burdens upon her when she was sick and dying ; we pestered her with our problems, our anxieties, our families, our ambitions, our love-affairs ; we over-worked and under-rewarded her ; we sent her forth on tedious and time-absorbing expeditions which varied from finding us lodgings to supporting us in elections ; we made her read our letters, speeches and manuscripts ; we constantly tore her from her own death-imperilled work to assist the progress of our less urgent activities.

Not one of us who loved her most dearly is guiltless ; not even one. But if ever we stand before the Recording Angel and bitterly confess the measure of our joint responsibility for her premature end, it will be her loving, distressed astonishment at our remorse which alone will save us from our just punishment for the wrong we did her.

That is why, as one of the offenders, I wrote in the Epitaph to the special edition of *South Riding* that I dared not dwell upon her unfulfilled promise, nor picture the heights to which she might have attained had time been permitted her, and a maturer wisdom taught her how to command the uninterrupted peace which her best work required.

But of this at least I still feel certain : that whether or not the spirit of man is destined for some unknown flowering in a life hereafter, the benevolence of the good and the courage of the undefeated remain, like the creative achievements of the richly gifted, a part of the heritage of humanity for ever. As such they attain their own shining immortality, though it is not without tears that we see them pass from our individual experience.

> *The splendours of the firmament of time*
> *May be eclipsed, but are extinguished not ;*
> *Like stars to their appointed height they climb,*
> *And death is a low mist which cannot blot*
> *The brightness it may veil.*

THE END

AFTERWORD

Testament of Friendship is Vera Brittain's biography of her closest friend, the writer Winifred Holtby, famous for her novel *South Riding*. Its title carries a conscious echo of *Testament of Youth*, Vera Brittain's earlier best seller. Years later, with *Testament of Experience*, she completed a trilogy which is as important taken collectively as individually.

Together they bring to life the experience not only of an individual but also of a segment of a generation as it lived through and subsequently responded to one of the most cataclysmic events of the twentieth century—the First World War, the "Great" War. It was a war which marked a historic turning point—everything else was "pre-" or "post-" it; it shook empires, gave birth to new political forms, and profoundly marked the imaginations of those whose lives it touched, transformed, or brought to an end.

Much has been said and doubtless remains to be said about the war's impact on the male literary and political imagination: Owen, Brooke, Sassoon, and the poets and writers of the thirties. Much less has been registered so far of its reverberations for the women who survived the loss and pain it inflicted. The Testaments of Youth, Friendship and Experience left behind by Vera Brittain are an invitation to do so and to re-assess the significance of the inter-war period.

In *Testament of Youth* we can share the anguish of the war's destruction of all hopes for the future through the loss of beloved young men, and can witness the start of a process of healing. *Testament of Friendship*, a study of "the best friend life has given me", explores yet another relationship dogged by death—this time with another woman writer who was herself sensitive to the disturbing power of social change. With *Testament of Experience* the author wrestles with an ideal whose aim is the abolition of war—pacifism—and confronts the problems and rewards it brings.

Perhaps because they deal with relationships with other people and not with an ideal, *Testament of Youth* and *Testament of Friendship* are the more forceful books. Within them Vera Brittain shows great courage as she takes hold of her deepest and most intimate feelings so as to show the crises which shaped her own thoughts and those of many of her contemporaries.

She put all of her developing skill as a writer and much of her historical training into this work of uncovering hard-won experience. The reconstruction of her own life and that of Winifred Holtby never falls into a hazy impressionism: using memoirs, diaries, letters, magazine articles and other sources she produces a highly detailed narrative in which not only personal dramas and high-flung ideals, but hats and dresses too have their place. As a method it has features in common with the new styles of documentary realism which were beginning to emerge in the late twenties and thirties in the novel, and the visual arts of photography and cinema. The canvas of the first book—that of the war and the war generation—is broader than that of the second—that of a network of women writers and political activists finding their feet in the postwar period. The appeal of the first has been enormous. Both are the results of an extraordinary effort of the imagination and will.

Although *Testament of Friendship* was published seven years after *Testament of Youth*, there is a continuity between them. In both, the chapters are headed by the poetry of the protagonists—Vera Brittain and Roland Leighton in the first book, Winifred Holtby in the second—and this poetry forms a *Leitmotif* to each, sounding notes of an internal emotional development. Both books, too, attempt to come to terms with the bewildering mystery of early death. They are held together by the continuing drama of Vera Brittain's emotional life and her continuing preoccupation with mortality—a preoccupation which perhaps explains why most of the poetry of Winifred Holtby chosen by Vera Brittain for quotation picks up the themes of death and loss.

The war's searing impact was potentially disastrous for Vera Brittain. Shaken by the twin loss of her brother Edward and her fiancé Roland Leighton, she felt thrust into a world "without confidence or security, a world in which every dear personal relationship would be fearfully cherished under the shadow of apprehension; in which love would seem threatened perpetually by death . . ." (*Testament of Youth*). In Winifred Holtby she found someone who was prepared to try to fill the place of this "composite lost companion" and by doing so, to help her to live in this world.

As Vera Brittain herself comments in *Testament of Youth*, she seems to have had two separate lives—one of which ended with Edward's death in 1918, the other of which started with Winifred's companionship in 1920. From *Testament of Friendship* it becomes clear how indelibly her friend was associated in her mind with those she had lost. In Brighton (where, in 1915, she heard of Roland Leighton's death) she learns of Winifred's deterioration, and goes to bed "with a dull, overwhelming sense of being in the war with doom close at hand". And she writes of her dead friend as if she is one last casualty of war—"she was one of the company whom age shall not weary nor the years condemn"—finally at rest with Roland and Edward.

It is with Edward Brittain in particular that Winifred Holtby seems to have been most closely identified by Vera Brittain and to have most closely identified herself. "You represent in my life," runs a letter quoted in *Testament of Youth*, "the same element of tender, undistressing permanence that Edward represented, and in the end, when passion is spent and adventures are over, this is the thing that comes out on top". There is a moving passage of *Testament of Friendship* in which she describes Winifred Holtby at a concert, comparing herself with the dead Edward and being struck by the thought that "I am his deputy". It conveys a feeling which must have been intensely strong amongst women of the war generation and is certainly a component of Vera Brittain's feminism as elaborated in *Testament of Youth*—the frustratingly impossible wish to replace their irreplaceable, fallen contemporaries.

In preparing her portrait of Winifred Holtby, however, Vera Brittain was setting out to depict someone who was not just a valuable friend to her, but who had a veritable gift for friendship and who was a successful writer and public speaker too. Winifred Holtby's capacity for friendship had been revealed three years before the publication of *Testament of Friendship* by the publication of *Letters to a Friend* (Collins, 1937), an edited selection of her correspondence to Jean McWilliam, whom she had met during the war in France.

Letters to a Friend presents an intimate picture of Winifred Holtby, and throws light on her crisis at the time of Vera Brittain's marriage. Interestingly enough, it presents a similar but different model of friendship to that of Vera Brittain's portrait of her friend. The relationship of Vera Brittain and Winifred Holtby is described in *Testament of Friendship* as being of the sort "which reaches its apotheosis in the story of David and Jonathan", the biblical friends whose love for each other surpassed the love of women. With Jean McWilliam the analogy is to Rosalind and Celia, the Shakespearian heroines of *As You Like It*, whose story, like the biblical tale, asserts loyalty to friends over and above filial duty.

It may be that in her relationship to Vera Brittain she was now taking up the position of Rosalind, the make-believe brother. The subject of friendship is difficult and complex, rarely investigated. As Vera Brittain justly comments, a friendship such as theirs is "not a monopoly of the masculine sex", but "hitherto, perhaps owing to the lack of women recorders, this fact has been found difficult to accept by men, and even by other women . . ." *Testament of Friendship* is a brilliant evocation of the range of emotions involved in close friendship, from exasperation to idealisation. *Letters to a Friend* demonstrates a deeply loving intimacy, with its own crises, misunderstandings and joys. Such friendships are not unique: it is their articulation which is unusual. They show great complexity of feeling and richness of associations. The tenacity with which they are attributed to a hidden lesbianism is therefore all the more remarkable. Vera Brittain alludes to contemporary gossip and speculation about her relationship with Winifred Holtby and in denying it points to an extraordinary blind spot about relations between women which would reduce all its forms to being mere variants, suppressed or otherwise, of one particular mode of sexual practice.

Generalised interest in Winifred Holtby, which could sustain such books and other memoirs, sprang from her success as a journalist and the spontaneous wit and humour which put her in demand as a public speaker. Through her regular contributions to the *Yorkshire Post*, *Manchester Guardian* and *News Chronicle*, her book reviews in *Good Housekeeping*, and her column in *The Schoolmistress*, journal of the National Union of Women Teachers, she reached a much wider audience than she did through her novels, none of which was really popular until the posthumous *South Riding*. A versatile and hard-working journalist, she altered her style and technique to suit newspaper and audience. In the *Manchester Guardian*, for instance, her articles are good tempered and often couched as appeals to good sense; in the *News Chronicle* she deploys the short paragraphs, disjointed non-sequiturs and associative logic of popular newspaper style then and now.

Her greatest journalistic commitment, through which we see best her politics and general stance, was to *Time and Tide*, the weekly magazine of which she was a director and occasional editor, and to which she made regular contributions throughout her short working life.

Founded in 1920, *Time and Tide* was the brain child of Lady Margaret Rhondda, feminist daughter of Lord Rhondda, coal owner and politician. She had been successful in the business world as her father's private secretary (one of the magazine's features was to be its weekly financial column) and had worked in the Ministry of National Service for part of the war, working on enlistment to the Women's Army Auxiliary Corps, WAAC (a link with Winifred Holtby, who joined). The magazine grew out of a feminist desire to create a weekly run by women and dedicated to continuing problems of feminism, but accessible to a general and influential audience. The model was the *New Statesman*. "When in 1913 the *New Statesman* was born," writes Lady Rhondda in her autobiography, *This was My World* (Macmillan, 1933), "I was enormously interested . . . to mould the opinion, not of the large crowd, but of the keystone people, the people who in their turn would guide the crowd — what a fascinating thing to be able to do. Perhaps the most fascinating of all. I envied the *New Statesman*." The policies of the two weeklies were not the same, however, a notable difference being their differing approach to feminism, which was not regarded by the *New Statesman* of that period with any particular interest or sympathy.

Against expectations *Time and Tide* was a successful venture, reaching its peak in the thirties, then declining until its absorption into *John O'London's Weekly* in the fifties. When Winifred Holtby was involved with it, its general orientation was parliamentary and its politics liberal-labour and anti-communist; its internationalism was formed by support for the League of Nations, its wish for peace by the hope that open diplomacy might be able to negotiate avoidance of war.

Time and Tide's feminism fitted a non-party stance. Lady Astor (Conservative), Mrs Wintringham (Liberal) and Ellen Wilkinson (Labour) were all supported because of the stand they took on women's issues (it is a myth that once women were elected to Parliament they took pains to dissociate themselves from feminist campaigns). Each election a list of MPs who had voted for policies supported by women's organisations was published, with the aim of influencing the electorate.

The voice that can be heard through the pages of *Time and Tide* is that of the liberal, concerned, reforming intellectual, a voice which has been excluded from many recent accounts of the twenties and thirties. By adding her own thought and work to its pages Winifred Holtby shaped its policies as much as she was shaped by them. She had enormous respect for Lady Rhondda. She joined the Six Point Group, the equality group Lady Rhondda had founded once limited suffrage had been achieved, and spoke on its platforms. It was to Lady Rhondda that she dedicated her collection of short stories, *Truth is not Sober*. During the twenties Winifred Holtby moved politically from support for Liberal candidate Percy Harris to support for the Labour Party, in particular its radical wing, the Independent Labour Party. As she identified herself more closely with socialist aspirations and noticed the tendency of the right to ascribe any desire for radical change to "bolshevism", her anti-communism was somewhat attenuated. (Its triggering cause was no doubt the disappearance of her child-hood friend George de Coundouroff inside Russia, where he had gone to fight against the Bolshevik government in the Civil War.) Like Vera Brittain she was a keen supporter of the League of Nations and lecturer for the League of Nations Union, and she reported on its meetings from Geneva for *Time and Tide*.

Her political commitments were arrived at through her own experience and thinking and that of her friends. The main principle of her political practice was belief in individual human rights. It informed her feminism, her commitment to the African struggle in South Africa, and her politics at home (she was, for example, a founder of the National Council for Civil Liberties).

As a feminist she was extremely influential. Harold Laski commented that "I always thought of her as not unlike what Mary Wollstonecraft must have been" (*Time and Tide*, Oct. 5 1935). *Women and a Changing Civilisation*, her history of women's position, went quickly through many editions. Within *Time and Tide*, in debate with other feminists, her writings provide useful insights into the shifts and transformations taking place in the women's movement in the wake of the war and with the gaining of the vote. Both these processes had contradictory effects on the position of women, but together they made them "curiously free", to adopt a phrase of Lady Rhondda's. On the one hand changes in social conventions meant that old barriers were removed: "we may not all turn out on winter mornings and run, ride, row, fly, play hockey or tame wild horses," wrote Winifred Holtby in the *News Chronicle*, "but the knowledge that, if we want to go, no human opinion can stop us, makes all the difference" (Dec. 1 1931). On the other hand, marriage bars were still in operation—in the teaching profession and the Civil Service for example—and full equality before the law was still to be achieved, particularly in marriage. Women still lost their nationality if they married an alien, and had not yet won equal rights in guardianship of their children.

As far as employment was concerned, women were being gradually displaced from the "male" occupations they had taken up in the war (the 1923 Report of the Chief Inspector of Factories and Workshops noted that the movement back to "women's trades" was almost complete). There was a widespread feeling amongst feminists that the trades unions were not doing enough for women, and that perhaps it had been a mistake to give up their separate union organisation for the sake of entry into the TUC. At the same time the success of fascism first in Italy and then in Germany showed how quickly feminist gains could be eroded.

Aware of these conflicting trends and the dramatic changes which had taken place, the women's movement was thrown into intense debate. The importance of this period is in general remarkably underestimated, but the battle between the "new feminism" and the "old", in which Winifred Holtby played an active part, was one of the formative moments of twentieth-century feminism.

The "new feminism" emerged from the National Union of Societies for Equal Citizenship (NUSEC), the name adopted by the National Union of Women's Suffrage Societies (NUWSS) in 1919, once the majority of women had been granted the vote. Its main proponent was Eleanor Rathbone, who succeeded Millicent Fawcett as President, supported by Eva Hubback, who took over from Ray Strachey as secretary. Its adoption by NUSEC in 1925 caused a split in its ranks and Mrs Fawcett's resignation from the organisation to which she had devoted sixty years of her active political life.

The "new feminist" argument was that a new direction for feminist politics was needed. The time had come to stop concentrating on equality, defined as demands for those things which men had and women were without, and to work for those things women needed "not because it is what men have got, but because it is what women need to fulfil the potentialities of their own natures and to adjust themselves to the circumstances of their own lives" (*Eleanor Rathbone*, Mary Stocks, Gollancz 1949). Since sex difference would always prevail and women would always have special needs in the area of maternity, emphasis should be put on issues connected with its economics and conditions—in particular on family allowances and birth control. These two were the main planks of the new feminist platform, and Eleanor Rathbone's dedication to the cause of family allowances eventually took her to Parliament and success in convincing her fellow MPs of her case.

One of the fascinating aspects of *Testament of Friendship* is the light it sheds on the role played by both Vera Brittain and Winifred Holtby in helping to shape feminist ideas in the twenties and thirties, that post-vote period about which so little has been written. Winifred Holtby was one of those who defended the "old feminism". "The division," she wrote in *Time and Tide*, "concerns both the aims and the policy of the feminist movement and superficially the New Feminism appears more tolerant, sane and far-sighted."

> Old Feminism, with its motto "Equality First" and its concentration upon those parts of national life where sex differentiation still prevails, may seem conservative, hysterical or blindly loyal to old catchwords. This is not the truth. The New Feminism emphasises the importance of the "woman's point of view", the Old Feminism believes in the primary importance of the human being ...
>
> Personally, I am a feminist, and an Old Feminist, because I dislike everything that feminism implies. I desire an end to the whole business, the demands for equality, the suggestions of sex warfare, the very name of feminist ... but while the inequality exists, while injustice is done and opportunity denied I shall have to be a feminist and an Old Feminist, with the motto Equality First (Aug. 6 1926).

These arguments represented the general position of Lady Rhondda's Six Point Group, which that autumn reaffirmed the priority it gave to equal political and occupational rights as objectives, and took up the slogan "Equality First". The issue was not one of support or not for family allowances and education in birth control techniques—both were supported by *Time and Tide*, but as generally desirable social reforms rather than as demands intrinsic to feminism. The issue was rather the politics of feminism.

The "old feminists" placed themselves within a long tradition. Mary Wollstonecraft had demanded women's right to be treated as part of humanity rather than being confined within their sex. Whilst the nineteenth-century suffrage campaigners had certainly stressed the enriching contribution women in politics would make to the solution of social problems, they had never claimed such areas to be of interest and benefit to women alone. Moreover, the objective of political, economic and social equality was paramount within nineteenth-century feminism, even if there was always an investment of energy in social reform. Winifred Holtby was fond of quoting Josephine Butler's reply to a questioner: "You ask me what I think the most important thing to place before the electors. I think the most important thing is equality, equality, and equality."

The debate between the "new feminism" of Eleanor Rathbone and NUSEC and the "old feminism" of Winifred Holtby, *Time and Tide* and the Six Point Group gives some measure of the ideological crisis into which the feminist movement was thrown by the limited amount of equality gained. From this point of view the twenties and thirties can be seen not as the quiescent period of feminist politics they are often made out to be but as a period of major ideological shifts.

Feminism as social movement, as "woman-centred" politics, making demands within the area of reproduction, has been such an accepted, if not dominant, part of the women's movement in the seventies that the recent origins of such an approach and the power of arguments opposed to it have been obscured. Yet it is important to be aware that feminists had always tried to distance themselves from the birth control demand, linked as it was to eugenicist and Malthusian ideas, and that its introduction into the women's movement stimulated deep and provocative arguments, since its connection to feminism was by no means obvious to all feminists. Such considerations point up the way in which feminism is not a political ideology for all seasons, but is constantly refashioned and given different content as circumstances appear to change.

Vera Brittain joined in the debate in *Time and Tide*, supporting the "old feminism" and analysing the timidity which, in her view, was deflecting feminists from the aim of complete equality and resulting in fragmentation.

> Today in England . . . feminists are still a little conscious that in 1919 they were patted on the head and given a limited franchise as a reward for having behaved so well during the war; they now fear that, if they venture to behave a little worse, they will lose even the partial benefits which were purchased at so heavy a price (Oct. 8 1926).

Many socialist supporters of the women's movement, however, supported the "new feminism" and Mrs Fawcett's objections were in part founded on suspicion of its "practical socialism". Free state provision of benefits and needs has been a stable component of the vision of socialism offered by the Labour and Communist parties in the twentieth century. It was not a vision with which Winifred Holtby was ever in wholehearted agreement.

One of her first contributions to *Time and Tide* contains her own definition of the key post-war concept of "citizenship". Stress is here laid on its elements of service and responsibility:

> citizenship means neither patriotism nor politics; it conveys a sense of the responsibility of man towards society and the development of social relationships, which is more than either of these . . . The greatest social danger in a free educational system lies in its suggestion to children that the individual may claim benefits from society without rendering service in return . . . (Nov. 4 1924).

Brought up at a time when the professional classes tried to instil in their children the habit of giving subscriptions to charity, and formed by the semi-feudal relations of East Yorkshire agriculture, Winifred Holtby had the desire to be socially useful inscribed deeply in her personality. *Testament of Friendship* provides many examples of her personal thrift and public generosity—of which her financing of the South African trades union whose formation she encouraged is perhaps the most outstanding. When she made her will she ensured that her practical philanthropy could continue, endowing a scholarship at Somerville College, Oxford for women who had worked for at least three years before going to college, leaving bequests to local libraries, and funding a reading prize at Pretoria High School for Girls. Her friends contributed similar memorials: a library for the use of Africans in Johannesburg (the first of its kind); the Winifred Holtby Prize for the best regional novel, administered by the Society of Authors from funds left by Vera Brittain.

Although there were those of her contemporaries who valued Winifred Holtby as a journalist and critic (her *Virginia Woolf*, Wishart & Co. 1932, sadly out of print, is still an illuminating and perceptive work), for many of her friends her literary ability came first and they mourned the political commitment which took her away from her work. They mourned and resented too the time given to helping others at the expense of her own creativity. This is a strong, compelling theme of *Testament of Friendship*. After a lapse of time it becomes possible to appreciate the grief and guilt felt by those who survived whilst speculating about the reciprocal nourishment of Winifred Holtby's personal, political and literary lives. Reading through her obituaries and memoirs of her it is remarkable how often she was called a "saint". Her attitude to her own sanctity, however, was more ambivalent. "I am not an angel—I am a debtor to life," she wrote in June, 1924, to Jean McWilliam, "one who without effort gathers in the gold, whilst others go upon their way weeping and bearing forth good seed, and I come again with joy and reap their sheaves. But they shall have their day and their joy. My heart is heavy for their sorrows and my joys" (*Letters to a Friend*).

Not least of the strengths of *Testament of Friendship* is the fact that although Vera Brittain benefited more than most people from Winifred Holtby's sense of indebtedness, she can also present her suffering. The person described comes alive, a many-sided enigma, as questions are opened up about her and the reader's curiosity is expanded—about her extraordinary relationship with Bill, the seemingly effortless purity and relentless kindness which may well have crippled her creative capacity. Desmond McCarthy reviewed the book for the *Sunday Times* when it was first published, and his comments are still appropriate. In particular he pointed out that "the reader can judge for himself what it was in her that won the devotion, admiration and trust of others . . . He comes to know her very well indeed; it is a privilege I would not have missed."

Rosalind Delmar, London 1980

Virago

If you would like to know more about Virago books, write to us at
Ely House, Dover Street, London W1X 4AH.

Please send a stamped addressed envelope

Book Tokens

Give them
the pleasure of choosing

Book Tokens can be bought
and exchanged at most
bookshops